D1559814

Patriotism Black and White

Patriotism Black and White

The Color of American Exceptionalism

Nichole R. Phillips

BAYLOR UNIVERSITY PRESS

Cover Design by *the*BookDesigners
Cover image © Shutterstock/brilliant eye

The Library of Congress has cataloged this book under ISBN
978-1-4813-0957-8

Printed in the United States of America on acid-free paper with a minimum of 30 percent recycled content.

The arc of history is longer than human vision. It bends. We abolished slavery, we granted universal suffrage. We have done hard things before. And every time it took a terrible fight between people who could not imagine changing the rules, and those who said, "We already did. We have made the world new."

—Barbara Kingsolver

To my parents, Alton Arthur Phillips (1941–2000) and Lorna Eleanor Phillips, for birthing a daughter with the faith, hope, and audacity and vision "to make the world new."

Contents

Preface

Patriotism Black and White is an interdisciplinary empirical study that attempts to answer questions about regional and American national identities from the perspective of patriotism, social conflict, and a politics of death. In so doing, it reveals a rural, Southern community's interpretations of their multidimensional identities under religiously inspired war conditions and under the presidency of Barack H. Obama. Both demonstrate how structural and global innovations and massive social transformations contributed to changing understandings of American national identity, signaling what was the onset of a crisis in American national identity. For that reason, new interpretations of American exceptionalism presently include the more triumphalistic and nativistic brand that *makes America great again.*

The research and findings support the implication that a politics of death underlies civil religion.[1] To achieve this result, the study explored the connection between religion and the sacrificial service and deaths of military personnel, fallen leaders, and common citizens who have given their lives to uphold the freedoms granted and preserved by the sacred founding documents of this country. The study also shows how whites and blacks in the rural Tennessee community of Bald Eagles produced assorted and differing public theologies of war.[2] This is particularly important because America, like many other countries, is now continually at war due to religiously inspired terrorist activity. Such distinct public theologies of war ultimately demand new interpretations of American national identity, interpretations capable of honoring nationalistic enterprises in a global market and of creating a "new" form of American exceptionalism anchored by a civil religion that can supply the moral and religious resources required for membership in a global civil society.[3]

Following are the questions that become the basis for comprehending how these rural dwellers construe and reconstruct American national identity and interpret American exceptionalism with respect to military service and in the midst of America's involvement with the War on Terror leading up to the start of Barack Obama's presidential tenure. How does soldiering in service to the country and sacrificing one's life in defense of the country reflect racial and American civil religious values? What hermeneutic drives the placement of secular symbols (e.g., the American flag and Tennessee state flag) and sacred symbols (e.g., the cross) in public and private "worship" spaces where community and congregational ritual life mirror and support each other and solidify regional identity? How should we interpret contemporary religious warfare theologically? Is war (even on terror) the best mechanism for preserving American civil liberties and constitutional freedoms? How does American exceptionalism connect with American national identity especially when an "exceptional" nation fights never-ending war against an "elusive enemy"?

These fundamental inquiries are at the heart of understanding the racial distinctiveness of whites and blacks in rural Bald Eagles and their Southern civil religious practices, political tradition of American exceptionalism, evangelical faith, patriotism, and public theologies of war. Answers to these questions are the basis for comprehending how these rural dwellers find themselves at the periphery of American society at the start of the twenty-first century. To interpret the community's civil religious practices under constant, albeit forgotten, war is to realize there are implications for *what it means to be American* in the present day and under the Trump administration.

The introduction is an overview that captures the meaning and import of evangelical faith and civil religious practices to Bald Eagles residents during wartime. Both subjects tie together the chapters in this volume. Both must be read in the shadow of definitive historical moments that continually prompt new conceptualizations of national identity and exceptionalist ideals embraced by Americans. A detailed account of military personnel, Corporal Keith Essary's funeral, is such an example launching chapter 1. Residents, visitors, and friends honor this soldier's ultimate human sacrifice for the protection of the nation by equating it to Jesus' sacrificial death. Death creates a moral community simultaneously solidifying national and regional identities of Bald Eagles' rural and Southern residents. However, wide-ranging interpretations of white and black patriotism in turn complexify evangelical faith and practice as well as American national identity. Patriotic "speech acts" turn consensus building into contestation and contradiction between the various segments of this rural American community. Such patriotic utterances signal the reality that Americans are living through "times of trial"[4] as discussed throughout chapter 2. Showcasing how the people of Bald Eagles integrate American exceptionalism and American national identity, chapter 2 additionally illustrates the particular ways in which reformulations of American exceptionalism begin to divulge rifts in American national identity.

Chapter 3 displays the regional and national identities of white townsfolk as observed through rites of faith that promote a theology and ethics of "good" and "evil." I argue that for these self-identified white evangelical Christians (who might also belong to historically liberal Protestant congregations), "good" and "evil" are oppositional constructs. The "devil" is a source of particular "evils" that require a "good" fight, meaning spiritual and temporal wrestling and struggles that will not allow the devil to overcome the "good" that resides inside of people. This ethic of "good" and "evil" attributes evil conduct to lax morals, secularization, and anything that disrupts a so-called orderly and balanced way of life.

In chapter 4, I argue for a theology and ethics of "good" and "evil" made evident through rites of faith that underline the regional identity of black townsfolk and the ways in which their regional identity grounds their national identity. Their theology and ethics of "good" and "evil" expresses itself through dialectical and conjunctive (i.e., syncretistic) thinking and practice. Self-identifying as evangelical Christians, their worldview accommodates and acknowledges the presence of the "devil" as the source of particular "evils" they suffer as a social group.

A social and demographic profile of the eighty-three research participants in this study is the focus of chapter 5. That includes members of both churches as well as white and black residents of the city and of the greater county of Bald Eagles. My descriptions of these self-identified evangelical Christians along with qualitative and quantitative data show how whites and blacks in this civil religious community are similar and how they are different. My goal, however, is to demonstrate that evangelicals of all stripes—white, black, male, female, single, married—are "made in the U.S.A." They contribute to and reinforce American national identity because of their investment in a republican *and* liberal democracy, market economy, and American civil liberties safeguarded by constitutional freedoms.

Chapter 6 highlights members of the First United Methodist Church to discuss the politics of dying on the battlefield and rites of war, based on their interpretations of patriotic service to the country. Such service is symbolized by the *ultimate patriot*, one who gives his or her life as a human "blood" sacrifice in defense of the American nation, freedom, and values. God and country for this group go hand in hand, for soldiers sacrifice their lives to preserve constitutional rights, including the guarantees of religious freedom, freedom of speech, freedom from want, and freedom from fear[5] that this social group holds at a premium. The unabashed display of ancient landmark insignia—the American flag, the Bible, and the cross—in public and private ritual spaces symbolically reaffirms the civil religious roots of the community, church members' commitment to their faith and nation and specifically to preserving our country. "In God we trust" holds dual meaning for these congregants. With respect to exceptionalist ideology, it indicates the country's special mission and destiny, when American interests are being served both domestically and abroad.

Chapter 7 captures the politics of dying on the battlefield and rites of war at home and abroad among members of the historic black Tabernacle Missionary Baptist Church. It relies on their interpretations of patriotic service to a country that often requires a "blood" sacrifice as an indication of one's loyalty. However, for these black members, their "blood"(-stained) loyalty is given and their fight for freedom is waged—to the point of death—in spite of America's broken covenant. While agreeing to enter America's battlefield(s), they do so with hesitation because of a less than perfect Union often defaulting on its promises to this segment of the American population, which identifies them as *not belonging*. Despite struggling to earn their "bars and stripes," the members of this social group remain true to their God and their native land and committed to realizing a more perfect Union. Consideration of what it means for black lives to matter to these black and rural Southerners who are still committed to a less than exceptional America closes this chapter.

Chapter 8 illustrates the civil religious loyalties of blacks and whites in Bald Eagles County who question and debate the meaning of a republican and liberal democracy in a postracial, post-9/11, militarized America, and who are feeling the effects of economic insecurity because of the housing crisis, market crash, and global impact of war. In chapter 8, both social groups display interactive, contradictory, and at times conflicting viewpoints, placing their public theologies at variance with their civil religious loyalties yet underscoring what it means to be American in a representative democracy and in a period of perpetual war. Moreover, each case study argues for group rights and responsibilities as freedoms that Americans exercise and must protect and uphold in "dying to defend the nation," thereby stressing *what it means to be American*. Interpreted from the standpoint of these rural Southerners on American national identity, "We the People," however, fails to function as a transcendent and enduring ideal for *what makes America "great."*

I conclude this volume in chapter 9 with a proposal for a more inclusive understanding of American national identity and a reformulated political tradition of American exceptionalism, rooted in the American dream, produced from diverse interpretations of rites of faith and rites of war, and with the capacity to honor the inclusive premise and constitutional principle of "We the People." Human "sacrificial" death features prominently in the narratives of these rural dwellers, for it exemplifies how they really do belong to a nation that however frequently disregards family histories of career military service.[6]

A "new" American exceptionalism recognizes this rural and evangelical community's service and sacrifice *to* and *for* the nation, regardless of racial group. "Remember the faithful and the dead"—*never forget*—is an enduring message about the values of this and other small-town moral communities. Feelings of isolation and alienation compounded by worldwide structural revolutions are hallmarks of twenty-first-century postmodernity. For these rural dwellers, especially many of those who are white, the election of Barack H. Obama embodied such tumultuous changes.

Mr. Obama was an unsettling figure for many whites—and even some blacks. While his election to executive office stood for human and racial progress, his "hybridity" was perplexing for many and nevertheless represented the discomfiting nature of twenty-first-century postmodernity manifested: as threats against national security because of religiously motivated terrorist activities. That, in part, precipitated fluctuating interpretations of American regional and national identities. Nevertheless, "fear" of the "other," uber-nationalistic avowals, and other strong patriotic sentiments corresponding to upticks in American triumphalism and nativism are not the only acceptable reactions or reasonable responses to extremely disruptive structural transformations.

Mindful of church members' and residents' struggles with the communal effects of our nation's endless war against terrorism, a reformulation of American exceptionalism and a novel and engaging approach to American national identity is in order. Such an approach would call for greater democracy at present and in our more global civil society and historical age. A new American exceptionalism would celebrate the ongoing moral discourse around divergent constituencies, civic debate, and social and religious diversity. In our growing and ever-changing democracy, it would tie together the dialectical interplay between civil religion and public theology. Such interplay would facilitate and enable cultural conflict in successive times of trial.[7]

Dying for country shapes social belonging. From this rural and Southern community's perspective, the fallen sacralize the land, preserve America from "enemies," and assist residents in their attempts to distinguish between *who belongs* and *who does not belong* in America. Yet that distinction also defies what it means to live in community and in America—a land welcoming of the dispossessed, immigrants, and any who yearn to experience "true" liberty. This new American exceptionalism requires democratic and (civil) religious work. As such, it holds the potential to create a more inclusive and just society where multiple global constituencies meet[8] and where the connection between race, ethnicity, and civil religion come to represent both reformulations of national identity and the more nativistic expressions of American exceptionalism.

Acknowledgments

Let America be the dream the dreamers dreamed—
Let it be that great strong land of love.
                    —Langston Hughes, "Let America Be America Again"[1]

Langston Hughes' classic poem stayed with me for the years it took for me to transform field research and a fledgling dissertation into this mature book. "Let America Be America Again" points out American *un*exceptionalisms, shortfalls that demand strivings after liberty, justice, and equality for many—blacks, poor whites, Indians (i.e., Native Americans), refugees, and those others who are seeking to "build a homeland of the free." Paradoxically, his poem not only reminds us but also definitively embraces and celebrates America's *exceptionalisms*—what makes her great. The People—they make up America's social fabric. The People are comprised of whites, blacks, Native Americans, and immigrants—persons of every race, ethnicity, and nationality. Also included in the People are Old World adventurers, farmers, entrepreneurs, and bricklayers representing workers at every socioeconomic level of society. Each social and cultural group has contributed and continues to contribute their respective share to developing "America . . . the dream [and what] the dreamers dreamed [it can and will be]." These are a few of my thoughts and reflections on what remains a rich and complex but glorious poem birthed from the 1920s Harlem Renaissance.

As much as researchers claim neutrality, research projects are still often (auto)biographical. Though my research started as part of a religion and politics project about the state of Tennessee, I suspect research on American national identity and American exceptionalism stems from the ruminations of my mind and heart. In both recesses, I frequently queried, *What*

xvii

does it mean to be American?, having grown up around immigrants and their first-generation children, with me, a first-generation black American woman, included in this latter group. And so, as readers turn the pages of this text, they will find me searching after and arguing for what that means—*to be American*—yet in a specific context, around a definite historic moment (and even further), and for particular groups of people: white and black, rural and Southern, politically populist, and evangelical Christian.

Even though this task exceeds the scope of these few pages, here I will begin to show appreciation for the institutions, groups, and individuals who have helped me over these very many years to bring forth this volume. I begin with the members of my dissertation committee who were invaluable to my research process and essential to my educational formation as both teacher and scholar. I want to offer enormous appreciation to my primary dissertation advisor and codirector, Volney P. Gay, who is retiring this year, after thirty-nine years, from Vanderbilt University and after forty-three years of teaching in higher education. He was one of the firsts who saw and did not hesitate to affirm my giftedness as both humanist and social scientist of religion. When I shared concerns about entering the professoriate, he was also the first to allay my fears and remind me that he had been teaching, at that point, for thirty-five years. In other words, once you repeatedly teach the same (but incorporate new) material for years, teaching those subjects becomes almost second nature. When a person, like me, is in formation and incorporating so many diverse and disparate experiences, she is in need of an advisor, guide, senior colleague, conversation partner, mentor—who will authentically approach challenging and sensitive subjects like racism, sexism, classism; identify her strengths and encourage her to develop in areas of weakness; mix in humor and model humility even in the face of human limitations. That is what Volney Gay did for me. I am both grateful and thankful for our teacher-student paths crossing, for him being seminal to my growth, and for all of the lessons learned during this process.

William Partridge is a cultural anthropologist extraordinaire as well as the codirector of my dissertation studies. From the moment I had enrolled in his ethnographic research methods course on the Peabody College campus (of Vanderbilt University), he not only saw my talent and voracious appetite for ethnography and scholarly research but encouraged it by recommending that I become a student participant in the Religion and Politics Project for which he was a coprincipal investigator. Through him and his teaching, scholarship, and ethnographic research and reading assignments on American communities, I was exposed and able to explore diverse worldviews, orientations, individuals, social groups, and cultures—perspectives different from my own.

From the start of my doctoral studies, I was confessedly starstruck by Bonnie Miller-McLemore because of her ability to rise to the top of her field as a highly regarded practical theologian, despite the challenges and demands of writing, researching, and producing scholarship while balancing this work with a family. Lewis V. Baldwin—a consummate researcher, writer, and Martin Luther King Jr. scholar—provided much of the historical evangelical Protestantism coursework that I drew upon to interpret and understand my community. I had come to realize a fact that he had come to affirm: my research questions were as much a product of this peculiar American religious history as were the cultural wars it contributed to producing.

By way of his research, teaching, writing, and discussions with me, Thomas Gregor gifted me with an appreciation for psychological anthropology and studies of indigenous peoples, myth, ritual, and symbol. All subjects have become seminal to my own research, teaching, and writing. It was always delightful and educational to be in the presence—and to procure the guidance, knowledge, and wisdom—of Paul Speer of the Department of Human and Organizational Development at Peabody College. I appreciate his sacrifice of time and energy and investment of statistical skills, from start to finish, into my project at Vanderbilt University—a graduate school, experience, and institution that will always be near and dear to my heart.

Without fellowships from the Center for the Study of Religion and Culture, the Center for Community Studies of Peabody College, Vanderbilt University, the Fund for Theological Education (FTE), now the Forum for Theological Exploration, and the Southern Regional Education Board (SREB), field research and subsequent work on this project would not have been possible. I give thanks for all faculty members and students affiliated with the Religion and Politics Project through the (now closed) Center for the Study of Religion and Culture developed and coheaded by Douglas A. Knight and Volney P. Gay. These faculty and student participants helped to cultivate this scholarly work at its earliest stages by way of critical conversations and constructive critique and by offering academic resources and opportunities for me to present select pieces to active and engaged listening audiences in small, closed settings and public, university-wide forums.

I am indebted to both congregations—the First United Methodist Church and the Tabernacle Missionary Baptist Church—as well as residents of larger Bald Eagles, West Tennessee. I have immensely benefitted from your openness and trust. I have endeavored to convey your stories and share your truths to the best of my abilities. I am humbled by the lessons you have taught me about religious, social, economic, and political life in a rural setting. These lessons have served me well. And so, for the myriad of participants who met, ate, spoke, heard, and traveled with me along this unchartered road—and for everything positive about this work, and none that is negative—I give you the credit for being willing partners.

A dissertation at its nascent stages would not have been transformed into a thoughtful and convincing book without the phenomenal and professional editorial assistance of Ulrike Guthrie. I would also like to thank the director of Baylor University Press, Carey Newman, and his team—Jenny Hunt, Cade Jarrell, Kingsley East, and Madeline Wieters—for accepting and having faith in my book project as well as moving it to the next level. I appreciate their strong boost, recognition of the book's vocation, and interest in my work. Additionally, the anonymous external reviews delivered by the press have only added to creating a stronger book.

Since I have been on the faculty at Candler School of Theology, the Center for Faculty Development and Excellence (CFDE) at Emory University has been invaluable to my growth and development as a scholar, professor, and writer. Toward that end, I was a beneficiary of a Scholarly Writing and Publishing (SWAP) grant awarded through the center. As well, I have had the good fortune of attending workshops, sharing conversations, and receiving welcomed feedback about my book and scholarly direction from Director and Vice Provost for Undergraduate Education Pamela Scully and Associate Director Allison Adams. Moreover, I was in a financial bind toward the end of the research, writing, and revising process. Dean Jan Love, Candler School of Theology, graciously approved a small grant to complete all three tasks. I am thankful. Besides this assistance, I want to acknowledge the following Candler faculty (retired and active)—Luther E. Smith Jr., Steven M. Tipton, Emmanuel Y. Lartey, and Ted A. Smith—for their generosity of time and spirit and for their availability as resources and wellsprings of information about tenure and promotion as well as the book and contract processes. Steve Tipton also garners special recognition and my appreciation for extensively and constructively critiquing the earliest draft of the manuscript and for offering useful feedback. I continue to reap the benefits of this hidden turned manifest—blessing!

Beyond Candler, the Mellon Foundation Faculty Fellows is a cohort that has provided me with additional conversation partners, encouragement, and emotional support as well as Emory University–wide networks. I and this cohort of individuals—Kate Winskell, Falguni Sheth, Daniel LaChance, Pablo Palomino, Kylie Smith, and Daniel Reynolds—were superbly coordinated and led by Office of the Provost's Senior Director of Academic and Strategic Initiatives Thomas E. Jenkins. A bold and innovative group deliberately appointed to be shaped into Emory's first cohort of humanistic and interdisciplinary scholars, members not only shared tips for navigating the tenure and promotion process but held my angst about getting the book completed while also listening, offering fruitful counsel, and nurturing the conditions for the scholarly community that I have desired and needed. For them, I am immeasurably grateful.

The following people were also important to my development as a scholar, teacher, and writer and deserve special mention. Evon Flesberg and Bruce Vaughn are wonderful clinicians, professors, mentors, and pastoral caregivers. During my Vanderbilt days, courses with each allowed theory to come alive in practice. For allowing teaching and theory to breathe and to live, I give thanks and praise! These circles of (then) student-scholars and interlocutors enriched my—at times arduous, sometimes long, at turns dull, but always comedic and never uneventful—"school days." Many still remain friends. Members of my Religion, Psychology, and Culture Program cohort were Christopher E. Jones, Karla Van Zee, Melinda McGarrah-Sharp, Elizabeth Zagatta-Allison, Leanna Kelley Fuller, Katherine Lassiter, Katherine Baker, and Eileen Campbell-Reed. Further, Monique Moultrie, Amy Steele, Keri Day, Kimberly Peeler-Ringer, Natasha Coby Earl, Kimberly Russaw, Tamura Lomax, Tamara Lewis, Angela Cowser, Lisa Thompson, Klem-Mari Cajigas-Chimelis, Febbie Dickerson, Bridgett Green, Charles Bowie, Christophe Ringer, Michael Brandon McCormack, Asante Todd, T. L. Gray, Arthur Carter, Asha Raziya Hunter, Karlene Griffiths Sekou, Alyson Dickson, Dianna Watkins-Dickerson, Kenya Tuttle, Cherisna Jean-Marie, Warren Chain, Almeda Wright, Albert Earnest Smith Jr., and James Logan comprised a network of graduate students, from Vanderbilt and other arenas, who metaphorically and on occasion became a "bridge over troubled waters."

The church can be credited for its faithfulness toward me while teaching me patience, trust, endurance, and hope as I walked the path to reach this point. For that, I extend my warmest appreciation. Bethel AME Church, Boston, has given pastoral vision, financial support, as well as inspiration to me—one of its "daughters" in the ministry—over many years even though I left Boston for the South in 2003. Assuming the role of "father" in the ministry, pastor, counselor, and friend to the multitudes is no easy feat, but Pastor Ray A. Hammond does so, unflaggingly. His tireless and exuberant support of my calling and my educational and ministerial pursuits I have treasured. Pastor Gary Gibbs and the Hyde Park Christian Church family, I am so glad I have inherited you along my spiritual way. This adopted church family continually waters my emotional and spiritual soil with preaching engagements, food, fellowship, love offerings, and prayers—especially when I return to the birthplace that brought me forth and fills me with many good childhood and adult memories, my home (away from home) East Flatbush, Brooklyn, NYC.

Elizabeth Pierre, Wendy Readus, and Kanisha Billingsley, thank you for standing in the gap with your intercessory and incessant prayers. Prayer (and fasting) changes things, people, and situations! That we know. Here, as well, I give special thanks for lifelong friends who have often inspired me to be my best self: Carla McGruder, Rita Wright, Leslie Greene, Richard and Abigail Uva, Brenda Dixon, Reggie Dixon, April Garrett, Carol Dufresne, Jeanine Lipscomb, Sharon Watson, and Candace Lewis.

A special and spectacular group of women have been friends par excellence from college to divinity through graduate school and beyond: Elaine Lalanne, Rachelle Barlow, Faye Holder-Niles, Ouzama Henry, Raquel Hill, and Helen Hayes. Your "friendship isn't a big thing; rather, it's a million little things" (author unknown).

Arriving to this point in my academic career and along my vocational journey would not have been possible without the love, patience, fortification, and understanding of my family. To Alton Arthur Phillips Jr., because you are special in God's eyesight, you are exceptional in mine. You move me to embrace "dis-abled" bodies as able-bodied individuals, bestowed with so many unique and godly gifts and talents. You fuel my desire to heal the brokenness of this world. To Andrea Ann-Marie Phillips, I treasure your sisterly love, your humor, and the nieces, Jenia-Renèe Steele and Lailah Steele, and nephew, Paul Steele Jr., that you have produced and that grace my existence. Keep pressing toward God's mark and high calling for your life, as will I.

To my parents, Alton Arthur Phillips (1941–2000) and Lorna Eleanor Phillips: Words cannot express how much your devotion, care, discipline, and nurture of my adventurous spirit means to me. From both of you, I have inherited my passion for learning, have acquired the skills to be strong and courageous in the face of adversity, and am inspired to be exceptional in all of my ambitions. Your life models this biblically based truism: "The race is not given to the swift, nor the battle to the strong, but to [s]he who endures to the end." And so, now I close this leg of my journey, eagerly anticipating the new, with unparalleled grace, vision, and gratitude.

Introduction

The United States faces an upsurge in nativism because of a return to certain forms of American nostalgia in the wake of the election of Donald Trump. A triumphalist variant of American exceptionalism has emerged because of this present national mode, engendering a crisis of American national identity. Citizens are at odds over how to understand the nature of the United States and its values. Traditionally, America has embraced a civil religion, frequently identified as a form of patriotism, which has been understood as unifying the citizenry, regulating its emotions, and sacralizing its communities and the nation. This civil religion has served as a means of national religious self-understanding[1] and has come to be associated with American national identity as illustrated in the motto "In God We Trust" as well as in the inclusion of the phrase "under God" in the Pledge of Allegiance.

Recent anti-immigration policies and travel bans, reneging on free-trade and climate-control agreements, the end to the DACA program, moratoriums on transgendered military personnel, massive budget cuts to social and disability programs, anti-Muslim sentiments, restrictions on refugee admissions and withdrawal from the U.N. Global Compact on Migration, white nationalist rallies, and an NFL-centered patriotism and race schism challenge American civil religion and a shared ethos. How various constituents of the nation conceptualize American national identity and belonging has become a pressing matter because of these far-reaching policy changes. In order to make sense of the social, cultural, and global changes that led to these developments, this book argues that we can trace the roots back to 2001 and the beginnings of the War on Terror.

1

Four years of research in the rural Southern community of Bald Eagles explores the ways in which both black and white rural dwellers found themselves feeling marginalized and isolated from the rest of the country at the outset of the new century. Understanding their reactions to the War on Terror and the election of a black president helps us to comprehend how these groups, bound by regionalism, responded both similarly and differently to these drastic changes. Both communities within Bald Eagles acted in response to these macrostructural changes by practicing a derivation of American civil religion called Southern civil religion.[2]

Southern civil religion acts like a social glue and spiritual anchor that pulls people together under common and abiding American principles and Southern regional experiences, regardless of race, ethnicity, and nationality. Other versions of this form of civil religion exist.[3] Racialized forms are ones that tie racial and ethnic groups to the land of America,[4] but they do so in different and compelling ways, ways that reflect the particular values and commitments important to each respective social and cultural group. Southern civil religion is further distinctive in that features of evangelical faith support regional and national commitments to America but disclose differences between white and black racial values. This book is therefore also a study of white and black evangelicals in this self-identified civil religious and politically populist community.[5]

Both communities additionally acted in response to the social turbulence by performing rites of faith that contribute to community contestation and consensus and rites of war that produce racially diverse and divergent public theologies of war. These rites are called rites of intensification,[6] and they reinforce the authority, identity, moral commitments, ideologies, values, and structures of social groups and institutions.

Religion, politics, history, and memorializing the dead together are forces that unify communities and inform Robert Bellah's investigations[7] into the ways in which political and sacrificial death—martyrdom— plays into the rebirth of a nation and shapes American civil religion. Concerning a politics of death implied as the *content* of civil religion,[8] the association between race, religion, and American national identity is made evident by examining the connection between religion and sacrificial service—and centralizing the deaths of military men, fallen leaders, and common citizens who have given their lives to uphold the freedoms granted and preserved by the sacred founding documents of this country. Polyvalent funerary rites of a civil religious nature, case studies on leadership and patriotism, and church sermons work in tandem to unpack racialized understandings of "blood-land-religion."[9] Studying the symbolism of these blood sacrifices and their ties to religion and to land shows this trifecta as reinforcing American nationality and regional communities, while also raising questions about the present resurgence and form of American exceptionalism.

Post-9/11 religiously inspired war conditions and the election of President Barack Obama produced a crisis in American national identity, for which reason the blood-land-religion trifecta remains central because the United States is in a perpetual and permanent state of war due to religiously inspired violent extremism. In responding to this civil religious politics of death, some Americans have embraced the nativistic and triumphalistic tradition of American exceptionalism, reintroduced by President Donald Trump. Distinct public theologies and civil religious interpretations of warfare related to Americans dying to defend the nation have become the substance of moral conversations and debate in American public life. These moral conflicts now demand new framings of American national identity.

The War on Terror and the election of Barack Obama have also contributed to restructuring America. We, the People, will consider those large-scale social factors that brought about these enormous shifts by providing a thick description that anticipated the incredible divide in the public's response to Trump's campaign (and why, though Trump's values were at variance to people who champion values, they still backed him); show how American's founding myths both do and do not explain religious and political behaviors; reveal the incredible complexity of being both white and black in America today (neither are stereotypical); and consider the politics of sacrificial death and how the blood-land-religion triumvirate (i.e., connection) has relevance to American national identity and American exceptionalism, particularly around questions of *who does and who does not count as American.*

We, the People, will uncover the microstructural and cultural realities that showcase the communal effects of America's War on Terror on rural and Southern dwellers; offer a richer picture of race and civil religion in the United States and a subtle understanding of the identity of American Evangelicals as a religious and political group; and determine the role of the public church (i.e., religious communities) in raising American consciousness and shaping American conscience—because the end result is to learn how to live in a more global civil society.

We, the People, must envision a "new" American exceptionalism for a global civil society that is in pursuit of the common good. For that reason, American national identity must offer greater democracy, not less. It needs to be diverse and inclusive enough to honor nationalistic loyalties even in a world market and typified by the democratic and (civil) religious service of rural subpopulations like those in Bald Eagles whose "boys come home in body bags."[10] It requires creating a path to peoplehood where a new American exceptionalism supplies the moral and religious resources required for common membership in (our) global and civil society and that *makes America better again.*[11]

1

Honoring the Dead

A Community Procession for a Fallen Soldier

On the morning of Friday, January 16, 2009, I jumped into my car to join the funeral procession honoring Corporal Keith Eric Essary. A few days earlier, the headlines of the *Bald Eagles State Gazette* had read: "Local Soldier Killed in Afghanistan." Around 9:30 p.m. on January 8, 2009, according to the newspaper account, two soldiers from Fort Campbell, Kentucky, had knocked at the door of Keith's grandmother, Anita Essary, to inform her of her grandson's death.

Essary was the second casualty from this area whose life has been taken in the War on Terror. According to the paper, he was the latest casualty in the United States' Operation Enduring Freedom in Afghanistan, which had lost 561 American military personnel since it began. Essary was killed in Maiwand, Afghanistan, a village fifty miles northeast of the city of Kandahar in Kandahar Province. While the details surrounding his death had not at that time been released, the cause of death was the result of the impact from an improvised explosive device while Essary was on dismounted patrol. As a consequence of this suicide bombing, also killed were another American soldier and three Afghan civilians. Essary was a 2006 graduate of Bald Eagles County High School who had enlisted in the army at the beginning of his senior year.

Based on the headlines of the Sunday, January 11, 2009, *Gazette*, which read, "Honoring One of Our Own," I went to observe how the city and county honor their military dead. It was a bitterly cold morning, yet multitudes of people of all ages saluted the hearse carrying the casket with Corporal Essary's body. The procession journeyed up 51 Bypass North toward Bald Eagles County High School. I joined the automobile procession at the corner of 51 Bypass North and North Sampson Ave. (which turns into Highway 211) where the grocery store, Country Mart,

5

is located because I could not find anywhere to park my car. Throngs of people three deep lined both sides of the streets, many with their hands on their hearts, to pay tribute to this fallen soldier.

The car procession included city and county police, fire trucks, civic leaders in cars, and other dignitaries. The air was solemn yet honorific. As we approached Bald Eagles County High School, it became evident that the students had been given permission to leave class for this event. They lined the road on both sides of the street. Especially significant was the salute by the JROTC as the procession passed by, for Essary had been a member of the group while a student at the high school. Once the hearse was completely out of sight, the students returned to their classes, whereas I continued in the procession.

The procession ended in the downtown area of the second city that comprises Bald Eagles County—Screaming Eagles—in front of the East Bald Eagles United Methodist Church. Downtown Screaming Eagles is a mere two-to-three-block stretch, and traffic slowed to a crawl as we approached the church. Even there, in that short stretch, hundreds of people lined the streets. No longer wanting to navigate the crowds in this small space, I decided to return to Bald Eagles.

A Civil Religious Funeral for a Local Hero

Corporal Keith Eric Essary, according to the *State Gazette*, received the lateral promotion from specialist to corporal, upon orders from Fort Hood, Texas, on the Monday morning after he was killed. The gymnasium of Bald Eagles County High School was the site of Corporal Essary's funeral and drew 500 to 700 community members from diverse segments of the city—diverse racially, economically, theologically, denominationally, and politically. The casket was draped with the American flag, a poster-sized picture of Corporal Essary displayed to its right.

Next to that was a podium with a microphone beckoning those who wished to pay tribute to this local hero. To my right, the Bald Eagles County ROTC cadets were seated. Attendees were solemn. Scattered throughout the audience were photographers and television media personnel. Army National Guard dignitaries faced the cadets and me.

Presiding over the funeral was Reverend James Wolfgang and First Lieutenant Ted Randall. Reverend Wolfgang opened the ceremony with a Christocentric reading and then a prayer committing Essary back to God in Christ. The first of many musical tributes followed, after which Wolfgang again approached the podium and began his comments with a reflection on Thursday's procession to comfort family and friends: "This nation honors and respects humanity and dignity," he said. "Guys like Keith give us the gift of life through their death. Our nation will continue until the Lord and Savior Jesus Christ comes. Sometimes men like Keith suffer the ultimate sacrifice. They also suffer emotional wounds that need healing: these wounds are also a sacrifice." He paused, then announced he would read selected verses from Romans 8. Wolfgang proceeded to recite the following verses.

> Now there is no condemnation for those who live in Christ Jesus [Romans 8:1]. But you are not controlled by the flesh; you are in the spirit, since the Spirit of God dwells in you [8:9]. We are heirs of God and joint heirs with Christ [8:17]. Consider the sufferings of the present time as not being equal to the glory about to be revealed to us [8:18]. If God is for us, who can be against us? [8:31]. Who will separate us from the love of Christ? Will hardship, or distress, or persecution, or famine, or nakedness, or peril, or sword? [8:35]. No, in all these things we are more than conquerors through him who loved us [8:37].

Following this, James, a member of the East Bald Eagles United Methodist Church, who had watched Keith grow up, rendered another tribute, this time the song "How Great Thou Art." As he sang, I looked to my left and realized I was sitting in a row of young people who quite evidently were Essary's friends. It was difficult for them to refrain from the quiet sobbing elicited by the loss of a loved one. Turning away from these mourners, I looked behind me and saw Tennessee state troopers lining the gymnasium wall.

Reverend Wolfgang then read Luke 12:32-38 and Ephesians 6:10-18 (the armor of God) from the New Testament. He highlighted that our struggles are not against enemies of the flesh and blood but instead against forces of evil. He encouraged us to take up the full armor of God and to fasten the belt of truth around our waists. He read from First Thessalonians 5:17 to encourage us to pray without ceasing; he exhorted us to put on the breastplate of hope and to don the helmet of salvation. After his exhortation, Reverend Wolfgang started his homily with an illustration:

> I had a friend named Ben Stout who observed that armor is placed in the front of the body but then you are left with nothing to protect your back except God who has your back. Soldiers combat wherever they are called. Paul, in Ephesians, shows us [that] the ideology we combat is an evil ideology. It is hard to conquer; it takes more than flesh to overcome spiritual enemies. We need to be neither hot nor cold about evil.

Christians must never surrender to evil. And why would we never do so? Because Christ's limitless love and compassion will always triumph over Satan. . . .

Why surrender to evil even if it is something that can kill your body? God gives to his children, such as Keith, his eternal life. With Christ, Keith is more than a conqueror.

Switching the subject and addressing the audience, Wolfgang continued:

With Christ, you can face the future. You can face what might attack and oppose you in life. No one ever knows when that great moment in life will be. You will never know when the greatest moment in life will be—when you depart this earth to meet Christ. Who better than our Creator would know what is best for us? Resting in Christ is your spirit's DNA. Living in Christ, you will have a restful and joyous life. It might be as short as Keith's twenty years—shorter or longer. If it was lived like Keith, however, it was lived well. . . .

To be with Christ is to be part of the triumphant church in heaven; that is an unmatchable gift. In spite of our sorrow, loss, and grief, we can still experience joy and peace. God's gift of peace is greater than sorrow. Keith lived his life with purpose and was therefore prepared to meet the Lord. Let us be like Keith who must have said, "I am prepared to meet evil, even the worst kind of evil in Afghanistan, because I have Jesus as Lord and Savior. Even if death takes me, I am more than a conqueror."

At the close of Reverend Wolfgang's sermon, musicians played "For You" by Johnny Cash and Dave Matthews. Captain Trevor Vogel, the company commander, offered a reflection after the song tribute ended:

I'm blessed to attend today.

The Taliban controlled the area [where Keith was killed] with no presence of officials for over a decade. Keith was a dedicated and loyal soldier. His dedication and loyalty were displayed to soldiers around him especially when he helped in constructing the floor at the local community center. His eyes would light up when he saw children around him. He was always willing to help. He was a man of character and loyalty. He knew what this meant and unhesitatingly defended our freedom. Let this flame of patriotism that burn[s] so brightly in this community never flicker. Keith joined the armed forces to serve this country. You, too, can serve this country as citizens of character, strong morals, and values. Our policemen, firemen, and factory workers serve this country by

exemplifying strong morals, character, and values. By being a good neighbor, you serve this community. This area truly represents America—
it is America—and it has never forgotten our sons and daughters! May
God bless you, your family, soldiers, and God bless America!

Army chaplain, First Lieutenant Ted Randall, then offered his reflections on Keith Essary, drawing upon a text from 1 Samuel:

In 1 Samuel, David mourns his fallen soldier friend Jonathan. The
mighty has fallen in the midst of the battle. The mighty continue to fall
in the midst of the battle. O, how the mighty fall in battle! However,
the Mighty One has *not fallen* in battle! God knows the depth of your
pain. He will sustain, provide for you, and uplift you during this time.
The Psalmist reminds us that "God is the strength of my life and portion, forever." For some of you, your faith is a comfort. Some of you are
angry because of this evil. Yet, God is not offended by your anger. God
is not intimidated by your questions. If you are wondering why this has
happened, ask [God].

I pray that Keith's closest friends will eventually be able to laugh
about the good times. A memorial garden will be established in his
honor. Keith's life must be celebrated even in face of the difficult days
ahead. In your grief, remember to tell his story. While you mourn his
death, continue to celebrate his life.

The chaplain's message closed with Trace Adkin's song "Arlington,"
inspired by the 2003 battlefield death of U.S. Marine Corps Corporal Patrick Nixon and sung from the perspective of a soldier killed in battle and
buried at Arlington National cemetery:

(Stanza 1) I never thought that this is where I'd settle down
I thought I'd die an old man back in my hometown
They gave me this plot of land
Me and some other men, for a job well-done
There's a big white house
Sits on a hill just up the road
The man inside
He cried the day they brought me home
They folded up a flag and told my mom and dad
We're proud of your son

(Stanza 2) And I'm proud to be
On this peaceful piece of property

I'm on sacred ground
And I'm in the best of company
I'm thankful for those, thankful
For the things I've done
I can rest in peace
I'm one of the chosen ones
I made it to Arlington

(Stanza 3) I remember daddy brought me here when I was eight
We searched all day
To find out where my grand-dad lay
When we finally found that cross
He said, "Son this is what it costs
To keep us free." [. . .]

(Final Stanza) Yeah, dust to dust
Don't cry for us
We made it to Arlington

As we neared the close of the service, Corporal Essary was posthumously awarded the Bronze Star and the Purple Heart. Members of the military stood in his honor. To end this two-hour, civic-minded, and faith-filled service, we sang a hymn and heard the benediction given by Reverend Wolfgang: "May the peace of God that surpasseth all understanding, guard your hearts, and minds in Christ Jesus."

Corporal Keith Essary's military funeral is first and foremost a compelling example of a rite of intensification, Chapple and Coon's term to describe events such as the one I observed in the rural West Tennessee community of Bald Eagles where I returned to conduct research at the onset of President Obama's tenure and at the height of the wars in Iraq and Afghanistan.[1] Enacted by both black and white subpopulations, these rites of intensification on many occasions—but to an exceptional degree on civic holidays like Memorial Day, Veteran's Day, Independence Day, and Martin Luther King Jr. Day—memorialize and recognize dead soldiers, political leaders, and ordinary citizens for their service to and sacrifice on behalf of the country. While reinforcing Southern, rural, and regional identities, these rites uphold residents' national commitments to democratic values and ideals, certain civil liberties, religious freedom, and protection of the nation.

Rites of intensification are ceremonies that reaffirm the identities, beliefs, values, commitments, ideologies, and structures of social groups and institutions. These rites foreground, describe, and explain the ritual behavior(s) of the community. Whereas rites of passage mark significant milestones in a person's life or restore order to a family unit after individual crisis, rites of intensification recover equilibrium after group disturbances.[2] Rites of intensification gather together disparate segments of a population and reintegrate members into group dynamics and processes. Notable examples of such reintegrating rites are speeches and patriotic displays (e.g., flying the flag and singing the national anthem) that mark American nationhood during special holidays like Inauguration Day and Presidents' Day; displays of military might and tradition exemplified by the changing of the guard at the Tomb of the Unknown Soldier at Arlington National Cemetery; and even special programming and events (e.g., prayer, fasting, Seven Last Words services, caroling) that distinguish religious occasions like Easter and Christmas.

Through the symbolic performance of values and commitments, rites of intensification remind participants of their group allegiances and loyalties. In Bald Eagles, such reminders typically occur on civic holidays like Memorial Day, Veteran's Day, and Juneteenth. Juneteenth celebrations occur annually on June 19 in acknowledgment and commemoration of the end of slavery in the United States because Texas slaves learned and were freed on June 19, 1865, a full two and a half years after President Abraham Lincoln's 1863 signing of the Emancipation Proclamation. Juneteenth and other civic holiday rituals foster social cohesion and solidarity of individuals whose group membership is easily differentiated along race, class, religious, and political lines. Moreover, these individuals might belong to social collectives with conflicting group loyalties; for instance, a person's membership in a particular political group could likely be at variance with that person's membership in a particular religious or civic group. Membership in groups with opposing group loyalties might prove dissonant and antagonistic. However, by reinscribing the continuity, power, and authority of social groups and communities, rites of intensification, especially those in the shadow of politically laden deaths, are instrumental in distinguishing between blacks and whites while also showing similarities in their belief and practice of Christian faith, civil religion, and public theologies of war. Ritual action in Bald Eagles is rich and pervasive, and it defines the life of this and other small towns.

The funeral of Corporal Essary additionally highlights the civil religious nature of rural Bald Eagles where features of evangelical faith support regional and national commitments to America yet disclose differences between white and black racial values. American civil religion, routinely identified as a form of patriotism, functions to unify, regulate the emotions of, and sacralize communities and the nation.[3] Civil religion is also fundamental to the character and personality of this rural community, and it manifests institutionally and structurally in the social behavior of the people. The civil religious and ritualistic activities of Bald Eagles towns-folk was on display for the four years that I conducted research, allowing me to examine the shifting interpretation and understandings of Amer-ican national identity in the midst of the post-9/11 wars in Afghanistan and Iraq and ushered in by a sea of sociopolitical change with the election of the first black president, Barack H. Obama, in 2008 and a year after he assumed the executive office.

"Bloodlines" are the primary means by which civil religion produces group cohesion, which next to violence is a unifying social force sorting groups and transforming members into Us and Them categories.[4] Rhys H. Williams extends the meaning of this concept and writes prolifically about the connection between bloodlines, land, and American national identity, bringing up the degree to which "blood" and its connection to "land" constitutes the *content* of civil religion.[5] Arguing for the association between race, religion, and American national identity when speaking of the *content* of civil religion underscores an implied understanding of nationhood as white, Christian, American. Bloodlines ascribe social identity via group membership, whether such belonging is genetic, nationalistic, religious, or to a primordial community.[6] Civil religious understandings of blood and land are integral to creating tribal identities and particularly applicable to American national identity,[7] especially in this current political climate.

The ties between blood and land and religion begin to explain why American's struggles with national identity consistently revolve around questions of who counts and who does not count as American. An often historically veiled debate, it resurfaced more publicly when this nation's panic button was triggered after Osama bin Laden's jihad-motivated, Muslim-extremist attacks—using orchestrated airplane salvos flown into the NYC Twin Towers, a Shanksville (Pennsylvania) field, and the Pentagon—propelled America into the War on Terror. The nation con-tinues to reel from the attacks and to fight on foreign grounds in order to protect domestic interests because on September 11, 2001, the blood of 3,000 dead and another 6,000 injured was unexpectedly spilled on Ameri-can soil because of the maneuverings of a religious ideologue—in the land of the free and the home of the brave.

On the strength of substantial ethnographic research, American national identity is characterized by investigating the faith practices, socio-political concerns, and civil religious loyalties of blacks and whites in Bald Eagles, and by focusing efforts on the connection residents make between human "blood" sacrifices and the land by their ritual actions, like that of

Corporal Essary. The chapters that follow capture how white and black social groups use religion: to memorialize the dead in the public square; to acknowledge the sacrificial deaths of military personnel who have served the country at the frontlines of war and the fallen honored on civic holidays; and to invoke messages about American freedom through the human "blood" sacrifices of past leaders and ordinary citizens. Study of the symbolism of these blood sacrifices and their ties to religion and to land show that blood-land-religion cements American nationality and regional communities, supporting but also at times questioning the political ideology of American exceptionalism.

Human sacrifices resulting from defense of country and American civil liberties translate into rites of faith that contribute to community consensus and contestation. Also representing the casualties of rites of war, they yield racially diverse and divergent public theologies of war. In this work, I assume analysis of both rites of faith and rites of war that produce such human "blood" sacrifices. What is more, Bald Eagles testifies to the moral community that emerges from this rural Southern town as it is being shaped by a post-9/11 world,[8] a community that identifies strongly with military and church cultures and that is changed by what many Americans wrongly presumed would be a postracial society after the election of President Barack Obama. By the close, the ongoing and very present crisis in American national identity is apparent, leaving room for distinguishable understandings of the ideals constituting American exceptionalism from the Obama years up to the present day.

Symbolic Acts, Beliefs, and Language in the Making of Moral Community

That the Bald Eagles County High School gymnasium functioned as the public's gathering place for Corporal Keith Essary's military funeral symbolizes the link between the secular and the sacred as well as the living and the dead and also introduces this constituency as a moral community. A sacred event being held in a secular space is a symbolic act that—alongside the mourning speeches, sermons, and language—elucidated the community's beliefs, allegiances, and values, reflecting their moral orientations and cementing their collective identities.

Establishing Bald Eagles as a moral community fulfills Émile Durkheim's description of how religion shapes moral identities; satisfies the drive to understand how residents construct meaning and ideas about belonging as self-identified evangelicals living in a civil religious town; aims to defy long-standing stereotypes of evangelicals as primarily lower-class to middle-class, undereducated and moderately educated, religious and political conservatives who are by default a biased social group; and illustrates that the norms and values that shape townsfolk into a moral community are maintained but also can be reconfigured by volatile social conditions that shift both regional and American identities. Thus, in his homily, Reverend James Wolfgang of the East Bald Eagles United Methodist Church remarks:

> This nation honors and respects humanity and dignity. Guys like Keith give us the gift of life through their death. Our nation will continue until the Lord and Savior Jesus Christ comes. Sometimes men like Keith suffer the ultimate sacrifice. They also suffer emotional wounds that need healing: these wounds are also a sacrifice. I would now like to read selected verses from Romans 8. . . . Who better than our Creator would know what is best for us? Resting in Christ is your spirit's DNA. Living in Christ, you will have a restful joyous life. It might be as short as Keith's—twenty years—shorter or longer. If it was lived like Keith, however, it was lived well.

From Reverend Wolfgang's perspective, Keith's life and actions are in some sense like those of Jesus Christ. Similar to Christ's sacrificial death to offer resurrection life and to unify those in the family of God, Keith—and the many like him—sacrificed human life and limb to defend and pull together the community and the nation. On the battlefield, Keith unselfishly gave his life for the longevity of the nation, which, in this community's understanding, also means he will receive eternal spiritual life. He will remain divinely immortal in the community's memory. By paralleling Essary's unselfish work to that of Christ, Wolfgang is also encouraging community members to live sacrificial lives.

Much like the martyred soldier, if they do live such sacrificial lives, they too will be held in high esteem by their community and country. Further, for American democracy to continue, community members must follow Keith's lead and die to their own preoccupations and interests. Their sacrificial service not only sustains but also regenerates American democracy under postwar conditions since: "Guys like Keith give us an example of the gift of life through their death . . . [because] resting in Christ's DNA is [resurrection] life. [His] and your spirit's DNA is in Christ's DNA."

Captain Trevor Vogel in his remarks takes a similar position, yet with a different emphasis than Wolfgang. That day, he not only identifies the "enemy"—the Taliban (i.e., Islamic fundamentalism)—but also highlights the theme of service by illuminating Keith's delight in being in the presence of Afghani children, his willingness to help, and his work building the floor for the local community center, all the while fulfilling his duties as a soldier by protecting American interests at home and abroad.

Vogel then pivots to ask something similar of his audience:

> You, too, can serve this country as citizens of character, strong morals, and values. Our policemen, firemen, and factory workers serve this country by exemplifying strong morals, character, and values. By being a good neighbor, you serve this community. This area truly represents America—it is America—and it has never forgotten our sons and daughters! May God bless you, your family, soldiers, and God bless America!

The relationship between the living and the dead predominates here as Vogel connects service to God, to humanity, and to country with the message of being "a good neighbor." Despite Keith's death, America is blessed because Keith exemplified "strong morals, character, and values" that anyone of the still living in the community can emulate. If, as good neighbors and godly soldiers on the battlefield, residents serve the American nation in their respective blue-collar professional stations—as police officer, firefighter, and factory worker—and through everyday acts of kindness, service, and character, they too will be called "family" (sons and daughters of God) and will be blessed likewise.

In his proclamations that close Corporal Essary's funeral, Army Chaplain Ted Randall delivers the following exhortation:

> In 1 Samuel, David mourns his fallen soldier friend Jonathon. The mighty has fallen in the midst of the battle. The mighty continue to fall in the midst of the battle. O, how the mighty fall in battle! However, the Mighty One has *not fallen* in battle!

He punctuates his sermon with the song "Arlington," which exemplifies the overarching message of this worshipful service and funeral in the county's public gymnasium, captured in the following stanza:

> I remember daddy brought me here when I was eight
> We searched all day
> To find out where my grand-dad lay
> When we finally found that cross
> He said, "Son this is what it costs
> To keep us free."

The language of the cross is that Christ died to set us free; the language of the song ties spiritual death to physical death, specifically death on the battlefield. The song reminds family, friends, and the public gathered that there is a cost to Americans for the nation to remain free. That cost is the cross, a symbol standing at the crossroads of life and death. The song's lyrics mesmerize, and the army chaplain reinforces them by reminding his audience of their responsibility toward the dead. Further, the song's lyrics symbolize, stress, and reaffirm this town's belief system ("[that] the mighty fall in battle! However, the Mighty One has *not fallen* in battle!"), meaning soldiers might fall on the battlefield defending the nation, but neither God nor America have fallen into the hands of the enemy!

The sermons delivered that day reflected the behavior and mindset of residents. Such behaviors and mindsets—a reflection of the religious actions and thoughts of townsfolk—form Bald Eagles residents into a moral community. Social groups and social organizations are religious in nature when they display collective beliefs, values, and practices that deeply and meaningfully shape moral identities.[9] Religion is a social fact that both reveals the ways people think and act and reinforces the social construction of human experiences; as a social force, religion also has the power to conform individual thought and behavior to that of society. The links between religion and society become clear when we consider the venue for Essary's funeral: the crowd. The crowd sacralized the Bald Eagles County gymnasium (which is not a church), where Reverend Wolfgang's language reiterated the community's beliefs in sacrifice and eternal life, which are suitable responses to honor the military dead and any member of the community who has fallen in defense of and for the good of the country.

In the making of moral community, religion is not necessarily a reflection of the supernatural, nor does religion account for humans' relationship with spiritual beings or gods. Religion transcends the supernatural and the gods. A religious theory of society is based on the unity of beliefs and practices, and it expresses the nature of sacred things. When beliefs are enacted—producing modes of action (i.e., rites) agreed upon by society and reflecting the emotions, shared values, history, and purpose—a moral community is conceived and established.

Knowledge of the emotions, shared values, history, and purpose of the Bald Eagles community is gained through Captain Vogel, who stresses Essary's service to neighbor *and* nation, yet not solely to America but also to one that is foreign—Afghanistan. In that instant, Essary's service to the Afghani community becomes symbolic action. It manifests the commitments and values not only of Essary but of Bald Eagles residents as a whole, who for twenty years shaped him socially and culturally for service. His service is a result of their service. So his service, whether of building up a devastated community or of fighting, not only fulfills his professional duties: his community through him also fulfills their obligations. Vogel closes by reminding that community never to forget the service to the living of those now dead. For in remembering that service, the living also receive God's favor.

The sacred and the profane are distinct but fundamental to all religions. Sacred things are consecrated, isolated, and protected by prohibitions, while profane things are marked by contempt and an irreverence for what is sacred. Although religious phenomena are categorized as sacred or profane, the power of sacrality manifests when the profane is placed in diametric opposition to the sacred. In brief, sacred and profane things are always separate, yet they function as a dyad in a study of the religious character of society.

When religion is defined as beliefs and rites with respect to sacred things, a moral community is formed and religion becomes a social glue—a common faith—prompting individuals to submit to the group, where common thinking and acting promotes unity with respect to the sacred.[10] Army Chaplain Randle's message instantiates my proposal that Bald Eagles is a moral community, whose religion—sacred and secular—guarantees its social structure, its "tribal" identity, its political power, and thereby its collective existence.[11] For Bald Eagles as a moral community, intertwined in the symbol of the cross are the beliefs, language, and symbolic actions of sacrifice, service, and resurrection life. Implied in the message of the cross is an enemy—loss, costs, and death—interpreted at both communal and national levels. What solidifies Bald Eagles as a moral community is their unwavering belief in the cross as a sacred and secular symbol and as a place where life and death collide. In the cross, the people of Bald Eagles choose and embrace good over evil, order over disorder, life over death, and they do so with respect to all aspects of their lives—spiritual, individual, communal, and national. This choice drives them to uphold constitutional freedoms and protections, even to the extent of bearing arms and entering war against the enemy. The religion they believe in and practice is both ecclesial and civic. The Christian religion thus functions to set this group apart as well as to project, regenerate, and re-create social structure, identity, and the mental states of members of this rural community.

Southern Civil Religion: A Way of Life

In 1967, the concept of an American civil religion was introduced to the American lexicon. Since that time, the scholarly community has both embraced and opposed the concept. America's present pressing political issues sparked by national debates about border control, immigration, increased national security, patriotism, and war have prompted a revival of interest in civil religion as an analytical tool among scholars. Robert N. Bellah defined *civil religion* as religious elements and an orientation shared by a majority of Americans and playing a critical role in the development of American institutions and democracy. This public faith is expressed in a set of beliefs, symbols, and rituals.[12] American civil religion can also be described as ritualistic expressions of patriotism.[13] Later, the concept was refined to include the religious dimension of a people through which the people interpret historical experience in light of transcendent reality.[14]

Prophetic and priestly forms of civil religion are notable but commonplace.[15] The prophetic grows out of a tradition of cultural contestation and criticism of America; the priestly is more conciliatory in its approach to critiquing America and more celebratory of individual responsibility through participation in a capitalist society and liberal democracy. Both forms, however, hold contested visions of America and the tensions associated with the critical and conciliatory dimensions of the term. Although there are diverse and divergent descriptions of American civil religion, such religion ultimately is belief in and practice of a nonsectarian faith that sacralizes social and political life through public ceremonies and rituals and that reaffirms American social identity through people finding ultimate meaning for collective existence in a religiously rooted national history. The strength of American civil religion is its supposed ability to unify Americans based on its capacity to be a cultural canopy for social diversity.[16]

However, a post–Civil War Southern civil religion developed in 1980, comprised of rituals, a mythology, and organization distinct from the national public faith known as American (Northern) civil religion. After losing the Civil War on a holy battlefield, disillusioned Southerners sought and found three values in their civil religion—affirmation, identity, and redemption.[17] Southern civil religion developed around death rituals as rites that commemorated and re-created a mythical past, and mourning rites that transformed dead heroes into esteemed ancestors.[18] These death rituals started as Confederate Memorial Day, identified as Decoration Day,[19] to honor the Civil War dead. On that occasion, Confederate widows and their Southern sisterhood placed wreaths and flowers on the graves of their martyred dead husbands, brothers, and nephews—a grim task particularly for the women who often sublimated and replaced the pain of their sacrifices on the national altar with joyous expressions of survival.[20]

Ironically, these death rituals became an expression of Southern civil religious loyalties because ritual participants were memorializing the death of a "political" (i.e., Southern) nation, in its practice of a religion of the Lost Cause.[21] Southern civil religion, a civic and cultural religion, became increasingly relevant to the development of a distinct Southern identity and of an ever-changing American national identity. In rural Bald Eagles, belief and practice of Southern civil religion—a regional form of American civil religion—is not only pervasive but a way of life that actively fortifies the Southern and rural identities of townsfolk.

A version of Southern civil religion that accounts for the history of American white and black racial dynamics also challenges the idea that American civil religion is a cultural canopy able to handle social diversity. Moving away from the Lost Cause version, yet extending the Southern civil religion concept, is a racialized form[22] that sprung up beside white civil religion and subtly grew alongside the black tradition of the American jeremiad, having historical roots in the nation's nascency and bringing about a messianic black nationalism meant to socially redeem white America.[23] A focal point of this progenitor form of black civil religion was the exodus motif, which occupied the imaginations of the enslaved and was central to abolitionist efforts, 1950s and 1960s civil rights campaigns, as well as later struggles for justice and liberty.[24] In light of David Howard-Pitney's 1995 study of the African American jeremiad tradition and momentous fights for freedom, this version of civil religion upholds and illumes the democratic commitments of racial (i.e., black) and other ethnic groups who are key to articulating notions of an ideal America.[25]

In later American and Southern history, desegregation had become pivotal to actualizing what American values were important to blacks and whites and to learning about each group's national commitments and espousal of principles salient to realizing the American dream. Here, racialized forms of Southern civil religion call forth an active black civil religion expressed as ritualistic forms of patriotism; determine and reveal the deeply held values, principles, and convictions of both white and black social groups; and highlight the potential for civil religious traditions to "contain" ideological fractures in the social and moral fabric of America.

Religious Patriotism, Race, and Memorializing the Dead

Field research was conducted in the 1950s on a prototypical New England town, producing five volumes of work identified as the Yankee City Series.[26] The first four volumes explored and theorized about social life and the import of status in community and about how American ethnic groups function as social systems (e.g., Polish, Russian, Irish, French Canadian), and they explained the particular sociology of the factory.

The fifth volume investigated the impact of religion, politics, history, and memorializing the dead on the residents of Yankee City, and it concluded that together these forces have a unifying effect on communities and the nation.

In that fifth volume, a regional study on symbol systems (e.g., political campaigns and conflict, cultural heroes, and Catholic mass), William Lloyd Warner posits that research done on one community, despite variation, holds for others because of the nature of symbolic life in this country where throughout all regions the basic meanings of our secular and religious symbols remain equal.[27] Such bold claims about examining the symbolic life of singular regions opens the way to interpreting and understanding the religious and civic behavior of Americans in all regions. Analysis of the Yankee City celebration of Memorial Day is described as a cult of the dead that organizes and integrates diverse faith, ethnic, and class groups. The sacrifices of dead soldiers compel the living to sacrifice their individual purposes to the common good. Symbolically, human sacrificial death for the public good is compared to the Christian church's sacrifice of the incarnate God. In sacrificing and dying, these men become powerful sacred symbols for organizing and reviving the collective ideals of community and nation.[28]

On civic holidays like Memorial Day, Independence Day, and Veterans Day where ceremonial rites memorializing the dead are performed, public and private arenas are transformed into sacred spaces because of the ways in which ritual participants symbolically (and usually unconsciously) connect human sacrifice on the battlefield to the human sacrifice of the incarnate God. By connecting both sacred and secular belief systems through ritual action (e.g., parades), social collectives are able to overcome anxieties produced by encounters with death and likewise are able to overcome death because of the euphoria recreated by the group, hearkening back to wartime service and reinforcing individual toughness, group strength, and (national) power.[29]

The significance of Memorial Day as a "religious day," which included messages about its meaning delivered during Sunday morning worship services, was made even more obvious because of its capacity to unify a religiously, socioeconomically, and ethnically diverse Yankee City population. The Polish, Russian, Irish Catholic, French Canadians, and Italians were members of the community despite being "new" immigrants to the United States in the late nineteenth and early twentieth centuries and were incorporated as those who would eventually achieve "white" status.[30] In the following exchange between a fieldworker and an older parishioner who was noting the decline in church membership because of these new "foreigners," the integrating effect of Memorial Day observances is quite clear:

> "Yes," he said, "there are not so many of the old New Englanders. It's these new foreigners who have come in that have spoiled it. That's what cuts down our church attendance. But there are some good foreigners. It's good once in a while to get a mixture of good fine stock, especially from Northern Europe, especially from Scotland. You know Scotland is the place where John Knox came from, who started Presbyterianism."[31]

In spite of their ethnic and religious "foreignness," the Irish, Germans, Scots, and Poles, and the Jews, Catholics, and Greek Orthodox were viewed as "'citizens'—the most equalitarian of Yankee City terms," and so their citizenship translated into the equally democratic status of soldier.[32] Contributing to their assimilation into the Yankee City community were the symbols, language, and rituals associated with Memorial Day that sanctified institutional spaces, then prepared to contain disparate and conflicting emotions, associations, and culturally diverse peoples, blending all parts of the community that would come to share a common mindset and spirit of sorrow and sacrifice.

And so Sunday morning messages on Memorial Day illumined the sacred and symbolic connection between the living and the dead, whether services were held at the Presbyterian or Baptist church; whether groups bore American and purple flags in the midst of a local cemetery or conducted a vacant chair ceremony in military style and regalia at a local church; whether veterans groups and lodges or the minister led the morning devotionals; whether the names of President Lincoln or President Washington or the Gettysburg Address was invoked during ceremonies throughout the town. By the 1950s, Memorial Day had come to represent a sacred day of the dead, not just a celebration of the military dead based on the regional conflict that had come to be known as the Civil War. Citywide participants— regardless of place, space, and position—heard, embraced, and heralded themes about "honoring the dead by being faithful unto death, because 'whosoever shall save his life shall lose it and whosoever shall lose his life in My name, shall save it'"; about "being true Americans by sacrificing and carrying on despite Death, [which] is not a conqueror [of humanity's spirits and souls]"; and in the name of the "suffering and sorrow [that] molded the nation . . . for the cause of liberty and of God."[33]

One speaker, after reading Lincoln's Gettysburg Address, asked:

> "Is patriotism dead? Why aren't these pews all filled?" He turned to the minister and said, "A few years ago there would have been crowds here

and now there are few. Isn't that right, Mr. Commander? Is patriotism dead? No, it isn't dead, it is sleeping. May we promise Thee, our Country, that our youth will not be exposed to pernicious influences, that the present evils will be overcome. Grant, oh God, that we may perform our duty. Amen."[34]

For this speaker, there is no conflict between religion and patriotism. His delivery of the Gettysburg Address primes his audience for the heart of his message: that true patriotism goes hand in hand with a religion; it is a religious patriotism that honors the dead while requiring the living to sacrifice for the cause of preserving American liberty.

Bellah's later work on American civil religion explains how history, religion, and politics in the public square bond local communities and connect segments of American society, and it adds a new dimension to Warner's piece on faith, politics, and the formative role of death on communities. American civil religion is situated alongside the institutional church and American political society, an appraisal that makes civil religion instrumental in capturing the values and commitments of Memorial Day participants.

In the end, Yankee City Memorial Day rites and ceremonies draw together three fundamental themes—starting with Memorial Day being a powerful civil religious event and symbol that regulates the emotions and organizes and merges Yankee City residents, organizations, churches, and associations into a whole unit. Their ritual activities stress the sacrificial death of soldiers for the country and identify the dead with the death of the incarnate God to encourage the living to respond with solidarity and service to the nation.

Second, Memorial Day rites in Yankee City expedited the process of melding diverse ethnic and religious groups that would eventually be grafted into the "white" American nationality and population; their incorporation into this "native" social and religious (i.e., Protestant) group would ultimately perform the task of cementing America's sub rosa social identity as a "white, Christian" nation.

Yankee City's Memorial Day rituals lastly generated an energy among residents that showed the value of war in solidifying communities and the nation. This implicit sentiment about war moreover suggests that Yankee City residents might have resorted to war as the only recourse and best possible mechanism for preserving constitutional freedoms and American democracy. Furthermore, the benefits to fighting war included the increased optimism of a post–World War II America that had survived a Great Depression and two war economies as well as the economic boom generated and maintained by prosperity derived from war efforts and international cooperation.

Yankee City Memorial Day investigations and theses are foundational to my research because these 1950s studies recognize that, taken together, death, ritual, religion, and politics unify regional communities and the nation. However, research on war and the civil religious loyalties,[35] faith practices, and sociopolitical concerns of residents in rural Bald Eagles is distinguishable from the Yankee City Series based on the historical and political moments marking American social change. That is, *when* research was conducted and *who* became research participants provided evidence for shifting interpretations and understandings of American national identity and the relationship between race, religion, and politics.

Data collection occurred during the height of two wars and in the midst of a sea of sociopolitical disruptions, precipitated by the election of Barack H. Obama as the first American president of African descent. Data therefore showed racial diversity to be a predictive factor for the interpretation and comprehension of American and Southern civil religions, a factor that neither Warner's nor Bellah's theories initially considered. Race (e.g., white, black), region (i.e., the South), and the particular "cultural" practice of civil religion (i.e., rural) and evangelical faith and American exceptionalism were crucial aspects of responses to my question of how we should live. How shall we Americans live together, given our social disappointments with wars spawned by violent extremism, struggles with undocumented immigration, questions about border control, increased national security, an economic depression blamed on an American housing crisis that triggered the 2008–2009 stock market crash, and perpetual post-9/11 economic instability?

More than a decade later, even with the benefits of an economic recovery, Americans still face the former disappointments and an added list of other sundry issues. Reports indicate that Americans are deeply conflicted about fighting never-ending wars, even wars touted as being about preserving constitutional freedoms. Americans are also profoundly troubled by the War on Terror, which was fueled by religious ideology and had neither specific military goals nor ground targets.[36] Moreover, that War on Terror is a different kind of war, one that has pushed America into the direction of flouting the rule of law and America's guiding principles by torturing prisoners of war and therefore not according them due process of law.[37] That war also raises questions in the minds of citizens about the legality and morality of the use of force as a counterterrorist strategy and option to make America safe. As James Madison warned, "No nation could preserve its freedom in the midst of continual warfare."[38]

Southern civil religion reflects the religious values and the social and political ideals of American Southerners, ideals that are centered around family, community, and evangelical faith. Though intellectual debate about religion, patriotism, and war is heightened among the broader population because of twenty-first-century religious pluralism and Christian ecumenism, for the rural farming community of Bald Eagles the frameworks of Southern civil religions and what it means to be American are religious patriotisms that offer them what American studies scholar Nicole Guétin explains as a unifying code of values and commitments tacitly respected by all citizens but not referring to a specific religion or God.[39] This local Southern community values religion's (i.e., Christianity's) role in both infusing and mooring American politics and public life: an ideology supported by the development of a post–Civil War Southern civil religion that was *not* antithetical to evangelical faith, unlike its American (civil religion) counterpart.

Religion assumes a role in leadership of the nation through its relationship to morality and politics. Research on religion and politics in the rural West Tennessee community of Bald Eagles in the late spring and summer of 2006 yielded regional and racial differences in evangelical faith and civil religion.[40] Whites were loyal to both Southern and American civil religions at the Memorial Day event held at the historic white cemetery in town, Fairview Cemetery. Conversations and speeches about the wars in Afghanistan and Iraq elicited a white Southern patriotism that supported America's fight for the preservation of democracy at home and abroad. On that day, program participants and spectators alike were transformed into preachers of American exceptionalism.[41] Yet, the history of the United States is far more intimately connected with the history of the rest of the world, and in particular with the history of Europe, than is generally assumed in the United States,[42] a cautionary note for those who tout America's political and moral superiority. Moreover, modern American social pride and political beliefs, especially core convictions about liberty and democracy, have been more troublesome than patriotic rhetoric claims. Far from what preachers of American exceptionalism suggest, freedom and democracy have not developed smoothly or easily. Both had to be fought for, and not only against strangers and foreigners.[43] Despite all great nations cherishing their national myths,[44] both propositions continue to strike at the heart of the often hubristic, exaggerated, and patriotic claims of American exceptionalism, forgetting or dismissing the historical moments where national struggles reveal America as less than exceptional.

Nonetheless, Reverend Branscomb, an army veteran turned Baptist clergyman who attained the rank of sergeant in the Vietnam War, preached a message prompted by Deuteronomy 32:7 about the virtues of having America's present generation draw wisdom from generations past, as did the Israelites who heeded Moses' message to remember the former days. Branscomb's sermon linked America's enduring symbols (e.g., the Declaration of Independence) to their meaning for present and future generations and to remembering to honor dead soldiers who had sacrificed their lives to maintain the values and principles represented by America's symbols, or what he calls its ancient landmarks. Branscomb encouraged the audience at the cemetery by reminding them what America stands for:

> God speaks through Moses to the younger generation. Ask the elders and they will tell you. Ask those with white hair what they have seen, what they have lived. Wisdom comes through the school of hard knocks, the school of black and blue. Ask the elders. Ask the veterans of World War II, pilots and those in the infantry. Glean wisdom from these experiences because profitable those words of wisdom can be. There are lessons to be learned from the elders of the Korean War; ask for those lessons.
>
> What would it be like to ask those who have been laid to rest. What would they say? I thank God for the legacy of a godly grandmother and mother. Their indelible impressions make me who I am. . . .
>
> What would the elders say?

Be of Service in Spite of Hardship

> The good ol' days were not so good. [The American public] faced the Depression and a 1941 surprise naval attack. These were devastating times of war and sacrifice. They knew about sacrifice. Women walked with babies on both hips to the church house. I would say that was a hardship, wouldn't you?
>
> Be of service in spite of hardship.
>
> Instill patriotism, love of God, love of nation. Instill this into our young people.
>
> Be of service in spite of hardship.

Remove Not the Ancient Landmarks

> The Declaration of Independence
>   Constitution
>   Word of God

Basic Human Values Are Found in These Landmarks

Stand up for the Judeo-Christian ethic.
   Stand for righteousness, morality, integrity.
   Landmarks set boundaries.
   The moral landmarks of yesteryear are boundaries for life now.
   Landmarks help you get your bearings.
   They are a compass.

Do Not Forget the Lord

There was a time when we had no problems saying "one nation under God," having prayer in school, and speaking the Lord's name in public places.

Leave a Legacy for Children

This cemetery is a well-maintained place and proof of the great effort on the part of many people. This has been purchased at a great price by the elders of yesteryear. People around the world would want to see America in a different place. . . . America stands for what is right—liberty, freedom.

Ask for Old Paths

The old book, blessed hope, precious blood of Jesus Christ. These are valid principles on which we order our lives: morality, love of neighbor, and righteousness.

   Don't neglect the Lord or the church. Join together around the word of God. Nation, home, church are ordained by God. Honor the memory of loved ones. And one day this wonderful grace of God will not be a memorial but reunion with him.

[Closing Prayer]

We give thanks for those who l[ie] at rest here. We owe them a great debt. . . . We give them the honor and respect they so richly deserve. . . . This we ask in Jesus Christ name. Amen.[45]

Blacks in the town held their own Memorial Day celebration at the historic black burial ground, Memorial Park Cemetery. Some citizens and political figures, including the city and county mayors, traveled across town from Fairview Cemetery to participate in the "black" Memorial Day ceremony. There, African American participants blended nationalism with a black racial consciousness that came alive as the preacher, Reverend Carter, a black veteran, delivered his sermon in the tradition of the American jeremiad.[46] His sermon, based on Ecclesiastes 3:1–8 and declaring "to every season there is a purpose, a time for every purpose under heaven," advocated for healing the American nation. The listening audience heard the following homily from Reverend Carter:

Every soldier takes the following oath:

"I do solemnly swear . . . to obey the officers and the
    President . . ."
Soldiers are defenders of the principles of the Constitution and
    liberty . . .
In the oath soldiers solemnly swear to defend the Constitution
    against enemies foreign and domestic.

They swear to uphold the Declaration of Independence . . .
Please honor their greatness in your hearts.
Not a day goes by without sorrow.
Honor their sacrifice by living fully.
[For they paid] the ultimate sacrifice for liberty.
These headstones with tiny flags remind us that many soldiers
    lived "unfulfilled lives, but their lives were filled with dignity
    and honor."

Some Americans [i.e., soldiers] will not live to see their home-
    land again.
Some return disabled, sacrificing mind and limbs for freedom.
Human costs of war are appallingly high!

Salute those who have given their lives!
Didn't James Madison say, "If men were angels, government would
    not be needed"?
2 Chronicles 7:14 proclaims "if my people who are called by my
    name will humble themselves, and pray and seek my face, and
    turn from their wicked ways, then I will hear from heaven, and
    forgive their sins and heal their land."

For the [American] nation to be healed, you have to humble your-
    self by admitting wrongs, pray to God for forgiveness, seek God,
    turn from sin.
Bring back the glory to America—pray for healing.
Israel/America have abandoned God and the glory of God.

[In order to be healed], we need . . . [based on Judges 9]
Gratitude, godly leaders, committed people.
Those committed to God and country [are] a source of glory.
America must turn back to God for her glory to be returned.
[We must ask God] to forgive us as a nation so that we can be
    healed again.

2 Corinthians 3:17 says, ". . . where the Spirit of the Lord is, there
    is liberty."
We, as a nation, must stand firm to what we believe and not com-
    promise with other nations.
[To the soldiers], we say "thank you" for your patriotic duty.
[We will continue to strive to be] one nation under God, indivisi-
    ble, with liberty and justice for all.[47]

Both memorial events centered on American landmark symbols, on
freedom as an attainable ideal, and on ritualistic expressions of death that
combined patriotism and evangelicalism while drawing upon the political
tradition of American exceptionalism. Both combined and drew attention
to the soldiers' sacrifice, prodding audience members to think hard and
practice the same level of service and sacrifice. And both combined scriptural interpretation with a defense of the nation.

However, the crowds that gathered at each ceremony had quite different perspectives on what it meant to be an American and therefore what
characteristics made America great. The white preacher and his listening
audience highlighted American democratic notions of freedom while also
fiercely embracing a Southern cultural identity rooted in white American
racial nationalism. This group championed a form of white nationalism
with cherished and popular founding and national myths, creating a climate for and making apparent what would be termed a *racialized town*.[48]
Their reaction nonetheless represented an interesting historical turn
because post–Civil War white Southerners have tended to stress democracy *less* than the conservative concepts of moral virtue and an orderly
society.[49] The black preacher and black attendees expressed American
nationalistic and social pride yet also racial and ethnic concern. At the
same time that the costly toll of war on human life rested on their minds,
they also pointed out the racial divide, and the inequality they perceived
still persisted and was the source of social deprivation and a discordant
lived reality for black Americans. And so, the black preacher reiterated the
vision of and need for a just society. For these reasons, both preacher and
participants pushed for the healing of the nation.

At the center of both white and black Memorial Day ceremonies were nonsectarian and Christocentric "death" rites, relating blood-religion-land to questions of *who belongs* (in America) and to declarations about the fraying of our country's social fabric. They also elevated residents' clear avowal of evangelical Protestantism and civil religion, attributes that defined the dualistic nature of rural Bald Eagles, a town that former mayor Bill Revell described as composed of friendly, God-fearing, and patriotic citizens living in a community atmosphere.[50] Indeed, the church has been the backbone of this community from the county's inception. Religiously, evangelical Protestantism reigns supreme.

In fact, evangelical Protestantism with its stress on a theology of inward conversion is not antithetical to the development of a Southern civil religion. In the South, each undergirds the other.[51] The sectarian nature of Christian faith is generally at odds with the nonsectarian faith of civil religion; intermingling the two can become a potential source of social conflict. American evangelical theologian Donald G. Bloesch grounds American Evangelical Christianity in the Protestant Reformation, Puritanism, and Pietism and notes that it is influenced by the Holiness Movement and dispensationalism. These historical roots contribute to the fundamental features of evangelical Christianity as a belief in the absolute sovereignty and transcendence of God; the divine authority and inspiration of Scripture; the radical sinfulness of humanity; the deity of Jesus Christ; his vicarious, substitutionary atonement; the eschatological and superhistorical character of the kingdom of God; a final judgment at the end of history; the realities of heaven and hell; and evangelization as the primary dimension of the Christian mission.[52] Elements of Protestant Christianity provide the framework for belief in and exercise of civil religion, a distinctive feature of evangelical Christianity, a conservative brand of American Protestantism.[53] Yet in Bald Eagles, religion and patriotism support each other, cementing the social glue created by a substantive ritual life that can "hold" ambivalences.[54] God's will is rooted in the eschatological and apocalyptic thought central to the evangelical theology practiced by many in this community and supported by Southern civil religion.

The Memorial Day celebrations I witnessed in 2006 further substantiate Wilson's claims about Southern civil religion. Both black and white communities' understandings of service to this country are an integral aspect of their civil religious loyalties, even if they differ as social groups. Such loyalties bind race, regional affiliations, religion, and culture and prompt questions about how historical and contemporary experiences with death relate to blood-religion-land. The ways in which this trifecta entwines death serve to influence townsfolks' worldviews about regional and national identities, their racial and identity politics, and their list of qualities that make America distinctive, as well as their interpretation of war. Without regard to race, for these rural dwellers the ultimate patriot is one who dies upholding and protecting democratic principles while in military service to the nation.

2

Religion, Race, Region, and American Exceptionalism

"Making America Great Again"

I reentered rural and Southern Bald Eagles in 2008 to continue to conduct macrolevel and microlevel studies of the county and black and white congregations in its most populous city.[1] Returning confirmed the need to complicate present-day understandings of American national identity, evangelical faith, American and Southern civil religions, and their relationship to American exceptionalism based on residents' participation in mourning and death rites during civic holidays and practice of alternating forms of civil religion. Public understandings of evangelical faith and civil religion, even among the educated elite, reveal that people often consider both from unidimensional perspectives. The American public, policy experts, and academic scholars fail to recognize the distinctive forms of evangelical faith, the racialized nature of evangelical faith and civil religion, and civil religion as a cultural religion—and how it functions differently in different communities. Applying regional and racial hermeneutics ultimately broadens and refines understandings of evangelical faith, civil religion, American national identity, as well as *who Americans are* in relationship to American exceptionalism—a guiding cultural principle and defining feature of the nation.

Bald Eagles County: Farming Rooted in Family Tradition

Situated in the northwest corner of Tennessee is the city of Bald Eagles,[2] the county seat for Bald Eagles County. Bald Eagles County is composed of three cities. From smallest to largest, they are Hummingbird, Screaming Eagle, and Bald Eagles. In 2006, Bald Eagles County had a population of 37,710 (approx. 18,000 males and 19,000 females), and Bald Eagles City had a population of 17,287 (approx. 8,000 males and 9,000 females). The county population was projected to increase to 38,013 in 2011, and while it increased by 625 to 38,335, the city's population has actually remained the same.[3]

According to the 2006 Census estimate, the county population by race was 85% white, 13.1% black, 0.2% American Indian / Alaska Native, 0.5% Asian / Pacific Islander, and 2.0% Hispanic/Latino. For the city of Bald Eagles, the 2006 numbers were 75.6% white, 21.9% black, 0.2% American Indian / Alaska Native, 0.8% Asian / Pacific Islander, and 2.4% Hispanic/Latino.

For 2011, Bald Eagles County's projections were 84.7% white, 13.2% black, 0.2% American Indian / Alaska Native, 0.7% Asian / Pacific Islander, and 2.8% Hispanic / Latino.[4] For Bald Eagles City in 2011, the projected numbers were 75.3% white, 22.0% black, 0.2% American Indian / Alaskan Native, 1.1% Asian / Pacific Islander, and 3.2% Hispanic / Latino.[5] Though field studies focused primarily on the city of Bald Eagles, both city and county were covered because of their close connection. For instance, the courthouse where the county offices are located is in the historical downtown area of the city.

Bald Eagles County is "100 miles from the geographic population center of the United States" and a "day's drive from 76 percent of the country's major markets." With 56% of the land used for agricultural production, farming is a $66.1 million industry in Bald Eagles County.[6] Bald Eagles County is Tennessee's primary producer of soybean and fourth largest for grain sorghum and wheat. The county also grows vegetables, rice, cotton, and corn, although farming no longer dominates its industry.

A diversity of manufacturing industries employs workers from around Bald Eagles County and outside counties, with manufacturing accounting for almost 40% of all jobs in the county. Industries are increasingly being added to this community, making it one of the fastest growing in Tennessee, according to Chamber of Commerce reports. The average household income in Bald Eagles County, according to 2011 estimates, was $49,056. For the city, the average income was $48,546. The median household income was $40,145 for the county and $33,752 for the city. Differentials exist according to race.

There is a solid wealthy/upper-middle-class white population in Bald Eagles connected to "old" money and "new" industry money. Middle-class whites tend to live on one side of town (along Highway 78 and 51 Bypass North) with working-class whites on its fringes. Middle-class and working-class blacks live on the other side of town, close to the "Historic Downtown District." However, the influx of black doctors and other professionals from outside the area has contributed to a very small but developing middle and upper-middle-class black population who tend to live among upper-income whites; similarly, working-class white and Mexican families live within the black working-class and poorer areas.

For political statistics, I visited the Bald Eagles / Bald Eagles County Election Commission and learned that (1) in primary elections, individuals are asked in which primary they will be voting (residents do not declare party affiliation); (2) in general elections, residents vote for individuals (candidates are not grouped according to party affiliation); and (3) voting by punch card changed on August 3, 2006, in local elections because punch-card voting is now outlawed in Tennessee. Bald Eagles City and County are predominantly white and politically populist, meaning townsfolk vote Democratic in local elections and Republican in state and national elections. Yet, some blacks do share the same voting practices as their white counterparts because of geographic and regional (i.e., rural and conservative) influences. That accounts for individual variations, from common social group voting patterns, within each of these racial collectives. For these reasons, voting patterns are also determined by race, ethnicity, and regionalism, so differentials will exist.[7]

The Outsider-Insider Ethnographer and America's Historical Turn

In 2008, after I had resided in Bald Eagles for seven months, the town had become for me a portrait of motorcycle culture and beauty pageantry, duck hunting and waterfowl gaming, faith-based nonprofits against the nostalgia of a strong military presence, city life mixed with farm life, and family at the center of a community grounded in love of God and country. I had returned to this community during a highly charged political season in our nation's history. In both church communities—white and black—I was viewed with a "hermeneutics of suspicion" because I was an "outsider," not having grown up in the South, much less in West Tennessee, and specifically *not* in Bald Eagles County. Like the rest of America, this rural and Southern locale was wrestling with notions of *identity*—racial, religious, political, age, and gender.

Presidential election politics defined the American landscape. Hillary Clinton had introduced herself into the race for the White House as an Ivy League–educated white woman with a Southern heritage, from Arkansas. John McCain, born in the Panama Canal Zone, Panama, entered the race for the White House having clinched the 2008 Republican nomination. As an older affluent white gentleman with a military background, he had secured an elite education (U.S. Naval Academy) and was a decorated military veteran and a respected former prisoner of war. Mitt Romney, a wealthy corporate businessman and former governor of Massachusetts, entered the White House race as the nation's first Mormon. Bill Richardson, former governor of New Mexico and of Hispanic descent, entered the presidential race on the Democratic ticket. Mike Huckabee came to the race as a Southern Evangelical and the sole candidate in the election primaries who represented any semblance of "true" Southern identity and values.

Against this political backdrop, Bald Eagles' identity and patriotic conceptualizations and notions of an "exceptional" America were being challenged and contested. The community at large and both church communities were trying to make sense of their communal and individual self-definitions being "turned upside down" and shifting with our country's political environment. During this tenuous period in our nation and the local setting, I had asked for their permission to explore five subjects among them: ritual, race, faith, civil religion, and death.

Barack Obama entered the American stage with "multiple" identities—biracial but self-identifying as black, born to a Kenyan Muslim father (precipitating questions about his religious identity although he had labeled himself a Christian), Hawaiian by birth (a geographical locale) but having grown up in Indonesia (a Muslim nation), and educated at Ivy League institutions (Columbia University and Harvard Law School) while wanting to connect with middle America. By Obama's second year on the election trail, I had settled into new living quarters where both church communities—white and black—were intent on questioning my motivations for studying them in their public and private worship spaces.

Members of the Bald Eagles First United Methodist Church, a white congregation, were welcoming and hospitable but did not hesitate to ask, "Why are you here?" On many occasions as I shook hands with parishioners and received warm smiles and other greetings, I could feel them wondering, "What do you want with us?" or hear them commenting, "Interesting for you to be here with us since worship is segregated in this community." As time progressed, I realized what I had come to represent—a liberal education and institution—ultimately subjecting this church group to doubts about my intentions. Would I pathologize or stereotype them as "stupid and conservative"? Embodied as female, black, and a researcher from a liberal and prestigious Southern university, yet originally from the North, I was received with a "playful" trope—*Yankee*.

Later in my study, I became concerned that members were hesitant about participating in my study; that would have hindered the completion of my work. I approached the pastor who was always open to meeting with me. As we discussed the issue, I attempted to rationalize why folks possibly would not want to speak with me. The pastor responded, "No, they have firm opinions on those subjects; they are able to tell you how they feel about the issues." I took his statement to mean that articulation of their views about religion and politics was not the problem. He joked, "The problem is too many of them are Republicans." I laughed and asked, "And you are 'Independent' or a 'Democrat'?" He proudly stated that he was a Democrat. His joke piqued my interest because of its implications. Many of his members were evidently conservative and because of this recoiled at divulging their true feelings about the questions I was asking.

His next comment, however, made me pause as I looked for a solution to my problem. Pointedly he said, "Well, the truth is that they may not be speaking to you because they are scared they will be cast as 'racists.'" Now, of course their apprehension about being stereotyped as such was in the back of my mind, but I did not say so. I am glad the pastor was forthright. He continued, "They are scared that they have 'latent racism' that may surface while speaking with you." Well, I immediately had two reactions regarding this: (1) I cannot write up a study simply based on a "cultural" group's racism or *fear* of being "outed," and (2) if there is a "fear of latent racism surfacing," then maybe they *are* racist. What other conclusions should I have drawn?

Yet, I responded empathically. This was certainly the first time I had been forced to confront the imbalance of power between me, as the researcher, and this community, as my research subjects. I was faced with their problem of me plausibly relativizing *and* essentializing them. Injecting my black and female body into this predominantly white community and their worshiping space obviously communicated an assortment of messages that evoked multifarious responses. Given the report, though, I felt I was not unlike Obama, who had entered the nation's spotlight as a lone black candidate in a mostly white and privileged political presidential playing field. That caused me to raise questions about what his presence would mean for nationwide politics, America, *and* this regional community.

Members of the Tabernacle Missionary Baptist Church, a black congregation, were also welcoming and hospitable; their initial queries had an edge that was attenuated because, immediately upon my Sunday return to this community, the pastor called a brief church meeting at which I was asked to explain my purpose for wanting to be part of their worship space. Yet that did not lessen their suspicions about me. A few months after first coming to the community, I attended a Tuesday evening church

meeting. That would have been my first. Out of the side of my eyes, I witnessed some members in the meeting silently but visibly glare at the pastor,
implicitly asking, "Why is *she* here?"

In response, the pastor stated that it was a delight to have me in the
meeting but gently added that the "church meeting is *only* for members
of the church." I knew that was my cue to leave. Here, as well, I was
the black female researcher from a *perceived* politically liberal and prestigious Southern university, yet who had come from the North, someone
who had entered their lives, it seemed, to study and civilize them. This
black community, like many others, had been historically conditioned to
respond cynically to scientific researchers because of the transgressions
and unethical conduct of mid-twentieth-century human-subject researchers toward Tuskegee blacks. Later, I learned that even members who had
become familiar and friendly with me would ask when I was absent from
their community: "What is that girl's name? Where is she?" My name-
lessness cemented my outsider status. I was definitively jettisoned to the
margins of their congregational community.

From their perspective, I was like the Northerners who had traveled
to the South after the Emancipation Proclamation to uplift the "ignorant,
uneducated, or undereducated" black masses. I would come to embody
Evelyn Brooks Higginbotham's "politics of respectability" *race woman.*[8] I
suspect that was the key reason why some of the church's female elders did
not immediately embrace me and instead handled me at a distance and
with caution.

The "Grotesque": "Alterity" and "Hybridity" in Disrupting Community

To both communities, I was determinedly an "outsider." As a perceived
race woman[9]—a Northerner conducting field research in the South to better understand Southern life and culture and moving there for educational purposes and in hopes of bettering the social condition of Southern
blacks—I recalled W. E. B. Du Bois' characterization of black existence in
early twentieth-century America, one of "Africanness" and "Americanness." I held in tension my Du Boisian double consciousness—this Africanness and Americanness—while doing research. It was palpable because
blacks and whites still apparently led segregated lives, though the ground
is shifting in this regard. When it comes to this dynamic, however, the rest
of America is no better.

How patriotism is defined in this community underlies the strain of
my Africanness and Americanness. White folks in Bald Eagles hold strict

conceptions of what a patriot is. Generally, a patriot is a Southern, male, white, conservative Protestant and has served the country as a member of the military. Black folks hold more fluid but racialized and social-justice-oriented notions of patriotism. Hence, a conversation about patriotism (i.e., Southern civil religion) and the characteristics of an exceptional America is inherently about the values associated with and what it means to be American.

At Tabernacle, I believe my Africanness and Americanness were regionally constructed. My Africanness, my black skin and folksy ways, enabled this church community to accept me more easily. Yet, my Americanness (read: Northernness) labeled me as an outsider. I was neither kith nor kin. I did not have family from that area or any other part of the South. My people do not hail from the South. They come from the South of the South—the Caribbean.

The complex political atmosphere of the nation was also at play in the minds of black people, here. Obama being a "wind of change" challenged African America on what it means to be a "true and authentic" (black) American. Blacks are not apolitical, nor are they monolithic. Their imaginations, like white America's, were being stretched by Obama—a biracial, self-identified black American and socially liberal Protestant Christian with no contemporary civil rights roots or history, and with a Muslim surname.

It is not implausible to conjecture that blacks, here and elsewhere, conceived that the first black president, after "Bill Clinton,"[10] would be someone like a Julian Bond or Jesse Jackson[11]—a black person with a charismatic and cult personality, whose family history is anchored in slavery, Jim Crow, and last century's civil rights movement and whose political focus is black mobilization and special interests. These have become the authenticating signifiers for being black in America or for what it means to identify as African American.[12]

I had disrupted both communities with my presence because I appeared when an American political arena was pressing the issue of *what it means to be an American*. For blacks, "American," both consciously and unconsciously, is generally identified as black, Christian, and Southern or black with some regional responsibility to the South, given America's racial history.[13] For whites, "American" is perceived as white, Protestant, and Southern with a military background, also because of the racial and religious history of this nation. For instance, our most recent commanders-in-chief have served in the military and/or have been Southerners: Carter, Bush Sr., Clinton, and Bush Jr.

"American" never or rarely includes being female. Community member Marshall Howard was the only speaker at the 2009 Martin Luther King Jr. Day worship service to trace Obama's political genealogy to Rosa Parks: "If not for Rosa Parks, there would be no King, and if not for King, there would be no Obama—Parks, King, Obama." In this simple statement, he not only includes gender in being "American" but also demystifies and deconstructs the notion that black racial uplift emanates solely from black men.

In terms of my white congregation, my Africanness and Americanness played out in a different way. Though I was accepted as one of the lone black members of the congregation, I suspect members of the First United Methodist Church were operating under another type of "politics of respectability," for the following reasons. Their faith and their Southernness required them to show hospitality toward strangers. This type of Southern lore had bearing because I was often asked by leadership and close members how I was being treated. I was accepted because I was categorized as similar to but also *unlike* many of the other blacks in the community. I was the seeming "exception," being an educated Northerner. They were operating under a "politic" fueled by anxiety around my potentially "inaccurate" representation of them. Such politics would demand I speak their stories about life in this community from their vantage point and with integrity. Through the research, they were aiming to debunk some myths about rural Southerners as well as white religious and social conservatives.

Akin to President Obama, I would come to represent the *grotesque*. In classical Western aesthetic theory, the grotesque is a concept with a long history dating back to the Christianity in Roman culture, where in paintings a style of intricately interweaving human, animal, and vegetable elements had evolved. In a move *beyond ontological blackness*,[14] Victor Anderson adopts the grotesque to argue for a "postmodern blackness," a reconstituted black identity transcending the circumscribed spaces commonly defining American black culture and life. The grotesque tensively holds oppositional sensibilities, such as attraction and repulsion, pleasure and pain, rather than having them be diametrically opposed. Leaving such sensibilities in tension, it does not seek to mediate or negate either one. Instead, the grotesque reflects the inherent disharmony that produces conflict, heterogeneity, and/or a conflation of disparates.[15]

Hence, the inability to synthesize binary attributes leaves the possessor of such myriad and disparate characteristics in a state of "alterity" or "otherness." In short, I was "othered" by both communities for different reasons. For the black community, my "othering" was based on regional affiliation. For the white community, it was based on regional and racial factors. Even I, as a researcher, participated in the tug-of-war of "other-ing" as I insistently compared the regionalisms of this rural community to more urban Northeastern attitudes, beliefs, practices, and actions.

Rather than accept the grotesqueries and contradictions of life, human beings instinctively respond to the grotesque by "othering." Perceived disharmony generates this response that can be countered if individuals begin to develop dual perception(s)[16] of humanity that include the grotesque as fundamental to human nature and worldviews.

The grotesque names and describes the double consciousness I was experiencing in Bald Eagles. It is this—the grotesque, grasped as diametrically opposed sensibilities—that is the root of cultural and social hiccups or conflicts and that can become a hindrance to actualizing the good person and the good society. Nonetheless, it is this—the grotesque, embraced as *lived contradictions*, as *hybridity*—that holds the potential for something new: greater democracy and a more inclusive society.

Hybridity provides more open spaces for the construction of a political object that is new, not defined as "other," and able to defy political expectations because hybrids are radically malleable and able to synthesize trends from diverse traditions and global cultures.[17] Ironically, hybridity disrupts community but in a very different way than alterity. Hybridity not only creates new culture but also incorporates the once-excluded culture while disrupting and deconstructing the dominant culture. Hybrids are the products of a cultural collision, and in their development a space of belonging is created where they can no longer be ascribed as "other." That is how commentators described Barack Obama's hybridity. Phillip Gorski observed commentators frequently remarking on Obama's hybridity. Noteworthy, for many, was his ability to bridge some of the deepest rifts in American politics through his complex personality and unique life story: black and white, urban and rural, ghetto and penthouse, and secular and religious.[18] Although a source of youthful frustration, Obama's hybridity metamorphosed into a strength in his adulthood.[19] Unlike Barack Obama's hybridity, mine was not evident, nor, do I suppose, did it have any real social, political, or religious consequence or effect on either of the congregations, at least none that I had known of while I was in the field, and definitely not measurable at the moment.

However, both communities and I watched as candidate Obama's hybridity became a source of power and authority, consistently opening the way for him to defy political odds and expectations, leading up to and consummating his win and election to the office of U.S. president. At the same time, his hybridity tapped into new dimensions of the human experience because his mere personhood resonated with so many different constituencies. He eventually came to represent a clean political slate because of his community work and background in grassroots political activism and to symbolize a wind of change in the eyes of an American voting public seeking a candidate with neither influential nor political ties to elites in Washington, D.C. Both features were instrumental to his definition of *what it means to be American* before he even assumed office. Another little-noticed aspect of Obama's hybridity was his ability to speak effectively in the timbre and rhetoric of American civil theology. This, too, was a result of Obama's unusual American autobiography.[20] His hybridity exposed Obama to a rich American civil religious tradition. Presumably because of his hybridity, he set out to cultivate knowledge about this civil religious tradition through his studies of constitutional law; the black church experience; writings of prominent and historic black leaders and thinkers; the works of American pragmatists; and the scholarship of Christian realists.[21] Being open to these political and religious ideals that continue to shape the nation prepared then presidential candidate Barack H. Obama to rearticulate both skillfully and artfully race, religion, national identity, and American culture in the vernacular of a 2008 pre-election "race" and political speech, "A More Perfect Union," where he cast a vision of *what he believed made America great.*

American Exceptionalism and the Crisis of American National Identity

American exceptionalism is a curious term with a correspondingly unique history, ideological composition, and affiliation with religion. The origin of the American exceptionalist tradition is contestable. American linguist Mark Liberman and other scholars and authors, whether writing brief or comprehensive histories of the term, attribute to Soviet dictator Josef Stalin the development of the doctrine to explain the failure of the American proletariat in the 1920s and 1930s to participate in a worldwide revolution that would have moved the United States from capitalism to socialism to communism—a political ideology that the Soviets believed was inevitable for Western societies. Stalin pointed to the "heresy of American exceptionalism"[22] when Lithuanian immigrant and leader of the Communist Party of America Jay Lovestone traveled to Russia and informed him of American workers' disinterest in a violent struggle that would have reoriented Western capitalistic interests toward communism in the shadow of World War I's social devastations and the Great Depression.

However, when comparing the post–World War I conditions in America to Europe, "the characteristics forged along the frontier [made Americans different]: individualistic, profit-crazed, broadly middle class and as tolerant of inequality as they were reverent of economic freedom"; they created a nation with "unlimited reserves of American imperialism."[23] Stalin did not hurl the phrase *American exceptionalism* at Lovestone as a compliment. In fact, both men used the term to demean America, and it came to represent the nation's "aberrant" and "abnormal" behavior.

The once derogatory *American exceptionalism* of Stalin's 1920s era would eventually enter into the 1950s post–World War II period as a term demonstrating American and European commonalities. American exceptionalism ultimately described the more positive characteristics that made the United States distinct from Europe. The most profound feature of this particular meaning of American exceptionalism pertained to working-class labor. In the United States, those in the working class could gain opportunities to rise above their socioeconomic class-related conditions because America was not an aristocracy, unlike the British Empire and the rest of Europe. Therefore, governing and economic privilege was not based on class interests (and invariably, class conflicts); rather, the United States was deemed a status society shaped by movements.[24] For example, Liberman cites anti-Marxists and postwar public intellectuals such as historian Richard Hofstadter and sociologists Daniel Bell and Seymour Martin Lipset for sharing what made America strong: "Diversity made a cosmopolitan liberalism dominant in American life particularly once the New Deal admitted the immigrant working class to a share of political and economic power. But the paranoid style [of Protestants] was the price America paid on its margins for the complexity, tolerance, and interest-orientation at its center."[25] In the parlance of immigrants and their American-born children, Hofstadter, Lipset, and Bell implicate the sources of the paranoid style as Protestants from the American hinterland—nativists, abolitionists, populists, and Klansmen. It was as if the children of immigrants were saying to their old-family targets, "You had the fantasy that our parents were dangerous to you; that fantasy made you dangerous to them. When America belonged to you, you tried to exclude us. Now with the New Deal, it belongs to us as well. But whereas you had only superstition and religion to delegitimize us, we can use modern, scientific methods to discredit you."[26]

Here, even though mostly European immigrants and their American children represented a "diverse" American experience and reinforced American "exceptionalist" ideals of freedom and equality built upon New Deal social relief and programming, their arrival on American shores also induced fear in members of "old-time" and "native" Anglo-Protestant communities. For these children of immigrants—Hofstadter, Lipset, and Bell—the racial reactions of "native" Anglo-Americans to these European "foreigners" and their American-born or naturalized children were both frustrating and unsettling, as Liberman's analysis suggests.

Surviving into the 1960s and early 1970s, the belief in American exceptionalism was initially and actively deployed by Southern Democrats, many of whom, feeling betrayed and abandoned, eventually shifted their loyalties to the Republican Party. In so doing, both political parties assumed more patriotic overtones as an unintended consequence of the intellectual and political upheavals of the 1960s,[27] making civil rights and the enfranchisement of Southern blacks a turning point in the Southern social landscape and politics of the nation. More generally, the political influence of Southerners precipitated the "Southernization" of American cultural and political life, which can be traced to activities such as the national enthusiasm for country music, the ardor and spread of the Southern zeal for sports (including NASCAR racing and hunting), and even a Southern style in attitudes to the military and to patriotism.[28] Southerners and in particular Southern evangelical Christianity held sway over society; that was not a matter of opinion.[29] "Southernization" happened simultaneously with the ascendency of social conservatism over liberalism throughout the South (and in many other regions of the country). The noticeable change in the Democratic Party, a shift from being socially conservative to more liberal, was brought about by new constituencies—such as African Americans, Hispanics, other ethnic minorities, and women—being added to its numbers.

In an effort to celebrate the reorganization of the Republican Party and its new nation-centered identity and Southern conservatism, conservative intellectuals looked to history to learn more about and to support their type of nationalism, a bold and uncompromising patriotism, lauding the greatness of America. What they found was French writer Alexis de Tocqueville's *Democracy in America*. Tocqueville's visit to America left him with the impression that this nation was distinguished from all others because it was settled as a class-less and status-less society, unlike Britain and other European nations.

Although he is often credited with coining the term *American exceptionalism*, and though he pointed out qualities that underscored America's uniqueness and specialness as a republic *and* liberal constitutional government, Tocqueville never intended the term to translate to the *extraordinariness* of America, an interpretation strongly embraced by later thinkers and leaders. In fact, Liberman suggests, for Tocqueville, *American exceptionalism* translated into the aptitude of democratic societies to cultivate an appreciation for science, literature, *and* art. For those 1960s socially conservative thinkers, nevertheless, Tocqueville's term and context would lend credence to the surpassing transcendence of America.[30]

Examining American exceptionalism uncovers how this ideology has been interpreted and understood over the years—namely as material success by dint of preparation, opportunity, and diligence; egalitarianism and democracy afforded to all segments of the society regardless of race, nationality, or gender and shaped by early frontier expansion and adventures; absence of an aristocracy comprising "true" and "strict" class divisions; consent of the governed at all levels of society dictated by voting and by elections at all governmental levels (i.e., local, state, national) and a market economy that, while encouraging competition, still is the pathway toward upward mobility and wealth; and the development of a global society attracting immigrants from all parts of the world because of four freedoms: freedom of speech, freedom of worship, freedom from want, freedom from fear.[31] When these characteristics are woven together, Americans can agree that America's high standing is a product of this nation's birth, growth, and development.

Such ideals, despite becoming an at times grandiose national myth, at root describe something that is neither pernicious nor inconsequential. At its best, American exceptionalism has been indisputably noble. The sovereignty of the people, the rule of law, and securing rights have worked in unison to subordinate political conflict to constitutional jurisprudence. These first-rate values have protected the United States from many of the political catastrophes that have plagued other great nations.[32] They have vexed men and women and inspired wise conduct and brave acts. In that sense, the strong belief that the United States has a special duty and destiny has worked in the past (and as other religions) to make those who believe in its principles more virtuous, ethical, and righteous.[33] Even so, when American exceptionalism encounters the political and religious realm, the most noble of civil religious traditions and political principles can be transgressed and thwarted. If the 1960s ushered in a more socially conservative nation as a reaction to civil rights gains, then the 1980s solidified a conservative revolution and the rise of the "New" (political) Right supported by presidential politics and the election of President Ronald Reagan, whose pronounced alliance with the political Right revived much of the de facto racial politics and dynamics of the 1960s, thus polarizing the nation.

The political culture of the 1980s was solidified by the "New Right's" mission to dismantle the welfare state and return to one more politically populist and traditionally moral.[34] Their strategy mobilized an aggressively antistate white electorate intent on preserving white privilege with respect to taxation, housing, and education. Legislation was achieved through the ballot box and by averting the conventional bureaucratic machinery like the courts, state governments, and even Congress. Traditional conservatives labeled the New Right's strategies "anti-political," even though they were using democratic means to channel their anger.[35] Hence, issues of race tied to "perceived" economic insecurity provoked the ire of working-class whites who had benefited from the New Deal and other post–World War II social welfare policies, programs that in large part had not provided services to or raised the status of people of color. But the civil rights reforms of the 1960s would come to include and benefit blacks and other peoples of color in the 1980s, proving ominous to members of the new political Right who recast the social policies as an attack on whites. The policies were reframed as a redistribution of resources away from whites—deserving, hard-working, family-values whites—and toward people of color.[36]

While foregrounding issues of race, Reagan's presidential politics was also notable because of his affiliation with the Religious Right through organizations like the Moral Majority, Focus on the Family, the Christian Coalition, and the Family Research Council, all of which strongly endorsed his candidacy for president, helping to bring him to power.[37] An outcome of his presidency was a more religious understanding of American exceptionalism.[38] Reagan revitalized American exceptionalism's affiliation with religion by popularizing John Winthrop's sermon "A Model of Christian Charity" during a campaign speech in 1974 to a group in solidarity with the Religious Right. Even though President Reagan anachronistically applied a seventeenth-century Puritan sermon and metaphor to a twentieth-century term and context, his repeated invocation of the metaphor of the United States being like a "city [set] upon a hill" captured the American public's patriotic fervor.

American exceptionalism is a distinctive cultural aesthetic often defended when the country's "superior status" is in question or seems to be receding; that is when Americans need to decide what "America" means to them and what it means to the rest of the world.[39] This brief history of the tradition validates the previous argument that explains *why* American exceptionalism emerges. The assumed and attributed "greatness" of America often surfaces in relationship to and/or in tension with worldwide disruptions, and more specifically in comparison to events happening in Europe. In these instances, when it appears, the concept is often attached to the question of what makes America distinctive.

What is more, Americans hold mixed feelings about the eminence of the nation when the country is facing grave economic issues and deemed economically unstable, contributing to class tension that can lead to conflict. In recounting the trajectory of American civil religion, what cannot be denied is recognition of its development during "times of trial,"[40] in the course of historical moments when Americans are grappling with *what it means to be American* to them and for the rest of the world. American renown and high standing is called into question when Americans become unsure about their national identity.

On the other hand, "American exceptionalism was nourished by the spectacular success of the United States in the twentieth century, and especially by the way in which America, alone, emerged strengthened by two world wars. It was encouraged by the ideological struggle with communism. For many, it was confirmed by the collapse of the Soviet Union in 1991 and the subsequent discrediting of socialist ideas. Sadly, in this century it has been soured and exacerbated by the shock of the atrocities of September 2001 and their consequences."[41] So while the rhetoric of American exceptionalism is rooted in enduring (but not always commonly shared) political beliefs, the aforementioned assertion acknowledges that the changing nature and philosophies of the American public redefine this ideology, demanding national leaders to rearticulate its meaning depending on societal concerns and the historic moment.[42] When it comes to American exceptionalism, political leaders and the public express convictions about the "greatness" of America in line with whatever democratic spirit prevails at the time. The language of exceptionalism subsequently has the potential to expose struggles with American national identity.

From 1980 to 2001, the American public enthusiastically embraced American exceptionalism, reaching its apex in 2001 following the tragedies of September 11 and the subsequent War on Terror. As time progressed, exceptionalist rhetoric persisted even though public expressions became less pronounced as the wars in Iraq and Afghanistan dragged on. In 2008, the nation again faced a significant trial, this time a sharp economic downturn and recession caused by the mortgage crisis. Republican presidential candidates responded by stressing what made America special, guiding the way for this ideology to assume new life in the public square.[43]

In that same year, Barack H. Obama entered the 2008 presidential field as a Democratic candidate. However, Republicans criticized him for allegedly not believing in American exceptionalism. Moreover, because of his association with Reverend Jeremiah Wright, his numbers were falling in the polls. Wright was accused of delivering a searing indictment against the nation for its historic maltreatment of black people, in a Sunday morning sermon where he had applied the American jeremiad form to comment on America's broken covenants and to address American's failings.

People who heard soundbites of the sermon accused Wright of implying that the 9/11 terrorist attacks were God's judgment on a wayward and unjust American nation. Seizing the opportunity to address and to quiet his critics, Barack Obama (then a senator) delivered a speech entitled "A More Perfect Union," inserting himself and his life story into American civil religious and exceptionalism traditions:

> I'm the son of a black man from Kenya and a white woman from Kansas. I was raised with the help of a white grandfather who survived a Depression to serve in Patton's army during World War II, and a white grandmother who worked on the bomber assembly line at Fort Leavenworth while he was overseas. I've gone to some of the best schools in America and I've lived in one of the world's poorest nations. I am married to a black American who carries within her the blood of slaves and slave owners, an inheritance we pass onto our two precious daughters. I have brothers, sisters, nieces, nephews, uncles, and cousins of every race and every hue scattered across three continents. And for as long as I live, I will never forget that in no other country on earth is my story even possible. It's a story that hasn't made me the most conventional of candidates. But it is a story that has seared into my genetic makeup the idea that this nation is more than the sum of its parts—that out of many we are truly one.[44]

Obama's hybridity gave him a powerful perspective on what makes America strong. His hybridity gave him access to the American exceptionalist tradition. His speech gave audiences at home and abroad insight into his perspective on America's special strength and power located in its attempts at inclusivity. Such inclusivity has traditionally incorporated the "huddled masses who yearn to be free"—regardless of tribe, sect, race, ethnicity, nation, or religion. Obama's *hybridity* additionally gained him access to America's civil religious tradition, as Philip Gorski notes. Obama cites the preamble to the Constitution, particularly the opening, "We the People," to affirm national unity over state sovereignty. In tandem with the dictum *e pluribus unum*, these words treat constitutional principles as more binding than a social contract. They hold great significance because they are covenantal, inspiring the nation to live up to ideals to which Americans must constantly return in times of trial.[45]

Obama relied on America's founding documents to interpret American national identity, a social identity he claimed includes and unifies. Despite inherent social fractures that derive from the challenges of living in a pluralistic society, Obama charged *all* Americans to "strive to be more perfect" by working together, which he reminded his audiences is part of our civic responsibility. From his standpoint, the Constitution's civil religious language calls the people of the United States to form "a more perfect union."

Interestingly, Obama's hybridity, though racially inclusive, and with cross-racial appeal, is not race specific.[46] To that extent, his hybridity had dichotomizing effects on blacks in America that, at certain moments, became a hindrance to achieving black political goals that can be tied to many black voters' disappointments with his lack of ability to address black special interest issues and racial inequality in the United States. Initially viewed on the campaign trail as "not black enough" to later a "black messiah" upon entering the U.S. executive office, Obama's hybridity factored into his race-neutral policies, policies that would ironically fail to make the United States "a more perfect union" and particularly because his presidential agenda did not necessarily target black and other racial minority communities for political empowerment or with remedies to mounting social and economic problems.[47] Many were expecting America's first black president to implement and create race-specific initiatives that would better their communities.[48] Still, Obama's hybridity exemplified the idea that despite human difference, the union still stands and is made "more perfect."

"Times of trial" cause Americans to call into question *who they are.* The prevailing sentiment and character of the American people in these same moments challenge the nation's prowess, prompting reformulations of American exceptionalism. Nonetheless, reinterpretation of *what makes America great* by national leaders also occurs beyond crisis moments. Seismic social transformations around the globe compounded structural shifts and social changes happening from 2001 to 2009 in America (and even before this period). These changes were destabilizing to the rural and Southern community of Bald Eagles, leaving whites and blacks, like many others in the rest of the country, to wonder *what it means to be American* and to struggle with conceptions of national identity.

Bald Eagle's residents articulated and practiced a political tradition of American exceptionalism rooted in nostalgia and nurtured through strong ties to local veterans and via family, *inter*generational and *intra*generational memories.[49] They maintained relationships with military personnel or remembered the community's dead, primarily military personnel who fought in World Wars I and II, by exercising "living memory,"[50] sustained by community stories and by those whose family members and friends still are on active duty.

As I write in 2017, Americans continue to endure "times of trial" that result from religiously inspired terrorism, one source of mass migrations of peoples of color and a subsequent refugee problem that has sparked a rise in right-wing extremism and supranationalistic reactions to these "foreigners." Added to those concerns are immigration and border-control troubles and unanswerable questions about how to treat and prevent Islamic radicalization in the United States, while simultaneously recognizing that it is not Islam as a religion that is the problem but its adoption by violent religious ideologues for disastrous ends. This is a mere short list of some of the challenges that were inherited by the new administration upon the election of Donald Trump to America's executive office in 2016. They became markers of a post-9/11 America and evidenced a crisis in American national identity. That is, they have become provocations for disputes about whom Americans are to *include* and whom they are to *exclude* from the American dream.

Such disputes have led to increased law-enforcement measures, whether in the form of bans on Muslims or a ban on immigrants and refugees from Muslim-majority countries, or raids on undocumented immigrants and immigrant communities. Strict(er) policing of black bodies has become part of the normal enforcement of "law and order" of the nation's present administration, displaying the nation's might, and is a form of dominance, power, and authority over racially marked bodies in this racial state.[51] Alongside those measures are President Trump's exceptionalist pronouncements about *making America great again*. His shibboleth, which began as a campaign slogan, now serves as a pervasive message about America's past supremacy, appealing to a segment of the U.S. population hopeful about America *again* rising to a place of superiority—as if our country has somehow relinquished its supreme and esteemed position on the world's stage. Unlike his predecessor, President Trump's definition of America's national strength is state sovereignty over and against inclusivity.[52]

Besides the fact that Trump's articulation of this ideology is coded with racial themes in its political messaging,[53] his most eloquent tool is *nostalgia*, a "memory of place" that leads us to invoke the following principle: "In remembering we can be thrust back, transported, into the place we recall."[54] By reorganizing the American public's temporal experiences around nostalgic activity, he grants permission for white middle America to recapture times when public and private social spaces were circumscribed by social controls to manage a growing population. Furthermore, his use of *nostalgia* recalls a former time when efforts to "sanitize" and "sterilize" unwanted, polluted, and *politicized* social bodies from the American body politic were legally allowed. By hearkening back to a "romanticized" past, Trump seems to suggest and "unofficially" sanction the formation of a racially differentiated society: one he proposes will *yet again* make America prominent. Coupled with this is his approval of *state* restrictions on "marked bodies," subjecting some individuals and groups to *exclusion* from the American dream in order for this country to *yet again* experience its political strength, military might, and vast power.

Although the brand of American exceptionalism that Bald Eagles community members honor and revere is rooted in historic and national values that differ from those President Trump espouses, Bald Eagles residents who have survived endless war still laud America as sovereign (with all of the exclusionary connotations), not only setting the country apart from much of the rest of the world but also setting the trajectory and tone for accepting an exceptionalism that *makes America great again*. Because their formulation of this American creed has been cultivated in a cauldron of continuous societal and global changes impacted by Islamism, immigration, economic insecurity, cultural pluralism, and "majority-minority" demographics in the nation,[55] such dislocation can elicit an "anti-democratic" reaction from these rural Southerners and other segments of the U.S. population.[56] More than that, shifts of such grand proportions impinge upon interpretations of American national identity, making the task of building consensus disagreeable while clearing the way for rhetoric and actions that purportedly will *make America great again*.

3

Fighting the Good Fight of Faith
Bald Eagles First United Methodist Church

In charting secularization over the course of the twentieth century, religious historians and sociologists have offered various theories about the relationship between religion and secularism in American public life.[1] Nineteenth-century orthodox Protestantism was institutionally secure, for evangelical Protestants directed and controlled denominations, seminaries, mission boards, and church-related volunteer agencies in America. They were active in various social and civic causes, whether temperance and prohibition, abolition, the rehabilitation of prisons, or the amelioration of dismal living conditions in orphanages. Along with shaping public discourse around public schools and the American educational system, including colleges and universities, evangelical Protestants had on all levels become the guardians of national morality.[2] For them, Christian faith and science existed hand in hand. Biblical literature asserted God's hand in science, and scientific invention confirmed God's existence. It was but a small step from Protestants' convincing, pervasive, and public presence to America's self-attribution of enjoying "manifest destiny" as a Christian nation, blessed with godly favor, and destined to become the kingdom of God on earth.[3]

Yet beginning in the 1920s, the influx of new immigrants along with the radicalism of urbanization, industrialization, and the introduction of German higher biblical criticism and intellectual skepticism into church settings brought sweeping social, demographic, political, and structural shifts and cultural change to America. Orthodox Protestantism, being not only a religious but also an American cultural institution, responded to such drastic social changes—by collapsing. The demise of this cultural institution signaled the rise of *modernity*.[4]

51

Modernity was destabilizing and ushered in the disestablishment of a common orthodox Protestantism. Emerging in its place were three Christian Protestant groups with roots in evangelicalism. Fundamentalists upheld doctrinal purity and exercised spiritual and structural legalism, and in this they were distinct from modernists, liberals, and, more generally, American society and culture. Neo-Evangelicals distinguished themselves from Fundamentalists in the 1940s by promoting a vision for growth and development rooted in effective evangelism, contributions to scholarly debates of their day, and an "engaged orthodoxy."[5] Liberal Protestants derived their faith orientation from a *social gospel*, a liberal theology that privileged individual conversion along with social activism and political reform as resources for social change.[6] "It is clear that over time," writes Christian Smith, "evangelicalism and fundamentalism developed into two distinct religious movements with major differences in orientation and style. By the mid-1950s, at the latest, the emergence of modern evangelicalism had affected a restructuring in the field of American religious identity."[7] Thus, modernity spurred the development of three religious movements in the mid-twentieth century, including that of liberal Protestants.

Fast forward to the early twenty-first century, and we find ourselves in a vortex of relational and structural disruptions precipitated by war and the rise of violent extremism; increased American militarization; technological innovations; and fears of widespread and sweeping economic instability that is a byproduct of globalization, massive migrations, and an international refugee crisis.

This chapter primarily examines church sermons to find meaning for the ways in which the regional identity of white townsfolk in rural and Southern Bald Eagles grounds their American national identity, an identity rooted in the religious strength of the Southern evangelicalism they believe and practice and exhibit in rites of faith that promote a theology and ethics of sharply delineated "good" and "evil." Evangelicalism among the white mainline Evangelicals at the Bald Eagles First United Methodist Church thrives despite twenty-first-century modernization and secularization.

Given present social and political conditions, how are we to interpret and assess the type of modern evangelicalism mixed with civil religious rhetoric that is practiced in the Southern community of Bald Eagles? What hermeneutic drives the placement of secular symbols (e.g., the American flag) and sacred symbols (e.g., the cross) in public and private "worship" spaces where community and congregational ritual life mirror and support each other and solidify regional identity? How do we translate our historical moment? Are we living in a postmodern period or in the shadow of a third wave of modernism? Under the conditions of modernity, it is plausible for cycles of religiosity and secularism to occur.[8] Specifically, I suggest that a theology and ethics of "good" and "evil" expressed through institutional leadership, thinking, practice, and rhetoric solidifies the regional identity and evangelicalism of this population.

While the topics of concern shared by the people of Bald Eagles come as a consequence of their engagement with American society and culture, sermons continue to deliver on the religious strength of the Southern evangelicalism that Bald Eagles residents believe and practice. These subjects are grasped by preachers who speak about America's influence on the rest of the world, question American leadership and authority at the moment of economic crisis, and introduce the practices of civic Americanism and a public theology of war in contradiction to parishioners' belief in Methodism, a "religion of the heart," promoting compassion and social missions. By way of professing the Christian faith, these preachers imply that "sacred umbrellas," reference groups that exhibit the same values, unify regional groups and reveal parishioners' anxieties about American national identity with the 2008 election results. Closing these sermonic subjects is their look at the role that rites of faith as communal theology and ethics of "good" and "evil" serve in sustaining the evangelical faith and collective identities of town residents and the people of Bald Eagles First United Methodist Church.

Bearing this in mind, "a religious movement that unites both clear cultural distinction and intense social engagement will be capable of thriving in a pluralistic, modern society."[9] Contemporary American Evangelicalism is strong because it strives with and struggles against forces that endanger its existence as demonstrated by eight principles that make up a "subcultural identity" theory of religious strength.[10] I showcase five of them to illustrate that these self-identified white evangelical Christians reinforce their regional and national identities and perform religious strength through rites of faith that bifurcate "good" and "evil" into oppositional constructs.

The five propositions advanced throughout the chapter argue for a "subcultural identity" theory of religious strength with respect to American Evangelicalism.[11] The first looks to social groups to provide membership, moral vision, meaning, and social identity to individuals. The second describes ritual, rhetoric, and church activity, for example, as "symbolic boundary markers" delineating one social collective from another. The third shares an alternative explanation of "community" as "a social network of individuals" rather than as a fixed location to offer a rationale for producing strong religious subcultures. The fourth looks at what role reference groups (called "sacred umbrellas") have in affirming the fundamental beliefs of a social group whose members adhere to the same ideals and principles. The fifth suggests that religion perseveres in modern, culturally pluralistic environments because out-group clashes typically fortify in-group strengths and dynamics.

To hear these parishioners vocalize the "devil" as a source of particular "evils" that require a "good" fight is to be persuaded about the effectiveness of a "subcultural identity" theory of religious strength. Further, an ethic of "good" and "evil" attributes evil conduct to lax morals, secularization, and anything that interrupts an orderly and balanced way of life (i.e., the good).

However, I begin by describing the church building itself as the immediate site where bifurcations become apparent through the architecture of the worship space and parishioners' interactions and clashes with American culture.

The First United Methodist Church: "The Church in the Heart of the Town with Town at Heart"

Driving down North Main Street toward McGaughey in Bald Eagles, West Tennessee, one encounters an imposing structure: the First United Methodist Church. At the North Main Street entrance, the building has one set of stairs that a visitor must climb before opening one of three sets of green wooden doors. The second stairway is flanked by an ivory-colored cement center encircled by black grillwork. Standing atop each of the four cement centers is an exterior lamp. To a visitor's left is a sign that gives a historical overview of the First United Methodist Church of the city of Bald Eagles:

> Robert M. Tarrant held a courthouse revival in 1840. The first church built in Bald Eagles County, First Methodist, grew out of this meeting. A frame church built in 1844, deteriorated from disuse during the Civil War. In 1864, a new structure at Church and Market Streets was dedicated by G. W. D. Harris. In 1923, this building was completed. First Methodist has built two churches: Boose Memorial named for the first woman ordained in the Memphis Conference, and Second Church, later Ross Memorial [a predominantly black Methodist church in town]. Strongly supporting foreign missions, county disaster aid, and community service, their motto is, *"the Church in the heart of the town with town at heart,"* erected by the Memphis Conference Commission on archives and history, 1994.

In 2006, when I first came to the community, I learned that the pastor, Reverend Dr. Phillip Cook, and many members are also city leaders. The First United Methodist Church is a flagship church. For instance, the former mayor of the city of Bald Eagles, Mayor Bill Revell, typifies the powerful and influential individuals who comprise part of the church membership and are drawn to this congregation. Upon my return in spring 2008, I also learned that some members attend more for social networking reasons and for the benefits of increased social status than for worship and catechesis. The church's prestige contributes to the somewhat guarded nature of congregants.

The First United Methodist Church owns land on which sit multiple structures, including the playground, the Family Life Center, and the Fellowship Hall. We discover vital differences when comparing First United Methodist Church's property to that of Tabernacle Missionary Baptist Church, another historic but black congregation in Bald Eagles. All church activities at Tabernacle are housed in one building that stands at the corner of a major intersection as visitors approach the historic downtown area of Bald Eagles.

The Fellowship Hall at the First United Methodist Church serves as an additional space where the 11 a.m. "contemporary" worship service, *Atmosphere*, occurs each Sunday at virtually the same time as the "traditional" service, which is held at 10:50 a.m. in the upper level of the building. Further, the Fellowship Hall is a place where other ministries, groups, and people gather throughout the week for social occasions and community and business meetings. Smaller in comparison to the First United Methodist Church, the two fellowship areas at Tabernacle usually cater to weekly Wednesday and Friday Bible studies and serve as social spaces for eating and conversation after special Sunday services of worship. The physical arrangements of the fellowship spaces at each church are dissimilar and differ in function yet meet the needs of each community.

Each building also reflects the denominational, regional, and racial culture of its inhabitants. At the First United Methodist Church, the stained-glass windows pay homage to deceased members of this church family, and a gold-colored cross hangs prominently from the front of the pulpit. Both artifacts remind visitors that the First is a place where worship is central, where congregants and community members are welcomed, making it a setting one can call "home."

For example, because the First United Methodist Church is a prominent church, members often make headlines in the local newspaper for their contributions to or leadership in the community. In line with that, the church addresses the concerns of its members while also offering a location where members of Bald Eagles as a whole can gather to address specific issues affecting the town's people. Community agencies like Alcoholics Anonymous rent space out of the church's Fellowship Hall to hold weekly meetings as members simultaneously schedule meeting space for support groups like the ministry to new and young mothers.

Entering the McGhaughey side of the church building, visitors walk on a slightly raised emerald carpeted ramp and at the top are greeted by one of two male ushers. Once inside, a visitor sees that the main sanctuary is divided by a wall that stretches from the ceiling to floor and that makes an archway. The archway separates the sixteen wooden pews (eight on the right side and eight on the left) with emerald-green and brown patterned cushions in the mid-to-rear part of the church from the twenty-two pews that comprise the mid-to-front part of the sanctuary (eleven pews on both the left and the right sides of the church). The middle aisle divides the left and right sides of the sanctuary; these divisions are relics of the church's beginnings where men and women were separated in the church's worship space based on seating arrangement.

At the rear of the sanctuary to the right side is the audiovisual equipment area where Mary Elizabeth Worthington, director of Christian education, records both services and where another member of the church operates the computer screen that faces the congregation. The church combines the traditional with the modern (here meaning technological), so that members can follow the order of worship in the paper bulletin and hymnals on the computer screen. On the backs of the pews are shelves that hold United Methodist hymnals and Holy Bibles. In the far left back of the church to the left of the audiovisual equipment area is a table and a wooden bench for extra seating.

Six stained-glass windows dedicated to deceased church members (three on the right and three on the left) decorate the front part of the sanctuary from the ceiling down to covered radiators. The stained-glass windows are huge and made of pale-colored pink, green, and violet glass. The tops of the windows form into the shape of an oval separated by a length of wood and morph into a rectangular shape with floral decorations. In the corner front left of the sanctuary the American flag is prominent, and in the right front corner is the Christian flag. In Bald Eagles, church members salute the American flag, the Tennessee flag, *and* the Christian flag on special occasions.

In the uppermost front and center of the sanctuary, facing the congregation, is the pulpit area. A wooden altar rail separates the front pews from this pulpit area. Entering the presbytery,[12] a guest walks up the center stairs either to stand at the lectern on the right or the pulpit on the left.

Behind the lectern and pulpit are five upholstered chairs—two on the left and three on the right. Looking up, a guest cannot miss the colossal gold-covered cross that hangs from the ceiling above this pulpit area. Flood-lights, vents, and other ceiling lights also fill the ceiling in the pulpit area. Under the cross is a table/altar that separates the upholstered chairs, and on it lies the Holy Bible flanked by two candles on each side.

A wall separates this space from the choir loft. Three rows of green cushioned chairs comprise the choir loft. On the left side of the choir loft is the piano. The men's choir leads the singing at the 8:30 a.m. service, and the chancel choir leads the 10:50 a.m. service each Sunday even if special musical guests and other selections are on the program. Clergy members can enter the presbytery from the 51 Bypass North side of the church by walking through that entrance and into the brown wooden doors leading into this pulpit area. In each front corner on the right and left sides of the ceiling surrounding the pulpit area hang small chandeliers. The ceiling design in the front part of the sanctuary looks much like that of the Sistine Chapel. A circle defines the front part of the ceiling.

Exit doors facing the congregation border the left and the right areas immediately outside of the pulpit area. Around these exits are walls with columns made of marble-like material that extend from the ceiling to the floor. These columns similarly adorn the archway separating the front and back parts of the sanctuary.

Contemporary Worship Generates New Atmospheres

The First United Methodist Church in Bald Eagles has a robust and grow-ing membership. At 600 members, this white congregation is primarily comprised of middle- to upper-middle-class and wealthy families. Three services—8:30 a.m., 10:50 a.m., and 11:00 a.m.—attract a healthy mix of people of all ages, from toddlers to the elderly. Its worship, education, music, adult, and youth ministries host programs tailored to parishioners. The Family Life Center is a venue for a number of community-wide events and programs like the summer youth basketball league, attracting residents from larger Bald Eagles County.

It was refreshing to start a conversation with a recently hired worship leader, Minister Darin Lightfoot, as I was passing through the church halls and to hear him say he wanted to invite a new "atmosphere" into this church house. As a minister of worship who had recently come from Fra-zier United Methodist Church in Alabama, Darin is developing a plan to create an environment where people can become more "real" by feeling less vulnerable about revealing more of themselves and their imperfections to others in the church community. During our conversation, Darin spoke further about the church's structure and ministries.

Sunday school classes have their own personas and function like small groups. Each class appeals to specific segments of the church population, according to their socioeconomic level, age, interest in serving, and the kind of Bible study they do. Minister Darin learned this by observing how the needs of the church are handled throughout the week. For instance, the church secretary will direct a person to a respective Sunday school class officer in line with the person's interest and the class' service to the church and wider community. Some classes are more visible in their ministries; others, less so. Some classes delve into the "word of God" (Bible) without being bothered by what they consider to be outside distractions, while others combine community service with their study of the Bible, applying biblical principles to their daily lives.

I was directed to enroll in a service-oriented class, the Sojourners. Members are mainly married couples in their mid-thirties to early fifties with families; these couples are active in the church, church leadership, and the larger community, supplying the larger community of Bald Eagles with a new generation of leadership. While I was living in the town of Bald Eagles, I noticed that they volunteered with the Salvation Army, participated in a live Christmas nativity scene, prepared and sent cards to the National Guard battalion that has been deployed from the area, and volunteered one night at the county fair located at the Bald Eagles County Fairgrounds. Unlike the Sojourners, some Sunday school classes give only monetary donations to specific causes, not their time and presence. Partic- ular Sunday school classes promote the town's religious personality and life by attending events that maximize social interactions and opportunities to develop relationships outside of the church's walls.

I ask Minister Darin how this traditional congregation has reacted to church leadership instituting the more contemporary worship service, *Atmosphere.* He responds that while the congregation has generally reacted positively to the contemporary worship experience, there are those who take exception to the idea that the *Atmosphere* service is "contemporary" worship. Their soft objections relate to "contemporary," meaning *here and now,* which might imply "traditional" worship is outdated. Labeling it "contemporary" worship, according to Minister Darin, is not what drives praise and worship in the *Atmosphere* service; rather, it gives members an alternative to more conventional worship.

Atmosphere is an attempt to create a new "atmosphere or attitude" in the congregation. Explaining why the name *Atmosphere* was selected, Minister Darin continues, "*Atmosphere* means my sphere is being allowed to touch your sphere; that can provide encouragement, acceptance of differences, and unity." Yet, he does not fail to point out the benefits of sitting in classes with individuals from similar backgrounds and with similar struggles. Minister Darin makes it plain that in those cases group members achieve intimacy via group dynamics and nurturing empathy for the spiritual, familial, and even financial burdens of group participants ultimately encouraging all members to lend their emotional support to troubled members of the group. Interestingly, these same small groups tend to become cliquish, which is also one of Minister Darin's reasons for wanting to create a new atmosphere to disturb the old.

Intergenerational Worship with the Billy Graham and Max Lucado Generations

Regarding the "traditional" versus "contemporary" worship, more senior women in the church weigh in on the debate during their women's Bible study. Every Thursday at 10:00 a.m., Pastor Cook leads a Bible study for the female retirees of the church. The women range in age from sixty to the early eighties. Many grew up Methodist (more specifically Southern Methodist Episcopal). The Methodist Church was historically divided into regions—the Methodist Episcopal Church, South, and the Methodist Episcopal Church, North. Quite a few of the women were members of the Bald Eagles First United Methodist Church even before Cook assumed his senior pastoral position. He had served the congregation as an associate minister for four years in the late 1970s, left to assume leadership responsibilities in other churches, and itinerated back in 2002 to the First United Methodist Church as senior minister.

I customarily joined these women for early morning Bible study and was the only "young'un" amidst this bunch of salt-and-pepper-haired disciples. They were always engaging interlocutors. The morning of our conversation about "traditional" versus "contemporary" worship, Pastor Cook was on his way to Florida, leaving a member of this cohort of women to lead Bible study. Though Cook was not present, the leader did an excellent job guiding participants through, interpreting, and explaining 1 Corinthians 1, with the assistance of academic resources.

These women, as they themselves mentioned, are part of the "Billy Graham" generation and are adept at handling scholastic texts like Barclays commentaries and the Interpreter's Bible Commentary, the Message, and the Revised Standard Version and the New International Version of the Bible. The member leading the study favored inclusive language substituting "brothers, sisters, and friends" in place of "brothers" to represent the "family of God," a non-gender-specific phrase. The women's interpretation of Scripture was at times conservative and at others liberal, always ending with what they understood as the simple message of the Christian Scripture: accept Christ as savior and be a good Christian.

More intriguing to me was their post-Bible study discussion about their preference for the "traditional" service and its rituals over the more relaxed nature of the "contemporary" worship service. One member explained: "I really don't connect with the words or the rhythm of the praise and worship songs in contemporary worship. I find the standard hymns easier to sing because I can read music but also the words are more meaningful to me." Another chimed in: "Contemporary worship is drawing members away from the 10:50 a.m. service, and younger couples seem to attend the contemporary worship more often because they have families." Still another participant responded: "I attend about once a month, and even though I get more out of the traditional service, contemporary worship appeals to the 'unchurched' and draws them into this worship community. The service is definitely growing."

I later have a conversation with Pastor Cook about the interplay between religion and culture. As we talk, he engages this particular issue from the perspective of culture impacting religious belief and practice:

> Well, on a very practical level, I think the kind of community organizations that want to use our church building, for instance, is one way that culture impacts our practice of religion. And, as well, the kind of things that are going on in society that our people find important to be involved in at this moment in the life of the church instead of simply being involved in the religious issues that are going on, is another example of the influence of culture on religious belief and practice.
>
> I think the culture around us is the culture within us. And it affects everything we try to do on a religious level as well. I think the *Atmosphere* service is an attempt to build a new bridge to the culture in the community, to the musical culture that is ever present on the radios, in the cars, in the homes, in the minds, and in the ears of the people. We are trying to say we want to build this religious bridge over. It may be the same beat that we hear on the radio and in our cars but we develop words that are different. Is that fair?

"The Culture around Us Is the Culture within Us":
On American Culture and Southern Evangelicalism

In describing the First United Methodist Church of Bald Eagles, West Tennessee, one cannot ignore this congregation's engagement with local and far-reaching American culture.[13] Parishioners' investment in both cultures is revealed through their social and political relationships, in their religious beliefs and practices, and, as Pastor Cook points out, in their ability to adapt some of their beliefs and ritual activities to a wider American society, their "cultural accommodation" to modernity and twenty-first-century globalization.[14] Here the influence of American culture on religious beliefs and practices is apparent.

For instance, the guardedness of this church's membership can be attributed to the size of the congregation but more significantly to the social position of the church in the community. It includes the community's doctors, lawyers, presidents of businesses and corporations, local politicians, and educators who are also the city's and county's leaders.

Social connections are part of the fabric of this congregation, much as they are in other churches similar in size and stature in the community. Thus, the president of the local bank who knows the CEO of a local industry will likely attend the First to be identified with this group, an important factor adding to its country-club vibe. A study participant suggested that social environment often distinguishes larger churches and especially white megachurches from their smaller counterparts in Bald Eagles. Established group patterns and social arrangements reveal that the corporate and professional nature of the First United Methodist Church contributes to some people feeling that the church is an insular place. However, Minister Darin appeals to the strength of religious tradition to recenter members on their faith rather than on their American culture.

Contemporary and traditional worship calls forth a "new" and changed atmosphere for religious activity and life in this congregation. In their willingness to let down their guards and openly share their views about the "traditional" and "contemporary" worship services, members of the women's Bible study exemplify how a level of commitment to and practice of religious tradition initiates and produces cultural change. By participating in the ritual of worship, church members counter the negative effects of American culture contributing to the congregation being described as "insular." Religious practice is the new social glue overriding the narrowness and restrictive nature of congregational life. At the First, members identify as evangelical, where "old line evangelicals" (i.e., older church members who adhere more closely to Christian tradition and practice) and "new line evangelicals" (i.e., younger members open to variation in Christian practice) relate to each other. Drawing both generations together is their practice of American Methodism as religious performance buffeting yet also being shaped by American culture.

Evangelicals populate both the Christian Right (i.e., Religious Right) *and* the Christian Left (i.e., Religious Left), delineated as political entities, although evangelicals are erroneously and perplexingly labeled a political entity.[15] This misnomer is a consequence of American society conflating religion and politics, a conflation also rooted in the confusion about the relationship between church and state. A further distinction of the First, this one attributable to its regional location, is its affiliation with a mainline denomination (mainline denominations are known for being informed by liberal theologies) and its ironic but firm identification as evangelical. Evangelicalism is associated with "conservative" Christianity. However, in the case of the Bald Eagles First United Methodist Church, regional association confers vitality to the people's exercise of a religiously orthodox Southern evangelicalism.

A marker of evangelicalism's religious strength is high levels of dedication to spiritual practices and church attendance at worship services, prayer groups, Bible studies, choir practices, potlucks, social events, and other ministries of the church.[16] In this way, the faith practices of people of the First United Methodist Church display the cultural distinctiveness of evangelicalism. Beyond that, their Southern evangelicalism withstands the secularity of American culture because their engagement with culture discloses the first feature of a "subcultural identity" theory of religious strength described as "the human drive for meaning and belonging [as being] satisfied by moral orienting collective identities."[17]

By faithful and robust participation in church activities, congregants at the First are able to survive the tensions produced by engagement with American culture. These religious versus political tensions derive from three spheres of activity: parishioners' attempt to forge relationships with individuals and organizations outside of their respective religious and social groups; their embrace of education and intellectualism; and their participation in the social and political life of an American nation whose loyalties, values, and mores are frequently at odds with the regional mindset of residents. Nevertheless, all of these secular activities remain defining features and qualities of communal living. Clearly, the creation of a congregation that provides social supports, emotional stability, spiritual nourishment, community outreach, practical assistance to families, and the means to foster casual and business friendships counteracts such religious versus political tensions by solidifying the regional identity of church members and townsfolk based on their abiding devotion to the practices of Southern evangelicalism.

Contemporary worship makes public the divide between the Billy Graham and Max Lucado generations at the church, best articulated by the opinions of the older women at their Bible study. The "Billy Graham" generation relates more to traditional worship, and the "Max Lucado" generation finds more inviting the contemporary service that attracts the unchurched and millennials. What ultimately binds the two together, however, is the religious strength of the Southern evangelicalism that both groups practice, in so doing reaffirming their rural, Southern identity and integrating them into American society as they defend against the infiltration of American culture into their communal ethics and living.

E Pluribus Unum, the Many Uniting into One: A Song for the Nations

I attended services at the First United Methodist Church two days before the Independence Day holiday during my first visit to the town to research townsfolk's interpretation of the relationship between religion and politics. Being unaccustomed to the practice of religious patriotism in church culture, I was captivated by the ways in which this congregation, other churches, and the rest of the city and county celebrated the holiday in their respective religious settings on the Sunday *before* the national holiday. Upon entering the church building for the 10:50 a.m. service, I was greeted by the organ prelude (a rendition of "The Battle Hymn of the Republic") and the opening hymn, "America." William G. McLoughlin asserts:

> The story of American Evangelicalism is the story of America itself in the years 1800 to 1900, for it was the Evangelical religion which made Americans the most religious people in the world, molded them into a unified, pietistic-perfectionist nation, and spurred them onto those heights of social reform, missionary endeavor, and imperialistic expansionism which constitute the moving forces of our history in that century. Both as motivation and as rationale, evangelical religion lay behind the concept of rugged individualism in business enterprise, laissez faire in economic theory, constitutional democracy in political thought, the Protestant ethic in morality, and the millennial hope of manifest destiny of white, Anglo-Saxon, Protestant America to lead the world to its latter-day glory. The national anthem of the evangelical movement was the "The Battle Hymn of the Republic," whose words, now empty

symbols, once surged with the emotional fervor of three whole generations of pious Americans.[18]

Orthodox evangelical Protestantism grounds the Methodism practiced at
the First United Methodist Church, Bald Eagles. This form of Christianity
was the spirit behind early social reform, missionary zeal, territorial expansionism, and the rugged individualism of Americans, breathing life into
a nascent republic that defined the contours of the American nation.

Southern evangelical religion lit the embers of nationalistic expression
in the worship service on that Sunday prior to Independence Day. During
the offertory, we sang "Song for the Nations," praising America's greatness and elevating the virtues of other nations. The praise song steadily
recognized America's partnership with allies and leadership role in chris-
tianizing America, while simultaneously being a "beacon of light" to and
missionizing the rest of the world. "America the Beautiful," the sermonic
selection, prepared the congregation for the morning message.

In tribute to the founding of this country and the July 4 holiday, Pastor Cook preached a message entitled "The High Cost of Freedom." For
this town and church community, the costs associated with maintaining U.S. citizenship and freedoms can never be forgotten. Cook launched
into a historical explanation of the *Statue of Freedom*—the small statue that
sits atop the Capitol dome in Washington, D.C.—in the first part of his
sermon. Danielle Scull of the United States Capitol Historical Society
describes the statue in the following way:

> This bronze *Statue of Freedom* by Thomas Crawford is the crowning
> feature of the dome of the United States Capitol. The statue is a classical
> female figure of Freedom wearing flowing draperies. Her right hand
> rests upon the hilt of a sheathed sword; her left holds a laurel wreath of
> victory and the shield of the United States with thirteen stripes. Her
> helmet is encircled by stars and features a crest composed of an eagle's
> head, feathers, and talons, a reference to the costume of Native Ameri-
> cans. A brooch inscribed "U.S." secures her fringed robes. Ten bronze
> points tipped with platinum are attached to her headdress, shoulders,
> and shield for protection from lightning. Her crest rises 288 feet above
> the east front plaza.
>
> The Lady of Freedom is a national treasure, crowning the United
> States Capitol Building's gleaming Dome. Her strength and beauty
> are a source of inspiration to all Americans. Standing a magnificent
> 19 feet 6 inches tall, weighing 14,985 pounds, the Bronze Lady stands
> upon an iron globe inscribed with "E Pluribus Unum," our nation's

motto. The lower part of the base is decorated with fasces (small bundles of rods, a Roman symbol of authority) and wreaths. The statue was erected in 1863 during the Civil War under the presidency of Abraham Lincoln.

There is a vast amount of artwork in the Capitol created by and portraying women. The Capitol is a symbol of our nation's history and the artwork conveys the importance of women as contributors to American society in the roles of creators, or onlookers in various scenes. The Statue of Freedom, atop the Capitol Dome, serves as a constant reminder of this important, but sometimes overlooked, fact.[19]

After Pastor Cook explains the significance of the Lady of Freedom, we take Holy Communion.

Cook delivers the second part of his sermon from Galatians 5:1: "Stand fast therefore in the liberty by which Christ has made us free, and do not be entangled again with the yoke of bondage" (NKJV). After sharing the history and purpose of this epistle based on the gentiles' conversion to Christianity and the resultant Jewish–gentile conflict, Cook moves into talking about the movie *The Patriot*.

The Patriot tells the story of a soldier who has fought in the Revolutionary War. The protagonist "long fears his sins would return to visit him," according to Cook, who then explains that this man's words represent the common experiences of humanity: we carry memories of guilt that make us slaves to our spirit. However, Cook concludes that we are free to be whole: "We are no longer slaves to things of this world. The yoke of the law has been removed, and the power and responsibility of the cross has been laid upon us. Genuine freedom comes from knowing we are children of God and living in that freedom. We are called to be custodians of this freedom."

Cook then makes a connection to the founding of the early American republic, by noting that Thomas Jefferson was selected as one of the framers of the Declaration of Independence because he was adept at summarizing and reflecting the sentiments of the rest of the Founding Fathers. As soon as the Declaration of Independence was signed, the Founding Fathers adopted the Bell of Freedom, rung to symbolize the freedoms this new land had to offer. Cook ties this civics lesson to the spiritual realm, declaring Holy Communion as the metaphorical ringing of this bell. The "ring! ring! ringing of the bell," he proclaims, "means individuals can now walk in freedom and no longer have to submit to the yoke of slavery." Cook closes his sermon by declaring, "We no longer are bound by the shackles of the Old World; we are free in Christ."

On that Sunday in July, I learned that evangelical faith and civic American devotion overlap in this church and rural area. Cook's sermon, framed in "God and Country" imagery and language, reflected the patriotic stance of the residents of this city and county, and of members of this rural congregation. Almost two years before my 2008 return, such images, songs, and rituals had elicited my curiosity and prompted me to revisit the First United Methodist Church in the city of Bald Eagles and to be active in worship services, Sunday school, Bible studies, and other events in the life of this church.

I connected to members of the First United Methodist Church as a researcher of Southern evangelicalism and Southern civil religion because I identified the civic creeds, religious myths and symbols, and cultural practice of religious patriotism in public and private spaces as distinctive collective identity markers that cement the regional identity of these Southerners and their national identity as Americans. Social groups construct their sense of self and distinctiveness from other groups via the cultural production of language, rituals, artifacts, creeds, practices, and narratives.[20] Socially constructed group markers not only display what members of a group have in common but also establish group boundaries,[21] differentiating in-groups from out-groups. The people of the First and the residents of Bald Eagles County are a group of American Southerners who maintain their rural and regional identity in contradistinction to Northerners and even other Southern subcultural groups, by defending against the secularity of American society through a customized Southern evangelicalism that incorporates civil religious images and rhetoric.

Here I argue for the second feature of a subcultural identity theory of religious strength. That is, symbolic boundary markers reflect group meaning, belonging, and the moral ethos of a people, distinguishing groups and their collective identities from each other. In this case, the images, rhetoric, rituals, and church activities of members of the First United Methodist Church showcase the religious strength of their variety of Southern evangelicalism with civil religious overtones, making manifest the statement inscribed on the presidential and vice presidential seals of the United States, on our U.S. coinage and currency, and on Lady Freedom, who sits atop the U.S. Capitol dome—*E Pluribus Unum*, "From many, one."

"'Who Says' . . . Our Nation Is in a Mess?": A Question of American Leadership and Church Authority

Reverend Terry Prosser is an associate pastor at the First United Methodist Church. Prompted to address the housing crisis and the economic recession facing the nation in 2008, Reverend Prosser chose the Sunday immediately preceding the stock market crash of Monday, September 29, to preach the following message: "'Who Says' . . . Our Nation Is in a Mess?" His sermon, about American leadership and church authority, finds its scriptural foundation in Matthew 21:23-32:

> [23]Jesus entered the temple courts, and, while he was teaching, the chief priests and the elders of the people came to him. "By what authority are you doing these things?" they asked. "And who gave you this authority?"
>
> [24]Jesus replied, "I will also ask you one question. If you answer me, I will tell you by what authority I am doing these things. [25]John's baptism—where did it come from? Was it from heaven, or from men?"
>
> They discussed it among themselves and said, "If we say, 'From heaven,' he will ask, 'Then why didn't you believe him?' [26]But if we say, 'From men'—we are afraid of the people, for they all hold that John was a prophet."
>
> [27]So they answered Jesus, "We don't know."
>
> Then he said, "Neither will I tell you by what authority I am doing these things."
>
> [28]"What do you think? There was a man who had two sons. He went to the first and said, 'Son, go and work today in the vineyard.'
>
> [29]"'I will not,' he answered, but later he changed his mind and went.
>
> [30]"Then the father went to the other son and said the same thing. He answered, 'I will, sir,' but he did not go.
>
> [31]"Which of the two did what his father wanted?"
>
> "The first," they answered.
>
> Jesus said to them, "I tell you the truth, the tax collectors and the prostitutes are entering the kingdom of God ahead of you. [32]For John came to you to show you the way of righteousness, and you did not believe him, but the tax collectors and the prostitutes did. And even after you saw this, you did not repent and believe him." (NIV)

Reverend Prosser ushered the congregation into his sermon, praying, "Lord, help us to see what's wrong in this world and help us to make it right." He preached that America's economic crisis stems from people's refusal to recognize God in their decision making, the country's lack of spiritual authority, and the failure of earthly leaders. Acknowledging the gravity of the situation, Prosser professed:

This is a serious time; we are living in a crunch time. Our nation is in a mess which extends from this issue of authority. *These are a sign of our times.* Parents, teachers, doctors, dentists, and leaders: "Do you feel like you have the same authority as you used to?"

Let's look back at our past. Let's look back at our heritage. Do you feel like you have the same authority you used to? We are in hard times. We are experiencing hard times. Who is running the household— the child or the parent? Educationally, are students dictating the rules of the educational system?

Let's look at the justice system. Criminals have twisted the law and blinded justice. And let's examine the economic system: What is the driving force behind our economic system? Greed and power seems to be driving our economic system. These are the sign of our times.

I am sure many of you are anxious about our economic condition. Some of you have been affected by the housing crisis; we know that some in our community have been affected. We have looked to the home, school, justice, and economic systems for answers, but now we have to look at the church. Too many churches today are not driven by the power of the Holy Spirit. They are in ideological, mental, emotional, religious chains.

We are bound by chains, oppressive chains of ungodly authority.

"How can we be viewed as soldiers of the cross when we look like a 'chain gang'?"

Satan holds the keys to the chains that bind us unless you know the truth. Too many church leaders who are called to stand up, do stand up and serve, but then often lose their sense of self and God. *They lose a sense of their authority.* Let's look at the words of Jesus: "There are going to be people outside of these walls to gain or get into heaven before you [i.e., prostitutes, sinners, gamblers, etc.]."

Authority and Love. If you don't pay attention to godly authority, you will be forced to obey ungodly authority. Is this not where we are? If you are confused about authority and ask, "Who should I listen to and follow?" Listen to what they [the leaders] in 1 Corinthians 13 say, "Unless you have love in your heart, then you are a resounding gong or a clanging cymbal . . ."

Why do people take positions of authority when they are not called to these positions? The Sadducees and the Pharisees asked Jesus: "By whose authority do you say and do such things?" Check your God-given gifts; you have the authority. Too many people have taken ungodly authority, even to the point of using God's word [the Bible] to support their positions.

Authority and the Church. Some people take positions of authority in the church because they have it in the world. And sometimes they take on authority because they do not have *any* in the world. God wants and needs business people in the church. Those who have the gifts and talents of business are needed in the church. But business ways of the world must be filtered so that we can fully offer our gifts to church committees and ministries.

Who says you don't have the authority? Who has the authority? Jesus has the authority. In Matthew 7:28, the people recognized that Jesus spoke with authority so they commented, "Wow, this man speaks with authority!" When people speak with authority, you know it.

Jesus and the Centurion. Jesus recognized that the centurion knew of Jesus' authority by his words and actions. If Jesus says, "Your sins are forgiven," then your sins are forgiven. In the name of Jesus, demons flee. When Jesus speaks, the poor are fed and sheltered. Stones roll away with the voice of Jesus; the dead rise up and the hungry are fed! Jesus' voice has authority! That is what the centurion teaches us!

Where is the voice of Jesus? The voice of Jesus is in the church. Jesus is the head of the church. And because Jesus is the head of the church, we are the voice of authority. Our father is coming back soon, and this issue of authority needs to be dealt with soon. We need to respond to God's authority.

As the sermon came to a close, Reverend Prosser prayed: "Embolden us with knowledge and power because things are not going well. Chase away the fear. This church can change the world today; let us believe that." Amen.

Millenarian Madness

Reverend Prosser's sermon both questions and critiques the contemporary administration and guidance of American households, along with the educational, judicial, economic, and executive systems of government. His exhortation suggests that the failures of national leadership and authority have propelled America into housing and market crises. That being so, his answer to the leadership and authority dilemma is offered in a nostalgic turn to the past, demanding that this Southern and rural church audience return to a place where power, guidance, and control of homes, schools, and the government is clearly delineated, defined, and undisputed. His sentimental yearnings find such direction and authority in the rich reservoirs of U.S. history and family heritage, American religion, and the local church.

To restore social and moral order to an America spiraling out of control, he encourages his parishioners to plumb the depths of American myths and foundational histories of bygone days that many Americans, including those in this rural community, still live by. However, sentimentalizing the past poses a problem; the problem with such thinking is the

> tendency to read religious history ahistorically: reifying this religious group's past into a sort of "golden age" of orthodoxy and ethics, one that never really existed. Set against a mythical past, it is easy to read the contemporary reality of [this religious group] as in decline, compromising and surrendering truths and standards to which generations past (supposedly) held firmly.[22]

While Reverend Prosser's sermon seeks to offer a panacea for the present housing, economic, and social crises, he and his constituents nevertheless tacitly express their discontent with what they believe are shrinking core religious, family, and institutional values once thought to hold sway over the American nation. Economic crisis is the consequence of such a decline, he insists.

Though parishioners process the nation's economic mess in the language of an orthodox and Southern Evangelicalism, this preacher uses nostalgia as a type of religious vernacular to expose what many are convinced is one of the harsh side effects of modernization pressurizing this small city in the early twenty-first century—*deinstitutionalization*, opening the door to secularism—in this period of rapid social change. Modernization has had deleterious effects on establishing and maintaining religious worldviews. Simply put, modernization reflects profound social, political, technological, and economic changes that *deinstitutionalize the religious reality* and orientations of modern peoples. If institutions support human thought, social patterns, and behavior, while providing intelligibility and a modicum of continuity, then the deinstitutionalization process disrupts social relationships and patterns. Such rattling of coherent and traditional patterns leaves people feeling unbalanced and in its wake with unpredictable and undependable human experiences. Modernity is characterized by increasing and unprecedented degrees of deinstitutionalization affecting both public activity and private spheres.[23]

Reverend Prosser implicates the twin forces of modernization and deinstitutionalization in America's decline and as the real causes for America's housing and financial crises, which have catapulted this community into spiritual crisis. Prosser confirms their spiritual upheavals using "God vs. Satan" language as code for the experiences of these white rural dwellers. God versus devil rhetoric translates into binary and moralistic thinking (e.g., good vs. evil) and commentary about social conditions that affect this Southern town.

According to Reverend Prosser, Satan is the source of anomie and chaos in all areas of American life—in the home, in government, and even in the church. It is Satan who exacerbates the spirit of greed that is driving the nation into a downward spiral. Satan also lures governmental and national leaders onto ungodly and rudderless paths in administrating this country's affairs. Without question, the people of Bald Eagles and members of the First, as garnered from Reverend Prosser's exhortation, are critical about the direction in which the country is headed. Using the religious lingo of God versus Satan, they take the opportunity to comment on the threat that a lack of leadership and lawlessness poses to their entire way of life: their perceived goodness and balanced lifestyle; their regional and American national identities; and their anticipated future prosperity. Communicating apocalyptic and eschatological urgency, Rosser declares, "These are the signs of our times."

This final comment reflects the millenarianism that is a hallmark of evangelical thought. Explaining millenarianism, Johann Peter writes that Christ will return at the end of time to bring together the just, to destroy hostile powers, and to establish a kingdom on earth for the saints to enjoy material and spiritual blessings. Christ will reign as a king and will call the just, including the resurrected, to participate in his kingdom. When his kingdom ends, the saints will enter heaven, and the wicked will be eternally damned. One thousand years is frequently earmarked for Christ's glorious reign on earth. This time period is usually known as the *millennium*, while realization of the future kingdom is called *millenarianism* or *chiliasm*.[24]

Millenarianism is the battle between good and evil materially recast as the fight between Christian saints and the wicked. Thus, good versus evil here once again refers to ethical conduct and specifically to the immoral behavior of American national leadership rather than to ontology in this Southern white community. Because of the perceived danger to the practice of evangelical faith and its anticipated decline, Prosser knowingly advocates for a showdown between "good" and "evil" as one solution to the domestic strife in American leadership and authority. In doing so, he calls forth the strength of this Southern community's faith to address America's temporal troubles.

Even though Southern evangelicalism was elementary to an emerging and growing Methodist Episcopal Church, South, Southern evangelicalism was equally and traditionally vital for furnishing an interpretive lens by which to understand America's most pressing social problems, similar to how Reverend Prosser is utilizing it presently—to critique American national and spiritual leadership. From the sixteenth to the nineteenth century, the issue of U.S. slavery and white-black race relations shaped Southern evangelicalism doctrine and activities. Although revivalism borne out of widespread Southern evangelicalism drew racially mixed audiences (i.e., whites; enslaved and free blacks) in the late 1700s and 1800s, white religious practitioners of Southern evangelicalism paradoxically and consistently both upheld and maintained institutional slavery based on scriptural understanding and authority, thus institutionalizing the segregation of white and black race relations.[25] Southern evangelicalism boasts a perplexing and complex past that serves both as a help and as a hindrance to healing the historical racial divide between white and black Americas. We see evidence of this in the historical development of Bald Eagles First United Methodist Church portrayed in the following sections.

From Revival Meetings to the "Church House": The History of the First United Methodist Church at Bald Eagles

Even though the county and town of Bald Eagles were formally organized in 1825, the introduction of Methodism into this area occurred earlier, following the westward movement of frontier pioneers who had signed an 1818 treaty with the Chickasaw Indians to settle surrounding land. Not until 1842 was the first Methodist society in the town of Bald Eagles formed—led by a young preacher named Reverend R. M. Tarrant—on the occasion of which Mrs. M. A. McGaughey, the spouse of one of the local doctors, wrote in her 1892 historical account: "R. M. Tarrant commenced [the society] by holding a series of meetings in the log courthouse, or a small building as such. Our preacher started out by asserting that God's grace is the beginning, increases, and is the perfection of all good. So eloquently and forcibly did he present the subject that he soon had the congregation too large for the house, the interest increasing daily."[26]

Under Tarrant's leadership, revival swept through the area, and between seventy-five and one hundred people joined the society. Exceeding the physical capacity of the log courthouse, these new converts in 1843 built a small frame *church house* that would eventually become the first church to be constructed in Bald Eagles:

> The church made an excellent meeting place for both the old and young. Six to eight young gallants would hitch up their lumbering old surreys and take their girls to church. It was considered scandalous to pair off in buggies. At the church, there were no street loafers after the conch shell had been blown for the audience to come into the building. Seated decorously at the right were the men and at the left the women.[27]

This small frame church house for years accommodated the members of the growing Methodist Episcopal Church, South, located in the center of town.

Civil War, Negro Methodists, and the Jackson Circuit

According to oral tradition, this first church was located at the end of "Church" Street (named after the construction of this new church). "Church" Street was near the banks of the Forked Deer River. Revival continued to produce a steady increase in membership from 1843 to 1861. During this period, the church at Bald Eagles remained an "appointment" on the Jackson circuit of the Memphis Conference. John Wesley's Methodist plan of multiple meeting places called "circuits" required an itinerating force of preachers. A "circuit" was made up of two or more local churches (sometimes referred to as societies) in early Methodism. In American Methodism circuits were sometimes referred to as a "charge." A pastor would be appointed to the charge by his bishop.[28] Methodist historian Robert Drew Simpson further remarks:

> During the course of a year [a pastor] was expected to visit each church on the charge at least once, and possibly start some new ones. At the end of a year, the pastors met with the bishop at annual conference, where they would often be appointed to new charges. A charge containing only one church was called a "station." The traveling preachers responsible for caring for these societies, or local churches and stations, became known as "circuit riders," or sometimes *saddlebag preachers*. They traveled light, carrying their belongings and books in their saddlebags. Ranging far and wide through villages and wilderness, they preached daily or more often at any site available be it a log cabin, the local court house, a meeting house, or an outdoor forest setting. Unlike the pastors of

settled denominations, these itinerating preachers were constantly on the move. Their assignment was often so large it might take them 5 or 6 weeks to cover the territory.[29]

In 1852, the trustees of Methodist Episcopal Church, South, at Bald Eagles were gifted with a plot of land "for the purpose of promoting Christianity."[30] No building was constructed on lot number 58, part of the original plan of the town of Bald Eagles, until after the Civil War. Yet, the Methodist Society weekly added to its growing numbers so that by 1853 the bishop established Bald Eagles as a "station," appointing W. J. Mahon as the first "official" pastor of this newly recognized church. Tarrant remained as a supernumerary preacher.

In 1854, Mahon was replaced by Samuel Hawkins as pastor. Under his leadership Bald Eagles' membership grew to include 130 whites and 30 "colored" members (likely the slaves of church members).[31] The church prospered from 1854 until the onset of the Civil War, when worship services ceased. Neglected and abandoned by members, the original frame church fell into disrepair. In 1868, the second small frame church house was built on the lot deeded to Bald Eagles' Methodist in 1852. Post–Civil War conditions proved difficult for attracting and rebuilding church membership. By Mrs. McGaughey's account:

> The old frame church (built in 1868) was dedicated by G. W. D. Harris (the presiding elder at that time); G. W. D. Harris is too well known for me to make any comment. The first to fill this new church was a soldier preacher, D. W. Priest. In the unsettled conditions of things he could do little toward building up the church. Then Allen, (replacing Priest), did less. Then W. T. Harris, zealous and eloquent, doing much to elevate the Christian character and restore unity and brotherly love.[32]

By 1875, a noticeable change to the church membership of 131 members was the absence of any "Negro" members. The absence of this population is attributed to Reconstruction conditions in the South. Nevertheless, changing times restored the stability of Southern and overall American society. That change again began to attract members to Bald Eagles Methodist Church. An expanding membership proceeded to leave the 1868 structure, which had become inadequate to house the people and activities of the church. Hence, in 1889, a brick building replaced the frame structure on the lot where the church had been located. For the next thirty years, the activities of the church were housed in this brick building, but, by April 21, 1919, the building was sold to the neighboring Church of Christ.

The membership of Bald Eagles Methodist had also outgrown this structure. A lot of land was purchased on May 3, 1919, with the intention of building a beautiful building at the north end of Main Avenue (then the main street that ran downtown). However, the agricultural depression during that period stalled the laying of the church's foundation. The completion of the new church building occurred in 1923. A Byzantine design, the building attracted a membership of 750 members by 1925. The architecture of the building was suitable for its place and space, making it unlike any other building in town. Adding to the $160,000 cost of construction was the $12,500 pipe organ purchased by the Ladies Aid Society. Total membership exceeded 800 people by 1941, when the building was dedicated by the bishop under the pastorate of Reverend G. C. Fain and the mortgage was burned.

"You Can't Fight the Flag"

In 1950, an educational annex and chapel were added to the church school facilities. This period further marked the church's support of its first missionary couple, Reverend and Mrs. Donald E. Rugh, who were sent to India. The Bald Eagles First United Methodist Church still today supports missionary endeavors. By 1963, to meet the demands of a burgeoning congregation of over 1,200 members, church grounds were once again remodeled and expanded to include a new education building, administrative offices, a fellowship hall, and a kitchen. In 1969, the church buildings again grew with the addition of a parsonage and youth center.

The Bald Eagles First United Methodist Church is presently still expanding its facilities to house the medley of church activities that serves its increasing membership. Church council members recently hired an architect for the church's expansion. The church's campus is enclosed by Troy Avenue, McGhaughey Street, and Elm Street. The front of the church is on North Main and McGhaughey Streets and welcomes visitors to a campus sitting on 4.5 acres of land. The sanctuary can seat 500 members and currently has 172 parking spaces between the Troy Avenue and Elm

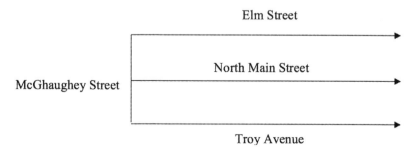

Street sides of the building to accommodate the membership. At any one time, there are usually no more than 200 members present in the building.

The church has a playground close to the childcare and preschool wings of the building. The main chapel opens onto the playground. The Family Life Center stands alone and was built in 1999. This center diagonally faces the lower level of the church building; interestingly, the lower-level entrance at Elm Street is one of the front doors to the community. There are nineteen entrances to the campus in total; the McGhaughey side of the building has an entrance to the administrative offices. The main social space for the church is the Fellowship Hall on the Elm Street side of the building. It accommodates 150 members.

The church wants to restructure and connect parts of the present campus to make room for an expansive alternative worship area for *Atmosphere* and for a children's worship area. To augment fellowshipping opportunities among parishioners, they anticipate designing shared fellowship and social areas between the alternative and traditional service spaces.

The history of the Bald Eagles First United Methodist Church is closely tied to the history of Methodism in this area. Decreases and increases in membership are responses to the social conditions affecting the town and wider America. In its most prosperous periods, the church has experienced an increase in the numbers of congregants who have benefited from larger facilities.

Given its history of community activism and missions work, I had a conversation with Pastor Cook and the youth pastor, Reverend Robert Craig, to ask about national and local social and political concerns important to this congregation. The purpose of the conversation was to learn about this church's current impact on the town and about its potential legacy in this new century.

I left the conversation with a sense of how the congregation explains history now—with an eye toward the mutual conversation between evangelical faith and civil society. "You can't fight the flag" is one way this congregation describes American national identity, suggesting that to be an "American" during the 2008 presidential election cycle was an exercise in religious patriotism. In addition, "You can't fight the flag" introduces their public theology of war.

I began the conversation by asking Pastor Cook:

> N: What do you think, what are the national sociopolitical concerns of the congregation, and/or what are the sociopolitical concerns you have?
>
> Pastor Cook: I think the level of interest and concern right now, within life of the community and the congregation, has to be on the war,

especially with our national guard that has just left the community and with members from this congregation who are a part of that. I think the whole . . . the last twenty-one to twenty-two months we've been through the election process nationally. You know that's been a part of the whole discussions that have taken place in addition to conversations about local political elections. And the economy, you know, both how it's impacting here and otherwise has been a part of the mindset. We have investment bankers and brokers and bank presidents, as well as people who are living on their retirement investments who are very concerned with where the national situation is going.

N: Okay, well the economy, everybody . . .

PASTOR C: Sure.

N: I mean, I heard it this past Sunday when Reverend Presson addressed it in his sermon. You have done it as well. I have also heard it in the black congregation that I'm participating in. Do you have anything to add?

REV. ROBERT CRAIG: I think that pretty well covers what I think are the top concerns at this particular time for the congregation; I think [Pastor Cook's] got his finger on that pulse real well.

N: How do people square their theology with war? And so, given that you're the head shepherd, how do you think . . . you can also tell me what are the attitudes toward the war in Afghanistan and the war in Iraq, but I'll just say the war. How do you understand your congregation's theology around war? How about that?

PASTOR C: I think their understanding comes a great deal out of *civil Americanism*, you know, as I'm sitting here looking at a flag right over your head.

 (*An American flag stands in the church conference room.*)

N: Oh, I didn't even see that, thank you.

PASTOR C: And I think it has to do with that and with the tradition of those who have defended this country—World War II and since. If you go into the sanctuary, one of the debates we've had is how, where do we put the American flag in the sanctuary?

N: You're not the only one having that debate, another congregation—

PASTOR C: Some would say it really doesn't belong in the sanctuary, as such. Others insist that it be in a very prominent place. We have, you know we put the Christmas tree up in the sanctuary, and sometimes we . . . One year, we had the flag behind the Christmas tree—the American flag, and that didn't sit [well] with some folks at all. (*Nichole laughing:* "wow.") So the location is of great concern because I don't think there is simply a religious and a patriotic separation; I think they're mixed and mingled in the American culture in a very real sense. And you know there are different theologies of religion and views of war, the Just War Theory and so forth. And it's, it's a balance. There's—there are ways to share the faith and (*sighing*) not alienate a lot of people. It would be easy to preach a sermon on peace to the point that the patriots would all be offended, you know?

N: Right.

Pastor C: And so while some of us are feeling that we need to be very careful to defend our rights, we also know we have a great responsibility not to abuse our power, forcing ourselves on others. There are other definitions of *American* that might exist within the life of the congregation, and I'm not sure that the pulpit is always the appropriate place to fight those battles.

N: Right.

Pastor C: Because you're not going to win.

N: (*Laughing*) Okay—

Pastor C: You can't fight the flag.

N: Definitely not in this community, you're not the only who has . . . I've been in quite a few churches here and that is [a question I've heard before]. You are raising the issue about where is the flag supposed to be.

Pastor C: That, it's symbolic, where do we put our civil religion? Whether we do "in God we trust," whether we do the Pledge of Allegiance, all those things in relation to the church: many pure religionists would say it belongs outside or somewhere, a fellowship hall, it belongs somewhere else.

Following this conversation, I interpret the concept of civic Americanism introduced by Pastor Cook, relating it to parishioners and Bald Eagles residents' public theology of war. In taking this measure, I intend to elaborate on how both groups justify their practice of civic Americanism and articulation of a public theology of war. The practice of civic Americanism in relationship to congregants' justifications for a public theology of war reaffirms their identities as people of faith, residents of this community, and Americans. Both concepts incorporate theories and conditions under which it is acceptable to wage war. Both concepts not only offer unique interpretations of their American national identity, but each also moves to solidify that identity, displaying the strength of their Southern evangelicalism as supported by civil religious practice.

Civic Americanism and a Public Theology of War

The Bald Eagles First United Methodist Church was birthed out of the revivalistic camp meetings that swept across the country and through the South during the Second Great Awakening. The fervor of itinerant preachers swelled the numbers of those joining Methodist societies. Their religious impulses also made Methodism relevant to the expansionist leanings of an American nation in the nascent stages of defining itself. Camp meetings were communal, and churches became centers of social life. Above all, although soul conversions required confrontation with God, Christian fellowship cultivated continuity while routinizing and canalizing parishioners' fervor into orderly social institutions.[33]

Bald Eagle's First United Methodist Church has the historical distinction of being the first church constructed in the town, where it continues to maintain the tradition of being a place for families, for the connection between younger and older generations, and for the social interaction of members. Its history is captured in the movement from a single-story small-framed building to a contemporary church complex that will eventually house three worship areas for traditional and contemporary services and for the youth. From pre–Civil War times to the present, the First has generated activities and developed programs to accommodate its increasing membership, who today primarily represent professionals, landowning families, merchants, as well as civic and political leaders in the community.

This group practices a "civic Americanism," like many of the white residents of this city and county, uplifting American myths, symbolism, history, and heritage while embracing evangelical faith.[34] Members have not experienced much cognitive dissonance with having the American flag in the midst of the worship space, supporting the pastor's insistence that "you can't fight the flag." Social networks are the mediums where religion and patriotism become inextricably linked to the extent that "one cannot fight the flag." The means for reifying particular religious and political ideologies in particular spaces underscores the third attribute of a "subcultural identity" theory of religious strength, which I will highlight.

The Southern evangelicalism of members of the First United Methodist Church thrives despite the challenges of contemporary modernity and secularization because of the strength of "community" as networks able to maintain religious subcultures. Traditional secularization theories propose that with the introduction of cultural plurality comes a decline in religious worldviews, which is a marked feature of modernity.[35] What parallels the decline in religious activity is also the decentralization of local cultures and communities because of urbanization.[36] In this "new" modern period, a postmodern era, the disintegration of local communities will more likely be attributed to globalization, not necessarily urbanization—or possibly a combination of both.

However, Thomas Bender argues for a new interpretation of community to contest the predetermined fate of religion and communities. Modernization paradigms propose that communities are linear and unidimensional. However, communities are not places—fixed locations like a small town, village, or neighborhood. Instead, community is an experience engaging face-to-face and intimate relationships and involving limited numbers of people in restricted social spaces and networks. Communities are held together by a shared understanding, sense of obligation, and affective and emotional ties rather than self-interest.[37]

The people of the First make no apologies for the Southern civil religious beliefs and practices that undergird their Southern evangelicalism. In fact, Bender's interpretation of community as a social network of individuals rather than as an immovable and fixed location gives a rationale to the role of communities in fostering and producing strong religious subcultures able to survive modernity, especially in this postmodern period characterized by globalization. And thus, the civic Americanism performed by members of the First is nurtured in the confines of community. That is, civic Americanism is fostered in social spaces and networks that reinforce and add to the strength of their rural and Southern evangelicalism, allowing for them to adjust their experience of and behavioral response to Protestantism without relinquishing religiously orthodox, moral, and cognitive orientations to the volatility of societal change.

As a further matter, being American implies "whiteness" and means being a patriot and a person of faith. For parishioners, civic Americanism provides a divinely guided justification for participating in war especially if American interests are at risk. Their public theology of war leans heavily on religious ideology comprised of a God-mandated defense of the nation against "foreign" enemies, at home and abroad—relying on the human sacrifices of veterans and of their families to a larger cause and recognizing the rights and responsibilities of American citizenship safeguarded by a sovereign entity that reigns above the sovereignty of the state. Fundamental to a civic Americanism is a millenarian, public theology of war and an implied definition of what it means to be American, at the heart of which is the concept "in God we trust." What is noteworthy is that members of Bald Eagles First United Methodist Church exercise a civic Americanism and public theology of war that, curiously enough, diametrically opposes the Wesleyan Methodism they vigorously believe, practice, and identify as a "religion of the warmed heart" promoting love of neighbor, life's purpose, and social missions, which is treated in the next two sections.

Methodism: A "Religion of the Warmed Heart" and of Social Mission

John Wesley experienced what many would call a religious conversion while someone was reading Martin Luther's preface to the Epistle to the Romans at a meeting in London at Aldersgate Street on May 24, 1738. Describing that experience, he explained that his "heart was strangely warmed." As a result of all the experiences leading up to this event, Wesley's focus turned to what would eventually become the cornerstones of Methodist theology: justification by faith only through Jesus Christ, holiness, and a converted heart manifested through social action—the love of neighbor.

This "religion of the warmed heart,"[38] of Wesleyan Methodism, is what consistently energized many of Pastor Cook's sermons. I recall, for example, one service and sermon in February 2009. Ushers handed me a church bulletin with the order of service as I settled into my pew. Enclosed in that Sunday's bulletin was a plea for Project 20/20. Project 20/20 is a United Methodist missions program supplying gently used sunglasses and eyeglasses to medical teams serving the poor in places with little or no medical care.

Approximately 200 individuals of all ages filled the sanctuary for the 8:30 service that morning. Betty Wagner, a church member who works with the youth ministry, illuminated the importance of Project 20/20 during the young disciples' moment, a time for three- to five-year-olds. Children are instructed in biblical principles and are celebrated during this part of the service. In addition, children begin to understand and participate in the ministries of the church during this time. This brief moment in worship prepares young hearts and minds for the day's preached message and provides a generational link to the beliefs and customs of older church members.

As he usually does, Pastor Cook outlined the day's sermon before the men's choir sang the well-known African American spiritual "There Is a Balm in Gilead." Afterward, Cook ventured further into his sermon entitled "Searching for Jesus." His homily was based on Mark 1:29-39, the story of a demon-possessed young man who approaches Jesus for relief from his affliction while Simon-Peter's mother-in-law (one of Jesus' disciples and apostles) also desires Jesus to restore her to good health. The crux of the sermon is Christian discipleship. To be a disciple, a person must display compassion toward those in lowly positions. Similarly, to be a Methodist requires focus, purpose, and compassion for individuals who clamor for assistance. One of the tenets of Methodist theology is regard for the other, which is the central lesson of this sermon.

Pastor Cook began with the following questions:

What does it mean to claim the name of Jesus? Does it mean to have the light of Jesus in us, transforming the world?

Living the life of a disciple means always being in a serving posture. In today's text, we discover the story of Jesus' compassion. Jesus spoke a word to Simon Peter's mother-in-law, took her hand, and restored her to health. Jesus' mind and spirit were always focused on people's needs. Restoring her health, Jesus was able to give back to Simon Peter's mother-in-law the desire to *serve*.

If we are called to follow a compassionate Christ, doesn't it mean we should have a desire to serve others?

Methodists are known for their compassion. Every day we find the needy at our door. That is why we visit the hospitals, serve at soup kitchens, deliver meals via Meals on Wheels, and work at food pantries. In this story, we see Jesus' compassion in his service to others, but we also see his devotional life. Jesus took time out from his eternally busy schedule to speak with his Father.

If you want focus, purpose, and energy in your life, then you must follow Jesus and make prayer a priority. We need to make time to commune with the Father. John and Charles Wesley awoke every morning at 4:00 a.m. to take time to pray. That is the heritage out of which we come. I challenge you to turn aside from the cares of the world and to pray so that you will become all that you are called to become.

Isaiah 40:31 says, "But they that wait upon the Lord shall renew their strength; they will mount up with wings as eagles, they shall run and not grow weary; and they shall walk and not faint." It takes waiting upon God to find that truth. Only a life lived in tandem with God knows that strength.

Jesus knew his focus, purpose, and his mission. In the early morning hours, Jesus was found missing from Simon Peter's mother-in-law's house. The manhunt for Jesus was on. The disciples eventually found him, but he was on a manhunt himself. When Simon Peter encountered him, he said, "Everyone is searching for you." Jesus gives an unlikely response: "It's time for us to be on our way." Jesus did not explain his actions, yet it was clear that he had just communed with his

Father because the house was yet again full of people with needs. Jesus knew the scope of his ministry. He did not come for one neighborhood or one community. He had come for the world. Jesus left Capernaum that day for you and for me. He knew his mission.

What is yours?

He was interested in preaching the good news and calling people to change. The good news is going to mean work, risk, and sacrifice. When Jesus confronted people, he demanded a decision. We are to be participants in the life and work of Christ, not mere followers of the crowd or participants in a throng.

The USC football coach tells the story of Joel, a student at USC, who felt he had no life's purpose. His coach directed him to a convalescent home where he met an elderly woman. Not knowing she needed company, he arrived at the home expecting to participate in something grand. As Joel walked up to her, she said, "Visiting anyone today?" He responded, "No." She said, "Good, I need someone to listen to me." Joel returned every week after that visit to sit with his new friend. And from that time forward, it was not surprising to see Joel leading his friends from the convalescent home to USC football games. We are called to lose ourselves in the service of Christ and this world. Will you accept the challenge?

It might mean saying, "I want to enlist in the army of God as a member of this congregation."

Pastor Cook then closed his sermon with a prayer and the benediction.

Compassion's Role in Methodist Theology

John Wesley concluded that the work of the Holy Spirit might occasionally move beyond, and work outside of, the established forms of church order. An important Wesleyan theological principle and evangelical priority is missions. Wesleyan theology perceives mission work as the direct work of the Holy Spirit in shaping and transforming both individuals and communities.[39]

Pastor Cook commonly preached self-actualizing messages such as this one to his congregation. He drew upon their shared Wesleyan heritage and theology to empower the people of Bald Eagles First United Methodist Church to cultivate hearts strangely warmed to serve the world. Using this approach, in the aforementioned sermon he introduced the stories of Jesus and USC student Joel to demonstrate that the catalyst for church members' passion, purpose, and mission should always be compassionate service to their neighbors. Throughout the homily, Cook elevated the movement of the Holy Spirit as being revealed through ministries to those outside of church walls—at hospital visits, soup kitchens, Meals on Wheels deliveries, and food pantries, and even abroad in the form of Project 20/20.

By stressing compassion's role in moving people to meet the needs of their fellow humans, Cook also illustrated the significance of Methodism as being a "religion of the heart." Believers who subscribe to a "religion of the warmed heart" are also buying into a "born-again experience" motivating them to examine their hearts' sinful spiritual condition and accept Jesus Christ into their hearts for the sake of righteousness. A spiritual heart examination and adopting Christ are starting points to unfolding a spiritual process that will initiate individual and, hopefully, social change, by firing up individuals to assume particular missions' tasks.

"Born-again" conversion experiences are pivotal to a free-will doctrine. American Methodists were the first evangelical body to embrace a free-will doctrine.[40] A free-will doctrine (by another name *Arminian theology*) ensured humanity's coparticipation with God in effecting its salvation; the doctrine advances evangelicalism by standing as one of the seminal features of the faith.

For Methodists:

> God had sacrificed his son in a spirit of free grace and love for human-ity, and all those who acknowledged their sins, repented and accepted Christ into their hearts were candidates for salvation. The emphasis in Methodism was on the human role in the process. God's desire for men and women to be converted and his mercy were constants; humans were the ones who had to be moved to acknowledge their sinfulness, repent, and accept Christ.[41]

Born-again conversion experiences are grounded in the love of God toward humanity.

This love is meant to produce individual transformation and to stimulate social action, also translating Methodism into a "religion of the heart." Methodists are compassionate, according to Pastor Cook, because renewal of individual hearts yields communal transformations and "transformation of the community was a deep concern of the Methodists, but it would come as a result of changing the lives of persons."[42] This, concludes Cook, is how Methodists "lose themselves in service to the world." Service and compassion are the focal point of the rites of Christian faith observed by parishioners of the First; these rites are deeply rooted in the established religious tradition of Methodism yet continue to flourish into the twenty-first century.

At the same time that service and compassion are hallmarks of Methodism, the evangelical nature of this congregation's and community's Methodism reflects the norms of the rural and Southern region where their religious institutions stand and the people reside. Southern regionalism strongly influenced and dictated the beliefs and behaviors of these religious practitioners, leaving them open to apocalyptic thought captured by verbal expressions of "God"-talk and "devil"-talk. Use of this religious vernacular to express opinions about U.S. domestic affairs also denoted "sacred umbrellas," keeping Bald Eagles' townsfolk connected to other regional groups and social collectives who share their same mindset, values, and commitments. In the following, I study rites of faith distinguished by "God"-talk and "devil"-talk to reinforce Methodism's adaptability to postmodern cultural conditions via these "sacred umbrellas" and to show how these rites of faith add religious strength to this social group's regional and American identities.

Brer Rabbit, Tar Baby, and a Family Feud

On a steamy, hot June morning, as I join members of the First United Methodist Church for worship service, Pastor Cook informs me he is conducting a series on "Journeying through Genesis." Yet this morning's preacher is Cook's associate pastor, Reverend Terry Prosser. His sermon, "Family Feud," is named for the game show that is a mainstay on television. However, his sermon is not about the game show; rather, it is about the consequences of family feuding. Identifying the source of family feuding as jealousy and materialism, Reverend Prosser's use of "God"-talk and "devil"-talk exemplifies how rites of faith that are bifurcated into the oppositional constructs of "good" and "evil" reaffirm the collective identities of this rural and Southern group and affirm the plausibility of their Southern evangelicalism.

At the start, Reverend Prosser presents a summary of Genesis 21:8-21. These Scriptures report the story of Abraham, Sarah, Hagar, Ishmael, and Isaac. God had promised Abraham and Sarah a child. However, after years of waiting without fulfillment of the promise, Sarah grants Abraham permission to sleep with her "slave girl"—Hagar. Hagar bears Abraham a son and names him Ishmael. Ishmael is not the "promised son," even though he is Abraham's son. Years later, Sarah produces a child—Isaac—who is identified as Abraham's heir. As the plotline develops, the relationship between Sarah and Hagar grows tense, and eventually it disrupts Abraham's household.

After summarizing the scriptural text, Reverend Prosser reminds parishioners that we are familiar with family feuding, but it is problematic when families get entangled with feuds especially because within family, we are made godly; we are sanctified. We must also remember there are different types of family. We have the church family, school family, and the birth family.

The musicians play the selection "His Eye Is on the Sparrow" (an old Negro gospel standard). Thereafter, Reverend Prosser prays and launches into his sermon proper:

Father, we thank you for the Word. We thank you for the Spirit tugging at us. Open our eyes so that we may see what you are trying to tell us. Bless this time in your presence. In Jesus' precious name. Amen.

Though it might be totally unrealistic to say this, family feuds are responsible for a good part of the hate, conflict, and suffering in this world. It is not totally unrealistic to blame what we see in American life today on the "family feud." What we see in American life today is a lack of communication, members of the family consumed in their own world, engrossed in television, caught up with the iPod, computer blog-gings, text messaging, and e-mails to name a few distractions.

None of these are bad except if they are put above *God and the family*. There is very little sitting around at the dinner table, today. In my past, Grandma and Mama expected us children to sit at dinner and have family conversation. To save today's family, some of us need to go to the family porch. Consider the different problems with the family. It may be that you have been in a "church" family for thirty years but start thinking, "No one has ever asked *me* to be an usher, teacher, or greeter." This contributes to the "family feud."

God has answers for the causes for family feuding in Christian work, home, and church.

One of the causes is jealousy. For instance, Hagar thought she ought to be treated better than Sarah. Ishmael was jealous about not receiving his father Abraham's blessings. Jealously is the cover for intro-ducing sin into the family.

Lucifer was second only to God in power and beauty. But Lucifer looked at the throne and thought he could be God. Adam and Eve felt they could be God. Cain looked at Abel and believed his offering was inferior to Abel's. Jacob's mother was jealous of her own son, Esau, and the position he held as the older of her two sons. In Jacob's family, Jacob's other sons envied Joseph. Saul was jeal-ous of David's victories. David was jealous of Bathsheba's husband,

Uriah, and had him killed. These are the effects of jealously on an individual.

Now let's look at the effects of jealousy on the family and the church.

Cain gave into jealousy and killed his brother, Abel. Sarah gave into jealously and ran Hagar into the wilderness. Saul gave into jealously and made attempts to take David's life. David gave into jealously and had Uriah killed. The religious leaders [in the New Testament gospel] gave into jealousy and stoned Stephen to death. And ultimately, the religious leaders gave into jealousy and crucified Jesus. Satan would like us to overlook jealousy, which is one of his best weapons, but we are here to uncover it.

Jealousy enters into the home when a wife says to a husband, "You don't look at me the same anymore. We don't talk the same anymore." It enters into the school system where I recently read about a mother who killed another girl to prevent her from filling her daughter's cheerleading spot. It enters when you know you've worked hard to get a promotion, yet the position you thought you earned is handed to someone else. It enters when you are a member of a group of pastors who meet regularly to support one another and suddenly Lucifer breaks the circle upon the announcement of you being selected as bishop. Watch the games begin!

Power and professionalism are the root of jealousy. But the main cause is *materialism*. The prophet Nathan confronts David about his jealousy and envy when he talks about the man with many sheep killing the man with only one sheep. What we have *not*, poisons what we already have. *Poison* is delivered upon the entrance of jealousy and envy.

I get so angry at myself about letting Satan in. We are content with things until our neighbor has something better. Phyllis and I were afforded the opportunity to be at the footprint of God last month. We got up to meet God, and God was ready to meet us. The human part of me saw cabins surrounded by boats and cars. And instead of praising God for this, I wondered, "Do these people not work? How is it that *sooo* many have *sooo* much and *sooo* many have *sooo* little?" Satan jumps right in there and we miss our blessings. I had to stop. God slapped me with "Terry, what is wrong with you? Look around you."

Jealousy and materialism make us lose all rationality.

You remember the *Brer Rabbit and Tar Baby* **story?**

We often lose when we strike something thinking that we will win. We could say that it is genetic, but we need to just call jealousy *sin*. We need to pray, pray for others.

We need to look at the cross. Instantly, I am reminded of God's great treasures.

God sent his son, Jesus Christ, to die for me just the way I am.

I must love God and love neighbor.

If we look at those below us, we will have no worries about those above us.

Reverend Prosser concludes his sermon with prayer and an invitation: your life could change if you are being called to be a part of this church.

"God"-Talk and "Devil"-Talk as Spectacle in Rural Southern Methodism

Lucifer is the primary antagonist in Reverend Prosser's "Family Feud" sermon. Satan is the source of familial divisions, social rupture, and global conflict. Members at the First United Methodist Church of Bald Eagle use "God"-talk and "devil"-talk to describe and to distinguish between good and bad action in their Christian experience, their local community, and the wider world. While "God"-talk and "devil"-talk is a display of evangelical theology in theory and practice, this folksy and religious vernacular also adds to the spectacle of a theologically orthodox, Southern evangelicalism, affirming the regional identity of the people.

Reverend Prosser's chosen topic is how family feuds arise when we allow the devil's talk to destabilize the white American family. Family feuds result from the following distractions: listening to iPods, blogging, texting, and e-mailing. Each member contributes to family rupture by being self-absorbed and distracted by worldly goods and by failing to communicate with one another.

Reverend Prosser argues that these disruptions shift the focus from God and the family to idolatrous practices originating from the wiles of the devil. Not only is blogging, texting, tweeting, and Facebooking upsetting to family dynamics, but such idols are also blinding people to the presence and existence of their maker and creator—God. Consequently, idolatrous practices lead to a lack of family conversation and cohesion.

Reverend Prosser advances another idea about Satan's machinations. Jealousy is one of Satan's strategies for upsetting family life. Once jealously enters the life of the Christian believer, then sin enters. He suggests that jealousy was at the heart of the New Testament religious leaders' stoning of Stephen and crucifying of Jesus Christ. Likewise, jealousy is always percolating in people's hearts, including those of church parishioners. This emotion can easily lead to the murderous thoughts of a mother, the irrational actions of a coworker, and even the poisonous and ungrateful attitude of a minister blessed to have the opportunity for a personal and spiritual retreat.

While Reverend Prosser hints at this in the earlier part of his message, as he comes to his close he solidifies what "devil"-talk ultimately represents for this church community and the white townsfolk at large: the threat of secularism. Prosser addresses this by verbally attacking materialism, pointing out its corrosive effects on family life. Fragmented households plagued by ungodly habits, venomous jealousy, and menacing materialism reveal an American society that has lost its spiritual moorings and moral foundations.

This rite of faith overlays an ethic of "good" and "evil" that characterizes "evil" as the "bad" conduct of society infiltrating local Bald Eagles culture and manifesting as jealousy, sin, materialism, and secularism, which seems now to be operating in local households. Other vices that interrupt the social order and plague the peace of the most basic of social units in America—the family—can also be included in this list of "evils." While some readers might be dismayed by how congregants at Bald Eagles First United Methodist Church and Reverend Prosser characterize "evil," their depiction leads to the fourth feature of a "subcultural identity" theory of religious strength that is important in interpreting the mindset and worldview of this group: "sacred umbrellas."

In contrast to the "sacred canopy,"[43] in a postmodern and pluralistic world, "sacred umbrellas" are small, handheld, portable, and accessible relational worlds. Like the faith-sustaining religious worlds that modern people construct for themselves, sacred umbrellas are religious reference groups that make a way for religious flourishing.[44] Because canopies are expansive and immobile, and reach beyond covered spaces, they are ineffective. People do not need large and overly encompassing sacred cosmoses to guard against threats, violence, and social disorder and to maintain their religious beliefs in a postmodern world. They need sacred umbrellas only to cultivate social relationships under which their convictions will make sense.[45]

Globalization is weakening traditional family values, an occurrence that people of the First find alarming. They find navigating an early twenty-first-century global (i.e., culturally pluralistic) and technological world distressing because secular values are permeating everyday life and having local impact on the systems these rural dwellers have put into place for stability and meaning.

Postmodernity and secularism are unsettling their sacred worlds. "God"-talk and "devil"-talk conjure up martial imagery. By denoting "good" and "evil" behavior as "God"-talk and "devil"-talk, they have put up *sacred umbrellas*. "God"-talk and "devil"-talk epitomize the regional and religious vernacular used and understood by those who serve as *reference groups* for the people in this region and of this religious subculture.

Reference groups are "a set of individuals whose standing or perspective is taken into account by an actor when selecting a course of action or when making a judgement about a specific issue," and they "serve as sources of norms, values, and standards of judgment, functioning as informal authorities in the process of self-evaluation."[46] The "god"-talk and "devil"-talk of these Southern Evangelicals are *sacred umbrellas*; they make use of this particular religious rhetoric to assess and judge "bad" *and* "good" social conditions in America, and this keeps them connected, regionally and religiously, to other groups who reflect their norms, commitments, values, and ethos. By measuring themselves against these groups, they are able to evaluate themselves and claim the religious strength of their practice of Southern evangelicalism, a practice that cements their regional identity and also their national identity as American.[47]

In closing his sermon with an implicit declaration about correcting unjust wrongs, Reverend Prosser draws upon the folklore of American slaves. "Brer Rabbit and Tar Baby" emerge from the social protest tradition of the slave. Slaves used the code of animal trickster tales to talk about the slave masters' injustices toward them. Lawrence W. Levine asserts that in animal trickster tales the animals, though retaining much of their natural characteristics, were humanized to inhabit the African and Afro-American world: "The world they lived in, the rules they lived by, the emotions that governed them, the status they craved, the taboos they feared, the prizes they struggled to attain were those of men and women who lived in this world." The primary feature of almost every trickster tale was their assault on deeply ingrained and culturally sanctioned values.[48]

Prosser leaves his audience with both a moral mandate and a warning: when the weak resist, the powerful do fall. His closing words indict the powerful and certain social structures as a peril and a threat to the flourishing of his rural congregants as they endeavor to give their best to America.

Similarly, the election of Barack H. Obama to the American presidency brimmed with possibilities of bringing out the best in America as his rise to power garnered jubilation from across the world. Yet, his election signaled a radical shift and potential change to American national identity and that of smaller communities and their regional constituencies. His winning revealed that some segments of the American population were tussling with the idea of a U.S. president of African descent. My study continues by showing how these white rural dwellers experience and translate into religious terms the rise of President Obama, who for many represented the destabilizing patterns of secularism and postmodernity, upsetting the social worlds of parishioners at Bald Eagles First United Methodist Church and other residents in the city and county.

Presidential Inaugurations, Barack H. Obama, and American National Identity: "A Change Is Gonna Come"

Anticipating the presidential inauguration of Barack H. Obama in 2009, Pastor Philip Cook preached the message "Jesus' Inauguration Day" at a Sunday morning service in early January. To prepare his church fellowship for the changes in American executive and governmental leadership, he connected the 2009 presidential inauguration to the commencement of Jesus' ministry. The inauguration of America's first president of African descent was highly anticipated around the world, and Pastor Cook's sermon records the historic nature of this event.

He stresses the significance of rituals associated with the start of each new year because inaugurations, he reminds his listening audience, represent new beginnings. To signal the start of a new year and new beginnings, Americans participate in making new year's resolutions, writing mission statements, and outlining visionary plans. Even so, a message about presidential inaugurations and new beginnings also highlights that this historic social and structural change might provoke anxieties in his Southern and rural parishioners since having a black president of the United States of America represents the dawning of a new day.

New beginnings modify "who we are." Fully endorsing the merits of seasonal inaugurations, Pastor Cook reflects to his audience that inaugurations provoke metamorphosis, establish fresh identities, and challenge individuals to live out a process of re-construction and re-creation. After this summary of his message, Cook proclaims:

> Millions are anticipating the inauguration, which always signifies a transition from one seat of power to another seat of power. When George Washington was inaugurated, the ritual of placing a hand on the Bible was also inaugurated; that happened in New York. Thomas Jefferson was the first president ever to be inaugurated in Washington, D.C. In fact, his inauguration was marked with the first ever inaugural parade. John Tyler was the first vice president to succeed a president who died in office. John Coolidge swore his son into the office of president of the United States in his home.

Jesus answered his calling as savior of the world by coming out of the waters of the Jordan; baptism was the ritualized washing away of sin. This marked Jesus' *inauguration into ministry.* Mark 1:4-11 professes:

> And so John came, baptizing in the desert region and preaching a baptism of repentance for the forgiveness of sins. [5]The whole Judean countryside and all the people of Jerusalem went out to him. Confessing their sins, they were baptized by him in the Jordan River. [6]John wore clothing made of camel's hair, with a leather belt around his waist, and he ate locusts and wild honey. [7]And this was his message: "After me will come one more powerful than I, the thongs of whose sandals I am not worthy to stoop down and untie. [8]I baptize you with water, but he will baptize you with the Holy Spirit."
>
> [9]At that time Jesus came from Nazareth in Galilee and was baptized by John in the Jordan. [10]As Jesus was coming up out of the water, he saw heaven being torn open and the Spirit descending on him like a dove. [11]And a voice came from heaven: "You are my Son, whom I love; with you I am well pleased." (NIV)

Jesus came from Nazareth of Galilee to be baptized by John. Upon coming out of the Jordan River, the Holy Spirit rested on Jesus. In the Markan version of the gospels, Jesus' ministry begins with John calling the people to "make ready for the day of the Lord, make his path straight." The story begins with the call of preparation (a call to readiness). "Make ready," draws us into a feeling of urgency indicating that God has acted in a decisive way, and also signaling we must respond right here and right now.

Like the Jews of old we often focus on traditions—with resolutions and plans, to signal the beginning of a new year. But we need Jesus' presence to bring us into a new year. We need to shake off the dust of our sinful lives and wade in the water like Jesus, in order to usher us into a new life. We learn of Jesus (who Jesus is) by the announcement made by his Father. Even before Jesus does anything, there is a revelation: "You are my beloved son and in whom I am well pleased." Here, Jesus is established by his identity and lives out this identity.

And that is how Jesus responds to his disciples. He asks the question: *"Who do you say I am?"* The answer they give is more complicated than what it needs to be. However, God's word to Jesus is, "You are my beloved son in whom I am well pleased." God's answer to Jesus' identity is not difficult. *Likewise, "who we are" is not as difficult as we make it.* If Satan could have kept Jesus from believing in who he was, then he would have been able to thwart Jesus' ministry. Satan tried to tempt Jesus by challenging Jesus' identity. He asked, "If you are the son of God then do this."

Instead of asking a question like that, I would like to challenge you with the following questions: What are we going to be in this new year? What are we going to do? Do you know who you are today? Once we know who we are, then we will know what we should do. God is saying to us today: "You are my son. You are my daughter. In you, I am well pleased."

Pastor Cook closes the sermon with a call to discipleship that includes a charge to receive the faith, to be baptized, and to become part of the church body. The congregation closes with the hymn "Where He Leads Me." Walking up the church aisle, Cook symbolically "sends forth" the parishioners to do the work of service in the world.

The congregation responds with the closing:

May God's blessings, God's grace, and God's glory be yours now and forever, amen, amen. May God's blessings, God's grace, and God's glory, be yours now and forever, amen, amen. Go in God's love, go in God's peace, go and know that God be with you! A-men, a-men, a-men.

Using narrative theology, Cook raises questions about personal and corporate identity by relating spiritual lessons to daily life practices. Accordingly, Cook says, "At the onset of his ministry, Jesus asks the following question of his disciples: 'Who do you say I am?' Likewise, replacing one president for another prompts Americans to ask a closely connected question: 'Who am I?' or more aptly, 'How is American being defined now?'"

Most storytellers pursue a practical interest in narrative traditions. What makes true stories distinctive are the teachable moments and lessons shared with the audience: a moral message, practical instruction, a rule of life. Storytellers know what to do with their listeners. Stories are based on experience of either the teller or other people that is transformed into the experience of those who listen to the stories.[49]

Like any good storyteller, here Cook translates religious myth into questions of social and national identity that are consuming the minds and hearts of his congregants, and he clearly links evangelical faith to civil religion. Hunter reminds us that "more extreme civil religious activism can be understood as an expression of protest against modernity, as a reaction against a secularized public sphere, as an attempt to reconcile the disjunctive worlds of the public and private spheres."[50] A query about Jesus' identity here elicits musings about individual and corporate American identity in an attempt to reconcile the listening audience's perceived disjointed worlds.

More significantly, Cook is exhorting his parishioners to prepare for the "new"—to be ready because God has acted decisively in the here and now. He is simultaneously attempting to allay their fears around what many, in this rural and Southern town, have perceived as a radical change in executive leadership that without doubt has implications for how America defines itself and for who *is* and *is not* considered American.

With the election of the first black American president, what anxieties are being provoked in these white parishioners and townsfolk? Why the trepidation? What did President-Elect Obama's rise to power signal for them? What do they stand to lose? What challenges were they facing regionally and to their twin identities (i.e., Southern and American)? Without having to articulate it explicitly, Pastor Cook addresses the disjuncture many parishioners must have been feeling between their private (i.e., Southern evangelical) and public (i.e., American) worlds. The rapid technological and global social changes that came in the early twenty-first century may well have precipitated such binary feelings even before this historic election.

The former questions might never be answered, but Cook's invocation of Satan's adversarial position in the temptation of Jesus is quite a telling metaphor about life for the people at the First and in this rural area. Satan tries mightily to assail Jesus by challenging Jesus' relationship to God and by taking issue with how Jesus defines—and identifies—himself. Satan attempts to hinder Jesus' ministry by pushing Jesus to do the miraculous in order to prove himself. However, God responds from heaven to Satan's attacks, declaring: "You [Jesus] are my Son, whom I love; with you I am well pleased." And, thus, by applying this Scripture, Pastor Cook is able to assure his congregation of their social identity as Americans, reinforcing that "who we are"—even with election results—is who we *say* we are, who we *have always* been, based on how *we understand* ourselves. Our identity *should not* change merely based on political situations and happenings in broader American society or events throughout the rest of the world.

That January morning in 2009, new beginnings demanded a major shift in how these rural inhabitants would need to relate to America's new president. A black head of state was *unanticipated* by this voting bloc, and how the country would relate to him was *unknown*, causing silent antipathy and upsetting their traditional construal of American national identity. All of this was happening against the backdrop of two wars started by religiously inspired and ideologically violent extremists as well as of a financial and housing crisis, leaving many throughout the nation and in this local community bereft and looking for answers. What could these Bald Eagles locals *not* anticipate about a postracial, pluralistic, and militarized America? Cook responds to their emotional and psychological tumult with an inadequate solution for some that is a righteous answer for others: he admonishes those in the congregation not to succumb to the wiles of the devil.

Even with such wise counsel, the parishioners of Bald Eagles First United Methodist Church still drew upon the resources of their Southern evangelicalism and civil religion to engage *and* to rebuff the social and political disturbances now characterizing the postmodern period in which they live. Their spiritual wranglings shaped them into fierce patriots prepared for a good fight and roused by rites of faith exhibiting a public theology and ethics of "good" and "evil." In this final section, we will witness the ways in which this communal theology and ethics of good and evil sustains these Evangelicals' collective social identities when confronted by the challenges brought on by early twenty-first-century globalization, setting the world on course for the major changes that, as Sam Cooke sang, "are gonna come."[51]

Shaping Fierce Patriots for a Good Fight

I am greeted with preworship service announcements on this spring morning as I await the beginning of the worship experience and watch parishioners visit with each other. The organist plays "When Morning Gilds the Skies" as the 8:30 a.m. prelude, followed by "A Lenten Call to Worship" led by the chancel choir. Afterward, congregants reaffirm their faith by reciting the Apostles' Creed.

The pastor recently instituted time at the altar for prayer to meet the needs of members emotionally and spiritually burdened and seeking God's guidance on specific issues. Following the altar prayer is our recitation of the weekly ritual prayer, the Lord's Prayer. A choral response closes prayer that is then followed by the offertory. After singing the doxology and celebrating the church's young disciples, Pastor Cook proceeds to the pulpit to preach the message "Nic at Night," based on Nicodemus' encounter with Jesus in John 3:1-21. A homily about God's grace and the necessity of being "born again," this sermon simultaneously pinpoints the "born-again" experience as seminal to shaping a fierce patriot. He declares:

Driving Ms. Daisy is more than a movie about an elder Jewish employer and her black chauffeur. Daisy and Hoke's relationship begins slowly, but they end up becoming best friends. The movie tells us about the challenges of being transformed and shares the confidence that as we continue to develop we begin to accept our lives the way it is. Today's lesson challenges us to be transformed in our relationship with Christ; that is the point to the Lenten season—to be transformed.

After the overview, the chancel choir sings "Jesus Keep Me near the Cross." Pastor Cook then sets in motion the reading of the sermonic passage for "Nic at Night," John 3:1–21:

[1]Now there was a Pharisee, a man named Nicodemus who was a member of the Jewish ruling council. [2]He came to Jesus at night and said, "Rabbi, we know that you are a teacher who has come from God. For no one could perform the signs you are doing if God were not with him." [3]Jesus replied, "Very truly I tell you, no one can see the kingdom of God unless they are born again." [4]"How can someone be born when they are old?" Nicodemus asked. "Surely they cannot enter a second time into their mother's womb to be born!" [5]Jesus answered, "Very truly I tell you, no one can enter the kingdom of God unless they are born of water and the Spirit. [6]Flesh gives birth to flesh, but the Spirit gives birth to spirit. [7]You should not be surprised at my saying, 'You must be born again.' [8]The wind blows wherever it pleases. You hear its sound, but you cannot tell where it comes from or where it is going. So it is with everyone born of the Spirit." [9]"How can this be?" Nicodemus asked.

[10]"You are Israel's teacher," said Jesus, "and do you not understand these things? [11]Very truly I tell you, we speak of what we know, and we testify to what we have seen, but still you people do not accept our testimony. [12]I have spoken to you of earthly things and you do not believe; how then will you believe if I speak of heavenly things? [13]No one has ever gone into heaven except the one who came from heaven—the Son of Man. [14]Just as Moses lifted up the snake in the wilderness, so the Son of Man must be lifted up, [15]that everyone who believes may have eternal life in him." [16]For God so loved the world that he gave his one and only Son, that whoever believes in him shall not perish but have eternal life.

[17]For God did not send his Son into the world to condemn the world, but to save the world through him. [18]Whoever believes in him is not condemned, but whoever does not believe stands condemned already because they have not believed in the name of God's one and

only Son. ¹⁹This is the verdict: Light has come into the world, but people loved darkness instead of light because their deeds were evil. ²⁰Everyone who does evil hates the light, and will not come into the light for fear that their deeds will be exposed. ²¹But whoever lives by the truth comes into the light, so that it may be seen plainly that what they have done has been done in the sight of God. (NIV)

After reading the Scriptures, Pastor Cook remarks:

Nicodemus belonged to the brotherhood; he was a moralist and was committed to living by the Torah. People looked to him for truth. If there was anyone who knew about God, it was Nicodemus. However, even as a ruler of the Jews, a Pharisee, and a member of the Sanhedrin [the Supreme Court during that period that made decisions about religious law and with regard to the person, Jesus], even with being pedigreed, Nicodemus was *empty*.

In all of his roles, Nicodemus was a fierce "patriot." He was looking for political solutions as he awaited the Messiah. Though he studied under the best teachers like Gamaliel [a premier instructor of that day], Nicodemus was a broken man who did not need more theories about God. Rather, he needed a "religion of the warmed heart," as described by John Wesley. Jesus knew that Nicodemus needed more than theories of God. He needed to be transformed. Did you happen to read the book *The Shack*?

The Word of God comes alive when we know Christ personally; it comes alive when we feel his love; and it comes alive when we return his love. Jesus said "to be born again" is mainly what is needed to enter the kingdom of God.

For example, Johnny Dean grew up in the South helping his uncle in the Delta region. It was hot and humid as they worked. During the evening, the night's heat and humidity forced them to stand still on the porch, but they soaked in the days when the breeze would make the leaves rustle. They did not know where the breeze or the wind had come from. That's like God's Holy Spirit and grace. Grace is a mystery. No one knows where it comes from and where it is going. That characterizes "born again" experience; it happens because of God's amazing grace.

Often we ask God to show us the Holy Spirit because we can't believe in what we don't see. *Then there is a story about a boy named Patrick.* One day Patrick asked his father about the Holy Spirit and where it comes from. Answering Patrick, his father said: "Patrick, I'll show

you the Holy Spirit if you can show me the wind. I cannot show you
where the Holy Spirit comes from much like I cannot show you where
the wind comes from. However, I can show you the effects of the Holy
Spirit on a person's life. Patrick, every time you feel the wind there is a
Christian in America praying for you."

    In Jesus Christ, God has brought history to a crescendo, which is
what John 3:16 tells us. God has the world in his hands although they
are pierced hands. God is waiting for you to give him control. Now is
the time to become a disciple of Jesus Christ.

Pastor Cook closed with the following prayer:

> Father, we bow before you conscious that we enter the kingdom by
> invitation. Lead us in the path to living out our kingdom work. Call us
> to commitments we'll have yet to keep or make. In Jesus' name, amen.

Rites of Faith as a Public Theology of Good and Evil: Pushing the Boundaries of the Good Fight

Pastor Cook implies in the "Nic at Night" sermon that fierce patriots are
birthed out of political and spiritual revolutions. Promoting this idea, he
declares, "Nicodemus was a fierce patriot. He was looking for political
solutions as he awaited the Messiah." Fierce patriots not only participate in
social and political upheavals but also are people with transformed hearts.
That is where God's grace enters. Pastor Cook preaches this evangelistic
and revivalistic sermon to encourage his listeners to experience what it
means to be "born again." Movement of the Holy Spirit and God's grace
facilitates being born again, resulting in a more intimate relationship with
Jesus Christ. Ironically, conversion experiences are also uniquely marked
by spiritual conflicts demanding the loyalty of a fierce patriot. Caught
between sin and salvation, believers work out their spiritual strife in their
physical bodies—the focal point of the battleground for mind, emotions,
spirit, and soul.

    Pastor Cook's rhetoric in public worship, his engagement with the
rites of faith in the church's sacred space, provocatively links the material
to the spiritual. Patriots are loyalists who stand for the individual rights of
citizens of a nation yet defend their country against outsiders. For members of Bald Eagles First United Methodist Church, patriots equally safeguard Christian faith. They are American and religious nationalists.

    In a sense Pastor Cook delivers two messages already at the fore-
front of the minds of his listening audience and reflecting the values and

commitments of this Durkheimian moral "church" community. First, born-again Christians are constantly endangered, always assuming a defensive posture to be ready for war with a secular world. Ergo, grappling with spiritual *and* physical enemies is a defining feature and a pillar of being evangelical Christian. Second, born-again Christians uphold the faith; protection of evangelical faith requires arming families and the homeland against adversaries. His message underscores the ways in which God and country, in this church and community at large, are constantly bound together.

In a religious sense, Pastor Cook's metaphor calls attention to John Wesley's theology of good and evil. Interpreting Wesley's spirituality, Jeffrey Williams explains that it preponderantly depended upon three notions: the conflict between saint and sinner, good and evil, the redeemed and the demonic. Believers moved from enmity to an intimate relationship with God through fighting the good fight. As God conquered penitents in conversion, they worked to effect communal transformation and to produce the fruits of eternal redemption.[52] Here spiritual conversion has a direct impact on the growth and development of communities. Williams insists:

> The battles Wesley found so important for the Christian life also came to shape Wesley's view of temporal struggles, whether in the form of England's wars or personal conflicts between individual human beings. Wesley often discouraged Christians from using force against other human beings. . . . Yet at various points throughout his life, Wesley allowed for the possibility that aspects of the Christian's fight might intersect with that of the state. In this intersection, the boundaries of the good fight became more permeable and contested as Wesley's followers struggled to apply the fight to their own lives and communities.[53]

Evangelicals' internal spiritual battles spilled into their political activism and entanglement with societal concerns and the administration of the nation. Their efforts to right public wrongs hostile to their way of being in the world placed them at odds with those whom they perceived as outside groups, domestic and abroad, both fictitious and factual. In mounting their counterattack, their actions illumined the "permeable and contestable" nature of moral conduct manifested as an "ethical" but physical fight for rights.

Having been forcefully pushed into the social realm, these spiritual struggles stretched the boundaries of a good fight, revealing a public theology and ethics of "good" and "evil" that sustained Evangelicals' collective identity in the face of earthly and secular challenges. How the Southern Evangelicals of Bald Eagles translated their rites of faith, supernatural wrangling, and social and political activism into interpretations of what is "good" and what is "evil" leads to the fifth feature of a "subcultural identity theory" of religious strength where religious groups grow stronger through the conflicts that arise between themselves and other groups and subcultures in a pluralistic context. These tensions strengthen their *own identities* and their members' commitment, unity, participation, and resource contributions. In this way, postmodernity's cultural pluralism can actually benefit religious subcultures by furnishing greater varieties and numbers of other groups and subcultures against which to "rub" in order to feel both distinction and tension, in a way that internally fortifies religious subcultural life. Whether fabricated or exaggerated, out-group conflict typically builds in-group strength and helps us to understand better the bases of the persistence of religion in the pluralistic, modern world.[54]

The inextricable link between God and country in Bald Eagles finds Wesleyan faith as one of its sites of inception because of the heavy influence of regional culture on area churches and city and county constituencies. The spiritual fights of born-again believers are an entry point into an early twenty-first century and postmodernist "engaged orthodoxy" and trigger the martial responses of Bald Eagles' Southern Evangelicals to cultural, social, and political upheavals, problems, and trends in a globalized America. From its start as a frontier revival meeting to its move into the first wood-framed church house built in Bald Eagles, the First United Methodist Church has been at the forefront of history in this rural and Southern community. Methodism was introduced into the area because of the fervor of itinerant preachers whose convincing, convicting, and born-again salvific messages drew crowds that welcomed both white and (at certain points) black members into the church community.

Several theologies are operating in the Bald Eagles First United Methodist Church congregation: a Wesleyan theology that stresses Scripture, reason, tradition, and experience; a Southern evangelical theology in which church members exhibit zeal for and robust commitment to spiritual disciplines like attending worship service, Bible study, and other activities; and a narrative theology that magnifies the power of myth and story, which, in collusion with theological doctrine, conveys the religious and civic orientation of this social group. Church members' engaged orthodoxy also becomes evident in rites of faith rooted in this town's military culture. It discloses parishioners' psychology, theology, and ethics of "good" and "bad" behavior, and it expresses such behavior with martial imagery.

Their public theology of war they express as a form of civic Americanism that embraces myth, history, and leadership authority as components of an authentic regional subcultural identity in tension with but against all others. Anything that threatens this identity is evil or devilish, and what-ever preserves it is characterized as good or divine. Categorizing "good" and "bad" behavior by using the religious rhetoric of "God" versus the "devil" also shows the strength of the Southern evangelicalism that these congregants and white townspeople practice. The ways in which such lan-guage creates and distinguishes between in-group and out-group cultures (whether real or mythic) nevertheless uniquely supports and elevates the regional and American national identities of the people of the First and the rest of the county.

4

Conjuring Black Evangelical Spirituality and Culture

Tabernacle Missionary Baptist Church

Tabernacle Missionary Baptist Church in Bald Eagles, West Tennessee, is a black working-class to middle-class congregation with an older membership comprised of school teachers, factory workers, business owners, service-industry employees, and veterans. There are few young families here. Middle-aged members whose children are college educated or just finishing high school are part of the church's demographic of approximately one hundred members.

It is a congregation primarily of extremes—the very young (e.g., infants and young children) and aging members (mid-sixties and older). Often the youngsters are the grandchildren of older parishioners or neighborhood children that members chaperone weekly to Sunday service. Tabernacle is an "ol' timey" Baptist church. There are no songbooks or hymnals. The songs are often spirituals, standard hymns, or gospel songs that older members remember from childhood and that the congregation knows by rote.

A visitor is expected to be familiar with the words; in the tradition of the black church, worship leaders do not "line out the hymns"[1] for repetition. The King James Version of the Bible—often humorously labeled black folks' "official translation" of the Bible—is used even though members have other versions (e.g., NRSV, NIV, NLV) in their possession. In public and from the pulpit area, Scripture is read from the King James Version. All in all, the church has a predominantly "older" spirit. Maybe it was to balance this that the pastoral search committee selected a young pastor, Reverend Mitchell Matthews—a tall (6'5") and slender, married African American man of forty-one years—to assume leadership of the church.

A prior conversation with the pastor and head deacon was instrumental to my being granted permission to conduct research among the membership of Tabernacle Missionary Baptist Church. It certainly eased my acceptance there. Each week as I entered the modern church's main doors, I was greeted by an usher who handed me the morning worship program. Typically, fifty to seventy-five members were in attendance; those numbers would swell to ninety or a hundred persons if members of another church visited for a Sunday afternoon service, as they occasionally did.

Seated in the choir loft on the first Sunday in June 2008 when I visited was the men's choir, which sang selections at designated times throughout worship. On that steamy Sunday morning, the air conditioning was not functioning properly, and consequently I was hot and sweaty when I approached Pastor Matthews after the service to reintroduce myself. He greeted me, quickly regathering the membership before everyone could disperse for the afternoon. Introducing me to the congregants, he told them I would be conducting a historical study of the church. While that was partially true, I proceeded to explain more fully why I had selected Tabernacle and the town of Bald Eagles for my research and study. I stressed the comparative nature of my project—that I would be observing religious activities in general throughout the town and county and also specifically at two congregations—one white, the other black. I told those assembled that I had selected Tabernacle Missionary Baptist Church as the black congregation because in my earlier visits to the area, residents had shared information about the historic nature of the church.

As I continued to explain my project, I added that I was planning to investigate the similarities and differences between black and white Christians by studying their beliefs and practices both in the public square and in more private church settings. I also wanted to understand how parishioners at both churches understood civil religion, which I simply explained as the relationship between religion, politics, and American values, and how this relationship is expressed, ritualistically and patriotically.

Though they listened intently, everyone looked quite dumbfounded, and, when I asked for questions, there were none. The pastor dismissed the congregation and, along with the head deacon and his wife, treated me to lunch at a local restaurant to become familiar with me and to ask some more probing questions about my project. Members might have exited the building puzzled that day, but apparently they were willing to take a chance on me and my strange explorations into their rural and Southern black culture—for the church and lunch meetings opened the door to my life as both a researcher and a member of Tabernacle Missionary Baptist Church and exposed me to the political mindset, social attitudes, and religious thoughts and practices of black residents who were also being affected by early twenty-first-century secularizing and modernizing forces.

Black congregants at Tabernacle Missionary Baptist Church in Bald Eagles navigate an American nation and world in transition in ways both similar to and different from their white counterparts in greater Bald Eagles and at the Bald Eagles First United Methodist Church. Rapid social and structural changes precipitated by the rise of violent extremism, technological revolutions, worldwide social movements, and increased religious and ethnic pluralism compound issues of race, gender, and human sexuality that parishioners contend with daily. What effect do such social ruptures to the fabric of American life have on the national and regional identities of these black townsfolk? How do these rural and Southern blacks navigate the social and political upheavals of a postmodern period? In what ways do their practices of a racialized Southern civil religion and evangelicalism contribute to a developing black public theology of war that also buffers black pain and suffering?

To engage and interpret their deeply held and abiding Christian faith and social values, this chapter studies how this local congregation applies different "moral logics" to social, religious, and political conflicts that arise during preaching moments, Bible studies, and personal experiences. A conjurational black evangelical spirituality and culture able to accommodate members' differing but shared moral expectations reinforce their regional identity and ground their American national identity. This conjurational and black evangelical spirituality and culture they observe through rites of faith that promote a theology and ethics of "good" and "evil"—a theology and ethics expressed through members' dialectical and conjunctive thinking and practice. Such a theology and ethics is less about "bad" and "good" (or immoral versus moral) conduct and more about how such conduct leads to black existential and spiritual crises while making room for the stability and beauty of black life.

Theophus H. Smith's important work explains a *black conjurational spirituality and culture* as that which transforms the sociohistorical realities of African Americans who use the Bible as a *conjure* book,[2] as a "kind of magic formulary for prescribing cures and curses, and for invoking extraordinary powers to reenvision, revise, and transform the conditions of human existence."[3] Basically, conjure is magic. Yet, the meaning of *magic* cannot be equated with the occult. Instead, *magic* is "ritual speech and action intended to perform what it expresses." Contemporary scholars regard magic as a primordial and lasting form of communication, a type of language.[4] Historically (and even now), African Americans sought out the black conjurer who would apply a "magical" system of manipulating human artifacts and herbal remedies and use their curative properties to transform social reality; hence, the black American conjurer ("hoodoo"/"root" doctor) was both magician and healer.

The meaning of conjuring culture includes indigenous spirituality (a blend of West African, Native American, and European derived practices) and cultural performances (i.e., religious and folklore practices) that use "biblical figures and biblical configurations of African American cultural experience"[5] to produce healing and to transform natural, social, and historical processes. As a consequence, the black American interpretation of *conjure* is differentiated from its English or European American counterpart that means only "witchcraft, sorcery, or occultism."[6] A black American conjurational spirituality and culture is based in black American folk practices and culture and not a heterodox form of "magic" concerned with manipulating the supernatural.

Further, a black conjurational spirituality and culture studies American blacks' "ritually patterned behaviors and performative uses of language and symbols that convey a *pharmacopeic* or healing/harming intent and employs the biblical figures of cultural experience"[7] by means of mimetic processes to transform black reality through acts of the imagination.[8] In this chapter, descriptions of conjurational spirituality and conjuring culture reinterpret the Christian thoughts,[9] rituals, and healing activities of African American congregants of Tabernacle Missionary Baptist Church, whose black evangelical spirituality derives from traditional white, Southern, and Christian influences as well as their own folkloric beliefs, wisdom sayings, and practices.

Sociologist Penny Edgehill Becker advances her own theory of how local congregations use moral rhetoric both to work out emerging social concerns and conflicts threatening to group identities and to negotiate social and religious identities and boundaries revealing "insider" and "outsider" status. Her premise finds its footing in Charles Y. Glock's 1993 claim that

> issues of race and ethnicity, gender roles, sexuality and sexual morality have become the primary arenas of conflict for churches in the United States throughout the [twentieth] century. . . . Perceived from the start as moral issues [Glock argues,] these topics have been difficult for religious leaders to ignore. Tensions over gender, sexuality, race and ethnicity reflect the reactions of national religious organizations to ongoing *modernization*, and, in particular, to the increasing *universalism* and *liberalism* of public life.[10]

Glock applies the terms *accommodation* and *resistance* to explain how these social issues—also labeled moral issues—speak of liberal and conservative churches' reactions to the modernization process and affect both the decline and the growth of national denominations. Though agreeing that Glock's argument is beneficial to interpreting denominational dynamics, Becker contradicts his accommodation and resistance proposal as well as the culture wars thesis,[11] instead explaining that neither theory effectively describes and rationalizes how local congregations broker the meaning of debatable social issues in congregational life. Becker further writes:

> At the local level, these issues are not, primarily, arenas for ideological battles between those who are more liberal/progressive and those who are more conservative/orthodox. At the local level, these represent issues of inclusion and exclusion, of boundaries and identity, of *who is* and *who is not* part of the moral community. . . . Liberal and conservative congregations alike tended to frame these issues as "moral" conflicts, or conflicts over, "What is the right thing to do here?"[12]

Hence, potentially divisive issues like race, gender, sexuality, and sexual morality—and in the early twenty-first century also issues of ethnicity, religious affiliation, and nationality—are reconciled by applying and balancing a "moral logic" of compassion and caring with a "moral logic" of religious authority.[13] Religious authority and judgment derive from social and cultural groups' interpretations of Scripture, religious texts, and the spiritual lives of congregants.

Rather than reviving the liberal and conservative conflict, a "moral logics" of compassion and religious authority bridges this divide to ensure that members who have transgressed the church's belief system(s) are not excluded from the fellowship of believers but rather remain socially included. Social inclusion is guaranteed by a recurring renegotiation of institutional boundaries. How does this apply to the black residents of Bald Eagles, in general, and to the black parishioners of Tabernacle Missionary Baptist Church, in particular?

For the black, Southern, and rural members of Tabernacle Missionary Baptist Church in Bald Eagles, the use of moral logics to interpret social conflict takes place in two identifiable ways. Alongside the Bible studies, and other spiritual experiences, a "moral logics" approach first illustrates the moments when African Americans are being excluded from the American social experiment and therefore calls for and demands their inclusion. In the second case, such an approach ensures that members who have moved beyond the bounds of Tabernacle's religious and moral belief systems are corrected but are sustained, remaining a part of the church fellowship.

At Tabernacle, through preaching, Bible studies, and collective cultural experiences, the membership's moral repertoire and active conjurational black evangelical spirituality was evident in many ways: in their endeavors to address subjects ranging from the preelection national crises in housing and leadership and American civic responsibility following the 2008 presidential results, in theologies of the disinherited, and in a black public theology of war for "peoples with their backs against the wall."[14] Together, these ways represent a black theology and eschatology rooted in African American existential experiences that normalize "evil" as an inherent part of human existence. While acknowledging the "devil's" negative effects on the well-being of African American people, belief in an eschatological hope celebrates African American victory over "evil."

Hence, this group's conjurational black evangelical spirituality and culture is observed in rites of faith that promote a theology and ethics of "good" and "evil"—a theology and ethics expressed through members' dialectical and conjunctive thinking and practices around black social and religious life in this rural community. A member of the church's Bible study group offers an example of this dialectical and conjunctive practice in her account of another black Christian who wears a necklace of copper pennies to ward off evil spirits. These devoted Christians practice a race-based Southern and evangelical Christianity able to hold both "good" and "evil" in tension with each other without succumbing to "evil." The borders of their race-based Southern evangelicalism are wide enough to accommodate the folk beliefs and practices that inform their spiritual development and life in a rural town. "Good" and "evil" are more about their ontological social reality than about "moral" and "immoral" conduct, although such conduct is included.

While their practice of a conjurational black evangelical spirituality acknowledges and accepts the "bad" of black pain and suffering, these religious practitioners still look forward to "golden crowns" of black joy and gladness both in the here and now and in the eschaton. Their dialectical and conjunctive faith shelters and houses tragedy and triumph, as well as telling of their regional and American national identities that play out publicly as ideas about who is included and excluded from American nationhood. With this in mind, I segue here into a preaching moment that defines and addresses social disruption to begin to illustrate how senior leaders and members of Tabernacle Missionary Baptist Church in Bald Eagles used a moral logics approach in concert with their conjurational black evangelical Christianity and culture to negotiate the fallout from the 2008 national housing crisis.

"What to Do in Times of National Crisis?": Use Your Time "Qualitatively" (Efficiently) and Number Your Days

Each week parishioners gather at 10:45 a.m. for Sunday morning worship services that begin at 11:00 a.m. This morning's order of worship is the same as usual—praise music to usher in the Spirit and to prepare the congregation for the movement of the Spirit, the call to worship by the pastor, and devotions led by the deacons. The worship bulletin or program identifies the time at which parishioners may enter the sanctuary by the phrase *worshippers may enter.* While church attendees are entering, the men's choir is singing two songs of praise—"When the Morning Comes" and "Jesus, I Love Calling Your Name." The responsive reading is from Psalm 24, in which a holy God claims ownership of the earth. Then the choir stands for another song of praise—"I Want to Be Ready when Jesus Comes."

During the altar call, deacons initiate the prayer, a line that stretches across the front of the sanctuary because no altar rail exists at which parishioners might kneel and pray. One member's hand securely clasps another's in anticipation of the minister's morning prayer that beseeches God to answer the prayers of the people.

Listed in the church program is the "Sick and Shut-In prayer concern list" that includes the Tabernacle church family, Christian missionaries, military families, youth, and elderly members. Also included are individuals and families with specific prayer concerns. Before entering the sanctuary on Sundays, parishioners seize the opportunity to write their names on another prayer list sitting on a table in the foyer of the building. That list is also submitted to the pastor and announced before prayer begins.

After this prayer, visitors receive a warm welcome, having introduced themselves and identified their church "homes" to the congregation. Immediately after welcoming the visitors, we march around the church to place our offering in the baskets being held by two deacons in the front of the sanctuary. The choir sings another selection before we stand for the reading of the Scripture, Psalm 90, in preparation for Pastor Matthews' message, today: "What to Do in Times of Crisis?"

Psalm 90:1-5 declares:

> [1] Lord, you have been our dwelling place
> throughout all generations.

² Before the mountains were born
or you brought forth the earth and the world,
from everlasting to everlasting you are God.

³ You turn men back to dust,
saying, "Return to dust, O sons of men."

⁴ For a thousand years in your sight
are like a day that has just gone by,
or like a watch in the night.

⁵ You sweep men away in the sleep of death;
they are like the new grass of the morning. (NIV)

As I sit in the pew listening and distracted by my note taking, much of Pastor Matthews' sermon becomes a record of paraphrases and direct quotes. He starts the day's message reporting Moses' reaction to personal crisis:

The eternal God is our refuge. This faith is what sustained the Israelites in the wilderness for many years. People looked to Moses for this type of direction. God was Moses' help in ages past. Psalm 90 indicates God's eternity and human's frailty. The difference between the immortal and the eternal is that man pulls off mortality and puts on immortality. That is how man is able to possess eternal life. God, on the other hand, is eternal. In God, there is no beginning and no end. Faith in Jesus Christ allows for eternity to set in.

Matthews continues:

If we ever lived in a time of crisis, it is now. We have leaders whose motives are messed up, and it is impacting the godly. *We are in a crisis!* Our government will spend $700 billion to better our banks instead of assisting homeowners in crisis!

We are in a crisis! When our men are fighting overseas, and there is no peace in our homeland, we are in a crisis! Yet, if we hold on to God's unchanging hand, we can survive crisis! For our days pass away under your wrath; our days come to an end like a sigh!

Our *sinfulness* causes us to decay daily. We pass away! Man is a creature of time who needs to be rightly related to God. We need to be hooked up to God to find our purpose and to live rightly!

Psalm 90 is a funeral Scripture, but this is a long funeral Scripture because the wages of sin is death. During Moses' generation, people lived longer than seventy years, but God placed a limit on the length of days that people lived because people were sinning. Their sinning cut their days short, as indicated by Psalm 90:9-10, which professes:

⁹ All our days pass away under your wrath;
we finish our years with a moan.

¹⁰ The length of our days is seventy years—
or eighty, if we have the strength . . .

Moses called the people to number their days and use their time qualitatively because of the limit that God had placed on the people. Moses realized that man without God had no purpose. So for those who don't know: there is no "pet" heaven. Pets have no soul; only men have souls. Man was made in God's image and desired life to mean something. Life is not meaningful until you place Jesus in the center of your life. Many live without purpose, but Paul said, "To live is Christ, to die is gain."

Moses tells us what to do in a crisis.

In verse 13, Moses says, "Pray to God for favor," because only God can help us. Moses tells us in verses 14 and 15 to pray for joy. We need to pray to God for joy. Each morning I wake up to news of people dying and losing their jobs. Whenever crisis comes, get on your knees to pray! I know we have no prayer in schools, but when there is a crisis in schools then we still need to start praying. That is our form of prayers in school. When there is a crisis in the White House, then people need to pray.

In the White House, they are facing a crisis. When men want to marry men, when women want to be with other women, and when men look to other men for guidance and leadership, that is not godly; there is a crisis! If we know how to pray to God, we can go through a crisis! We need to hold on to God's unchanging hand! We need to praise God. Praise God and he will see you through! Sin is all around us! Praise God and he will see you through! If you don't start praying now, you will be like the children in the wilderness and fall to your death! The children fell to their death! By holding on to God's unchanging hands, we can survive tornadoes, hurricanes, and earthquakes! We will survive other natural disasters!

What to do in a time of crisis? We need to pray! We are in a crisis! Our children are falling by the wayside, killing one another. We got to pray and trust God, and he will change things. He will see you through!

The pastor closes the sermon enthusiastically, invites nonmembers to join the church, and afterward makes the church and community announcements.

Conjuring God for Freedom from
Sin and Economic Hardship

Pastor Matthews addresses America's housing/mortgage and thereby economic crises more broadly in this sermon by implicating "sin" and human "sinning" as the source(s) of these crises. He considers that this mortgage crisis triggered not only the stock market crash and the resulting 2008–2012 Great Recession but also the country's acceptance of homosexual marriage, ungodly leadership, and the lack of prayers in school, all of which he identifies as human sin. Americans are living through crisis situations that by all accounts are affecting local communities, homes, and schools. Matthews suggests that African American communities are particularly affected and in crisis. Black families are caught at a crossroads between ungodly White House leadership and the failures of black family leadership, which together result in community crisis. The fact that black children are killing one another in major cities and rural towns puts at risk future generations of blacks, impacting the viability and longevity of the black community.

Solving these problems requires the people to be more vigilant about their time, efforts, and labors. Substituting the Israelites that lived in Moses' period for the members of Tabernacle Missionary Baptist Church, Pastor Matthews asserts they are to use their time efficiently, effectively, and wisely. That furthermore implies their labors must not be in vain; hence, they are to *number their days.* To avoid falling into sin, members must additionally pray for God's favor and for the joy that only God can bestow. Pastor Matthews' preached message is replete with dialectics and conjunctives: immortality and morality, humanity and divinity, flesh and spirit, war and peace, life and death. Dialectical and conjunctive belief and practice exemplifies how this community denotes "good" and "bad." For these rural dwellers, "good and evil" are opposing social forces legitimating American blacks' social experiences as lived "in between"—"in between" distress, suffering, and anxiety but also joy and hope.

Pastor Matthews draws on Moses and the exodus narrative to explain the experience of his African American members especially during this span of economic hardship. Biblical scholar and cultural critic Allen Callahan shares the Greek etymology of the term *exodus*, literally meaning "the way out."[15] Particularly during slavery and throughout American history, *the exodus* became a major trope to explain how both white and black Americans saw themselves. For whites, the exodus from England landed them in New England, their promised land. For African Americans, their exodus would be as a people like the ancient Israelites in Egypt, whom God would deliver from the bondage of American enslavement. Each of these American racial groups subsequently adopted and adapted exodus to shape their collective identities and for purposes of theological and political strategy.[16] The enslaved kept alive a mythic past by praying for deliverance and incorporating the Old Testament exodus narrative into their spiritual imaginations. Appropriation of the exodus story shaped their sense of peoplehood and historical identity because Israelite enslavement linked them to a group of biblical peoples with a common heritage. Having identified with Israelite exodus out of slavery, these Christian slaves created meaning and purpose out of a chaotic and senseless existence. Through the exodus, God's history of liberation would be repeated in the American South, making the event archetypal for this enslaved group.[17]

Pastor Matthews' sermon shows us that African Americans continue to link their social experience to biblical figures and narratives and especially to that of the Moses figure and exodus narrative. Werner Sollors' term, *typological ethnogenesis*,[18] showcases a literary history of Puritanism's influence on whites, ethnic and immigrant groups, as well as peoples of color who connect biblical figures to their cultural experiences in America. Typological ethnogenesis encompasses the ways in which each of these groups relate biblical narratives and characters to postbiblical people, places, and events.[19] On that Sunday, the listening audience fully apprehended and appreciated the different crises this group of black rural dwellers were confronting when Pastor Matthews conjured the God of Moses. These are crises to which they are being held captive and for which they need "a way out."

By conjuring (i.e., summoning, invoking) the God of Moses, Matthews participates in a form of typological ethnogenesis in which God is a deliverer of these present-day bondsmen and bondswomen. As stated, to conjure or to "induce a deity" is a "device for inviting us to make ourselves over in the image of the imagery" or "to image or reimagine the self."[20] Hence, Matthews exhorts his congregants to reimagine themselves as a people emancipated from economic constraint and freed from the sins that have led to American social and political disruptions as well as black family and communal crises.

What does Pastor Matthews articulate as the moral obligations of community through his preaching on this Sunday? In this setting, he communicates a conjurational black evangelical spirituality and culture that recognizes the unique social experiences of African Americans as a people tied to a legacy of American institutional slavery and whose current communal experiences of black children murdering other black children comes as a reminder of the constraints and limitations of being black in America, especially in the rural South. These constraints are based on a confluence of factors including socioeconomic status, discrimination, and other social privations.

Overlaying such experiences of blackness are those of being American, made explicit in Pastor Matthews' sermon by his pointing out the failings of the White House and executive leadership, more broadly speaking. Members of Tabernacle Missionary Baptist Church in Bald Eagles live out the moral imperatives of being black, Christian, and American by following the God of Moses whose strong hand has historically cared for and guided this rural black and Southern community into better days despite the stressors of racialized American living. In the next section, the social geography of Tabernacle's worship space lends background to the dialectical and conjunctive Southern civil religious and evangelical faith church congregants exercise. This space is the means by which a conjurational spirituality and rural black culture is nurtured.

Stained-Glass Windows and a Black Jesus Holding a Long White Staff: A Visual Dialectic

Whenever I walked through the front doors into the foyer of Tabernacle Missionary Baptist Church, doors of heavy steel that belied the beauty of the church's interior, I was greeted warmly by an usher. In the foyer, the wallpaper is white with a floral decoration running through its middle. Two striped sofas line the main entrance of the sanctuary and are in full view as visitors walk through the front doors of the church building. At the left of the front doors and inside the foyer is a table with Afrocentric pamphlets with titles like "A Healthy Weight for You" and "High Blood Pressure: Facts for You."

Around the corner from the front doors on the left is a room adorned with pictures appropriate for school children, along with a few chairs. I learned that the monthly church newsletter is generated in this room. As a guest member of the congregation, I later have my photograph taken in this room. My picture is printed alongside a brief biography that appears in one of the church newsletters not long after my arrival.

Leaving this room, a visitor notices two square windows above the left sofa. When glancing across the main doors of the nave toward the right side, one cannot miss two square windows above the right sofa and parallel to the left windows. In one of the left windows is a mini-display of the birth of Jesus with all-black characters. Also noticeable is the green marble-topped and dark-wood end table with gold trim that is standing next to the left main door before entering the sanctuary. Bathrooms as well as a drinking fountain adjoin the foyer. Windows are lined with gold trim on both left and rights sides of the foyer. On the right side of the foyer, below the windows, and adjacent to the sofa on each side, are white lamps with white lampstands.

Upon entering the green-carpeted sanctuary, a visitor encounters three rows of wooden pews separated by two central dividing aisles. The sanctuary is a modern-day structure whose construction cost over a million dollars. The three sections of pews are each comprised of eleven red-cushioned benches for comfort. Two more red-cushioned benches stand on the interior of the main sanctuary and at both sides of the main entrance. There is an audiovisual "island" in between the back bench and the last pew where the worship service is recorded.

The interior of the sanctuary is off-white with natural-colored wood trim. Both left and right sides of the sanctuary are decorated with stained-glass windows. Five natural-colored wooden beams furnish the infrastructure for the upper sanctuary of this church from its carpeted base to a triangular shaped apex at the roof of the upper sanctuary. Long rows of natural-colored wood intersect and run perpendicular to the beams.

Toward the ceiling in the front of the upper sanctuary is an elevated stained-glass window. Unlike the windows at eye level, this window depicts a black Jesus / black shepherd holding a long white staff with two white sheep flanking him on either side; this stained-glass black biblical figure reflects the racially conscious, dialectical, and conjunctive Christian faith practiced by these black evangelical believers. Moving down from this stained-glass window to the front of the sanctuary, a visitor sees on the floor of the church a communion table and a smaller statue with a wooden crucifix carved atop the wooden block. Also located on the floor of the church on the visitor's right is a standing podium as well as a black piano.

By walking up five green-carpeted stairs, visitors enter the chancel where the pulpit is located. Behind the pulpit are five chairs. Three majestic red-cushioned chairs are situated directly behind the pulpit that is flanked by a red stole embroidered with a gold-colored cross. Of the three majestic chairs, two are separated by small tables used for a pitcher of water and other miscellaneous items for visiting guests and the main preacher. On the right and left of the three chairs are two other red-cushioned but more simple chairs. Dividing the pulpit area from the choir loft is a white wall with natural-colored wood trim.

The choir loft has approximately twenty seats for members. Behind the choir loft is a covered wading pool frequently used for church baptisms. A beautiful mural is painted on the back wall behind the choir loft. The mural is painted in blue. Blue hands that stretch toward the congregation transform into a blue dove and become the background for a black Jesus in a light-colored tunic/robe embracing a black man, probably a new believer. The mural is framed by a natural-colored wood-trimmed wall that separates the wading pool from the mural.

To the left of the pulpit, in an enclosed area, are the drums and other percussion instruments. Standing on the floor in a corner to the right of the pulpit area is the American flag, commonplace for this area of the country, even though it is not a regular sight in African American congregations throughout many other parts of the nation. As one turns to leave the sanctuary and looks upward, five more small stained-glass windows come into view. Each of these windows has a biblically related image. For instance, in one of the windows is a dove diving toward the earth. A visitor returns to the outside world by leaving through the main doors of the sanctuary and walking through the foyer toward the front steel doors, then exiting. In the end, the biblical figures in the stained-glass windows and wall mural are permanent reminders of the traditional rural and Southern evangelical faith that members of Tabernacle Missionary Baptist Church profess and practice—yet shaped by racial experiences that make living "black and Christian" in America an enduring dialectic.

Local "black" Historian Mrs. Johnnie P. Whitelaw Talks Race Relations in Bald Eagles

The documented histories of both black and white communities in this town and county are mainly oral histories. Representatives of the Bald Eagles Historical Society, established in 2004, were resourceful in providing me the names of the local black and white historians in town. In a 2007 article from the *Bald Eagles State Gazette*, the local newspaper, the newly elected president of the society refers to the Bald Eagles County Museum that spurred the founding of the historical society. The journalist (who is also the local white historian), Earl L. Willoughby Jr., writes:

> The beginning of the museum and the historical society go hand-in-hand. The Downtown Bald Eagles Development Association began the historical society. But it was actually the museum aspect that started it. During the first years of the McIver's Bluff Celebration, Bald Eagles' residents shared their pieces of the county's history in a makeshift museum

at the Bald Eagles County Courthouse. That interest led to the creation of the historical society in April 2004. Since officially opening
on March 17, 2005, in the basement of the Professional Development
Center, the museum has housed several exhibits including the Nancy
Timmerman Memorial Dollhouse Collection, a collection of military
artifacts from the Civil War to Desert Storm, Bald Eagles Fabrics' items,
and new exhibits that will be displayed soon.[21]

After I located Mr. Willoughby, he encouraged me and confirmed my
inclination to speak with the town's local black historian as well, a woman
named Mrs. Johnnie Parker Whitelaw.

Mrs. Whitelaw, a member of Tabernacle Missionary Baptist Church,
is also identified as the church's historian. We met at 8 a.m. on the west
side of town (one of two black areas) at Carol's Restaurant, an establish-
ment patronized predominantly by the black residents of Bald Eagles. It is
a simple but warm environment where people gather to eat and fellowship
during lunch hours.

Mrs. Whitelaw is a slender, silver-gray-haired, light-brown-skinned,
eighty-four-year-old African American woman who does not look a day
over seventy and still has a very sharp mind. She reminds me of the late
Rosa Parks—in physical features, stature, intellect, and commitment to
certain causes. Mrs. Whitelaw, who is a shade darker than Parks, participated in chartering the town's local NAACP chapter and in establishing
race relations in the city of Bald Eagles.

Mrs. Whitelaw often travels between this town and Memphis to stay
with family. Formerly a schoolteacher in the Bald Eagles school system,
she served children in the local white and black schools, when the school
system was segregated. Through our conversation, I learned the history of
Tabernacle Missionary Baptist Church's relationship to the early years
of the developing Bald Eagles community. In the following passage,
Mrs. Whitelaw reports on Tabernacle's beginning:

Tabernacle was *a* leading church dating back to when it purchased its
first building in 1880. It was a leading church because it was the largest
black church in the community. However, that is not the case now.
Initially, the CME Church drew the black professionals; it was what we
would call the "style shop" because its members were the black elites in
town. Tabernacle also drew professionals—doctors, lawyers, and dentists, but it was still essentially the "poor man's" church. It was a "poor
man's" church, yet it drew many members. Under the leadership of Rev.
G. W. Tyus, the church nurtured a lot of young boys and shaped them

into young men. You had to belong to the church in order to be a
"young ambassador" [which was] an early church activity for the young
men or to be on the baseball team. We belonged to a lot of associations.

Since Rev. G. W. Tyus left, the church has changed its name several
times. We have no mothers' board anymore; we don't have a "church
aide" or a "pastor's aide." Previously, the church paid the pastor, the
landscaper, and the secretary. I was the secretary for a long time; [at that
time], I thought that if you had [such] skills, you were giving back [to
the community] what God has given to you. Now *everyone wants to be
paid.* Black church culture at Tabernacle has changed.

Mrs. Whitelaw explains the role of the mothers' board and deacons in
the church:

> MRS. WHITELAW: Our mothers' board sat to the left, and the deacons'
> board sat to the right, filling the first few pews in the church. Before
> the service officially started, the mothers' board would sing, and the
> deacons' board would pray. But now the whole musical composition
> of the church is led by the choir. The mothers' board used to set the
> tone for the service. When those sistahs got to singing and praying,
> you *knew* you had been to church.
>
> N: Who comprised the mothers' board?
>
> MRS. W: The wives of the deacons and the older mothers of the church
> made up the mothers' board. The pastor and the congregation chooses
> the "mothers' board" based on a woman's dutifulness, life lived, and
> whether she can be a role model for the younger folks. You can be
> any age and be selected to serve as a "mother" of the church. It is all
> based on lifestyle. Usually, deacons' wives were chosen as "mothers,"
> regardless of age.

Mrs. Whitelaw continues the conversation by speaking about her participation at Tabernacle and the Bald Eagles school system:

> When I was growing up, we had a special day where we dressed up in a
> long dress and sang our little hearts out. We had quartets for the young
> men, chorus, and the young ladies choir. We had to dress to the best of
> our ability because we were on the program. Regardless of how good
> or not so good you were, you received the applause and approval of the
> adult congregation and they thought you were great! As I look back and
> think about it, those were really good programs. In addition to Taber-
> nacle, we had the "sanctified" churches in the community; they became
> the Church of God in Christ. We had the Presbyterian Church, and we

also had Ross United Methodist Church which is located on the east side of town. [That is the other designated black area in Bald Eagles and on Fair Street.] The "sanctified" sisters could dance, and there were times when I would join them.

Whitelaw's comment about the role of the black church in socializing children into the social graces as well as instilling self-confidence is confirmed by Mrs. Mai Mai Watkins, a member of one of the leading families at Tabernacle. Mai Mai Watkins is a sixty-nine-year-old retired school teacher who has attended Tabernacle from birth and been a resident of Bald Eagles for fifty-nine years. She informs me about her family's participation in Tabernacle:

> The six of us grew up in Tabernacle. And, I was baptized at age thirteen in the old Tabernacle Church. And, um, in that church we had Sunday school, Baptist Training Union [BTU], and a program led by a woman by the name of Willadee Porter. She had a group of girls from the community who met at her house every week, and she taught us to make cookies, how to say thank you, how to shake hands, how to smile, be friendly to each other. And one thing she taught us was to never do anything to someone else that you would not like to be done to you. And even though the Bible says to do unto others as you would have them do unto you, she said don't do anything to anybody you don't want them to do to you. And we learned Bible verses. Um, we went on field trips, and that was what the, the people of Tabernacle did, especially the BTU teachers. Baptist Training Union, we had every Sunday evening at six o'clock, and it was as full as the Sunday school morning classes were.

I resume the account of my conversation with Mrs. Whitelaw where I was asking about Bald Eagles' educational system:

> N: Tell me a little about *the educational system*, here, in the community.
> Mrs. Whitelaw: I taught at both the black school, Bruce, and Jennie Belle, the white school. They integrated Bruce in the early sixties by bringing white students and white teachers there [an interesting reversal of integration]. The year they closed Bruce, we were not informed. I was wondering what was going on as I saw schoolchildren carrying pictures and other memorabilia. That stuff could have been saved for the archives. We didn't know they were going to close the school just because the enrollment had dropped [after integration].
>   Bill Thomas, Sammie Lee, and I started the local NAACP chapter in Bald Eagles. There have been two or three chapters since. The

chapter was founded and meetings were held at Salters AME Church. Tabernacle Missionary Baptist Church was a leading church in the community; however, the pastor, at that time, was apprehensive about holding NAACP meetings there. During the fight for civil rights, Bald Eagles did not have sit-ins. Members who participated went to Jackson, Tennessee, and became involved through Lane College [a historically black college].

   In terms of *race relations*, it was about whom you knew and who knew you. I grew up in a segregated neighborhood, but some Caucasians also lived in the neighborhood. There were quite a few who would come and eat breakfast with you. In fact, one of our neighbors, who is white, was born on the predominantly black side of town; he worked in the cotton mills. His midwife was a black woman, and to prove his place of birth, he showed me his birth certificate.

N: Allow me to revisit "race relations" in the community so that I can gain a better understanding.

Mrs. W: Black people in Bald Eagles enjoyed many privileges. Black people lived on Sampson Ave. and East Court Street. They went to moving them out during integration, but those white folks still took to taking care of those black people. They saw that they had a job. They saw that they had food. They saw that they had clothes. For instance, when my cousin was sick and died, her white employer came back and walked me down the aisle at the funeral.

   My dad got his first job from one of the members of a very well respected white family, here, in Bald Eagles. There was a relationship between white and black families, here. Relationship building occurred between families. It came down from the families. That was true in many families. If our church was in a financial bind, you knew who you could turn to. It is the same now with certain white and black folks and for those who fostered such relationships.

Mrs. Whitelaw moves into talking about the black church and politics—who was involved and not involved during the civil rights movement:

The Methodist Church [Salters Chapel] has a history of being involved in civil rights. At Tabernacle, some of our deacons felt that politics ought to be kept out of the church because the deacons who were in leadership before them had used the politicians to line their pockets. Of course, there was a mixture of people, ideas, and beliefs in the black churches in this community, and there still continues to be. There were also some blacks who were just as bitter against whites as whites had been against blacks. I don't see people as white and black. People are people. We all have our shortcomings and we all have our good parts.

Black church history in America affirms such accounts of black-white relations. That history has been immeasurably solidified by sociologist E. Franklin Frazier's treatment of religion's evolution in the development of American Negro life, facilitated by his reading of American religious history and leading to a sociology of religion's role in institutionalizing the black family. Though Frazier's theories continue to be debated, much of his scholarly acclaim finds its mooring in his observation that the spread of evangelical Christianity during the 1740s Great Awakening became the social glue for the enslaved community.[22] The Christian religion razed language and social barriers among the enslaved population because it introduced a set of common beliefs and traditions into plantation life.[23] An "invisible [religious] institution"[24] took root amongst black bondsmen and bondswomen, creating solidarity and fulfilling the social need for connection while valuing the ties of kinship formed in the New World. The invisible institution made possible the emergence of the Negro preacher as leader and guide of the people. Moreover, slaves' practice of evangelical Christianity was coded, conferring a countercultural morality to that of their white slaveholders. In their practice of this coded religion, a new theology oriented them toward the world in which they lived while simultaneously helping them to interpret and understand complex experiences including their human existence in chains.

Before and during the Civil War, the Negro Church came to be made of the enslaved Southern population's invisible church and the Northern freedmen's independent black church. Post-emancipation, the Negro Church served as a "nation within a nation," in which black life was privileged, making possible black self-determination, community and educational development, and the dawning of black political leadership. A safe haven against white hostility, Negro Church leadership prepared the black American masses to speak out against racial barriers and obstacles.[25] Religion became the anchor for black institutional and social structures like the church, schools, fraternal organizations, mutual aid societies, and the family. Religion moved to the epicenter of black social life.

In one of our exchanges, Mrs. Whitelaw communicated the Baptist Church's role in developing the gifts and graces of young people and adults in this rural and Southern community, not unlike the goals of the Negro Church for enslaved and post–Civil War blacks. C. Eric Lincoln later extends and elaborates on Frazier's argument, asserting that the 1960s Black Church was extremely different from Frazier's post–Civil War and survivalist Negro Church. The "Black Church," more radicalized than its former counterpart, arose from the civil rights and black power movements. Religion held an active role as part of the fabric of black institutional social structures that precipitated social change.[26] Confirming the rise of the 1960s Black Church is Mrs. Whitelaw's oral history of the political activism of select Bald Eagles' black churches in the fight for American civil rights, churches that were essential to the inception of Bald Eagles' local chapter of the NAACP.

Yet, given what Mrs. Whitelaw shares, I believe she expresses a moral logic of caring and religious authority incongruous to her *lived* experiences of race relations in Bald Eagles. However, that incongruity is addressed by the aforementioned conjurational black evangelical spirituality and culture characterized by dialectical and conjunctive thinking and action. Black liberation theologian James Cone captures such incongruity well in his own reminiscences:

> This black religious experience, with all its tragedy and hope, was the reality in which I was born and raised. Its paradoxes and incongruities have shaped everything I have said and done. If I have anything to say to the Christian community in America and around the world, it is rooted in the tragic and hopeful reality that sustains and empowers black people to resist the forces that seem designed to destroy every ounce of dignity in their souls and bodies.[27]

Since Mrs. Whitelaw admits the need for Bald Eagles' Black Church political activism during the 1960s, a need affirmed by her involvement in the founding of the local NAACP chapter, her lived experiences counter her statement about the congenial relationship between blacks and whites, thus implying that race relations were actually tense in Bald Eagles during the civil rights period. Her declaration ("I don't see people as white and black. People are people. We all have our shortcomings and we all have our good parts") further substantiates the paradoxical nature of her moral reasoning and group experience. Though Mrs. Whitelaw's moral rhetoric is incongruent with the reality of past race relations and experiences, it serves her and others well for sustaining commitment to and inclusion in the Bald Eagles and church communities while bestowing upon her and others the power to resist forces designed to destroy dignity in their souls and bodies. Handling paradox exemplifies the magic and healing intent of a conjurational black evangelical spirituality and culture that additionally distinguishes the regional and national identities of these rural and Southern black folks.

Old Tabernacle: By Mule and Wagon / New Tabernacle

Tabernacle was established in the 1870s after the end of the Civil War. Former slaves who remained in Bald Eagles needed a place to worship. Accordingly, a group of men and women who identified themselves as Baptists initially gathered at different homes to hold worship meetings. "Money was scarce, but each individual gave a part of his meager earnings toward a dream—to own their very own place, dedicated to God, where people of the Baptist belief could gather and worship according to the dictates of their hearts."[28] With these monies, early members of Tabernacle rented an old four-room frame house that was once the site of the town's jail. Unfortunately, they had to vacate the house in late 1879 to make room for the county's jail.

This news galvanized the membership and the appointed leaders; once again, they gathered meager financial resources to make a move. Since their desire was to purchase property, on March 3, 1880, with the guidance and bargaining power of the deacons, the church bought a building and the surrounding land. "The deed to the property provided Tabernacle with historical data about their first deacons, the first purchase made in the name of Tabernacle Missionary Baptist Church, and solidified their role as part of Bald Eagles early history."[29] This first church building was located on the early east-west connector routes that would take residents and visitors toward and away from the Bald Eagles historic downtown area to points north and south of the town.

Tabernacle grew and prospered during the late 1880s to the 1920s. An agricultural area, Bald Eagles drew black day laborers to the house, fields, and other areas of commerce. Yet, there were also enterprising African American men who started their own businesses as draymen, physicians, barbers, blacksmiths, and carpenters. This group of men provided leadership to Tabernacle during this period. Meanwhile

> members were not bothered by the church facing a westerly direction or that it sat on a dead end road. Nor did it cause any raised eyebrows when negroes who lived all over Sampson Avenue to the north had to cross a plank to get to the church from the Bald Eagles–Teapots Road. Sunday mornings saw the crowds gather in time for service. Walkers came on foot, visiting with one another as they trod the rutted road to the church. Those who could afford them, rode gracefully in their buggies. Yet others came by mule and wagon, picking up passengers as the slow procession made its way to Sunday service down the narrow dirt road known as Baxter Street.[30]

Though Tabernacle experienced the Great Depression along with the rest of the country, between 1920 and 1940 the church witnessed significant growth. Under the pastoral leadership of Reverend W. M. Harris alongside the board of deacons and trustees, in 1922 they demolished their first church building and constructed a church basement where the growing membership could participate in church activities. The church basement was the initial phase of what eventually would have become a new church building. Tabernacle would also experience a changing of the guards starting with Reverend W. M. Harris, as a series of senior pastors, once assigned to the church, either retired or moved on to other churches. On August 20, 1940, Tabernacle once again purchased a new church building, this time for $4,750.

On the first Sunday of September 1940, under the leadership of Reverend C. E. Davis, members moved from the basement to the new church building. The record shows: "At promptly 11 o'clock, the pastor, Rev. Davis, dressed in full clerical garb, Bible in hand, stepped out followed by the Deacons in their best Sunday suits. Trustees, Mothers Board, Ministers, and Deacons Wives, all other officers, organizations and members followed in order. The march led from the basement to the new church, where it officially ended with the pastor's arrival at the church steps. From there, he and the members entered their new home together."[31]

"How You Want the United States to Go?": Mai Mai Watkins on America's Dialectic

Tabernacle's early history demonstrates the church's ability to attract the professional and working-class crowds fundamental to the growth of Bald Eagles and its black community. Because the archives do not record the church's activities beyond the 1950s, much of my conversation with Mrs. Whitelaw focused on race relations in Bald Eagles and on Tabernacle's role in civil rights and beyond that period. However, when comparing notes from my conversation with Mrs. Whitelaw with those from my conversation with Mrs. Mai Mai Watkins (another prominent member of Tabernacle and the black community), I learned other residents have different memories of Bald Eagles' race relations between blacks and whites, memories more reflective of the historical times.

> N: How did whites and blacks interact during the 1950s and 1960s, and moving forward?
> MAI MAI WATKINS: People from the east side of town, across the tracks, went to Kennedy Rogers; it was as big as Walmart. It was a little

store, but as far as names go, it was as big as Walmart because people from all over town, especially people from west end of town, came to Kennedy Rogers to buy groceries. I knew that Kennedy Rogers was next to Tabernacle.[32] Now, that was a white person's store, Kennedy Rogers. And . . . and the stores downtown, Gravis—black and white—all the stores downtown we went in, and Brewers, we went in and out of. And then you had the farmers—we worked in their fields. Now when you think about the farmers, they were very kind people and accustomed to being around blacks. That's the way I look at it, more than anybody else. But you also had the women working in the household, doing housework for white women. And, even though we didn't come in contact with that side of the white people, very often, we were in contact with the farmers very often. And the farmers chose to be in contact with us.

N: And this was during segregation.

MMW: *Before.*

N: Before *de*segregation.

MMW: . . . before desegregation. Because when you got up into desegregation, things start to change in terms of working in stores downtown and other places. Before you didn't see a black person working at the cash register anywhere 'cept when you step into some little corner cookie or candy store on the west side or something. Something like that. But your question was . . . was it interacting with white people?

N: Yeah, you're answering. You've answered it.

MMW: I'm trying to see, to answer your question. I think we all kept our distance. Even though we did certain things together such as in the fields and working for . . . but then there was, you know, you knew as blacks which side of the street to walk on.

For instance, going to the movies, we had two theaters here, the Francis and the Capital—and even though they were open for us as well as the whites on the same day—that's where the shoe store is, I think that's the right place. I think that was the Francis theater. To enter we went around on that little alley, alley-like side. That was the door there, and we had to go upstairs. And on the Capital theatre, it [the entrance] was around the corner on Main Street, and you had to go upstairs there. Now we didn't buy popcorn, even though you could smell the popcorn; the white kids bought popcorn, but we didn't buy no popcorn.

N: Hmm . . .

MMW: And uh, we just, we knew where to go and where not to go and when we went into those stores downtown and went shoppin' on Saturdays, and we knew what to do and what not to do.

N: Mm hm. So, so, blacks and whites led separate lives. I mean during segregation and the only time there was real interaction was in a working relationship.

MMW: Mm hm. And that didn't come until the kids started going to school together.

N: What didn't come?

MMW: The change in, uh, feeling comfortable saying, uh . . . we grew up in that "Yes, ma'am" and "No, ma'am" period.

As our country moves into another historic direction with the election of President Barack Obama, I ask Mrs. Mai Mai Watkins to consider the impact of his election on the church, more generally, and Tabernacle's mission to the community, specifically.

N: Okay. So, uh, contextualize Tabernacle for the future especially in light of yesterday's inauguration. How do you see Tabernacle? What role do you think it will play in the future? What role is it playing now?

MMW: In light of the election and the inauguration yesterday . . . well, let's go back to the election. I think that the election opened up, uh, minds. . . . Yeah. But I think the inauguration yesterday slapped those minds in the face. To the point we're saying, "Hey, it happened!" And then seeing all those people on TV who were there [in Washington, D.C.], simply for the fact of being there, and like Grandmamma Stokes was not caring whether she saw . . . she just had to be there. And many people traveled for that reason, they probably didn't know the historical impact at the time that they had uh committed to [traveling], but being there they had to realize for themselves what was happening in this season and time of change. I truly think that it did not faze many people until after the words were spoken in the inauguration, until he actually became president, and not president-elect.

N: Yeah. He's President Obama.

MMW: Uh huh. I think people . . . you see, yesterday people were crying and shouting, and I don't think they really knew why; it was the Spirit in them that just caused them to do that. But I think today they are, today, on the twenty-first of January, they are calming down and realizing that *"I have to do my part to make the change that he feels is gonna take place."* And even though he's saying that it's not gonna happen overnight, and it's gonna take time, but if I do my part, it will help to make it quicker. And I feel that people are beginnin' to feel that way right quick. (*clears throat*) Excuse me. And I think that preachers will be able to teach and preach toward that type of change in their different denominations: both black and white. That is what I envision happening at Tabernacle, also. I believe that many white people who did not vote for President Obama are willing and ready to support him in a way that has surprised even them. Realizing that this is a season of change, for instance, I ordered my prescriptions from Super D; I handled ordering my prescriptions differently yesterday. The pharmacist said, "Uh, you know, I believe uh everything is gonna be alright." And I told him, "Sure! He's in God's hands, everything's gonna be fine." Then the pharmacist said, "Well I didn't vote for him! But I'm gonna support him," and I told him, *"Well you're tryin' to be a true American, aren't you?"* He told me again, "I'm gonna support him but I didn't vote for him." And I said, "Well, he won the election. He is the president of the United States. And you are a member of the United States simply by being an American and living in one of the states of the United States. So it's up to you. *How you want the United States to go?"*

Mrs. Mai Mai Watkins' willingness to try something new and her verbal exchange with the local pharmacist makes evident that Watkins relates the church and civic responsibility to *magic*—the transformative power of social change, all of which historically have been part of the prophetic role of the African American church in the United States.

Dialectical tensions typify the black church tradition. C. Eric Lincoln and Lawrence H. Mamiya's 1990 sociological study of the black church confirms the need for a "dialectical" social scientific model for interpreting this social institution. Mai Mai Watkins' focus on civic responsibility and social change illumines the dialectic *between the priestly and prophetic functions* of the black church. Every black church engages both priestly and prophetic functions. Spiritual life and care of members are priestly functions concerning maintenance of the worship community. Church involvement with political and social justice activities in the broader community are classically prophetic. Operating to pronounce God's judgment on a wayward society, the prophetic also expresses hope for change and amelioration of bleak social conditions. Churches often stress one function over the other. Priestly churches are characteristically fortresses of survival, and prophetic churches are liberation networks. Yet both types of churches also demonstrate both functions, which means that liberation churches also perform the priestly functions and priestly churches contain liberation potential.[33]

What Mai Mai Watkins envisions for the future of Tabernacle and its contribution to the Bald Eagles' community is good citizenship and each member's participation in a continuously shifting social landscape. Involvement with the political process is her hope for the refinement and building of a better American society. Her hopes are driven by traditional black church dialectical thinking and social processes.

How do you want the United States to go? is a provocative question that, for Mrs. Mai Mai Watkins, underlies what it means to be "American." In the vernacular of a conjurational black evangelical spirituality and culture, being American during that historic moment and for the purpose of moving forward requires *magic*. To conjure new social realities or to reenvision old realities demands *magic*—the performance of ritual speech and action *and* belief in such action to come to fruition in order to alter present reality and circumstances.

The election of Barack H. Obama, as the first person of African descent to ascend to the American presidency, was *magical* for many Americans, including Mai Mai Watkins, one that equally represented an American dialectic. For many, having a black man eventually come to symbolize "America" or American national identity was an anomaly. Melayne T. Price talks about Obama's *magic* in terms of national curiosity over his *hybridity* or multifaceted racial history that, every time he shared his story, would reframe American history, not in exclusively racial, but in inherently racial, terms.[34] Further questions were raised about his unconventional lineage and with respect to the African American community because he lacked a historical connection to American slavery, in not being a descendent of slaves. Would African Americans identify with him? Alternatively, many argued Obama might be viewed as exceptional by white Americans and therefore different from other blacks.[35] How would his blackness (and whiteness) play out for white voters?

However, Barack Obama's election to chief executive officer in 2008 and his 2009 inauguration happened a little more than forty years after Attorney General Robert Kennedy made a 1961 public pronouncement articulating the possibility of a black president of the United States in the future, which also came after hearing black leaders vocalize this hope on numerous occasions. Their very public avowals arose during the social tumult of a civil rights movement, a visually and graphically challenging historical period revealing the soul of America.

Mrs. Watkins suggests that with President Obama's election *and* inauguration, to be "American" is to be a person, regardless of race, who participates in and does her or his part in making change a reality for all Americans. In addition, Mrs. Watkins implies that the *American church* has a responsibility in reshaping America. Hence, her conversation with the pharmacist promotes a definition of being American that encompasses civic responsibility—at individual, communal, and institutional levels—and that is a basic and essential part for an improved, socially progressive, and inclusive American culture and society.

Conjuring black evangelical Christianity and culture encourages exceptional faith and hope but also dialectical and conjunctive thoughts and action for the black folks in this rural and Southern community, enabling them to speak into existence anticipated and new social realities. That is what Mrs. Mai Mai Watkins' actions and speech represented at the pharmacy the day after President Obama's inauguration and what came to represent the ways in which this racial group was choosing to live out their regionalized version of being black, Christian, and American.

The next three sections of this chapter study the role of the (black) American church in shaping a future America from the perspective of a conjurational black evangelicalism (with moral logics at its center), and from the vantage of advancing rites of faith that elevate a theology and ethics of moral community formed by the social experiences of these rural blacks and their interpretations and articulations of what is "good" and "bad" for their community.

Black Baptists and Theologies of the Disinherited

What follows is analysis of Wednesday evening and Friday noonday Bible-study sessions as well as Sunday morning sermons to describe theologies of social justice, a black public theology of war, and the black liberation theologies operating at Tabernacle Missionary Baptist Church.

Go Out to Where the Fish Are and Cast Your Net

Every Wednesday at 7:00 p.m., there is Bible study at Tabernacle. On those evenings, I would enter the rear door to the basement of the church and walk into a large room with the other participants. After entering, I would settle into my chair, anticipating the evening's discussion. On this night, the pastor returns to a study entitled "101 Bible Reasons Why I Am a Baptist." Tonight, we start with number 71 of 101. We close the evening parsing number 71 because of participant interest. This congregation strongly identifies with being Baptist and, more specifically, with being Missionary Baptist. That warrants instruction on Baptist theology led by Pastor Matthews who, after taking the pulse of his students, sees that members want and need to be educated about what Baptists believe.

The annals of American history record that the largest conversion of slaves happened during the Second Great Awakening. Albert Raboteau explains:

> The increase in conversions of Negroes under the impact of revivalism was due to several factors. The evangelical religion spread by revivalists initiated a religious renaissance in the South as a somnolent religious consciousness was awakened by revivalist preachers. The revival itself became a means of church extension for Presbyterians and, particularly, for Methodists and Baptists. The mobility of the Methodist circuit rider and the local autonomy of the Baptist preacher were suited to the needs and conditions of the rural South. . . . The individualistic emphasis on revivalism, with its intense concentration on inward conversion, fostered an inclusiveness which could border on egalitarianism. Revivalists had little doubt—indeed they were enthusiastic—about the capacity of slaves to share the experience of conversion.[36]

Bondswomen and bondsmen were attracted to the Baptist tradition and Methodism because of the missionizing efforts of revivalists, their focus on transformation of the heart, and slaves' recognition of their membership and inclusiveness in the human family and family of God ensuring spiritual equality with slaveholders, albeit with their physical reality of remaining in bondage. Thus, this week's exploration of Baptist theology recalls the history of the development of the Baptist Church among the enslaved to interpret present-time missionizing efforts.

Seventeen regular Wednesday-night attendees of the Bible study are present (including me and the pastor), ranging in age from the mid-thirties into the early eighties. Deacon Parsons starts this evening's Bible study with prayer. Afterward, participants sing "What a Friend We Have in Jesus." The pastor follows with a prayer for "all the residents of Bald Eagles, the soldiers fighting the war, for both sides in the war—the enemy and our men, the cyclone victims, the earthquake in China, and the floods in Iowa and Missouri." Deacon Wilcox requests a volunteer for a scriptural reading, testimony, or "to say a word" before the pastor assumes the rest of the evening's responsibilities. A member rises to read Matthew 7:12-20; with no other additions, Deacon Wilcox gives the study over to the pastor.

Pastor Matthews declares:

> Many Baptist churches are taking the "missionary" out of their names. But if you take the *mission* away, then you might as well take *the Church*

away. You can start a mission in your house, next door, the community and then spread. One thing, we have a serious dilemma in—Baptists want to "GO" and travel, but they do not want to do the mission in their home. Missions work starts at home and spreads abroad. Are we [Tabernacle Missionary Baptist Church] doing Christ's mission? We are supposed to do it—in our home, communities, state, and the world. Often we understand missions as [being in places like] Ethiopia and other faraway lands. But missions are for the rich *and* the poor. You can't look and determine who is who.

The pastor's question leads into a round of discussion about the role of missions at Tabernacle:

DEACON WILCOX: Our last mission as a church was to ask the Lord to send us an undershepherd [a pastor].

JEFFREY GREEN: At the convention for National Baptists, the poorest night for turnout is missions night.

DARRYL TODD: We often think about missions as something big.

JOY SNOW: Pastor, you have visited the sick, shut-in, and given them Communion.

DEBORAH GRANT: In my side of town near the Bruce projects, and across the tracks, three new families have moved in, and I have been talking to the young people.

PASTOR MATTHEWS: There is a difference between ministry and mission. Ministry goes along with missions except your ministry includes issuing Communion to the sick and the shut-in. The purpose of missions is to evangelize. When you go out and evangelize, "you can't catch a fish that's already been caught." When you evangelize, you have *"to go out where the fish are and cast out your net."*

JOY SNOW: Evangelize, baptize, and educate. The Holy Spirit must go with you on missions. He will send you to the right place at the right time. But before we go, we must ask, "Am I educated enough? Have I heard the voice of the Holy Spirit?"

PASTOR MATTHEWS: In my Bible, I have six reasons to evangelize. *The first* is that God has commanded us to do so, according to Acts 1:8. We have already acknowledged you should not go out before you have been endowed with the Spirit of Christ [Holy Spirit]. It's a difference between joining a denomination and being saved. This is a mandate. Christ has commanded us. *The second* is based on John 14:15. It demonstrates our love for Christ. If you love me, like you say you do, you will keep my commandments. These floods and these earthquakes we now have are signs that we are living in our last days. Christ is showing us we need to get our house in order. We should be concerned because it's too many who don't know Christ. Hell does not have to be a sinner's destination. That is, you can be living in hell and yet be out of hell [on the earth].

The third is found in Romans 3:10, 23. There is none righteous, not one. We all have fallen short of the glory of God. "You have been thrown the life preserver, you caught it; now don't you think they deserve it too?" As a Baptist, are we doing God's mission?

The fourth requires us to share our faith with others as God's chosen method to redeem sinners, as found in Romans 10:14-17; Acts 8:3. Only redeemed sinners can tell lost sinners about Christ. We are the redeemed and our mission is to help save the lost. "We can throw the life preserver out. What is the life preserver? The Word of God. In our mission, when we need to be talking, we usually don't say nothing. But when we don't need to be talking, we say so much." *How many of you have spoken to one child out there? Do you know why they hold so much faith in gangs?*

The fifth is "because God destines to save all people." We find that in Acts 4:12 and 1 Timothy 2:4.

The sixth is because someone once shared his faith with us, according to 1 Corinthians 15:3. Others have the right to expect that what was done for us, we will do for others.

"Should we not throw out a life preserver to someone drowning?" *For instance, let's take* [*our*] *gang problem.* A bus driver saw a five-year-old [child] throw up gang signs. Some five-year-olds can cuss you out in five different languages. *They have been shown that* [gang life]*, and they believe that.* "The devil is on his game, but we are not on ours." Romans 10:14-17 and Ecclesiastes 12:1 indicate the following: *It is easier to catch a tap-water fish than a big fish. The tap-water fish represents the young, and the big fish is symbolic for the old.* The old fighting fish is a big fish that you sometimes have to throw out a big net for, in order to catch. "Am I throwing this out for free?" You don't have to be called and be ordained to be a preacher. The reason we can all be preachers is that "if you can open your (*pastor points to his mouth*), then you can spread the Gospel."

When you evangelize, remember that you are "one beggar asking another beggar for a piece of bread." We often come up with excuses around evangelizing, but it is only when you do what you have been commanded to do, it is then you no longer have excuses.

> However, when it comes to gossip, we have no excuses; there is nothing to stop us.

With this, the pastor implies human frailties do not prevent gossip. Likewise, members should not stop evangelizing in the streets because of human weaknesses. Matthews proceeds with "in going out on this mission, the only thing you can do is to offer Christ, and if people reject Christ, that's on them. People don't want to hear this, because they don't want to be held accountable."

Pastor Matthews concludes the evening's discussion on missions:

> Salvation carries a bigger paycheck than any job. You take abuse from the job, for that forty-hour-a-week paycheck, but salvation carries a bigger paycheck than that job. People willingly suffer abuse on the job for a paycheck but shy away from spreading the gospel with its lesser degree of suffering.

He ends the study with his initial question: "Is the Baptist Church a missionary church?"

Yes, it starts with us. If we were hauled off to court and charged with being a Christian, would some of us be found *not* guilty?

Speaking in (Un)Known Tongues: When Gangs Are Catching Our Tap-Water Fishes

Tabernacle is a Missionary Baptist Church, meaning one cannot be Missionary Baptist without doing missions work—the work of evangelism. Bible-study participants stress evangelism, hearkening back to the historic mode used by revivalists to convert slave masters *and* slaves to Christianity. During the Great Awakenings, as we have previously read, evangelization changed the unconverted hearts of whites and blacks, attracting some of them to the Baptist faith.

As a dimension of Tabernacle's group theology, Matthews teaches about evangelism by appealing to the black and rural culture of the people, speaking in parables and resurrecting folk sayings of a former generation. His metaphors resonate with this Bible study group, who are residents of this agricultural community; by speaking in their regional language and terms, the pastor draws attention to and is verbally highlighting the regional identity of his members. "Catching a tap-water fish" is a rural regionalism for evangelizing young that equally shines a light on an actual community problem—black youth being seduced by gang membership. The moral obligation of this community, as laid out by the pastor, is to speak in known tongues to the town's black young people so that they do not deliberately fall into the trap of the enemy—gang life.

Nevertheless, the pastor points out that church members *and* many other blacks in this town are better at gossiping than speaking a life-saving word to the youth. There he points out the moral boundaries of not only membership in the black community but particularly the *black and Christian* community in this rural area. The pastor uses this rite of faith, Bible study, to vocalize the life-threatening social experience of the young while censuring church members and the local black communities for failing their youth. Bible study is his venue for raising this theology of the disinherited, a theology of social justice targeting black youth, in the hearing and presence of his members.

In doing so, he demonstrates the ways in which a conjurational black evangelical faith, with moral logics as a focal point, underlines a theology and ethics of "good" and "bad/evil." For if spreading gossip does not stop idle talk from reaching its final destination, neither should the affirming words from elders of the church toward their future—young blacks. What the pastor concludes is that a "good" word from people of faith spoken to a "bad" situation—youth gang membership—becomes a spiritual "life preserver" that can save "tap-water fish" (i.e., young people) and bring a dimension of healing to this rural and Southern black community.

Fight the Devil with the Sword: Biblical Messages for "Peoples with Their Backs against the Wall"

As another dimension of Baptist theology practiced by these black Baptists of Bald Eagles, this next Bible study yields a different message. It delivers biblical and theological messages to "peoples with their backs against the wall."[37] So, on this night, we cover two more characteristics on the list of "101 Bible Reasons Why I Am a Baptist":

> The first attribute is: "I am a Baptist because the weapons of the Baptist Church are spiritual and not carnal." (Ephesians 6:10-20; Romans 12:17, 18)

The pastor explains there is no need to use "physical" weapons when an individual has the word of God as their sword. However, Brother David Jordan, a participant, declares: "Pastor, there are going to be times when you must fight if the devil keeps at you." Pastor Matthews responds, "If you are a Christian, you must as much as possible lean towards the peace side."

Deacon Wilcox joins the conversation, reminding Brother Jordan of the Ephesians passage that exhorts the believer to "step back and resist" if the devil attacks. Wilcox continues:

Ephesians teaches us our responsibility. It encourages us to understand our responsibility and to learn the truth. The truth should hold us together. The gospel is our peace. It is our stability. The key phrase in the Scripture is "for you to resist." The word of God is a "sword" used to sharply cut—divide lies from the truth. It is also a "shield" which allows for resistance.

Pastor Matthews responds: "If you don't have on the full armor [of God], then you will react from 'self' or the 'flesh.'" He then proceeds with the next religious trait of Baptists.

The second attribute is: "I am a Baptist because Baptists believe in and die for religious liberty." (Romans 14:5)

He explains:

Even though salvation is free, religion is a freedom of choice. The same way that you have the choice to serve God, another has the choice to serve the devil. We have a choice between right and wrong. If I live for God, then you can't make me be convinced otherwise. However, it is a matter of being convinced. If you are fully convinced, you won't allow for threats and intimidation to sway you from your belief. For example, we will know if we are fully convinced of our faith as Christian believers in the face of persecution. Those fully convinced are willing to die for their religion. If not, in the face of persecution, they may decide to leave the church.

Brother Jordan chimes in:

What is going on over in Iraq [suicide bombing], those people are convinced of their religion, which is why [American] servicemen and servicewomen have their hands tied. You've got to be persuaded in your mind, but you can't take that persuasion and force it on someone else. You should not be mad or upset if people don't want to go the way you go, in terms of your religion.

Agreeing with Brother Jordan, Pastor Matthews uses his children to exemplify Jordan's point: "All I can do is convince them that Christ is the way, but in the end, they will make their own choices."

He then refers to Aretha Franklin, who exercised her choice, what the pastor defines as liberty, to sing rhythm and blues as opposed to gospel music. "Reverend Franklin was a big Baptist preacher who had problems with his daughter being an R&B singer. He did not like his daughter's choice but [had to respect her liberty to make that choice]." Brother T. Russell, another member of the Bible study, follows with a question about the structure of the army and how it defines religious liberty. He wants to know why Catholics and "everyone else" are categorized as Protestants.

Pastor Matthews answers: "Formerly the armed forces distinguished between Jews and gentiles, which allowed for Catholics to be defined as Protestants." Both continue and close this Bible-study conversation by explaining the ways in which the armed forces must now provide spiritual leaders for Catholics, Jews, Protestants, and adherents of other religions, including Islam and those they identify as "anti-Christ" (agnostics, atheists, and children of the devil).

The Religion of Jesus and an Armed Christ: A Black Public Theology of War

The exchange between Pastor Matthews and Brother Jordan illustrates the limits of Jordan's tolerance for "evil" or for the anthropomorphic devil whom he identifies as people who incessantly *keep at him*. Although Pastor Matthews and Deacon Wilcox encourage Brother Jordan to broaden his perspective about weapons, Jordan in his response implies there are times when a Christian must fight with physical weapons regardless of and in addition to the availability of spiritual weapons. Brother Jordan's answer calls to mind the numerous ways the dispossessed and disinherited have interpreted the religion of Jesus. Howard Thurman's *Jesus and the Disinherited* is predicated on two questions. First, what is the significance of the religion of Jesus for "people with their backs against the wall?" Second, why is it that Christianity is impotent in dealing effectively with the issues of discrimination and injustice on the basis of race, religion, and national origin? For Thurman, these questions are not about the moral duty Christianity lays before those who possess much. Rather, they hold Christianity's existential meaning for those with very little or nothing. Thurman continues: "The masses of men [i.e., suffering blacks] live with their backs against the wall. They are the poor, the disinherited, the dispossessed. What does our religion say to them? The issue is not what it counsels them to do for others whose need may be greater, but what religion offers to meet their own needs." The question is who Jesus is for the downtrodden.[38]

From Brother Jordan's view, a devil who constantly keeps at him is an entity that for Thurman "pushes his back against the wall." We learn from this particular scenario that God and the devil are a dialectical pairing that explains threats against black livelihood; because God is the more powerful of this spiritual pairing, the Almighty provides a way out of such despair as captured by the image of a New Testament Jesus who will fight on the side of the oppressed. Thurman teaches that the religion of Jesus is not impotent. Rather, the religion of Jesus grants Brother Jordan permission to fight, to fight spiritually against people and repressive institutions. Christianity is vibrant for suffering blacks because Jesus carries not peace but a sword.[39] Yet the sword Jesus brandishes is a sword of peace that, simultaneously and ironically, reconciles humanity and God but divides nonbelievers from believers, good from evil, light from darkness, justice from injustice.

Because this is so, the sword throws people into battles that might also summon up the use of physical weapons to oppose enemies in response to a call to defend the nation and to protect constitutional liberties and rights. The sword of Jesus at times even divides black believers one from another on their particular interpretations of the Second Amendment's right to bear arms to safeguard personal property, personhood, and the state. That difference of opinion is made apparent in the exchange between Brother Jordan, Pastor Matthews, and Deacon Wilcox. In this exchange, Jordan starts out on the other side of the moral logics argument being presented by Matthews and Wilcox. All three would, however, agree that from a spiritual perspective, the sword Jesus brandishes represents the cost of discipleship, is in *defense* of the Christian faith, and is an instrument of minorities and the mistreated used to secure victory when waging war against an anthropomorphic "devil" who is *keeping at them* as their enemies *press their backs against the wall.*

Yet, black Christians uphold and cling to more than one image of a sword-bearing Jesus.

In the same way that they have embraced a nonviolent but resistant Jesus, they have also historically welcomed the divinely sanctioned violence of a martial Christ. Allen D. Callahan writes:

> The armed Christ of the book of Revelation who rides into battle on a milk-white horse had been a venerable image in black Christianity from the days of slavery. . . . The Bible has offered slavery's children a martial paradigm for liberation by divinely sanctioned violence. . . . In the Bible, Jesus is the son of [an] angry God. At the close of the New Testament, Jesus becomes that god's most distinguished general. The

book of Revelation renders Jesus waging war on the enemies of the Lord "with the sword of his mouth," riding a white stallion through a deluge of blood that would rise "even unto the horse bridles" (rev. 14:20). . . . Informed by the rich biblical imagery of the Last Days, African Americans have anticipated the return of the militant Jesus as the righteous arbiter of human destiny.[40]

However, Pastor Matthews and Deacon Wilcox caution against Brother Jordan's implied (physical) call to arms by recalling and teaching that the word of God serves as the primary and most formidable form of resistance against the devil's schemes. Here, their moral rhetoric of caring and religious authority realizes Brother Jordan's position and corrects it, while serving to confirm his membership not only in the body of Christ but also in this specific congregation. More important, by pointing him back to the New Testament Scriptures, their verbal exchange models how blacks, like Brother Jordan, *conjure* the religion of Jesus, who they are convinced is acquainted with their selfsame experiences of brutality, dehumanization, and crucifixion.[41] They intentionally claim Jesus as a *man of war* and liberator as well as an *arbiter* of humankind because of their convictions.[42]

This eschatological and apocalyptic Jesus is realized in the here and now and is a revolutionary who will always fight on the side of the marginalized and the dispossessed. "The militant tradition of African American Christianity in the South [is] rooted in the Christian slave revolts and church organized armed resistance during Radical Reconstruction."[43] Although there exists a black and Southern tradition of armed conflict inspired by and compatible with a revolutionary Jesus, Pastor Matthews and Deacon Wilcox refrain from that image of a physically armed Christ while still invoking a revolutionary Jesus bearing nonviolent, pharmacopeic, and healing properties. Still, Brother Jordan's nonviolent but resistant Jesus is a historical figure whose exhortations to "turn the other cheek" and "go a second mile" do not mean that people with their backs against the wall should be doormats for others.[44]

This rural black community appropriates the Bible as a pharmacopeic book filled with prescriptions for how to exercise the nonviolent religion of Jesus. This becomes the basis for a black public theology of war that also addresses religious liberty, a crucial aspect of life in Bald Eagles, located in the interior of the Bible Belt. The need to countermand the most toxic forces impacting its communities both internally and externally remains black America's primary pharmacopeic project.[45] Whether for these rural and Southern blacks what menaces them is found within the community in the form of broken homes, addiction, and domestic violence or outside of the community in the form of racism, lack of educational opportunities, joblessness, and poverty, a black public theology of war describes a revolutionary yet nonviolent religion of Jesus that preserves religious freedom and negates and resists those social and cultural forces of American society and culture that lead to black victimization and death. Christian freedom demands action through the risking of one's faith but not to the extent of suicidal martyrdom. A black public theology of war that draws on pharmacopeic properties, the religion of Jesus, and Southern tradition will promote the bearing of arms, out of necessity and by fiat, in so doing distinguishing what it means to be black, Christian, and American in this rural community.

Reviving Prophecy

In addition to this black public theology of war, today's Sunday morning sermon, "We Need to Pray for Sight," showcases the black liberation and existential theologies that operate in the lives of these rural black Baptists. Pastor Matthews begins:

> Sight is the most essential of all our senses. Through sight, we gather information. The Bible speaks of *sight* as spiritually being able to *see*.

Elaborating upon the three types of human sight, Matthews explains:

> We have *physical sight*, which relies upon retinal activity. This sight can be evaluated by an eye doctor who uses technological advancements to tell us if our sight needs correcting. If our sight needs correction, we rely on eyeglasses, our second pair of eyes, to alter how the eyes in our head see. The second type of sight we have is *mental sight*, which is different from retinal activity. Our mental sight deals with our mental comprehension. Mind readers exercise mental sight. And mothers and fathers, who are endowed with "eyes in the back of their heads" also exercise such mental sight. The last type of sight is *spiritual sight*, which is the providence of God. How God enters into our presence in the midst of trials and tribulations requires spiritual sight.

He proceeds:

> If God is for me, I am stronger than the whole world against me. The person who spiritually walks and talks with God is able to impart that everything is going to be alright. For instance, suppose someone gets into a car accident? The woman with spiritual eyesight knows God is

behind the scenes even in the midst of escalating medical bills. Our foreparents possessed this eyesight even in the midst of trials. With the auction blocks and cotton fields prominently in their faces, even with all they were going through, they could sing "Trouble Don't Last Always."

By virtue of a black evangelical theology, this body of Christian believers use their "God"-talk to reflect the particular and peculiar lived experiences of blacks, in America and in this agricultural community. Their "God"-talk communicates the black theology idea that God as spirit is not opposite to the idea of God as person. Rather, they are complementary. Humans connect to God as being both human and divine because of their needs for relationship and intimacy. Such connections complement and reinforce black folks' humanity while avoiding the isolation, alienation, and objectification that comes with being black bodies in Christian theism. African Americans theologically interpret God's providence as being closely associated with God's creativity. When African American Christians declare God cares for them, the proposition that follows is God created them. In African American religious expression, creation and providence are intertwined and implied as God's *work* in history. "To work is to accomplish something in spite of resistance. To work is to enter into a formative relation with someone or something outside oneself. One cannot act in the abstract. One works in the concrete reality of history."[46]

Pastor Matthews captures these points when he professes:

> In 2 Kings 6, Elisha prays for his servant to receive sight. Sometimes you gotta go through some storms before seeing the rainbow. The king of Syria is convinced there is a traitor in his ranks because every tactical move he makes against Israel fails. Acting on its foreknowledge, Israel mounts offensive attacks before Syria has a chance to strike. The king of Syria eventually finds there is not a traitor in the ranks. Instead, God is telling Elisha every move the Israelites should make.
>
> "If you listen to God speak, he will allow you to be able to be one step ahead in many areas of life—your finances, your marriage, your family, your home, your life!"
>
> The king of Syria had equipped his army to go after Elisha, but "Why would a whole army have to come after one little man?"
>
> The institution of oppression is always threatened by those whom God has given spiritual insight.
>
> If Jesus had his Pilate,
> If Caesar had Nero,
> If M. L. King Jr. had J. Edgar Hoover,

Then we will have to face our own enemies.

What should be our response? When Maya Angelou wrote her famous poem "And Still I Rise," she didn't know this would serve as an answer. She declares, "You may write me down in history with your bitter twisted lies, but still I Rise!" If you can't see, hold on a little while because when prayers go up, blessings come down! Leonardo da Vinci *saw* flight 200 years before the Wright brothers flew the first plane. Thomas Edison *did not* physically see electricity but still became the father of electricity. George Washington Carver *saw* something already in the peanut.

Stevie Wonder was once asked, "Is there anything worse than being blind?" He responded, saying: "Having eyes and *not being able* to see." We only *see* the problems but not the solutions. Likewise, sometimes we see the faults of friends and not their strengths.

Have you ever heard the story of the buzzards?

The Female Buzzards bring gossip and exclusion.

The Male Buzzards bring racism, oppression, and victimization.

However, in all of the "-isms" you do not have to succumb to victimhood.

If you do, you may fail to see the only person stopping you is you!

Pastor Matthews ends his morning message, declaring:

After the prayers of Elisha, the servant is able to see that God was there. God is not absent. He is always there. When you see God, it is impossible to see defeat. We see victory, victory is mine! God's grace is greater than any sin! God's presence is greater than any fears! God's resurrection is greater than any death! The devil may have come to take your life last night, but I'm glad that I have mercy, goodness, protection and grace around me to take care of me. We need to pray for sight, because God will hear and answer our prayers.

"Sight-Seeing" as Conjuring Black Social Prophetism and Action

A God who grants sight to seekers is providential and creative. God is made known to Tabernacle's black congregants and community members by God's ability to care for, strengthen, and empower them as they labor against a recalcitrant and in many instances unyielding world. Donning the prophetic mantle, Pastor Matthews "sees" and boldly calls out the deforming powers of unjust people, situations, and systems as enemies of families, finances, and marriage. These enemies are not unlike Pilate, Nero, and J. Edgar Hoover, having the force to devastate their victims. Slavery, gossip, exclusion, racism, fear, and segregation are "buzzards"— brutal social institutions, outside and within, that possess the might to exact a heavy toll on the black home and community.

Though these foreboding and disquieting people, events, and institutions produce black suffering and distress, Pastor Matthews, by virtue of his prophetic office, "sees" his people's pain and speaks to the people's trials and tribulations by extolling and invoking the name of a God mightier than any human or spiritual power and able to bestow a resurrection hope greater than their heaviest burdens. Along those lines, James Cone considers: "The resurrection conveys hope in God. Nor is this the 'hope' that promises a reward in heaven in order to ease the pain of injustice on earth. Rather it is hope which focuses on the future in order to make us refuse to tolerate present inequities."[47] Pastor Matthews spotlights God's work of giving sight throughout human history to the likes of da Vinci, Edison, Carver, Martin Luther King Jr., and Stevie Wonder as those whose social projects contributed to shifting and changing the face of America.

To the question, "What is worse than being blind?" Stevie Wonder answers: "Having eyes but *not being able to see*." And so throughout this preaching moment, Matthews assumes the role of a "seer," employing "prophetic oratory" to look beyond the social, political, and historical problems of his church members. Prophetic oratory is a fusion of African spirituality and biblical religion.[48] Pastor Matthews reads his congregants into the Old Testament text where Elisha conjures up God, a God that bestows onto Elisha exceptional sight to the degree of his seeing past the tactical maneuverings of the Syrians and ultimately to win the contest between him and the Syrians.

History reports that black and Christian slave insurrectionists and folk prophets Nat Turner and Denmark Vesey exhibited the traits of seers given to mystical experiences. Both preachers strongly and self-consciously identified with Christianity and opposed conjuration. Nevertheless, these men with their mystical sense of prophecy and divine intervention that both laity and clergy found in the Scriptures—particularly the apocalyptic writings—were able to invoke a power that gave them license to become oracles against whites in vindication of their own people, which was a power that required no human justification.[49]

While not a seer in the sense that Turner and Vesey were, Pastor Matthews too is part of the tradition by being an *oracle*, a seer who acknowledges his religious constituents' hardships but *sees* past these difficulties to offer liberation theology as an antidote to their stressors. That is, he encourages this conservative black evangelical community to push beyond their present circumstances and to act in their own best interests in order to see a brighter future.

Tabernacle's practice of black theology more closely resembles Martin Luther King Jr.'s faith and integrationist philosophy than the black nationalist liberation theology of James Cone.[50] Cone's black theology of liberation names the gospel of Jesus Christ as emancipatory by placing Jesus at the center and in the midst of liberation struggles of blacks and other oppressed groups, and by locating and identifying the black power and black consciousness raising movements with the birth, life, death, and resurrection of Jesus Christ.[51]

Cone's theology of black liberation embraces a God who is not color-blind because doing that would be metaphorically saying that God is blind to justice and injustice, to right and wrong, to good and evil.[52] Instead, he makes Jesus pivotal to the liberation of African American and other oppressed communities throughout America. As an ontological symbol for oppression, "blackness" is not only a theological construct but also a political one.[53] In 1970, Cone wrote:

> From the very beginning to the present day, American white theological thought has been "patriotic," either by defining the theological task independently of black suffering (the liberal northern approach) or by defining Christianity as compatible with white racism (the conservative southern approach). In both cases, theology becomes a servant of the state, and that can only mean death for blacks.[54]

His words ring true, even now. Nevertheless, for the folks at Tabernacle and the blacks of Bald Eagles, their more conservative version of Christianity does not really politicize God or Jesus Christ of the church in the ways Cone suggests, even if their wall murals meld blackness with God.

Black theology was made palatable to them when religious language centered on Jesus Christ. The freedom about which Martin Luther King Jr., his predecessors, and his contemporaries in the civil rights movement preached was grounded in a theological and political message of Jesus Christ that stressed a theology of integration and race relations. As well, this black theology, primarily invoked by black men, had as its goal to raise up the interrelatedness and interdependence of human life because God, from their perspective, was concerned about everyone's welfare.[55] Nevertheless, congregants of this particular church did fully embrace and practice a political black consciousness outside of church walls through membership in social justice organizations like the NAACP or black fraternities and sororities.

At Tabernacle and in Bald Eagles, God is still familiar with the African American experience. Through the preached word, God enters into the events and lives of this group of believers to empower them to defeat the enemy. God is conjured by prophetic social preaching, such as Pastor Matthews does when he asks his congregation to reimagine their hard social realities and to take action against debilitating social, economic, and political conditions by moving beyond the limits of what their eyes can actually see. Conjuring God, in this sense, stipulates church members become active agents in improving their social standing in spheres outside of their control and current realms and even resistant to their involvement to produce social change. Conjuring God through social prophetism and action gives them the advantage to win the showdown with evil, key to progress in their own lives.

Their liberation theology has the same spirit as that of early black leaders and ministers like Benjamin Elijah Mays, Howard Thurman, Mordecai Johnson, and Martin Luther King Jr., and it adds to the meaning of conjuring a black evangelical Christianity among the members of Tabernacle. That being so, these final sections illustrate the ways in which a conjurational black evangelical Christianity and culture simulates divine activity, honors black social experience, and resists devilish tactics and behaviors to fill out the meaning of black, Christian, and American in rural and Southern Bald Eagles through rites of faith that advance a theology and ethics of "good" and "evil" and that embody the peoples' dialectical and conjunctive thinking and practice.

Devilish Religious and Cultural Practices: Black Magic, White Magic, and a String of Dimes

At tonight's bible study, the pastor continues his study of the spirit of divination, which is a section in the book *Strongman's His Name . . . What's His Game.*[56] Present at Bible study are approximately twelve members of the church. At six thirty in the evening, we have prayer meeting before the official opening of Bible study at seven o'clock by a church deacon, who follows with a song and other prayer requests, and thereafter Bible study is eventually taken over by the pastor.

The study is based on Titus 1:1-11, which treats the appointment of elders or overseers as administrators over God's household and silences detractors of the faith who were leading the Christian community astray by their false teachings. These false teachers were identified as fortune tellers whose beliefs and actions opposed the lifestyle and teachings of the early Christian community.

In the group's workbook, *divination* is defined as "the practice of attempting to foretell future events or discover hidden knowledge by occult or supernatural means. God's Word goes a step further by showing that people who divine are controlled or possessed by supernatural spirits, which enable them to receive information beyond the human realm at a particular time. God's prophets receive their divine revelation by the Holy Spirit. On the other side of the spectrum are demonic spirits feeding information to fortune tellers and sorcerers."[57]

In tonight's study, we focus on fortune telling, hypnotism, and magic as the antithesis to divine revelation. Pastor Matthews asks for a definition of *fortune teller*. A member responds that a fortune teller is a predictor of the future and prophesier. The pastor agrees, reinforcing that Satan is also involved in fortune telling based on Micah 5:12: "I will cut off witchcraft out of thine hand; and thou shalt have no more soothsayers." Pastor Matthews queries:

> How many of us have thought of binding fortune telling in the name of Jesus? Do Christians have the right to bind the fortune telling business? Why? [He answers his question with Matthew 18:18:] "Whatever we bind on earth will be bound in heaven and whatever we loose on earth will be loosed in heaven."

Pastor Matthews testifies:

> We have authority to bind non-Christian elements. For instance, the store Pure Passion located in Memphis was recently closed down. Christians in that area also prayed for the club to be closed and it was. I can understand you going to a strip club and not being saved. But if you are saved, you should not be found in the strip club! Another example of binding non-Christian elements on earth is the abuse of alcohol. Alcoholism is something that must be bound because it is an addiction. According to Micah 5:12 fortune telling is considered witchcraft. Don't you know that a lot of businesses stay open because we as Christians won't bind those businesses?

After ending his discussion on fortune telling as a form of witchcraft, Matthews moves to hypnotists, charmers, and passive mind states. He defines hypnosis as the strongman that Satan uses to alter a person's mind. Hypnosis is dangerous because the mind is left unguarded and susceptible to any spirit that may be waiting for just such an opportunity. He admonishes his Bible-study students not to leave their minds open for Satan to manipulate them, and then he references the workbook lesson on the topic, which declares: "Not every case of hypnosis results in demon possession, but it can be the beginning of a very negative experience that can affect the person spiritually."[58]

Once again Brother Jordan adds colorful commentary to the study: "I listen to jazz music, easy listening jazz, to relax. I do not consider my habit of listening to jazz as a form of hypnosis." Debate ensues among Bible-study participants about opening oneself up to Satan by listening to easy jazz because of the potential for seductive and harmful subliminal messages to come through easy listening music. Because the listeners are in a relaxed state of mind, considered by these black Christians as a semihypnotic state, the listeners' guard against "Satan" is down, seemingly leaving them unaware of their spiritual surroundings and condition. As such, to Brother Jordan's statement, the pastor responds: "Relax by reading the word of God. That is how I relax, and it makes me fall asleep. When we are meditating on God's words, it is not hypnosis. Instead, it is an exercise of the spirit. It is God's way of speaking to us. We can meditate on God's word without opening a door that needs to be shut later."

The pastor then proceeds to read the definition of black magic from the printed lesson. Black magic is an attempt to produce evil through the particular methods of curses, spells, the structure of models of one's enemy, and an alliance with evil spirits. He gives an example of black magic found in black culture such as the use of voodoo dolls to harm individuals. The pastor reminds Bible-study participants that the devil will use spirits to get into you. People controlled by the practice of witchcraft, the source of which is the devil, are similar to believers controlled by God and who practice Christianity. White magic, on the other hand, is used to get somebody to undo the magical spell originally cast on an individual.

As well, the pastor introduces sorcery as a form of witchcraft. Witchcraft, accordingly, is the magical practices associated with witchery. Pastor Matthews warns the group about the consequences of practicing any form of sorcery, black magic, or white magic, by guiding them to Galatians 5:19-21, which declares:

> Now the works of the flesh are manifest, which are these: fornication, uncleanness, lasciviousness, idolatry, sorcery, enmities, strife, jealousies, wraths, factions, divisions, parties, envyings, drunkenness, revellings, and such like; of which I forewarn you, even as I did forewarn you, that they who practice such things shall not inherit the kingdom of God.

At this juncture, members begin to share different stories of familiarity with black magic. One participant recalls that black women and men of earlier generations practiced forms of witchcraft like hoodoo. Others also begin to share their experiences with black magic. Sister Yvonne Brent talks about a spooked book that a neighbor had while she was growing up. The pastor talks about an experience with a woman whose daughter had a voodoo doll. We also learn that practitioners of Christianity would wear a string of dimes as anklets to ward off bad spirits. The conversation becomes extremely interesting when members of the Bible study talk about their childhood and adult experiences with sorcery. With that, the Bible study closes with prayer.

Rites of Faith: An Africanized Cosmology of Good and Evil

The devil lurks behind practices of divination, hypnosis, and magic. Through an exploration of the hypnotic power of smooth jazz, this group identifies Satan as a "strongman" yet not mightier than God. This study is yet another example of how these black evangelical Christians parse "good and evil." Antithetical to Christianity, black magic, white magic, and all other forms of witchcraft represent evil and thereby the devil. As such, their recognition of "evil" through their special Bible-study focus on the occult is also an admission that the anthropomorphic devil is a dimension of this group's cosmology and Christian belief system.

Black magic is an integral part of this community's worldview because members practice a conjurational black evangelical Christianity and culture attuned to its presence. Sterling Stuckey would likely identify the religious practices of these rural and Southern black folks as an Africanized Christianity.[59] An Africanized Christianity is syncretistic; it reconciles conjurational black spirituality and culture with traditional Western Christian practice. I believe this form of black Christianity exemplifies a dialectical and conjunctive faith because of its capacity to merge the folk wisdom of these rural blacks with their active and abiding, white-influenced Christian belief system. African American Christians who wear a string of dimes to ward off "bad" spirits, an example offered by one of the Bible students, exemplify this. By virtue of their practice, these members showcase a melding of their black (i.e., race) and Christian religious identities with their Southern (i.e., regional) and American (i.e., national) identities.

For Tabernacle's black evangelical Christians, black magic and sorcery contravene Christianity, yet the magic (i.e., socially transforming power) of conjuring a black evangelical Christianity and culture is made transparent by their genuine acknowledgment and lively confrontation of the evils that beset persons and groups in their community. An Africanized cosmology grants them permission to combat unchecked "evils" like racism, gang warfare, and mass incarceration, by invoking the presence of God and other biblical figures like Elisha and by applying biblical religion and rites of faith to desperate situations. God is deemed more powerful than the "devils" that may hold them back. Their behavior can be attributed to

> black North American culture's general *continuities* of tradition that derive from elements common to a broad number of West African peoples. . . . Two broad areas provide the ethnographic basis for such continuities: . . . beliefs and practices. In this instance, the beliefs concern *spiritual beings* and the practices comprise *magical and ritual performances.*[60]

Black magic and sorcery do exist and are real. Conjure theoretically explained the mysteries of evil, but it was also a practice for doing something about it. Their doing something about it begins, first, with confessing their belief in spiritual beings, both in God and in the devil as well as in principalities and powers having the authority and strength to affect human lives, and, second, with evaluating the difficulties and joys of living black in the Southern part of the United States and in rural America. The anthropomorphized devil is absolutely at fault for human actions that cause ill will and for the evil that affects individual and community prosperity. But God is greater than any devil in the heavens above and on the earth below. And, as our Tabernacle Bible-study participants imply, God will always prevail.

Peeking into Heaven

Wednesday evening Bible studies deal with Satan, while Friday noonday lessons investigate the apocalyptic literature of Revelation. Revelation 4:4 is the focal point of a study attended by twelve members in early spring 2009. This Scripture declares: "Around the throne were twenty-four other thrones; and upon the thrones I saw twenty-four elders sitting, clothed in white garments, and golden crowns on their heads." From the sheet the pastor has handed to participants, we learn Revelation 4 is "A Look into Heaven."

Pastor Matthews explains:

> The word *throne* appears twelve times and the book of Revelation makes it clear that the throne is the throne of God who rules in the universe, not the thrones of men. The elders are church representatives who will stand in place of specific churches from Pentecost to the rapture. These elders will wear white raiments; these raiments signal their triumph over

evil and symbolize the righteousness of Christ. They will also wear gold crowns connoting the church's rule with Christ.

By correlation, Pastor Matthews seeks to convey that Tabernacle's membership has the potential to reign with Christ in God's future kingdom. The crowns, which are divided into five categories, are rewards that will be given to saints in heaven. The first is the Crown of Righteousness (2 Timothy 4:8). Added to that are the Incorruptible Crown (1 Corinthians 9:24-27); the Crown of Life (James 1:12); the Crown of Rejoicing (1 Thessalonians 2:19); and the Crown of Glory (1 Peter 5:4).

As Pastor Matthews continues instructing, he talks about the importance of the elders and follows by distinguishing between elders and angels:

> There is a difference between elders and the angels. Our writer gives us eight reasons why elders cannot be angels. *The first* is that you will never see an angel on the throne. *The second* is that you will never see angels with crowns because angels do not wear crowns. *The third* is that Revelation 7:11 distinguishes between angels and elders. This Scripture sets angels apart from elders. Elders are assigned. Angels are identified. *Fourth*, Revelation 5:8-10 says that elders sing the hymn of praise. We have no records to show that angels sing. However, we also have no records to show that they do not sing.
>
> *Fifth*, in their song, elders claim to have been redeemed. Since Christ died for sins and the church, by Jesus' blood we are redeemed. Angels can never say that they have been redeemed, meaning that they have been bought or purchased by the blood of Jesus. *Sixth*, Revelation 7:2-3 says that angels speak while elders sing. Angels speak but do not sing. *Seventh*, Hebrews 12:22 reminds us that angels are never numbered, *but* the elders are numbered. There are twenty-four elders. *Finally*, elder signifies maturity and angels are timeless beings. When you speak of elders, you speak of maturity.

Conjuring Black Evangelical Christianity and Culture: From Genesis to Revelation

A conjurational black evangelical spirituality rooted in the wisdom of rural and Southern black folk culture paves the way for these Tabernacle members to peek into heaven, where white raiments of purity and triumph as well as golden crowns are the rewards for physically and spiritually prevailing against the burdens and daily affairs of living a racialized social existence. The eschaton is in the future; yet the eschaton for these black Christians is in the here and now. Tragedy and triumph mark black

American social reality. Consequently, for these black Missionary Baptist congregants, tragedy and triumph call for resurrection hope, hope in God and in the religion of his son, Jesus, to work on behalf of the disinherited and to make straight a skewed social order. The inseparability of material and spiritual dimensions of life is key to understanding the complexity of African American eschatology.[61] Language such as "new shoes" and "white robes" reflects black Christians' hope for better things to come. Such talk juxtaposes concrete earthly images with sovereign objects of "crowns and wings." This points to the worldliness and concreteness of the black religious imagination.[62] That is, objects associated with everyday life draw out tropes of transcendence meant to satisfy physical needs *and* satiate spiritual hunger.[63] Thus, on display is the religious and intellectual imaginations of these black Baptists of Bald Eagles who embrace the "white raiments" and "gold crowns" of an eschatological and transcendent hope that connects the mundane and the divine. The community's focus on material and earthly articles like "white raiments" and heavenly "gold crowns" signals their desire to satiate the physical and spiritual hunger that comes with battling life's daily challenges and that produces weary souls, even as they strive for contentment by envisioning better days ahead.

For these reasons and many more, Friday meetings at Tabernacle Missionary Baptist Church in Bald Eagles were spent exploring the book of Revelation to pinpoint the eschatological hopes of these black Bible Belt believers, and Wednesday evening Bible studies were spent parsing religious literature and Scripture to grasp more fully the wiles of Satan. Though seemingly paradoxical, taken together these Bible studies produced rich discussion about the pains and pleasures of black life in this rural, Southern American community. Both meetings displayed the conjurational and black evangelical spirituality and culture of this congregation comprised of four important elements: rites of faith that expressed the ontological realities of their blackness in rural Bald Eagles and America via diverse configurations of "good" and "evil" held together and interpreted dialectically and conjunctively; their appropriation of Old and New Testament biblical religions to guide their comprehension of the providential and prophetic nature of God and to confirm the presence of the devil, an anthropomorphic and inescapable entity believed by these blacks to affect all aspects of human existence; a black public theology of war that enjoined civic responsibility and furnished the tools to work toward freedom for all in a raced America; and a "moral logics" approach that demanded that these rural, Southern black dwellers be actively included in the economic, social, and political prosperity of the South and their local community as well as in the promises secured by simply being American.

5

Made in the U.S.A.

American Evangelicals and Identity Politics

W ho and what are American Evangelicals? The term describes a heterogeneous mixture of denominations with diverse institutional
histories, doctrinal systems of belief, and behavioral patterns. Evangelicals are only one religious grouping of conservative Protestants among
many. Other denominational sects widely associated with conservative
Protestantism and therefore historically considered evangelical include the
Churches of Christ, Charismatics, Holiness, Pentecostals, Baptists, Wes-
leyans, Nazarenes, Black Methodists, Lutherans of all types, and Seventh-
Day Adventists.[1]

Because such a medley of subcultures comprises American Evangelical
Protestantism, sociologists, historians, and theologians alike continue to
conduct research to codify the characteristics of evangelicalism, fitting
religious practitioners of evangelical Christian faith into typologies that
explain and define who an Evangelical *is* and *is not*.[2] More important,
their research describes why Evangelicals remain religiously vital in this
technological, global, and postmodern world. Regarding evangelicalism's
encounter with cultural pluralism, Hunter writes about the pressure on
Evangelicals to be tolerant, and to a limited degree accepting, of those
who hold different beliefs. Yet, this pressure is contrary to evangelical doctrinal beliefs. Orthodoxy is an enduring feature of evangelicalism because
of adherents' monopolistic and strict claims to religious truth. "From the
Evangelical perspective, the issue is clear-cut: orthodox Protestantism is
the only true faith, and all other faiths either deviate or are manifestly
false—the tools of Satanic deception." Adherents must show belief in
Jesus' forgiveness of sins and anticipate a future glory in him or risk the
fires of hell. Contemporary American evangelicalism remains essentially
unchanged because these doctrinal beliefs comprise the core of a religious

system that has been culturally edited to give it the qualities of sociability and gentility. It has acquired a civility that proclaims loudly, "No offense, I am an Evangelical."[3]

What Hunter established as truth in the 1980s remains true today. Contemporary evangelicalism continues to be religiously vital, active, and growing in a postmodern and global society despite *and* because of Evangelicals' exclusive claim to religious truth presented in a civil and socially acceptable manner. In spite of that, defining Evangelicals along the boundaries of history, theology, and even sociology proves challenging; nevertheless, scholars still press toward a precise definition of evangelicalism and who belongs to this group, irrespective of the maze produced by twenty-first-century splintering of the evangelical community and organizations.

Theologian Robert E. Webber finds a typology that works. For his fourteen-group categorization, he employs a social compositional framework to "ideal-type" Evangelicals because, he explains,

> all these groups reflect a theological unity at the center—in their confession of Christ and the doctrines which the Protestant Church has always believed. But because of their various historical origins and cultural shapes, they reflect a diversity of expression in theological particulars and practice in areas where differences of opinion have been tolerated.[4]

Two of those fourteen subcultural types categorize members of the First United Methodist Church and the Tabernacle Missionary Baptist Church in Bald Eagles, many of whom self-identify as "evangelical." Bald Eagles First United Methodist Church, as a church body, is assigned to *mainline* evangelicalism. Mainline Evangelicals stress a historic consciousness that returns as far back as the Reformation,[5] and they are classified by movements in major denominations: Methodist, Lutheran, Presbyterian, Episcopal, and Baptist.[6] In contrast, Tabernacle Missionary Baptist Church is designated as a *black* evangelical body, although questions emerge about the degree to which members embrace the National Association of Black Evangelicals as a symbolic presence.[7] Nonetheless, in their everyday speech and actions, they emphasize a "black consciousness" that cannot be denied.[8]

Clearly, the public, media, and even scholars possess overgeneralized and colorblind conceptions of American evangelicalism. Therefore, this chapter critically considers moving beyond the constructs of theological and social conservatism that frequently reflect and reify social thinking about Evangelicals and no less the white mainline and black Evangelicals of Bald Eagles who, for the most part, embody much of the conservatism of their "Bible Belt" region. Offered, here, is a social profile of a few of the eighty-three research participants in this study—members of both churches, white and black residents of the city and the greater county of Bald Eagles, along with qualitative and quantitative data to show how these self-identified white and black evangelical Christians are both similar and different. (More information about the research methodologies applied to this study of white and black evangelical Christians is located in the appendix.)

Further tested is the validity of what is considered an enduring historical and sociological conviction about the religious beliefs and political positions of white and black Evangelicals—that evangelical white Christians are "socially conservative and theologically conservative" and that evangelical black Christians are "socially liberal and theologically conservative." By gaining entrée into their stances on sociopolitical, theological, and moral concerns like working-class labor and economics, sexual reproductive rights, poverty, teenage pregnancy, affirmative action, employment, and education, what is argued is that Evangelicals of all stripes—white, black, male, female, single, married—are made in the U.S.A. and thus contribute to and reinforce American national identity because of their investment in a market economy, in American civil liberties safeguarded by constitutional freedoms, and in a representative democracy that, at times, is a questionable and elusive liberal democracy.

Conservative, Progressive, and Emergent Evangelicals: Moving beyond Constructs

American evangelicalism is color coded, and in its contemporary form it is coded white.[9] These white Evangelicals cannot escape the "conservatisms" related to the "evangelical" identifier. Fundamentally labeled "social" and "theological" conservatives (particularly because of their relationship to the Religious Right), they tend to exhibit moral intolerance on issues like homosexuality, pornography, abortion, divorce, school prayer, imprisonment, and capital punishment.[10] The wider American public perceives them as politically intolerant toward particular populations like undocumented immigrants *and* documented immigrants, because these conservatives deny protection of the civil liberties of these social and cultural groups.[11] Despite this characterization, white Evangelicals are unquestionably politically astute, as candidates for office garner their support during election cycles because of their strength as a primarily Republican Party–based voting bloc. In fact, during the 2016 election cycle and season, 81% of white Evangelicals voted for Republication presidential candidate Donald Trump.

Another distinguishing feature of white evangelical conservatism is an intolerance to difference. Studies show that conservatives often support racial discrimination in housing, employment, and marriage.[12] Such studies provide theoretical justification for depicting them as racially intolerant based on their fears of radical social change that will upset the status quo.[13] Though they think like their white counterparts on some issues, black Evangelicals are still frequently abstracted from public policy conversations because of factors like America's historical legacy of slavery and struggles around the social-justice–oriented civil rights and black nationalist movements, factors that represent the social change that many conservatives strongly dislike and avoid. As well, the American public fails to ponder the relevance of black evangelical voices on issues of importance that impact the nation.

Race and gender become fault lines in conservative Protestantism, and particularly in evangelicalism,[14] when "Evangelicals" are intractably labeled "monolithic" and when considering the historical mistreatment of marginalized groups in America who have gained traction and constitutional rights by putting into practice a "social gospel." In a push beyond the presumed religious practices and political leanings of white and black Evangelicals and to reorient our thinking about Evangelicals on a whole, we do well to heed the words of philosopher of religion Andre C. Willis:

> U.S. evangelicals of all stripes are deeply modern; they presuppose liberal values of individual agency of human subjects, embrace rational propensities of the human animal, confirm the constitutionality of representative democracy and its concomitant market arrangements around private property, and they prioritize freedom as a necessity for subjects, communities, institutions and nations. They have a strong desire to influence democratic culture and politics along the lines of Christianity as they believe it has been revealed to them.[15]

With Willis' declaration comes the recognition that Evangelicals in the early twenty-first century are now separated into three groups: conservative, progressive, and emergent. If Evangelicals, white and black, can be typified theologically by membership in each of these three groups, then perhaps a similar argument can be made politically. This is indeed the case. Ideologically, conservative Evangelicals lean toward the moderate and extreme right, while progressives and emergent (i.e., millennial and younger generations) Evangelicals lean toward the left and far left. Bald Eagles residents and members of both churches can also be classified along the lines of these three groupings, even if these rural townsfolk tend toward the more moderate and conservative sides of the spectrum.

Reductionism marks our interpretation of Evangelicals when it comes to race and their religious orientations and political persuasions. To learn more about Bald Eagles' white and black Evangelicals and to challenge such reductionist thinking, especially about Americans who live in rural areas of the country, an in-depth exploration of sociopolitical issues of paramount concern to these white and black townsfolk was conducted. Interviewing the eighty-three participants in this small study showcased the community concerns of the *mainline* Evangelicals of the First United Methodist Church and other white members of this community expressly about (1) the local economy, job creation, and mentoring young people to prepare them for the future job force; (2) young people and the moral life; (3) the threat of secularization on the well-being of family, church, and community; (4) the welfare state and American dependence on the federal "big" government; (5) family values and issues related to the sanctity of life (i.e., women's role in society, teenage pregnancy, and abortion); (6) the defense and leadership of America (i.e., safeguarding the American flag and American way of life, constitutional freedoms: freedom of religion, school prayer, bearing firearms, freedom of press and speech); and (7) the relationship between church and state.

Surveying the black citizens of Bald Eagles along with the *black* Evangelicals of Tabernacle Missionary Baptist Church displayed the subjects that black townsfolk cared about: (1) the national economy and the recession's impact on the country; (2) the implications of delimiting social welfare programming and its potential effects on increasing poverty; (3) constitutional rights and "rights" abuses; (4) American military power and the military industrial complex; (5) educating black youth; (6) African American youth, drugs, and gang culture; (7) black men and the penal system; (8) the demise of the black family; and (9) the social, economic, and ideological implications of a "postracial" society.

The study clarified that regardless of race (and gender), these Evangelicals as well as other white and black residents in rural Bald Eagles shared similar concerns about the length of America's presence in the wars in Afghanistan and Iraq. Both racial groups also held strong positions on the growing gay rights movement. Evident are the common civic and political perspectives shared by members in both congregations, even if the dominant social perspectives are unique. In this rural community, these are the ties that bind whites and blacks together. These are the ties that establish that whites and blacks interact but hold different and also similar sociopolitical and theological positions on various issues that affect all Americans. These are also the ties that demonstrate that religious exercise and the political processes of Evangelicals should not so easily be stereotyped by race.

The Theology and Politics of Race: On White and Black
Social Conservatism and Liberalism

In the article "Scripture, Sin, and Salvation: Theological Conservatism Reconsidered," authors Lynn M. Hempel and John P. Bartkowski posit:

> Race is a second critical fault line within conservative Protestantism. . . .
> Black theological conservatives exhibit more liberal attitudes on social
> justice issues (e.g. racial equity and social welfare policies) while the
> theological conservatism of whites is tied more closely to political and
> social conservatism.[16]

Hempel and Bartkowski's contention has become a truism not only in black and white conservative Christian circles but also among more liberal publics—a universally accepted axiom that proclaims that black Americans are theologically conservative and socially liberal while their white counterparts are more theologically, politically, and socially conservative. Their statement can be applied to the mainline and black Evangelicals in rural Bald Eagles. In this study, Hempel and Bartkowski's premise is put to the test. Table 5.1 measures race against sociopolitical perspectives and theological position for the eighty-three participants in this study to gather information about this historic contention and to illustrate the range of religious varieties and political permutations that potentially exist within white and black populations of American society.

Conducting *intragroup analyses* on the data collected based on the contemporary evangelicalism practiced in the rural and Southern town of Bald Eagles revealed that 91.7% of African Americans are strongly drawn to social conservatism and theological conservatism, representing eleven of twelve African Americans who identify as *social conservatives*.[17] Sixteen African American respondents identify as *social moderates*, contributing ten of the sixteen African Americans, or 62.5%, who classify themselves as social and theological moderates, and followed by social liberals and theological moderates at 60% (i.e., three of five identify as *social liberals*). Small but equal in number are African Americans who classify themselves as social liberals and theological conservatives and/or social and theological liberals at 20% (i.e., one of five social liberals in each category, respectively).

By performing intragroup analyses, the social and theological conservatism of these rural and Southern white Americans was made apparent, standing at 94.4%, representing seventeen of eighteen respondents who identified as *socially conservative*. Social and theological moderates measure at 86.4%, by calculating the nineteen white respondents against the twenty-two who label themselves as *social moderates*. Further away are *social liberals* and theological moderates at 60%; that represents six of ten individuals who identify as socially liberal. Only 40% corresponded to the socially and theologically liberal group (i.e., four of the ten respondents), and none of the research participants for this intragroup analysis corresponded to the social liberal and theological conservative category, leaving this category registering at 0% for these white rural dwellers.

Regardless of racial groups, when theological and sociopolitical orientation is measured against age groups, 20–70+ years old (Appendix 2, "Theological Orientations and Social Perspectives against Age Groups"), what is notable is that social conservatism controls more of the worldview of these rural residents than does theological conservatism. Broadly speaking, the findings indicate that theological conservatives are more fluid in their outlooks than are social conservatives. This means theological conservatives have a greater chance of being socially liberal and moderate than do social conservatives being theologically liberal or moderate. If applied to all voting-age Americans, these results imply that social conservatism is more strongly linked to a conservative mindset than is theological conservatism. Exploring the data along the lines of age groups offers yet another dimension to and way of interpreting white and black social conservatism and liberalism. In other words, whites tend to be more socially conservative, and blacks more theologically conservative.

In fact, returning to the previously recorded results, if we are to examine the data based on the total number of research participants (n=83) in Table 5.1 from a macrostructural perspective, results show that thirty individuals identify as social conservatives, fifteen individuals as social liberals, and thirty-eight as social moderates. These numbers are significant because social conservatives, liberals, and moderates comprise our democratic nation and champion a *liberal democracy*. However, Americans and the media pit conservatives against liberals, often stereotyping liberals and their agenda as unchristian and corrosive to religious and moral values and by the same token conservatives as intolerant of social diversity, justice, and human differences. More striking is that my statistics (albeit based on a small sample of individuals) signal that *social conservatism* abounds across the country although the vast majority of the American population eagerly accept and embrace our *representative and liberal democracy*. Nevertheless, the degree to which most of the nation is conservative makes very plausible the clash between the tenets of America's representative democracy with the principles of an American liberal democracy.

When *comparing* white Americans and black Americans (i.e., Evangelicals and non-evangelical Christians) in this research study and conducting *intergroup analyses*, we find that white Americans are one and a half times more likely to be social and theological conservatives than African Americans (60.7% vs. 39.3% respectively). Yet, white Americans are four times more likely than African Americans to be socially and theologically liberal (80.0% vs. 20.0%). In contrast, black Americans are four times more likely to be social moderates and theological conservatives than are white Americans (80.0% vs. 20.0%). Furthermore, blacks more readily identify as socially liberal and theologically conservative (100%).

What do these demographic findings suggest? White Evangelicals are frequently typified as "social and theological conservatives" and black Evangelicals as "social liberals and theological conservatives" because we have developed a habit of comparing the *groups* though *individual members* of each racial group represent a spectrum of ideological and theological perspectives. Comparing groups inclines Americans to develop an understanding of each cultural group solely in relation one to the other, eviscerating essential group features and social personalities, rather than interpreting and understanding each racial group as sui generis social and cultural entities. Some uses of sociological data have led to perceptions that groups are monolithic while they contain significant variation. Individual variations across the three domains (i.e., race and theological and social perspectives) are evident among members of the Bald Eagles community and two congregations. The demographic findings suggest that though the results strongly support the historic premise about black and white evangelical Christians and Americans and reaffirm how they are conventionally identified theologically and politically, there remains a need to recognize and develop categories beyond such constructs and to better interpret paradoxical ideological positions. That opens the way to gain better footing and greater understanding of each group's religious and sociopolitical realities. That adds value and insight into each group's racial and national experiences of being American. For example, political scientist Tasha S. Philpot lays out a rationale for why the correlation between party identification and ideological self-identification tends to be lower for African Americans than with other racial groups. An American public cannot begin to understand the relationship between black ideology and political party affiliation until the mix of six issues, which are tools enabling blacks to self-identify as liberal and conservative, are accounted for.[18] That is also the starting point for deducing why blacks to a greater degree than whites tend to simultaneously hold more conservative theological positions (on particular issues) and liberal social positions (on others) and how such paradoxical and tensive ideological positions might translate, politically.

Table 5.1. *Theological Positioning, Race, and Sociopolitical Perspective for N=83*

Social	Theological		Ethnicity		Total
			African American	Caucasian American	
Conservative	Conservative	Count	11	17	28
		% within groups	39.3%	60.7%	100.0%
		% within ethnicity	91.7%	94.4%	93.3%
		% of total	36.7%	56.7%	93.3%
	Moderate	Count	1	1	2
		% within groups	50.0%	50.0%	100.0%
		% within ethnicity	8.3%	5.6%	6.7%
		% of total	3.3%	3.3%	6.7%
	Total	Count	12	18	30
		% within groups	40.0%	60.0%	100.0%
		% within ethnicity	100.0%	100.0%	100.0%
		% of total	40.0%	60.0%	100.0%
Liberal	Conservative	Count	1	0	1
		% within groups	100.0%	.0%	100.0%
		% within ethnicity	20.0%	.0%	6.7%
		% of total	6.7%	.0%	6.7%
	Liberal	Count	1	4	5
		% within groups	20.0%	80.0%	100.0%
		% within ethnicity	20.0%	40.0%	33.3%
		% of total	6.7%	26.7%	33.3%
	Moderate	Count	3	6	9
		% within groups	33.3%	66.7%	100.0%
		% within ethnicity	60.0%	60.0%	60.0%
		% of total	20.0%	40.0%	60.0%
	Total	Count	5	10	15
		% within groups	33.3%	66.7%	100.0%
		% within ethnicity	100.0%	100.0%	100.0%
		% of total	33.3%	66.7%	100.0%

(Continued)

Social	Theological		Ethnicity		Total
			African American	Caucasian American	
Moderate	Conservative	Count	4	1	5
		% within groups	80.0%	20.0%	100.0%
		% within ethnicity	25.0%	4.5%	13.2%
		% of total	10.5%	2.6%	13.2%
	Liberal	Count	2	2	4
		% within groups	50.0%	50.0%	100.0%
		% within ethnicity	12.5%	9.1%	10.5%
		% of total	5.3%	5.3%	10.5%
	Moderate	Count	10	19	29
		% within groups	34.5%	65.5%	100.0%
		% within ethnicity	62.5%	86.4%	76.3%
		% of total	26.3%	50.0%	76.3%
	Total	Count	16	22	38
		% within groups	42.1%	57.9%	100.0%
		% within ethnicity	100.0%	100.0%	100.0%
		% of total	42.1%	57.9%	100.0%

Note: In this cross-tabulation of three variables, race is measured against theological and sociopolitical positions. The "% within ethnicity" shows the intragroup statistic for each racial group against sociopolitical and theological dimensions. Reading horizontally, the "% within group" produces the intergroup statistic for both racial groups along theological position and against sociopolitical status.

Blacks have created a special set of criteria (i.e., ideological dimensions) that they use to self-identify as *liberal and conservative* that when applied explains their conceptualization of a hierarchical liberal-conservative continuum.[19] These six ideological dimensions are racial, military, social welfare, religious, moral, and laissez-faire economics.[20] Given their multidimensional nature, "race" does not solely define what it means to be a black liberal versus a black conservative.[21] However, another identity that must be considered alongside the others is racial group consciousness. These ideological issues are multiple and competing identities that blacks must negotiate; tensions arise because of these various identities often conflicting with political party attachment but that ultimately affect black voting decisions.[22] Philpot explains:

> Blacks' ideological self-identification is shaped by the historical relation-
> ship Blacks have had with government and politics. Because Whites have

not been privy to these experiences, they use a different set of dimensions in determining their ideological self-identification. . . . Blacks are not uniformly liberal. While Blacks are significantly more liberal than whites when it comes to racial, social welfare, and military issues, there is no meaningful differences (statistically or substantively) between the two racial groups on moral issues. Furthermore, Blacks' mean placement on military and moral issues indicated they were fairly moderate in these areas. Finally, blacks were significantly more conservative than Whites on religious issues.[23]

In other words, blacks' ideological issues and attitudes do not neatly map onto the general electorate because of their distinctive position in society, consequently resulting in a complexity. This complexity not only displays incongruences between voting behavior and ideology but also reveals heterogeneous social and religious discourses and attitudes.[24]

In closing, the manner in which white Americans and black Americans perceive themselves is frequently at variance with how others understand them. This warrants acknowledgment about the array of black and white religious and political behavior exhibited by both publics. It shows the necessity of extending to both social groups more opportunities for claiming traditions of liberalism and conservatism—or at least recognizing the diversity that exists within the spectrum.

Wrestling with this subject matter and engaging in this data analysis is imperative to uproot traditional ways of thinking about mainline and black Evangelicals, specifically, in addition to whites and blacks, more generally. Even though research is based on a small, rural, Southern, and mainly theologically conservative community, the findings disclose and echo the national trend.

Consider, for example, the article authored by social psychologists Haidt, Graham, and Joseph, "Above and below Left-Right: Ideological Narratives and Moral Foundations." In this psychological study of how specific left-right ideologies reveal the moral foundations of individuals and cultural groups, four cluster groups describe and articulate the liberal and conservative split. Although more illustrative than definitive, this research in the psychology of political and moral behavior categorizes people into groups to aid comprehension about the ways in which political ideology can predict and reflect moral values.[25]

Having collected survey responses from the database YourMorals.org, from 25,000 people who completed a Moral Foundations Questionnaire related to moral or political psychology, these authors then mapped five virtues/values/norms/vices and so forth (Harm/Care, Fairness/Reciprocity,

Ingroup/Loyalty, Authority/Respect, Purity/Sanctity)[26] onto liberal and conservative ideological dimensions to perceive how individuals and different cultures build on these psychological foundations to build a moral life and then to understand the meaning of moral debates in culture wars.[27] Their initial analysis of the questionnaire produced two clusters that clearly fit along the liberal/conservative split; however, further analysis yielded two more clusters as alternative groupings that did not neatly fit along liberal/conservative dimensions but did produce knowledge about the continuum of left and right morality.[28]

In cluster 1 (people labeled *secular liberals*), high scores on Harm and Fairness values were noted but low scores on Ingroup, Authority, and Purity. People in cluster 4, identified as *social conservatives*, typically had high scores on Ingroup, Authority, and Purity but low scores on Harm and Fairness. It would be erroneous, however, to conclude that *secular liberals'* high scores in Harm and Fairness as well as *social conservatives'* high scores in Ingroup, Authority, and Purity mean that the other virtues are not in operation. It is more accurate to say that both groups display all the virtues but that the most prominent moral values showcase each political group's strongest commitments. In other words, *secular liberals* are not oblivious to the importance of in-group loyalty, respect for authority, or the values of social discipline and self-restraint, which holds a different meaning for them. Likewise, *social conservatives* are mindful of care of society and basic concerns for reciprocity, which have a distinct meaning for them.[29]

In between these groupings are clusters 2 and 3, considered moderate groups. Those persons in cluster 2 are characterized as *libertarians* and scored low on all five moral values: Harm, Fairness, Ingroup, Authority, and Purity. Because of their low scores across the board, they are a hybrid of "liberal" and "conservative" clusters, and their moral foundation settings seem to deny the general value of externally imposed moral regulation of any kind.[30] People in cluster 3 are *religious liberals*. This group uniquely combines liberal *and* conservative norms, contrary to cluster 2, by having high scores on Harm and Fairness as well as on Ingroup, Authority, and Purity—although not higher than the *secular liberals* or *social conservatives* that their values emulate. In this case, participants have a "high" moral outlook in which people are obligated to each other and members of the group.[31]

The research of Haidt and colleagues not only shows how political ideology sheds light on moral commitments; it also uncovers the range of moral belief systems and political orientations present within the conservative/liberal *divide* and *continuum*. "These four [groupings] and narratives can yield insights into the shifting and often puzzling dynamics of American politics."[32] By that account, the fact that white evangelical Christians are fundamentally characterized as socially and theologically conservative and black evangelical Christians as largely socially liberal and theologically conservative translates to narrow typologies that evolve into stereotypes and continue to foreclose opportunities for members of each group to move beyond these constructs, typologies that furthermore prevent each group from fully exercising the strength of their moral and political mindset, theological positions, and public voice.

This data analysis moreover indicates and maintains that black and white American Evangelicals represent an array of complex ideological, moral, and theological positions not reducible to any sort of identity politics. That unquestionably has ramifications for how both groups play their American politics.

The next sections represent the diverse array of moral, theological, and political positions of white and black Bald Eagles Evangelicals. Four cases and subsequent evaluations advance a new hermeneutic about white and black Evangelicals, supporting Willis' earlier claim about the nature of American Evangelicals.

Tom Belkin: Churches Rank Sin

Tom Belkin is a fifty-year-old white American worker who has been living in Bald Eagles five years. A family man, he is actively involved with the ministries of the First United Methodist Church while also attending law school in Memphis. He identifies as a social and theological moderate. Asked about his stance on evangelicalism in addition to the national and local issues of concern to him, he comments:

> I don't identify with the term as it is used by our media today. I am not a social conservative bent on interjecting my personal religious and moral standards into [the] law of the land. That is what I perceive as the usage of [the term] Evangelical Christian by the media now.
>
> I do believe that most Protestant churches are evangelical in a biblical sense. I am not exactly sure about the Methodist Church. We do believe in baptism of infants, and we don't then require a public confession of conviction of sin and remorse to be considered a church member. I personally believe there is a time when each of us becomes aware of our personal sinful nature and realizes we can't save ourselves. We must turn to Christ. I don't think this must come as some blinding, sudden, and traumatic event. It can be the result of teaching and eventual understanding.

The issues that are of primary importance to me are related to economic opportunity in all of the diverse groups in our society. The extreme stratification of our society by economic level is causing a new generation of people to feel abandoned by all of the existing social institutions, including our churches. The existing churches in poorer levels of society are struggling to reach the young people in the neighborhoods because of the alienation they feel. The jobs that were available for people to have an alternative to welfare, that gave the opportunity for a decent life within their community, are vanishing. They are faced with the option of giving up their cultural identity and trying to break into closed ranks of another culture or falling into a culture of welfare and/or crime. This is a national problem manifested on a local level.

The injection of religion into the issues regarding birth control is also a concern to me. I see this as an ethical issue, but not a religious one. Our modern society has pushed back the age of adulthood to a point that is actually several years past the age when our bodies naturally start telling us to bond together and mate. We have created a structure that makes it very difficult for young adults with children to continue their education to the level necessary to prosper. This has driven society to recognize the need for birth control, even for married couples.

Pre-conception birth control, by whatever method available, is generally accepted now by most churches, but abortion is a major issue where the churches seem led to take a front-line position. I don't understand or agree with this. The Bible is filled with examples of God ordering the death of huge groups of people for one reason or another. We currently have many other types of killing in our society that are not viewed as murder under law or perceived as a religious. And even if we do choose to consider it a sin, we don't try to criminalize all sin. Why is this issue one where the churches feel the need to demand criminalization of sin?

Tom Belkin is a white mainline Evangelical who is more progressive in his thinking and actions than his peers in this region of the country. He critiques the media for reducing the term *evangelical* to a religio-political entity and for characterizing Evangelicals in general as socially and theologically conservative. Taking exception to that caricature, he makes clear his desire for economic parity among diverse groups; his resistance to making birth control a religious rather than a medical or ethical issue; and his objection to the church ranking of "sins." Belkin appeals to the brand of American populism that Gary Gerstle defines as "civic nationalism":[33] a belief in the fundamental equality of all human beings; in every individual's inalienable rights to life, liberty, and the pursuit of happiness; and in a democratic government that derives its legitimacy from the people's consent.[34]

Although he self-identifies as a social and theological moderate, Belkin's critique of the media, the church, and American social structure is more liberal because he advances a conception of "We the People" that transcends race, ethnicity, and gender. Further, his sensitivity toward class stratification manifests as his defense against lower-class economic struggles and the American worker who he believes is being "left behind" in our current economic state and structure.[35] *Who is American?* signals the fight for economic equity and justice (although he does not seem to be in favor of a governmental social welfare system) that is a major part of his sharp critique of a nation facing the reality of diminishing job opportunities for the working majority in the middle and lower economic echelons of American society. Belkin closes by advocating for those whom he regards as marginalized for making certain sexual reproductive choices without going so far as to say he is pro-choice (which he might not be even if he is fully in support of a person's right to exercise choice). He reconfigures the abortion issue—a "culture war" matter—into religious talk rather than political conflict, concluding with: "We don't try to criminalize all sin. Why is this one [abortion] where churches feel the need to demand criminalization of sin?"

Rebekah Coleman: Follow the Rules

Rebekah Coleman is a forty-year-old white American and married mother of three young boys who has resided in Bald Eagles for nine years after moving from Memphis. Actively involved with the First United Methodist Church, she represents a new generation of lay leaders at church. Rebekah is a theological and social conservative. She begins this exchange by sharing her desire to improve the lives of inner-city black youth through her church work. The conversation turns to her position on teenage pregnancy and its linkage to cycles of poverty.

> REBEKAH COLEMAN: I have a real heart and passion for inner city, the inner city. [I] worked there for three years in Memphis and just had to recruit tutors to come and tutor the inner-city children. It just breaks my heart to know that these inner-city children have to live on junk food because they don't have access to fresh vegetables and fruits. And have a mother that doesn't want them, and a dad that they don't even know, and there's just a real burden in my heart for that.

And, it's just so hard to break the cycle. And I don't know how you go about doing it, and I don't know how, how it ever stops.

There's a family in our church that came, and there's like twelve of 'em, and there's just lots of anger issues and volatile situations and, and our church opened up our arms to 'em, but what we tried to instill in these children is there's rules. There's rules for our kids, and there's rules for you. And they didn't want the rules, so they left. Yeah, which is sad.

They had a free meal offered to them every Wednesday night. We had Bible activities planned, and they chose not to obey the rules. And it's really hard in situations like that, but I have, I just have a little burden in my heart for that. I'm real sensitive to that, and it breaks my heart. I don't know how you break the cycle, because it seems like it's neverending.

N: So, so are you talking about the cycle of poverty, or the cycle of lack, or . . .

RC: Well, the cycle of poverty, because they're not educated, they don't have a mother who will sit there with them and read their Accelerated Reader books. And, then, they get so behind in school. With this No Child Left Behind in school, a lot of times they're just bumped, and so they get so frustrated that they just end up dropping out of school and getting pregnant and having another child and here goes the cycle.

Repeat, then repeat, then repeat. And I don't know how to fix it. I don't know how you fix it. But . . .

N: Yeah, I don't know either.

RC: And, I promise you, and I hate to say this, one of those little girls was already startin' to dabble, in promiscuity, and so, I just see before long that she will be a young, young pregnant mother.

N: More than likely a teenaged mom.

RC: Mm hm. If she makes it to teenaged years.

N: Oh. How old is she?

RC: She's like ten.

N: Oh. Okay.

RC: It's very sad. But, that . . . that is a real passion of mine.

N: Okay.

Rebekah's social burden is inner-city poverty. She wrestles internally with the dilemma of finding effective ways of addressing and preventing the cycle of poverty caused by limited educational opportunities, school dropout rates, sex, promiscuity, and teenage pregnancy. What stood out to me is her judgment about why the black family under her church's care left the congregation. Said simply, they left because "they didn't want to follow the rules."

Without explicitly articulating it, her position speaks for many who believe that cycles of poverty produce or reproduce the welfare state. Bald Eagles' residents share a strong communal belief in individual responsibility, hard work, and self-reliance, and they often challenge the idea of a welfare state. Their resistance to the federal government's role in "taking care of you"—primarily in the form of federal-assistance programs for low-income women and children—is revealed through conservative attitudes toward the poor and racial minorities who are stigmatized as abusers of the social security system. It does not help that throughout the nation political rhetoric becomes a push for such branding, demonstrated by local intolerance toward both groups. Religiously, Rebekah is a mainline Evangelical who surprisingly and unexpectedly does not represent the views of the Christian Left; instead, she is theologically conservative, and her statement reaffirms her identity as social conservative, thus representing more closely the perspectives of the Christian Right.

Political scientist Karen Stenner's article "Three Kinds of Conservatism" gives a fuller definition of conservatism, and it further differentiates between "status quo conservatism," "laissez faire conservatism," and "authoritarianism" (commonly known as social conservatism), not as "political ideologies but rather as psychological dispositions akin to universal personality dimensions."[36] More than studying how such "conservatisms" work politically, her purpose is to address the medley of value commitments that individuals hold in tension as they exercise these distinguishable forms of conservatism, and to show how authoritarianism (i.e., social conservatism) in American society is both *harmful* and surprisingly *helpful* to maintaining social hierarchy, structure, and order.

Rebekah's comment about the family "not following the rules" illustrates Stenner's definition of authoritarianism (i.e., social conservatism). Authoritarianism is the form of conservatism most familiar to the American public because it conventionally combines "preservation of the status quo over social change; preference of a free market economy with limited federal government interventions; and a predisposition of conformity (sameness and oneness) and obedience in political and social matters over freedom and difference."[37] Stenner further separates this definition of "social conservatism" into its component parts, delineating distinct forms of conservatism and naming them "social," "status quo," and "laissez faire" conservatism. With respect to authoritarianism / social conservatism, authoritarianism is an individual predisposition—a system of *functionally related* stances addressing the appropriate balance between group authority and uniformity as well as individual autonomy and diversity.[38] Authoritarianism is far more than a personal distaste for difference (and libertarianism more than a mere preference for diversity).[39] Instead, it becomes a standard worldview about the social value of obedience and conformity (or freedom and difference) demonstrated as the prudent and just balance between group authority and individual autonomy,[40] and the appropriate uses of (or limits on) that authority.[41] Authoritative constraints are exercised in the forms of political demands on, personal coercion of, and bias against those who are different, such as racial and ethnic out-groups, political dissidents, and moral "deviants." Typically, that will appear as and include legally discriminating against minorities and restricting immigration, limits on free speech and association, and regulating moral behavior—for example, policies regarding school prayer, abortion, censorship, and homosexuality, and their punitive enforcement.[42]

Authoritarianism (i.e., social conservatism) favors group loyalty, authority, obedience, and behavior over the individual. Authoritarians are boundary maintainers and norm enforcers who respond to the threat of a complex and diverse society by delineating between "us" and "them." What makes "us" an "us" are common authority (oneness) and shared values (sameness).[43]

Threats to unity and uniformity activate this latent predisposition. To maintain social order and stability, social conservatives prefer the cohesion of the collective over the uniqueness of the individual. As a response to threat, they invoke group authority. That is what drives Rebekah Coleman's more socially conservative bent, reflected in her comment about the family who left the church: the kids did not want to follow the rules, rules that were for their own children. Authoritarians work at structuring society and social relationships around *sameness* and *conformity* rather than diversity, difference, and expressions of uniqueness, all of which are minimized.

A need for social processes and detectable moral values, over and above individual processes and anomie, fuels and justifies how Rebekah rationalizes the family's departure from the congregation. With that in mind, classical social conservatism responds to "normative threats" to the social collective, what Stenner identifies as the "authoritarian dynamic."[44] A rise in intolerant behavior by authoritarians (i.e., social conservatives) can be attributed to threats they perceive to the moral order and to the social system that they safeguard. "In conditions of normative threat, authoritarian fears are alleviated by defense of the collective 'normative order': positive differentiation of the in-group, devaluation of and discrimination against out-groups, obedience to authorities, conformity with rules and norms, and intolerance and punishment of those who fail to obey and conform."[45] Hence, Rebekah reacts to the presumed threat against the social collective of which she is a member by activating and enabling an authoritarian dynamic, a threat she unconsciously determines has been precipitated by the family that she believes lacks moral vision and moral allegiance to her social and cultural (church) group because they will not follow the rules. As a mainline Evangelical and social conservative, for Rebekah what it means to be American is to be a person who "follows the rules," communicating shared norms and a sense of identity as well as shared moral commitments with the group.

Roger Charles Courtney:
Affirmative Action Has Run Its Course

Roger Charles Courtney is a college-educated retiree from the West Coast who worked as a telecommunications engineer. He moved to Bald Eagles two and a half years ago. Though he is not presently active in a local congregation, he identifies as a Christian. An African American, he served in the armed forces from 1955 to 1959. At seventy-one years of age, he is a social and theological conservative.

Frances Trumpton is a black American, college-educated, and retired auto dealer. He has lived in Bald Eagles for twenty-four years, is sixty-two years old, and is a veteran of the Vietnam War. He serves in the leadership of one of the local Baptist churches. He is a social and theological moderate. In this conversation, Roger Charles Courtney speaks with Frances Trumpton and me. Affirmative action in a postracial society is the topic under discussion.

> N: The historic moment in which we now live is being defined by Representative Harold Ford Jr.'s appointment as chair of the Democratic Leadership Council and the election of President Obama—two extremely powerful U.S. governmental positions, so do we live in a postracial society? Yet, I'm going to nuance the question for you a bit and ask, does a postracial society include other people and ethnic groups?
>
> ROGER C. COURTNEY: My experience has been a little different from his. I worked for the government all my life so I never had any problems. I always got my raises and my promotions and what I wanted, so I guess I got it pretty easy. So, I've never felt any pressure in being different or being otherwise, because I was treated just like

everybody else was. So, that's my attitude. I just hadn't had to deal with that.

N: O.K., but you also grew up in California.

RCC: California, yea. No doubt about it.

FRANCES TRUMPTON: Allow me to ask a question so that we can all get a better understanding. Would you have experienced the same occupational and career deal had it not been for the equal opportunity law et cetera? The government ain't always been straight up because the government is the same one that had segregated armies in the forties and the fifties or whatever.

RCC: You're right.

FT: So, yeah, our experiences have been different, but whatever level you have attained in government services, had it not been for the Hank Aarons and the Jackie Robinsons of the world . . .

RCC: . . . had it not been for the people who had gone before me. Of course, the place where I worked, people had gone before me and opened doors for me. But I was the first African American [in] my department, ever. And that company had . . . and that department had been there for the vehicles and buses—the transportation department had been there for a while. I was a telecommunications engineer, and I helped to put together their communications system for all the trains, buses, and trucks. There had never been an African American in that department; I was the very first in 1972.

FT: O.K., what did your dad do?

RCC: He was a driver with the city of Los Angeles.

FT: So, he worked in government, in a sense. So, like what I was talking about in private industry.

RCC: Oh yeah, yeah, we all got different situations.

FT: I look on my experience, for example. I became a corporate representative for Ford, and I showed up to be the representative for an area down in Dothan, Alabama; and I would get out of my car, back in those days everybody wore a dark suit, necktie, and I got out and carried a briefcase—my boss and I. So, after I had been in that territory for several months and they had gotten comfortable with me, they said, "Man, we are so relieved to find out that y'all weren't from the NAACP because we had just fired a black guy." And this is in south Alabama in the early seventies, so that's the kind of things that we had to face back then so that we have to now position ourselves so that our children don't have to go back to these same kinds of things.

RCC: Umm . . . huh . . . sure.

FT: So, that's why affirmative action and those kinds of commitments from the courts that say, "You got to treat him equal," like the EEOC and affirmative action and those things are a *must* as we go forward.

N: O.K., so I got that. But I still am asking you, I hear the two experiences which are different and also regionally, I mean, out West has a different history. And in terms of black people it has a totally different history. But, today, do you believe we live in a postracial or postracist society? And is that inclusive of other races and ethnicities?

RCC: Yeah, I think we do, I just don't think that people have the time to plot and scheme and sit around and think about how they are going to hurt people of another race and ethnicity. I do believe we live in a postracial society because my experiences have been different. I have prospered and have seen those around me prosper. I have a different experience.

There was talk about "quotas" where I used to work—people were not thought of as good enough. "Quotas" / "tokenism" / "affirmative action" had bad connotations. When affirmative action started to change, it included other minorities and women. But, the original intent of affirmative action was to secure employment for black males. Recently, those marching for affirmative action—especially in California, where I am from—have been Asians, for example, at UC Irvine. Affirmative action has served its purpose. Before Coretta Scott King died, she said the new frontier of the civil rights movement is the gay rights movement. Supreme Court justice nominee Sotomayor recently ruled against eighteen whites and one Hispanic who took the test to become captains in the New Haven Fire Department because no African American had passed the test. These men were denied their promotion. Because this stuff is divisive, we need to get away from it.

Affirmative action is confusing because you don't know who is favored from one day to the next. Since we have these positions, those who are qualified (regardless of race and ethnicity) should be considered. Thinking about representation in society and other issues that arise around affirmative action is problematic. It has run its course.

For instance, let's return to the Supreme Court nominee Judge Sonia Sotomayor. The feeling is that because she is a woman and a Latina she will make better lawful decisions and these decisions will be based on her experiences. Personal experiences should not be involved in making law and especially constitutional law. The thought is: "Get rid of all the white guys and put all the women in there. Get rid of all the Hispanic guys and put the black guys in there." It has run its course.

The only reason Sotomayor was chosen is because she is Hispanic and a woman. That is playing into identity politics regardless of qualification. Other people have her similar story. But, they were not chosen because it's not their turn. Once again, I say, it has run its course.

Roger Charles Courtney is black, evangelical, and a social conservative. His social conservatism shows through his ideology on affirmative action. Never disregarding the historical weight of forebears in paving his way to a successful career in the Los Angeles city government, where he was the first African American in his department in the 1970s, he is still vocal about its limitations (e.g., "quotas"/ "tokenism"/ "affirmative action" have bad connotations for him) and confident that affirmative action is a vestige of an American past. The death of affirmative action would be proof that we live in a postracial society.

Affirmative action is puzzling for Courtney, who disagrees with any sort of privileging of race and gender over qualifications and merit. His contestation of such preferential treatment extended even to Supreme Court nominee Judge Sonia Sotomayor, who had been portrayed, during the media's frenzy and within public circles, as the president's choice because she is a woman and Latina. Courtney outspokenly deviates from black racial group political standards, even after acknowledging his historical forebears. His level of racial group consciousness might give a rationale for his distinctive divergence from the majority of blacks on the issue of affirmative action. His policy preference suggests that Courtney, a black social conservative, possesses a low level of group consciousness, meaning that he does not necessarily employ racial considerations in social policy affairs.[46] That also suggests Courtney will deviate from other blacks when making political party evaluations and decisions.

Because he does not view social and political issues from racialized lenses, he might not consider black political interests in public policies and voting. Black conservatives with low racial group consciousness are not bound to the same political preferences as other blacks.[47] As such, Courtney sees no room for ignoring qualifications and merit in the fight for equalizing an unbalanced system; we hear it in his biting criticism of affirmative action: "Get rid of all the white guys and put all the women in there. Get rid of all the Hispanic guys and put the black guys in there." In his final analysis, affirmative action no longer serves any valid purpose because it is not based on the value of diversity and inclusion; rather, its basis is representation in American society where the "representative" is arbitrarily selected to meet the needs of people during particular historical moments, leading to Courtney's proclamation that affirmative action has run its course.

Since this is so, it is plausible that regionalism over race more strongly influenced Courtney's political decision-making processes and that of other black social conservatives exhibiting low racial consciousness. Some likely bought into the triumphalistic and nativistic brand of patriotism that was slowly developing and expanding yet still on the ground during the Obama years and as the wars ensued. Yet, Philpot reports that the numbers of black social conservatives with low group consciousness are a small proportion of the black electorate. That is why blacks still tend to be a strong Democratic voting bloc.[48]

Ronnie Janoff-Bulman's research compels consideration of Courtney's position from another angle. She writes about the psychological tendencies that make those on the political Right distinct from those on the political Left. "To Provide and to Protect: Motivational Bases of Political Liberalism and Conservatism" contends that these psychological tendencies are actual moral motivations that specify how conservatives access the political arena (from an *avoidance orientation*) and how liberals enter politics (from an *approach orientation*).

Both orientations are aimed at addressing the interests and the needs of the larger group, and so the research shows that political conservativism endeavors to *protect society's members from harm* and that political liberalism *provides for the social welfare of members*.[49] In line with Janoff-Bulman's investigations, Courtney, a political conservative, sounds the alarm about "quotas"/"tokenism" by being attuned to what he discerns are the dangers of affirmative action as it currently stands. Affirmative action is entrenched in "representation" politics and not authentic diversity and inclusion, says Courtney, and therefore institutions are acting prejudicially when they apply the principles and procedures of affirmative action to cases meant to deliver on a more equitable American culture and society. He senses a normative threat when this type of social programming and others like it are put into place, programming based not on merit but rather on history and social context, shaking the foundations of a discrete moral order.

Courtney's critique prompts the following questions: If affirmative action requires overhaul, can we trust the American public, Congress, and the Supreme Court to find or come up with a suitable replacement that is equitable for all? How would that system be constructed to fit social needs for representation, diversity, and inclusion? In the end, Roger C. Courtney is flat-footed in his practice of evangelical faith and social conservatism around an issue provoking serious debate among women and men, racial and ethnic groups, the federal government, individuals in the educational arena, institutions in corporate America, and mostly all areas of American social life. And thus, Courtney offers his interpretation of constitutional equity by treating affirmative action as a negative lifestyle issue and by delivering his opinion about equal treatment of people under the law. Equal treatment implies no one is favored, regardless of social impediment. Courtney consequently wants to see an end to affirmative action, delivering on his message that to be an American means *we are all the same.*

Angela Love: Capitalism's Economic Engine, Education, and Jobs (for Black Youth)

Angela Love is a thirty-two-year-old African American divorced mother of four who moved to Bald Eagles County fourteen years ago from Chicago. With spiritual roots in the Church of God in Christ, she presently attends a charismatic nondenominational church in the area and ministers as an evangelist. Additionally, she writes Christian novels and works in one of the area's banks. Angela identifies as socially liberal and a theological moderate believing that human-made rules sometimes overshadow and hinder God-inspired religious belief and practice. In our discussion, she articulates her aspirations for the solid education and employment of Bald Eagles' African American youth.

> ANGELA LOVE: My name is Angela Love, I am thirty-two years old, I am not originally from Bald Eagles. I was born in Mississippi and raised in Chicago. However, I've been in Tennessee for about fourteen years. I'm a writer. However, I do work commercially. I am a mother of four children. I have a sister that lives, I guess, within a twenty-mile radius of where I live. And some distant family, but I don't have any close relatives that live locally at all.
>
> N: So what do you think are the benefits of living here?
>
> AL: I think the benefits of living here as opposed to Chicago is the smaller . . . town, the community type environment. I don't tend to worry about violence as much as I would in the city. I like being able to raise my children in a more relaxed environment, and I believe Bald Eagles provides that. I like that pretty much everything that you want to do is accessible. You know, I'm not one that does a lot of flashy type things, so you know going to the movie theater, shopping at the local stores, everything I need is pretty much here in Bald Eagles.

N: What do you understand are the drawbacks of living in Bald Eagles?

AL: Everybody knowing everybody is a strength, but it is also a weakness, because a lot of times when people feel like they know you, you know they may not know you on the inside, like you know yourself. They just know what they've heard or they know what they have apparently seen. But they don't know you and your true function or even your heart. People tend to stereotype and they may say, "Oh well he or she is a part of this family or that family" . . . and they'll classify you as such and not see you as an individual. And sometimes when people feel like they know you, you know they tend to judge you based on that. They don't give you much room for change. They don't give you much room for advancement. They put you in a box and say that's where you have to stay. So, I think that's one of the drawbacks.

N: What are some local social and political issues that are of concern to you?

AL: One thing that concerns me is that although I find this is a great place to raise my children, I don't know that this would be a great place for them to establish themselves as adults. And the reason I say that is because of the lack of attention given to African Americans. My children have proven in school and in everything that they are very intelligent, and that they could obtain very good jobs in the future. But I don't feel like those employment opportunities will present themselves here. I have often told them that. And to prove my case, I'm going to take them to other cities to visit and on vacations and things like that, so that they can see African Americans in a more positive light than what is actually displayed here.

The place where I work, I would say between both [bank] branches we have maybe twenty-plus employees. However, only two of them are African American. I've been there three years, and the other lady has been there over thirty. But she has spent, I would say, 95% of those thirty years being the only African American employee there. And so, because of that I don't feel like the employment opportunities are such.

I mean I'm making contacts because of where I work, which made it easier for my daughter to obtain a job. So you know if you have a good name then they tend to be more lenient with your children. However, if you are unknown, or if you're known for something less than positive, then your children will have a hard time because they don't know you and they don't care to know you. My children were raised here. They will be able to say, "Well I'm from here." However, I still feel like they will be limited in their opportunities to advance and develop.

N: It sounds like race still is very much a prominent issue.

AL: Yeah, very much so. Very much so. Even in the schools. I've noticed that even in the case and especially with my oldest daughter in high school. I've noticed some of the situations that have arisen, you know some of the things. . . . She's an honor student. However, some of the things that she has been disciplined about have been just ludicrous and absurd. It makes no sense. So, I find that even in the school system they're limited in how far they can go because there's only so much they're gonna allow them to have.

N: Can you give an example of that?

AL: A good example is—

N: Without giving too much away.

AL: Right, a good example was something that happened in class. Although the room was filled with hundreds of students, because she [my daughter] laughed . . . at something that was going on the film screen, she was called to the office and told she [had] disrupted the whole class. But I inquired and later found out that everybody was laughing. But because her voice carried, they placed harsh disciplinary actions on her. She said everybody was laughing because of what was going on, because what was on the screen was funny. But because her laughter was loudest, and because they thought she was signifying, they picked on her.

N: So, so you feel like no matter what, black kids are still kind of treated differently.

AL: They are.

N: And picked on.

AL: Yes.

For Angela, living in small-town U.S.A. is a relief from the violence that often plagues large and complex cities like Chicago. The benefit of Bald Eagles' uncomplicated and quiet living is that it provides a safe environment for Angela to raise her children and a place where entertainment and shops are in close proximity to each other. Still, small towns are akin to looking glasses, and Bald Eagles is no less a metaphorical looking glass. For it is a place where everyone knows everyone else—whether white, black, or member of the very small percentage of Asians and Latinos (primarily migrant farm workers), as well as others who live in this residential community. Because of this, Bald Eagles can also be a place where people come to know their neighbors based on perception, on conceived images that do not accurately reflect persons as they really are. As Angela says, this can result in people being unfairly judged.

In this rural and Southern town, racial discrimination can occur without much protest or recognition. Interestingly, however, prejudicial behavior when noticed is more glaring in smaller-town environments, although it does not happen any less frequently than in large cities. Angela reaches the conclusion that prejudice is prevalent in Bald Eagles by drawing attention to her work setting, where she observes African American adults are not being extended the same opportunities at promotion as their white peers—or so it seems. And so, in her verbal exchange with me she remains focused on the imbalances she sees and discerns, eventually bringing up cracks in the local educational system, where race still matters. By articulating her grievances with the educational system, Angela voices her misgivings about her own children's future job potential in this small town, realizing the benefits and drawbacks to being known and/or having a bad reputation.

Angela is verbalizing the ideologies of socially liberal Evangelicals. Social liberals' emphasis on social welfare concerns draws attention to issues such as health, education, and employment. Thus, liberals are more likely than conservatives to support government welfare, social security, and affirmative action. Liberals more than conservatives prefer equality, which is even apparent in their more egalitarian and less hierarchical orientations.[50] Features of social liberalism are evident throughout Angela's commentary about small-town life. Implied in her views about the lack of opportunity for educational and upward career mobility for African Americans in Bald Eagles are the concepts of social justice and equality. More than once, Angela stresses that African Americans are not being treated justly or equally—which gravely concerns her. That is why she wants to expose her children to another way of life for blacks in America by taking them to cities where blacks are socially and visibly advancing.

Ironically, equality holds a different meaning for Angela than it does for social moderate Tom than it does for social conservative Roger, illustrating the existence of a conservative and liberal continuum that includes moderates. This continuum also shows that those on the political Left, in the political Center, and on the political Right are all motivated by similar values, one of which is care for community and the nation; but each group is oriented quite differently and handles these values altogether distinctly.[51] Because this is the case, for Angela, American nationality infers access to a good education and guarantees the economic gains that come with entry into the job force, a sign of adulthood that she desires not only for her own children but also for all black American young people.

The Cultural "DNA" of Contemporary Evangelicalism and American Democracy

Diverse Protestant denominations and Christian and racial groups constitute what it means to be "evangelical." How the phrase "conservative Christian" translates in contemporary American society tends to limit religious understanding of the term *evangelical* and to blind most Americans to Evangelicals' participation in the American political process as members of the political Left, Center, and Right. New constructs or moving beyond the old require more expansive and fluid definitions for what it means to be "white," "black," and "evangelical." "Right or Left" and "liberal or conservative" are binary categories that just do not cut it when describing Evangelicals, because these political identifiers do not adequately capture *who* or *what* an Evangelical is. Evangelicals cannot be strictly classified by political ideology, and even to a greater degree by theology.

Evangelicals are white but also black, male and female, old but also young, rural and urban, social conservatives but also social liberals, theological conservatives as well as theological moderates and liberals. An Evangelical who is both a social and a theological liberal might be a rare find in traditional politically conservative milieus and rural regions of America; yet they do exist, thus proving Andre C. Willis' point: Evangelicals are part of the American fabric.

However, even before Willis, sociologist Christian Smith and colleagues articulated the following closely related claim:

> The evangelical tradition's entire history, theology, and self-identity presupposes and reflects strong cultural boundaries with nonevangelicals; a zealous burden to convert and transform the world outside of itself; and a keen perception of external threats and crises seen as menacing what it views to be true, good, and valuable. These, we maintain, go a long way toward explaining evangelicalism's thriving.[52]

At the dawn of the twenty-first century, Evangelicals face the pressures associated with globalization and a technocratic and culturally plural American society and world. As a Christian collective, their strength is found in their ability to continue to thrive because of distinction, active civic engagement with American culture, as well as a recognition of the perceived political threats that bear on and shape their moral and theological worldviews. Their passion for representative *and* liberal democracy reveals fault lines that expose them to warranted and harsh criticism; yet, their vitality is likewise attributable to fault lines showcasing the exceptional varieties of races, ethnicities, nationalities, and genders who participate in the American political process as Evangelicals, an identifiable group and moral community, holding diverse viewpoints and opinions, that cannot be dismissed or ignored. This is evangelicalism's historical and cultural "DNA," its sociological and theological legacy, that has taken root and will endure, making Evangelicals relevant and reinforcing their status as Americans—those made in the U.S.A.—in this new age.

6

For God and Country

Bald Eagles First United Methodist Church

The idea of a civil religion stemmed from Jean-Jacques Rousseau's *Social Contract* and spread to late eighteenth-century America, where Benjamin Franklin, Thomas Jefferson, and their deist compatriots used the concept to set up a government that stressed the moral utility of religion as indispensable for political prosperity.[1] Natural law and biblical religion written into the Declaration of Independence entitled human beings to freedom and equality based on being endowed by their creator with inalienable rights.[2] In the process of crafting the Constitution, this burgeoning American republic would continue the tradition of recognizing the sovereignty of the nation as resting with the people but ultimate sovereignty as resting with God.[3]

When Robert Bellah set out to develop the concept of an American civil religion, he therefore interpreted Presidents George Washington and Abraham Lincoln's religious language as well as the religious rhetoric in the later political speeches of John F. Kennedy and Lyndon B. Johnson in the light of Rousseau's religious and political philosophies and that of the early democracy's founders. The God they invoked was not the personal, loving, and salvific God of Christianity. Rather, the God of American civil religion these presidential leaders introduced to their public was a "unitarian, austere God centered on moral order, law, and right and who acted in history with biblical authority and covenantal concern"[4] for America.

In Bellah's Durkheim-influenced 1960s definition of the term, he initially described American civil religion as the religious dimension of American public life, including the political sphere, and as being displayed in an assemblage of beliefs, symbols, and rituals with respect to sacred things and institutionalized by the people.[5] Historical precedence was enough for that religious dimension to be translated into an actual means of national religious self-understanding.[6] It legitimized the nation as a political entity with an accompanying political ethic that was guided by the motto "In God we trust" and the phrase "under God" in the pledge to the flag. From its earliest beginnings until now, American civil religion has been instrumental in bridging the gulf between "God and country" while cementing the two into a viable and lasting ideal despite debates about the relationship between and separation of church and the state.

Later, American patriotism would be classified as a form of civil religion and exemplified by the death, sacrifice, and rebirth of the nation around historical events such as the Civil War and martyrdom of Abraham Lincoln.[7] Lincoln's martyrdom was symbolically Christian, calling forth a spirit of public sacrifice to uphold America's mission and vision. The Civil War turned Northern and Southern fratricidal battle also proved to be a testing ground for national meaning and identity.

Accordingly, Bellah writes: "With the Civil War, new themes of death, sacrifice and rebirth entered into [America's] civil religion . . . [linking] Lincoln to the [Union] war dead, who gave their last measure of devotion" to supporting democratic and constitutional tenets.[8] In other words, those who sacrificed their lives for Jeffersonian principles of freedom and equality did so in order that the nation might prosper. Even though historically distant from the War on Terror, the Civil War era is a reminder to us that war can "test" American civil religious loyalties and stress national commitments, identity, and meaning. Thus, the public theologies articulated and rites of war enacted by the predominantly white church members of the First United Methodist Church and other white Bald Eagles' residents are hallmarks of a civil but religiously inspired American patriotism.

Although American civil religion shaped the convictions and actions of townsfolk, Bald Eagles' residents practiced an alternative form of it called *Southern civil religion.* It pulls together these Southern and rural inhabitants around Southern regional and American national experiences. Yet racialized forms of Southern civil religion also exist. Blacks, whites, and other ethnic groups tend to express civil religious understandings based on their differing racial experiences in America; nevertheless, racialized civil religion reflects the ideals, values, and commitments of each social and cultural group.

Institutional "legitimating" structures frame white town life and are critical to making sense of white leadership and authority in rural and Southern Bald Eagles and the surrounding county. Community leadership is exercised via "legitimating" and "landmark"[9] (i.e., historic and national) institutions like the church, family, school, government, and military that provide stability by reinforcing social relationships, social hierarchy, culture, and the social arrangements that constitute community. Within these infrastructures, individuals promote their moral norms and positions that contribute to the development of cohesive working groups and networks.

This chapter offers four case studies on leadership and these "ancient" landmark (i.e., historic and national) institutions to ascertain how white members of Bald Eagles and of the First United Methodist Church congregation relate their patriotic commitments to decisions about their homes, local community, and country.

Patriotic practices are "legitimating" and "landmark" (i.e., historic and national) oriented, as well. The Ten Commandments, public prayer, the American flag, and plaques and stone monuments paying homage to prominent figures in this county's development and to Southern regional history more specifically are reminders and celebrations of American identity and ideals. Community members display their allegiance to the country by elevating these symbols. In their descriptions of patriotism that follow in this chapter, white residents of Bald Eagles express their worldviews about the indissoluble connection between God and country and about constitutional rights and freedoms by referencing these landmark symbols. Deaths of servicemen and servicewomen represent the sacrificial spirit townsfolk foster and treasure; moreover, these deaths are emblematic of an enduring, influential, and landmark military culture that characterizes this local area. In this chapter, three case studies also reveal the patriotic mindset and ethos of these white rural dwellers.

To understand these case studies is to interpret religion's role in legitimizing the American republic. Bellah's essay on the relationship between religion and politics comprehends and explains how the church / First Church relates to the state.[10] To address the confusion around church–state relations, the essay first clarifies the nature of the American republic and then asserts religion's role in managing the tensions that emerge at the intersection of two forms of American democracy: U.S. republicanism and liberal constitutionalism.[11] On the nature of the American republic, political customs evolve from the behavior of a democratic and participatory public, grounded by egalitarianism and guaranteeing wide distribution of small to medium goods and land.[12] All are meant to foster a sacrificial and charitable American spirit and a purposeful public working for and toward the common good.

Yet liberalism is a byproduct of republicanism. With its focus on self-interest, liberalism becomes the seedbed for economic growth and competition. Because of this, republicanism ends up being diametrically opposed to liberalism. The economic side of our liberal state undercuts public participation, essential to the proper functioning of a republic. To address this contradiction, Bellah proposes that religion can mediate a civic republic and liberal democracy.[13] Offering the early republic as an example, he examines religion's "superstructural" and "infrastructural" roles in developing this nation-state.[14] Religion's superstructural role is found in the civil religious language of the Declaration of Independence and the Constitution that elicits the ethical commitment of citizens. The civil religious rhetoric of these two seminal and sacred American and political documents points to a sovereign God that is a "suprapolitical"[15] entity; as such, God stands above, judges, and justifies the American republic.

In the realm of the "superstructural," this deistic God also works through public theology especially because civil religion is formally but not securely institutionalized in the American government. Further, civil religion hardly meets the religious needs and demands of the republic.[16] Public theology has its origins both in religious communities that are described as located outside of the church and in formal political structures. Yet it also possesses national commitments that influence the making of public and social policies. These church communities gained power from rendering countercultural political interpretations of social issues.

Martin Marty's explanation of "civil millennialism"[17] distinguishes between the civil religion embedded in our nation's overarching political documents and the public theology practiced by these "national" religious communities comprised of self-selected segments of the American population. This public theology breaks through civil religion to become "the purest expression of ethical values, principles, and dynamism,"[18] because it is an outgrowth of the rhetoric and activity of leaders and followers in movements ranging from abolitionism to the Social Gospel, from Martin Luther King Jr. and the 1960s civil rights movement to the farm workers movement led by Cesar Chavez and Dolores Huerta.[19] Americans continue to exercise vibrant and active public theologies recognizable through cross-racial, religious, and multiethnic demonstrations. Such demonstrations are, for example, against the nuclear arms race, capital punishment, and the kinds of social and economic inequalities that were central to Occupy Wall Street and the Black Lives Matter campaigns and now protests against Trump's governmental immigration reforms and refugee bans. Bellah reminds us that "every movement to make America more fully realize its professed values has grown out of some form of public theology . . . [but] so has every expansionist war and every form of oppression of racial minorities and immigrant groups."[20] Ultimately, the "superstructural" role of religion is meant to advance America's republican virtues.

Religion also serves an "infrastructural" role in promoting our liberal democracy but one that is constitutionally weak and therefore problematic for encouraging republican character and virtues. For this reason, the "infrastructural" role of religion's work in the state socializes the American people into being law-abiding citizens. Here, too, civil religion works alongside and combines with public theology, although public theology has the advantage. Republicanism permitted the founding of public schools, religious congregations, and communities; eventually, these organizations developed into self-governing bodies.[21] Outside of public schools, "the church" is valuable not only to the process of inculcating moral and spiritual principles but also for teaching individuals the importance of participating in American public life.

Steven Tipton elaborates on this last claim: "Precisely because [religion / religious communities] contributed so centrally to creating the character and consciousness of American citizens and the moral order of life they shared, Tocqueville concluded that religion should be considered the *first* of our political institutions."[22] In other words, religion has a role in nurturing and creating good citizens. Churches generate public theologies that represent American people's "way of life"[23] and in relationship to our political organizations. Said another way, "public theology unfolds as both argument and conversation within communities of faith as well as among them and in their [communities of faith] relationship to public dialogue in the polity."[24] This occurs as diverse public theologies *contest* the *content* of civil religious ideals even though civil religious discourse structures the various moral claims and judgments made by public theology.[25]

Bellah's argument leads to the following point: conflicts around the relationship between church and state could be significantly reduced were people knowledgeable about religion's "superstructural" and "infrastructural" history and roles in the development and survival of our American nation-state. Religion's role can be divisive, but when taken together, the various dimensions of the nation-state—civil religious, national and religious, including the church—can anchor and strengthen religion's role by offering social values and moral commitments that become the cornerstones of community and peoplehood in our nation. Each of these, separately and together, also socialize individuals into the American culture, citizenry, and society.

Thus, the civil religious, communal, and church loyalties of Bald Eagles' white, rural, and Southern residents become exemplars of how "God *and* country" work together to legitimize their region and the nation. In addition to "God and country," "blood sacrifices" tied to religion and land serve that purpose, too.

The town's patriotic character legitimizes the local community and the nation by granting unquestionable spiritual authority to the "martyred dead." This patriotic ethos consists of nationalistic and celebratory displays of American pride that are mainstays of the leadership and authority of rural and white Bald Eagles; such displays unite and fortify the community. Further, the "martyred dead" celebrated on civic holidays and in funeral processions unconsciously transform into "landmark" symbols that come to epitomize regional and American national identities. They validate "who we are" as a "people"—namely, an America that wields military power through social and political hierarchies, an America tasked with realizing national and state interests by securing and protecting our land.

As we shall see in the case studies, though members of the church name other forms of patriotic service to the country beyond military service, for many at Bald Eagles First United Methodist Church and for the rest of the community a soldier sacrificing his or her life in defense of America remains the ultimate form of patriotic service. The *ultimate patriot* is one who gives his or her life as a human "blood" sacrifice in defense of American norms, freedoms, and the nation. Throughout this chapter, white townsfolk imply that fighting war produces "blood" sacrifices—military men (and women) who have died in the line of duty to guarantee the continued existence of our country. Rites of war capture the sacred nature and the civil religious sentiments surrounding such military sacrifices.

In writing about blood sacrifices, the nation, and American civil religion, cultural theorists identify American patriotism as a religion of borders and a religion of blood sacrifices, especially during wartime.[26] Borders are compelling to social theorists because cultural identity and the image of society develops or is particularly and strongly visible at borders, at the limits where territorial edges contain power to reward conformity and to repulse attack. Energy is in unstructured areas.[27] However, defense of borders and territorial edges requires violent "energy" and blood rituals to ensure that nations and social groups endure. Equating nationalism and sectarianism, Marvin and Ingle explain that most people name as morally repugnant those religions that both kill an identified enemy in the name of a deity or deities and those that require self-sacrifice of religious practitioners and devotees.

Yet, moral opposition to violence dismisses a more profound reality. The most deeply committed religious devotees are bound to faith structures that organize killing energy (i.e., violence).[28] In the same way that religions have a violent character, American patriotism possesses a "religious" character with a sacred center for which members of communities willingly kill and die. "What is really true in any community," declare Marvin and Ingle, "is what members can agree is worth killing for, and what they can be compelled to sacrifice their lives for . . . when there is a serious threat."[29] That is to say, during wartime the boundaries surrounding the nation-state and religion collapse. No longer does the nation-state stand for unyielding force and organized religion, unassailable truth. Wartime conditions oblige organized religion and the state to combine their powers. As a result, rituals that celebrate blood sacrifice give expression and witness to faith and sacrificial death that ultimately defines both sectarian faith and national identity.[30] For these reasons and more, American patriotism is a religion of borders and blood sacrifice. And for these reasons and more, as we shall see, often sacred and secular symbols overlap and even become conflated.

In the cases that follow, members of Bald Eagles First United Methodist Church discuss rites of war and the resultant "blood" sacrifices as part of a conversation on the politics of death and patriotic service to the country. Servicemen and servicewomen[31] capture this notion of God and country by being willing to forfeit their lives to preserve constitutional rights, including the guarantees of religious freedom, freedom from want, and freedom from fear[32]—liberties this social group holds at a premium.

The unabashed display of "ancient" landmark insignia (the American flag, the Bible, the cross, and statues of fallen Confederate leaders) in both public and private "ritual" spaces, as well as residents' fearless and strong embrace of legitimizing and landmark social and cultural institutions (family, school, church, government, and military), are "key" symbols that reaffirm the civil religious roots of the community; church members' commitment to their Christian faith and their regional identity; as well as the fight to protect our country. In fact, even in their public critiques of American culture and society, landmark insignias and institutions mostly reign supreme and persist, reinforcing the continued survival of the nation and solidifying national identity.

Thus, the motto "In God we trust" holds dual meaning for this rural, white, and Southern public. A civil religious aphorism, it relates American national identity to the civil liberties and rights identified in the country's landmark and sacred documents. Yet, this catchphrase also expresses the political tradition of American exceptionalism, signaling the country's special place in and mission to democratizing the world. Up to now, this mission has been guaranteed and characterized as *Pax Americana*.[33] However, in 2017, world leaders were noting the demise of *Pax Americana* because national security and other global issues have instead disrupted worldwide peace, precipitating a restructuring of international politics and social orders.

Regarding America's "greatness," white residents of Bald Eagles typically believe and practice a political tradition of American exceptionalism rooted in nostalgia, a tradition that is developed and nurtured via strong ties to local veterans and perpetuated by the family, *inter*generational and *intra*generational memories of townsfolk.[34] Longstanding relationships alongside active "living memories"[35] are instrumental in family members and friends' remembrance of the sacrifices of the living as well as the community's dead, primarily military personnel who fought in World Wars I and II but also in later conflicts. Community stories shared by those whose family members and friends fight in the ongoing War on Terror further sustained the exceptionalist tradition, even if attacks against American interests at home and abroad have declined somewhat.

Ironically, like many citizens throughout the rest of the globe, Americans are living under a permanent state of war because of terrorist activities. Accordingly, the American exceptionalism these residents practice and continue to cherish was fostered in a post-9/11 environment. Residents' interpretation of this American creed has been cultivated in a cauldron of continuous societal, cultural, and global changes instigated and impacted by Islamism, immigration, economic insecurity, cultural pluralism, climate change, and "majority-minority" demographics in the country and abroad.[36] Social ruptures and political upheavals of this nature unlock the potential to elicit an "anti-democratic" reaction from these rural, white Southerners and other segments of the U.S. population.[37] If left vulnerable to war conditions and endless structural shifts, their ideas about America's greatness have the potential to morph into the type of exceptionalism that is directed at *making America great again*.

Good Parenting as Leadership Practice

The first of my case studies on "legitimatizing" and "landmark" institutions is on Burt Harger and Pete Smith. Burt is a seventy-year-old retired Vietnam War veteran who has lived in Bald Eagles, West Tennessee, for twenty-four years. He worked with the state of Tennessee and keeps busy with the men's ministry at the First United Methodist Church. Pete is a wheelchair-bound seventy-eight-year-old World War II veteran. He has lived in Bald Eagles for fifty-eight years, is a retired school teacher, and is actively involved with the men's ministry at the church. As we converse, both men share their views on parenting as a cornerstone of family structure and community leadership, even reaching into the educational realm.

N: Okay, do you think just secular values enter the urban churches and that's maybe one of the reasons why there may be a decrease [in church attendance]? Or should we blame it on street issues?

BURT HARGER: I think just street issues. I can't see just secular values messin' with it that much.

N: Okay.

BH: I think it's street issues. You're talking about the internet and stuff like that. I'm sort of a firm believer in "train up a child in the way he should go and when he's old he won't depart from it" [Proverbs 22:6]. And therein is the absolute major problem that this country faces. It has to do with a lack of parenting.

PETE SMITH: As a school teacher, and working with elementary kids for over twenty years, you can always just look at a child and see whether their parents are involved or not. And, most of the time, I had a special education class that I would teach. I had prekindergartners and kindergartners, and I would teach them skills like if they couldn't walk, couldn't bounce a ball, couldn't jump a rope. To enter my program, I had to go to their home and get permission from their parents. It was unusual for me to realize that, uh, these kids live in homes without screen doors. No screens in the window. I had a third grader and I asked him, "Well, how come you smell so bad?" He said, "Well because the water's fifty feet out the back door." I said, "Well, who's bathing you?" He answered, "My seventeen-year-old sister."

N: Oh.

PS: I said, well, Sammy, I understand. So, I took him into the restroom and I sprayed him pretty good so he could smell pretty good. And, uh, one day, he brought marijuana cigarettes to the classroom, so I took him to the principal. He had a druggist who sold marijuana. So, I just asked him, "Where'd you get it?" He said, "Well this is from my sister's boyfriend's hubcaps." So, we called the sheriff and we had a stakeout. I said, "Sammy, go home and keep your mouth shut, because your life depends on it. If he knew we was rattin' on him. . . . To make a long story short, the boyfriend was arrested and so forth but fled Bald Eagles. He is still in Nashville probably. But that's what Sammy had to deal with—his environment. I realize that all kinds of people have problems. He was a good runner. If you'd let him to take off his shoes, he'd beat everybody! He became a track star! He got a four-year scholarship to college just because he could run.

N: Okay.

PS: So, the hope is that you've managed to instill—even if Sammy was raised by a seventeen-year-old sister—she did the best job she could!

> But that's just pitiful! Broke your heart! But, you don't have a lot of control of things like that, just have to take advantage of what you can.
> N: Okay. I get what you're saying, I get what you both are saying. You think family environment influences membership activity at local churches.

Burt Harger and Pete Smith point to what they consider a major source of lack of leadership in the home, family, church, and community—lack of adequate parenting. Though environment might factor into a child's development, Smith's account tells us that environment does not necessarily determine a young person's destiny. An alternative to Sammy's debilitating home environment is his school setting, where Sammy realizes his gifts and talents. That milieu primes and gives Sammy the blueprint for success; that is where he is "trained" to triumph. In that environment, Sammy encounters his school teacher, Pete, whose religious convictions inform his guidance of Sammy. Although Pete holds a "secular" occupation, his religious practice is not secularized; rather, it is inherent to who he is. It is a byproduct of American society, suggests Tipton, and is—thereby—public. Along those lines, Tipton explains Bellah's understanding of "modern religion."

Modern religion comes at the end of a "religious evolutionary" process relating religion's development to American society. In our fast-paced society, American religion has oriented individuals in church pews toward transcendent truths while holding the family close, forming moral communities made up of people with similar mindsets and social backgrounds, and reaching across a plurality of denominations to gather the faithful together. Moral order remains an enduring feature of American culture, even though American religion has not imposed specific institutional behaviors on this complex society. "However close the meshing of such 'private' religious life with traditional 'overtones of home, mother, and childhood,' religion in America is neither 'privatized' nor captured by a secularized alien culture. American religion is public as well as personal, and religious tradition has generated much of American culture in both realms."[38]

Smith and Harger's religious beliefs and behaviors are not confined to church walls. That is evident from their response to Sammy's case. They are "likeminded" individuals whose religion is both personal and public and whose religion informs and influences their understanding of moral principles and social order. Even if both do not articulate it as such, both men agree that the "traditional" family and schools are institutions that operate to extend religious action in the world. Regardless of the possible "enmeshment" of public and private life, the family and schools remain places where moral values are instilled, resisting the ways in which secular society and culture entrap religion.

Sammy's home experience defies the community's presumptions that the family is a place where moral standards are established and shared, because Sammy's home lacks parental supervision, participation, and leadership. Sammy nonetheless wins a four-year college scholarship. That paves the way for his eventual escape from the dismal conditions of home life as reported by Pete Smith. Smith's religiously inspired actions, although controversial, strengthen Tipton's premise: "Reformed and dissenting Protestantism has played a central role in shaping the ongoing development of modern American society as a whole."[39] As an educator, Smith expresses religiously motivated concern for Sammy because it is evident that Sammy's parents are not involved in giving him guidance and instilling moral values. Smith sounds an "alarm" (i.e., expresses dissent) to alert officials that his parents are missing from Sammy's life.

For Smith and Harger, family and schools are "landmark" and "legitimating" social institutions that furnish not only a moral framework but also the elements to launch a person into successful stable relationships and an emotionally healthy life. Upon further analysis, Sammy's story also answers the question about why urban churches are experiencing a decline in membership. From Smith and Harger's point of view, the church that lacks member participation and engagement is much like the "parent" who fails to participate actively in a child's growth and development.

America the Beautiful's Shrinking Mainline Congregations

My second case is of Abby Taylor, Rebekah Coleman, and Suzanne Dell. At fifty years old, Abby is married with children. A tall, lean woman, she is a hospital professional and homemaker who has lived in Bald Eagles for forty-three years. She is friends with Rebekah, a forty-year-old married mother of three young boys. Though she has lived in the town for only nine years after moving from Memphis, Rebekah is very active in the church. Suzanne is a friend of Abby and Rebekah. She, too, is married, with one child. She is a petite, thirty-nine-year-old homemaker who was born and raised in Bald Eagles; although she left the town for college, she later returned. All three women represent the new generation of leadership emerging at the First United Methodist Church. Here we talk about America's status as a Christian nation and the implications of that for the future.

N: Do you think there's a threat to religion *not* being in our country?

ABBY TAYLOR: I, I think, yes, I think the Christian faith is dwindling. I mean, you know, I mean when you look at things that talk about the numbers of Christians, and, and you know . . .

SUZANNE DELL: What'd that just say, we're not a Christian nation? What did I recently read? We don't consider ourselves a Christian nation? That quote just came out in the news.

REBEKAH COLEMAN: I don't know, but I read that somewhere.

N: Hmm. Okay. So, so there is a threat? I don't wanna put words in your mouth. There's a threat that, we're no longer a Christian nation, or there's a threat that—

REBEKAH COLEMAN: . . . that Christianity might be *taken* out of our nation. I think, permanently.

N: Okay, Okay. But I guess I don't understand where that threat comes from.

ABBY TAYLOR: Well, I mean I don't think that . . . I think it's just that people are falling away from it. You know? You know we just have a lot less Christians in the w—in America now than we did . . .

REBEKAH COLEMAN: Well, and I think statistically speaking, church growth is deteriorating, and new believers, they, everything is just dwindling, the numbers. If you look at the numbers, it's like we're not growing in our religious faith and our churches aren't growing. They're dwindling. I think with that—

ABBY TAYLOR: And part of it [the decline] just, it falls on us, not on . . . I think it's . . . I think as Christians we have to represent the Christian faith. Because if somebody looks at somebody that calls themselves Christians . . . I mean they're out there, just being, I don't know what all. No, just being, *not me*—just, not doing things that you would think of as Christian, you know, just anything. Showing prejudice is one problem or even just . . . there are so many things that people can look at to define a Christian and, people call themselves Christian, but then they're out there trying to scam somebody. Or try, just different . . . there are just so many different things that, that you know [can be a problem] and so I think, so these actions make people that are non-Christians say, "Well why would I wanna do that?" They don't, you know, they're not, so, I think it's our responsibility.

Taylor, Coleman, and Dell are anxious about the potential loss of America's "Christian" character. Spurring their fear are the steadily declining numbers of parishioners in mainline denominations. Findings of the Barna Group and the Pew Research Center—which conduct research at the intersection of society, religion, and culture—support these women's eyewitness accounts of decreasing membership in mainline Protestant churches.

In December 2009, researchers examined the condition of mainline Protestant churches (i.e., United Methodist Church; American Baptist Church, USA; Evangelical Lutheran Church in America; Presbyterian Church, USA; Episcopal Church; United Church of Christ; and others) and found that these denominations had seen a reduction from 80,000 churches at the height of religiosity in the 1950s to around 72,000 congregations by 2009.[40] In that same year, only about 15% of all American adults were affiliated with mainline Protestant traditions, a sharp downturn from 18% in 2007.[41] When the Pew Research Center conducted the 2014 Religious Landscape Study to measure changes in religion across demographic groups and all regions of the country, survey findings attributed a fall in the Christian portion of the population from 78.4% in 2007 to 70.6% in 2014 largely to reductions in Catholic and mainline Protestant shares of the population.[42]

In 2007, approximately 178 million American adults identified as Christian out of a total population of 227 million. Even though the United States experienced population growth between 2007 and 2014 to around 245 million adults (an increase of 18 million people), adults who identified as Christian in 2014 only totaled 173 million people, a net decline of 5 million people to just under 71%. More specifically, the major subgroups within mainline evangelical Protestantism accounted for 41 million members in 2007 as compared to 36 million in 2014, a decrease of 5 million members.[43]

Thus, Taylor, Coleman, and Dell's fears are not unfounded. Their conversation is a reminder that a large segment of the American population regards the church as a legitimizing and landmark institution because of American religions' (especially Christianity's) role in authenticating national and regional identities via civil religious discourse and in producing and maintaining culture and community. Implied in this discussion is their fear of the nation losing its "Christian" character because, as Bellah states, Western Christianity has predominated our interpretation of modern religion in America, and the church has therefore come to symbolize humanity's relationship to ultimate conditions of existence.[44] No one institution holds a monopoly on ultimate conditions of existence; at a certain point human beings must take responsibility for themselves and their behavior and look to a variety of institutions to supply meaning for them and to symbolize ultimate conditions.

Moreover, Taylor, Coleman, and Dell communicate an unstated but underlying anxiety about the nation's multireligious makeup that is all the more pronounced in their post-9/11 world. In truth, America has always been religiously and confessionally plural. When illustrious church historian Sidney E. Mead wrote about what made America unique, he quoted the words of lay theologian and English writer G. K. Chesterton. Chesterton, upon his arrival in America, described the American social experiment as a "nation with the soul of a church" because, at the nation's inception, religious sects were equal to each other and to the civil (i.e., political) authority.[45] And though religious plurality to a certain and large degree conveyed and connoted Christian ecumenism in America's early years, the question of "What is pluralism?" also denoted "many different sects, each a religious interest group, and civil neutrality based on the recognition, as Reinhold Niebuhr put it: [that] 'it is dangerous to give any interest group [in a nation] the monopoly to define the "truth" which was the practice in nations with established churches.'"[46]

Further, in Chesterton's time, religious plurality meant accepting the diverse religions that English settlers and other people brought with themselves from the "old" world to the "new" nation. Mead's writings, and Chesterton's before him, would ultimately chronicle pluralism and religious freedom as core to American ideals and greatness, even if religious, racial, ethnic, and other forms of sectarianism persisted. Yet, because of this nation's spiritual core, America has the fortitude and resources to transcend and to include people's national and religious particularities as they regularly set foot on American shores, arriving from throughout the rest the world in order to become "American."[47]

On a Dot-Com Generation Displacing Moral Leadership, Conduct, and Christian Faith in Modern Society

My third case is of Peter Crockett and Harry Ray. Reared in Bald Eagles, Peter Crockett attended a highly selective American college outside of the area, eventually returning to his hometown after graduation. A self-employed fifty-year-old corporate businessman, he is married and active in his Sunday school class and in programs outside of the church community. Harry Ray is a forty-seven-year-old business executive with a wife and three adopted children. Company moves have exposed him and his family to different parts of the United States, but he always calls Bald Eagles home. For forty years, he has been a resident and is also actively involved in church life.

> N: Do you believe that American culture in forms of the internet, television, videos, and the like affect religious belief and practice, and how?

PETER CROCKETT: Mm. I wish you hadn't thrown in videos. Well, video games *is* I guess what you meant by that.

N: No, I was talkin' about *music* videos, but tell me about video games.

PC: Alright, well, no . . . I just—'cause my son kills more people than, you know . . . (*laughing*) and I think that's not really good for your religious [formation] . . . but that's his pastime.

N: That's his pastime, right?!

PC: Yes, yes. But, well I think it *has* to affect us. I think if you go back to the romantic part of, or you look back at the United States, we had this nice religious culture—I don't know, you're the historian, you probably know a lot better than I do . . .

N: Mm hm.

PC: But it seems like Harry and I grew up in a world where it did . . . you know you watched television if there was something on the three channels to watch, but we don't watch network television anymore. It's not because I have anything against network television, but there's nothing worth watching on network television anymore.

N: You mean in your home?

PC: In our home. Well, I mean, we're on History Channel, we're on Discovery, we're gonna be on something like that; we're not gonna be on ABC, CBS, something like that. It's not because—if there is something like American Idol or something we can sit down and watch with our kids, [then we'd watch it] but there are very few things on primetime television that you want to sit down and watch with your kid. I know like in a lot of families, they do sit down and watch these shows that do affect their view of what's right and wrong. But like I said, my son's not sitting down watching that; he's going in on the computer killin' people. So, I shouldn't be pointing fingers, we're not innocent here, we're part of the problem. But . . .

N: You're the first one that's said that!

PC: But I do feel like it does affect people's ideas of what's right and wrong. The entertainment world, and, they don't, they don't necessarily reflect my ideas of morals. And religion, I guess it flows out; I think it's possible that it doesn't affect my [personal] religious belief and practice. Yet, I can't tell you how it affects it, for sure. But I think it affects society's religious views; it affects their moral views. I think those are pretty connected.

N: Okay, that's what I was about to ask you. So, you see a connection between religion and morality.

HARRY RAY: Very definitely.

PC: Now, we're not perfect, like I said . . .

N: No, no—and that's not, no, it's not a human question; it's more, I think I'm listening, but I think it's more technical than that, you're tying them in . . .

PC: I think your morality is based on your religion, and probably vice versa to some degree. Because if the church is too far from what you think is right and wrong, you're not gonna walk in the door.

HR: If the idea is too radical for you, whatever you think is radical, then you're not gonna stay there. For me, what I see or hear or do not see or hear at this stage of my life doesn't affect me that much; I guess I'm more (*chuckles*), I'm not a finished being by any means, but I'm more . . . I am really glad, though, that the avenues, that some of the avenues and options that are available now weren't available when I was a kid. You know it's one thing to, when I was a kid, to watch the season opener of *Charlie's Angels* and talk about how cool that was and how great that looked; it's another thing now to see the season opener of the latest show and then go on the internet or YouTube and download the opening clip of somebody jumpin' into bed eight or ten times.

I think the repetitive nature of all that has a way of desensitizin' [us], and I think probably the younger people are more susceptible to that than someone our age. But, I mean, now that we can download anything we want to download; now it's more of a "right now" society. Back then, you thought about something, and, say you wanted to go find a picture of a movie star, you'd go to the main store that was open, search through all the magazines, find a picture or two, maybe. Now, you decide you wanna picture of a movie star and see 35,000 of them in the space of about fifteen seconds. It's, I think that kind of thing can desensitize and cloud the morality. So—

In this conversation with Peter and Harry, together we explore the role of American culture on religious belief and practice and find media images bear heavily upon religious thought and moral behavior. Both men agree our contemporary times are different from the past in terms of mass media's influence on American religious and political life. Harry's critique of America's "right now" society is an implied critique of technology's role in aiding people's abuse of web images and downloaded information.

What is most curious about Peter and Harry's discussion is what is left unspoken—the fact that electronic media shapes how people live out a public faith. Mass media's power complicates the degree to which legitimating and landmark institutions function in this community. Religious communities and electronic media are vying for the attention of parishioners—indicating trouble, especially in a place like Bald Eagles where traditionally religious communities live out and embody their faith in public, which informs public rhetoric of religion and influences the moral arguments of public life.[48] Moreover, religious communities and the mass media industry in modern society often have competing interests. Whereas formerly electronic media was in sync with family values, now a simple click of a computer mouse or keypad on a link to the worldwide web opens knowledge seekers to exposure to both desirable and undesirable web material. As such, both Peter and Harry are left to struggle with trying to decide between which of two pressing social issues to be vocal about—sexually explicit images on the television and internet or the pervasive violence in American culture. Both are subjects of heated debates in the public sphere that form the basis of public theological and moral stances in many religious communities.

Furthermore, technological advancements are opening the way for Bald Eagles' church communities, rural Americans, and all others to receive floods of information shaping them in both positive and negative ways. Take, for instance, Peter's son who goes to play (video games) on the computer where he is always "killin' people." Without parental monitoring, Peter questions what values violent computer games might be imparting to his son and what conduct such games might be affirming. Though unstated, I suspect Peter is asking these questions also out of his concern for all American youth.

Media violence is popular and sells because, whether the American public accepts it or not, violence is the greatest threat to the survival of, but also vital to maintaining, social groups.[49] Particularly in cases of groups that participate in rituals of blood sacrifice, people are committed to a system of organized violence that forms and sustains the social group.[50] Some readers might wonder whether Peter's son along with many of America's youth now fascinated with computer gaming are being socialized into and primed for participation in an American civil religious tradition and culture founded upon a religion of blood and sacrificial violence. Media tools and other modern communication technologies constantly rehearse and ritualize structures of sacrifice and their supporting myths.[51] That being the case, mass media can without warning hijack the spiritual and ethical formation of religious believers and other citizens who originate from families that conventionally relied upon the church to assume such socializing roles. What's more, and as indicated by this example, while playing a role in moralizing contemporary political issues, mass media's social influence profoundly complicates and severely constrains the traditional role of religious tradition in legitimizing the community and nation.

Gay Rights Are "the Beginning of the End"

Burt Harger and Pete Smith are veterans more than seventy years old. They are the final case study on "landmark" and "legitimating" institutions and their connection to social authority and leadership. In the following excerpt, they are commenting on how they figure the Bald Eagles First United Methodist Church fits into the wider United Methodist denomination with respect to the gay rights agenda taking shape in America's churches, and with specific focus on the United Methodist Church that at the time of our conversation was discussing this topic throughout the country.

> N: Okay. I also wanted to ask you—the United Methodist Church in *general* is considered a liberal body, and so it's interesting that you had brought up the issue of same-sex unions, same-sex marriage I guess, which is not unique to the United Methodist Church. I mean, we know that that is an issue throughout the country, and Iowa just passed a same-sex marriage law. We'll see if it's gonna end up like California in terms of it being turned back. But I'm wondering how does that impact . . . how do you see this church fitting into the more liberal United Methodist Church?
>
> BURT HARGER: (*chuckling along with Pete Smith*) The way I see it, this church *doesn't*.
>
> PETE SMITH: That's right.
>
> BH: This church is not liberal!
>
> PS: That's right. Not in our age group!
>
> BH: Most of the people that I know, and being fortunate enough to be an usher, I know most of the people, there's not a lot of, there's not a whole bunch of liberals amongst us. Now, there are, there are certainly—I'm liberal—but, you know, I consider myself liberal on some things, but even the liberals, I don't think, are just really big into this gay rights business. But I realize, I realize that we may be the exception to the rule, okay? It's just like—we're Northwest Tennessee, and there again, you're talking conservative from the get-go. And maybe that's what it is. I know the last General Conference in Texas, I think it was, that was a major issue. And, there's enough dissension about it, that it didn't go anywhere.
>
> PS: Okay. Okay. And it's an issue because, because, some bodies are looking to, to have their clergy participate in same-sex marriages?
>
> BH: I wouldn't even go, I wouldn't even narrow it down to that small of a group. I'm just saying with respect to the gay rights whole movement,

we won't have gays as preachers, or gay marriage, we won't have gays
as boy scout leaders, it doesn't go where I'm goin'!
PS: No way!
BH: Okay. So, it's not just limited to same-sex marriage, it's the whole
gay rights, that just—
PS: It's the beginning of an end.

"It's the beginning of an end"—that's how Pete Smith constructs the
gay rights movement. Not immediately clear is what the gay rights agenda
signals the end of—the American church, the family, or the society? He is
not alone in his stance. Identifying himself as more liberal than Pete, Burt
Harger confesses that even liberals at the First do not support same-sex
unions or rights. The reality is that both men identify as theologically and
socially conservative and/or moderate. Neither is liberal with reference
to geographical location—living in Northwest Tennessee. As a result, the
liberal theology of the United Methodist denomination does not super-
sede the more conservative nature of this Southern and rural region.
By default, regional conservatisms have more social and cultural impact on
the First of Bald Eagles than does the moral and religious orientation of the
United Methodist Church.

The First United Methodist Church is a religiously and socially conservative church in a liberal mainline Protestant denomination—regional
alliances are more compelling than are denominational ones. That puts
into context Burt Harger's proclamation: "We're Northwest Tennessee,
and there again, you're talking conservative from the get-go. And maybe
that's what it is." This situation brings up Tipton's critique of "communitarianism."[52] Communitarianism is understood as advancing a dualistic
argument: "Either we are unencumbered selves or we are totally constituted by community. Either justice must be totally dependent on society
or totally independent of society. . . . Communitarianism misses a real
dilemma: that real people can disagree about the good life."[53] Tipton
writes: "[*Communitarianism*] relies on oversimplified consensus models of
culture and community to grasp the nature of moral unity within social
diversity."[54] In other words, the social and theological conservatism of
Northwest Tennessee and Bald Eagles First United Methodist Church
offers a different model for interpreting community, culture, and morality. With this recognition comes the acknowledgment that though this
church's religiously oriented moral positions are opposed to the more
social and theological liberalism of the United Methodist denomination of which it is a member, this church and others like it still contribute to and must not be dismissed from complex and important moral

conversations that are happening. That moral consensus and unity might never be achieved is factual especially when such conversations are occurring in the church and society.

How members of Bald Eagles First, like Pete and Burt, conceptualize the civil and gay rights movement in America is likely in direct opposition to the general sentiments of their denominational body. Both models of community, tensively coexisting, illustrate that consensus models of culture and community are distorted, raising questions of the moral unity of communities while showing evidence for the nature of moral unity as being oversimplified. The heritage of organized religious communities is that they offer religious and moral orientations that invariably affect American social behavior and society.[55] Democratic politics requires both the moral commitments and practices of many and diverse moral communities that comprise our pluralistic culture. Even as the institutional bodies of church and state remain distinct, moral communities can normalize the link between religion and politics via cooperation and overlapping consensus. Only then can their core commitments support rather than subvert democratic politics.[56] A problem surfaces, however, when the communal beliefs and ethics of certain moral communities defy moral mandates for social change.[57] This is made plain in the case of the culturally conservative congregation of the First, whose communitarian responsibilities furnish security, stability, and care of members in the community but also a moral center that could be perceived as resisting social change and thus undermining the efforts of democratic politics.[58]

War Calls for "Blood" Sacrifice and a Belief in Country

My first case study on patriotism is of three men: Larry Jones, Edward Smith, and Campbell Scott. Larry Jones is a married fifty-eight-year-old executive in the banking industry. He moved from Memphis to Bald Eagles eighteen years ago and is more active in the community than the church because of his travel schedule. Edward Smith is in his sixties, married, and a retiree from the service industry. He has always been an active Boy Scout leader. Having himself been a Boy Scout, he believes scouting builds character and leadership in young men and women. He also participates in the Bald Eagles Civitan club for special-needs youngsters and young adults. Another constructive use of his time is spent in church activities. He has lived in the town for thirty-five years. Like Mr. Smith, Campbell Scott is married and a dedicated leader of the Boy Scouts and the Girl Scouts. Scott is a retired human resource manager who spends time in the church and working with the community-oriented Transitions Program that partners with and is a ministry of the Bald Eagles First United Methodist Church. The Transitions Program trains and teaches life skills to formerly incarcerated women.

In the following exchange, all three men regard death on the battlefield while protecting America to be a sacrificial act. They admire and relate this type of death to a strong belief in country. In the midst of conversation, they also point out that Americans have more regard and respect for veterans of the Iraq War than those of the Vietnam War. For them, *special patriots* are men and women who have chosen to serve our country via military duty. Even beyond *special patriots* are those who die on battlefields. These men name them *ultimate patriots*.

> N: How do you define *patriotism*? And if you determine that military service is the highest form of patriotic service to this country, why? But then are there other forms of patriotic service to the country?
>
> LARRY JONES: I guess I haven't thought about that in terms of defining the word. I mean I do believe for a young man or woman to give their life in defense of our country is the ultimate patriotism. I do believe that those people who are put in harm's way are *ultimate patriots*. But we have patriots who are not necessarily in military service. We have patriots that are in the intelligence [i.e., CIA]. We have patriots that are the in foreign diplomatic corps. *It is a belief in country*. But the *ultimate patriot* is the one who gives her life for the country. They may disagree with why they're there. But theirs is ultimately not to question. It's to defend the interpretation [of the events or the law]. So, you can be a patriot and not be a military person. But *the ultimate patriot* is the one who is willing to give their life for the freedom of others. Whatever you define that to be.
>
> EDWARD SMITH: I think patriotism to me is generally love of country, it's a love of your country. I agree with Larry. You don't have to be a military person to be a patriot. But those military people are *special patriots*, and the ones that give the ultimate sacrifice are heroes; they really are. I've not served in the military, but several of my brothers have and many friends. It's a sacrifice. And it's something that I truly, truly appreciate as an American. And I'll be honest with you, since the first Iraq War, I travel a lot. I run into those guys in airports. I try to always go up and thank them for their service. And my wife tries to buy 'em lunch (*laughing*). But it—patriotism—to me is love of country.
>
> N: Okay, okay.
>
> CAMPBELL SCOTT: I agree with you both. I'm amazed, however, that just a few years back when people came home from Vietnam we didn't

have that, or whatever it was, we didn't appear to have that collective attitude towards our military when they did the very same thing. But they rank up there very, very high. Training to die must be part of the military process, but I've never been in the military either. The U.S. military must have a tremendous method of driving the whole [system] or embedding that whole idea because a man just doesn't want to go out and get himself killed. It's almost as if you have to learn that; and they learn that as part of training in the military. And that's a sacrifice they make. And the amazing part is there are people who went to Iraq, came home, re-upped, and went back again—a do over, a repeat. And that's amazing. But it is a love that they must have that we can't even comprehend. But, and I agree with Edward, Sue does the same in airports and stops; she'd be hurrying through but she'd find the time to walk and give everybody a hug.

Marvin and Ingle propose that violence unifies social groups and that blood sacrifices hold societies together.[59] Totem myths are creation-sacrifice stories with corresponding group-forming rituals that give rise to group identity. These myths give meaning to and are organized around violent events to which blood sacrifices are central. With respect to American experience, the American flag is the sacred totem-object (in totem taboo theory), around which war as ritual sacrifice is fought in order to maintain the groups that constitute our national identity.

"The flag soldiers carry into battle signifies their willingness to go to the border and die."[60] The sacrality of the flag is marked by patriotic rituals producing a reverence and respect comparable to the Christian cross that Jesus carried that

> stands at the border between life and death and also signifies sacrificial willingness, and recalls the origins of European nation-states within the sacrificial systems of Christianity. The myth of the sacrificed Christ who dies for all men makes every sacrificed soldier a remodeled Christ dying to redeem his countrymen. Every soldier becomes a redemptive sacred figure to subsequent generations of celebrants.[61]

Border regions mark the crossroads of death and life. The border region is where the group (i.e., Americans) will ritually defend what it means to be a group and where members will sacrifice themselves in order for the survival of the group. Border experiences facilitate group sorting, enable designation of an enemy, and distinguish between Us and Them. Moreover, border experiences are transformational. At the border, the American patriot is akin to the religious devotee who violently sacrifices his body in the act of crossing over into death.[62] Sacrificial death creates an in–group experience, a kind of loyalty to which soldiers pledge themselves. Implicit to the sacrificial pledge of the few is the longevity of the many, solidifying group identity. At the crossover point, the human transforms into divine, the profane turns into sacred, and the center shifts to the periphery.

Larry Jones and his friends speak of the *ultimate patriot* in honorific terms because the *ultimate patriot* is a border crosser. He is the "insider" who has been changed into and consequently dies as the sacrificial outsider because we construct our identity as a nation from the flesh and blood of sacrificial group members.[63] By succumbing to death at the border, the soldier displays *belief in country*, morphing into the transformed totem, not unlike the revivified totem of Christianity identified as the risen Christ.[64] His soldiers' willingness to submit to death renders him holy. That being so, the military dead are totem objects who legitimize the nation through rituals of war that make them blood sacrifices, paving the way for national restoration throughout and at the culmination of war.

Periodicity implies regularity, connoting cyclical and seasonal occurrences; something that happens at regular intervals is a function of periodicity. Hence, periodicity is one quality of ritual life, and war is very much a part of the activities that characterize the spheres of life of highly ritualized humanity and societies.[65] In fact, significant "bloodletting" is one feature that makes war ritually successful.[66] The "identity-producing" blood sacrifices of Southerners are kept alive because they exercise the practice of sharing public and social memories of soldiers whose lives were lost in previous wars even as far back into the past as the war between the Confederacy and the Union.[67] "Though competing histories of bloodletting continue to vie for Southern loyalty and identity," comment Marvin and Ingle, "it is fair to say that blood sacrifice to the nation as a whole has become the primary sacrificial identity of Southerners"[68] and particularly because of the Confederate states' shocking losses during the Civil War. Such devastating losses facilitated white Southerners' ability to maintain a separate identity despite the United States being a single nation whose identity had been forged in the blood of its own.[69] Eventually, the pain of losing would recede from public memory due to the progression of time and Southerners fighting on behalf of the United States in more recent wars.

Nonetheless, regionally speaking, the *ultimate patriot* is an adaptable and modern metaphor for the many rural and white (male) Southerners who have gone to war and died on behalf of their regional identification, commitments, *and* belief in country. National restoration happens when remaining community members and citizens of the nation communicate shared meanings and social memories of the "blood" sacrifices of fallen combatants and heroes. Such sacrificial acts unleash regenerative power.[70] "In the funeral ritual, the dead warrior will be reassimilated and transformed from a father owed for sacrifice who needs future blood tributes, into a child embodying the renewed life of the community, on whom its future depends," because the border also defines and encircles the generative center of community and the universe from which the "violent" dead have been expelled.[71] Hence, the meaning that Larry Jones, Edward Smith, and Campbell Scott place on the "blood" sacrifices of *ultimate patriots* exemplifies how a politics of patriotic death reveals itself as civil religious behavior simultaneously reaffirming and validating the Bald Eagles community and the U.S. nation. Indeed, "boys become men by touching death."[72]

"Patriotism's Gotta Be Something You Live"

Earlier we encountered Peter Crockett and Harry Ray. Both are business executives and are of similar age. In the following excerpt, Peter and Harry elaborate on patriotism and the salience of the flags in the sanctuary.

> PETER CROCKETT: To answer your question, I think patriotism goes way beyond military service. Military service is a wonderful way to show patriotism, expression of your patriotism, assuming that's the reason you're there. But, I think supporting your country, not blind support, but supporting your country, a healthy support for your country, is patriotism. Being involved at least to some degree in the goings on of your community, your country, whatever government level you wanna work in, is an expression of patriotism. I think anything you do to promote the country is an expression of patriotism. So I'd think military service is one aspect; I'm not sure that most people in the military—most might not be right, but a good number in the military—are there for patriotic reasons. Or is it that they're just shopping? I don't know, I don't have the answer to that. It'd be interesting to survey that.
>
> HARRY RAY: Well, job training, last chance—
>
> PC: Exactly, there's lot of reason to . . .
>
> HR: Patriotism is not the reason for them.
>
> PC: And not that they don't love the country as much as me, but is that reason enough?
>
> HR: I don't know. I think military service is and can be *a* sign of patriotism, but not necessarily *the* sign of patriotism. I heard a statement in

a movie one time, and it's one of these things that in an odd moment it brings it into focus. And, it defines for me what I believe; *patriotism is a way of life. It's an attitude, it's a feeling. Patriotism is—if you hear somebody doing or saying something that makes you so mad you can't see straight, but yet you're willing to fight and die if necessary for their right to keep doing it—that's patriotism.* Patriotism can't be just a Sunday afternoon feelgood. *Patriotism's gotta be something you live.* I mean I tell you somebody can get up and exercise free speech about how they wanna bomb the Pentagon, well, I hate it. I think they oughta be boiled, but the fact is we gotta be willin' to fight for their right to do that or patriotism doesn't mean anything. So, that's my thoughts on it.

N: Okay. I think the example about bombing is an extreme, so I won't use that, but I'm wondering: Can you criticize your country, but still love your country?

PC / HR: (*in unison*) Absolutely.

HR: I think it's your responsibility to criticize what's not working right. That's how it gets better.

N: Okay, okay. Allow me to ask you some other questions. So, when I walk into the First on Sunday morning, I see the American flag to my left and the Tennessee and Christian flags to my right. You know, wherever I'm sitting, that's how it is. The first question is: What does that mean to you to have the American flag, the Tennessee flag, and the Christian flag in your worship space?

HR: Is the Tennessee flag there?

N: Uh, it was there a while ago, or maybe it's not there. Maybe it's just the Christian flag.

HR: I think it's just the Christian flag.

N: Okay, well the American flag and the Christian flag, but what does it mean for those flags to be in your worship space? How do you understand that?

PC: I rarely recognize they're there. But, I think that, if they're there, that at least that historically they're there, it just shows they support the church as another American institution that supports the country. As well as communicating Christianity. I don't know that there's, I wouldn't read a lot into them being there, personally.

HR: No, in fact it's, to me I mean, not so much the flag, itself, *but the fact that it can be there is a reminder to me that we can come to a place and worship in the open with our symbols important to us all out in front of us, and we don't have to hide them under the floorboards or hide them in a case somewhere. That we can, we can do that and have the Bible and the cross and everything out in the open. They can sit there in a prominent place. That*

says a lot to me for the freedom that we've got. So . . . but, I can't honestly
say that I sit there and think about, "Oh, there's the American flag.
I'm reverent for it." But I think it very much belongs because it's a
representation that we, here, can do that.

N: Okay, so it's an identification of being American *and* Christian.

PC: Yes, and the freedom to be able to profess that.

Harry explains his perspective on patriotism by saying: "Patriotism is
a way of life. It's an attitude, it's a feeling." Patriotic talk elicits a swell of
emotions in Harry. Such intensity is revealed in his statement about the
abuse of U.S. constitutional rights. Love of country should encourage a
person to defend and die for the right of fellow citizens to exercise their
freedoms, even if such liberties infringe upon this selfsame person and
seem to dishonor what it means to be American. Hence, Harry's response
to patriotic behavior is: "If you hear somebody doing or saying something
that makes you so mad you can't see straight, but yet you're willing to fight
and die if necessary for their right to keep doing it—that's patriotism."

This opinion about the patriotic nature of supporting the right to
free speech is addressed in ritual studies. For in describing ritual, distinguished anthropologist Roy Rappaport highlights the performative
nature of speech.[73] His definition of *ritual* is "speech acts" whereby "rituals 'say something' about the state of the performer and 'do something'
about it."[74] That being so, the fundamental function of ritual is to initiate
transformation of ritual participants by virtue of connecting both saying
and doing. The messages being performed and communicated are key
to bringing about change; yet, in a seeming paradox, ritual performance
of speech acts is dependent *not* on belief but on *acceptance and conformity*
to these speech acts.[75] Rappaport asserts that "the acceptance indicated
by liturgical [i.e., ritual] performance, being independent of belief can
be more profound than conviction or sense of certainty, for it makes [it]
possible for the performer to transcend his or her own doubt by accepting . . . it."[76] In that case, although Harry does not necessarily believe in
unrestrained free speech—say, to the point of an individual expressing a
desire to bomb the Pentagon—Harry *does accept* freedom of speech as a
constitutional right, so much so he would willingly defend the individual's constitutional right to unrestrained and free expression even if he
disagrees with its content. As a result, speech acts as ritual performance
support Harry's words despite Harry's doubts about making civil religious
American patriotism something that a person "lives."

Further, Harry and Peter risk making the claim that a patriotic person
has a duty to criticize the country if problems arise resulting from unfair

policies and unjust social systems. Such thinking feeds into a discussion about the meaning of flags in the church. Though they confess to having paid little attention to the public display, Harry and Peter declare that the American and Christian flags, like the other sacred symbols such as the Bible and the cross, guarantee freedom of religious expression. He celebrates "that we can come to a place and worship in the open with our symbols important to us all out in front of us, and we don't have to hide them under the floorboards or hide them in a case somewhere."

In studying the symbolic nature of culture, anthropologist Sherry Ortner labeled the American flag a summarizing "key" symbol. The flag is a "key" symbol of this community because it is embedded with cultural meaning. As a "summarizing" key symbol, it represents and condenses the emotions, ideas, values, and attitudes of the people of Bald Eagles. Summarizing symbols operate by centering and focusing power on respondents. These convergent powers consequently impact the recipient. In this way, major commitments take shape and crystallize because the symbols speak primarily to people's attitudes.[77] The American flag is a key and summarizing symbol, yet Harry's and Peter's exuberance concerning its placement in the church sanctuary raises a moral dilemma about America's civic republic and liberal democracy and religion's divisive role in navigating the tension. The presence of the cross, Bible, and Christian and American flags in the sanctuary of the First testifies to a republican tradition of self-government, where religious freedom presumes the spirit of an American republic that, with the governance of citizens, conceives and decides on the meaning of the common good.[78] In this case, the flag's prominence in the sanctuary, and in most churches throughout Bald Eagles, speaks for the common good. Nonetheless, a competing liberal tradition of American democracy ensures that the practice of religion is unencumbered by a political state and that people are allowed to choose their own values and ends,[79] thus protecting against imposition of religious values on others. That mandate includes and covers *all* congregational members. One cannot infringe upon the rights of others even if individuals share the same belief system.

The American flag's placement not only sparks debate about the ways in which religion is politicized at the First and throughout Bald Eagles but also reveals the dialectical nature of civil religion. It is a conflictual landmark and legitimizing symbol in this community of rural, white, Southern, and Christian believers because its presence promotes, conflates, and confuses profound and varied moral, civic, and democratic traditions. Still, it is plausible to support the flag's existence in the church sanctuary by using Rappaport's ritual typology to interpret its placement in this space. Rappaport's three-level typology can refer to ritual beyond "techniques of the body"[80] to include *high-order meaning*. High-order meaning produces a "unitive consciousness,"[81] meaning that it unifies ritual participants and grounds group identity.

This "unitive consciousness" can be likened to Durkheim's "social effervescence," which is the emotional state precipitated by ritual actions of social collectives that engenders social solidarity from among individual members who adopt group culture. In doing so, the group creates both moral and social bonds and orders. I argue similarly for the mystical potential of the American flag in the church's space. Its centrality to ritual life at the First and its pervasiveness in church sanctuaries in the city and the county of Bald Eagles is incontestable. The moral center of ritual life at the First is the church's sanctuary. Positioning the American flag in the worship space and at the center of the church's ritual life around which members repeatedly gather is a pivotal decision.

The American flag is a symbol that induces collective emotions and produces social cohesion. By virtue of such social bonds, the group is capable of subsuming individual concerns. That the American flag is found in so many spaces is a measure of its mystical power and significance. Symbolically it straddles the *middle- and high-order meanings* of Rappaport's typology.[82] Creative expressions and symbolic meanings are primary to *middle-order meaning*. Surrounding ritual's "techniques of the body" are the likes of art, poetry, and music, from which symbolic meaning is extracted. Even if the repetitive nature of ritual does not convey much information, it does "link realms of experience and feeling that might have become disconnected in the daily activities of life."[83] The American flag might not be artwork, but it is a landmark and a legitimating American artifact laden with real and symbolic meaning.

By straddling both levels of meaning, the American flag's placement in Bald Eagles' churches, while at times contentious, not only reaffirms the identity of these rural, Southern, and Christian whites but also forms society. Having it positioned in church settings defines Bald Eagles as a church and civil religious community where "patriotism's gotta be something you live."

"I'm a Patriot . . . I Hear 'The Star-Spangled Banner' and I Get Tingles"

Amanda Martinez—a seventy-one-year-old white woman, retired educator, and Hispanic Lay Missioner for the Memphis Conference—speaks with Mary Elizabeth Worthington, a fifty-six-year-old church employee who is director of Christian education at the First. In this final case study on American patriotism at the First, both women engage me in a conversation about the ways in which the U.S. Pledge of Allegiance, public prayer, and "The Star-Spangled Banner" serve as patriotic and legitimizing rituals that honor constitutional principles. In relationship to war, these three landmark (i.e., historic and national) symbols reinforce what it means to be American. The two women nevertheless conclude: "War isn't good. . . ."

N: How do you define *patriotism*? If you say that military service is the highest form of patriotism, tell me why. However, are there other forms of patriotic service to this country?

AMANDA MARTINEZ: Do I think that military service is the highest form of patriotic service to the country?

N: Please also include your definition of patriotism.

AM: That's not my definition of patriotism. *My definition of patriotism is that I believe in a country that wants to be fair to everybody, to give everybody a chance. My idea of patriotism is that we go to unbounded lengths to look for peace instead of going to war.* And I don't think the American flag should be in the sanctuary. I don't believe there should be prayer in school. I don't believe that's what made us behave ourselves. As a child, we would read the one hundredth Psalm, a thousand times (*mumbling a rote prayer*), and then we said the Pledge of Allegiance and then sat down. I think that if we're going to do something, then we should have the Pledge of Allegiance, every day. *Then children would know the reason why they say the Pledge of Allegiance. That you are in this school because people have paid their taxes and that the country is interested in everybody having an education.* And prayer, I can pray any place, and I used to tell my students. This is a way I would get around that. I would say, "You will now have a moment of silence." And I would always tell the students we're going to have a moment of silence. I would also say, "I know what I'm going to do during the moment of silence. You may do anything except disturb me while I'm doing it." You must be silent, you must be silent, that's right. And you can do what I do, and it was very obvious what I was doing. *I would bow my head and I would pray for those students for that day, which I think is very important. But that is something that you would know.*

N: So, in other words you're saying that military service for you is not necessarily the highest form of patriotism?

AM: No, and at the same time I had two husbands that were in the military, and I had three children who were in the military. *And they were all extremely glad that they had been in the military and thought that it was a good idea for young people to go into military service. That, that was a wonderful growing-up opportunity.* On the other hand, I had a husband who had a complete nervous breakdown because during the Korean War he was the first gunner on a destroyer. And he said the noise of that gun just, you know . . . and they were in waters where they shot and they knew that they had hit submarines and that they couldn't tell whether it was theirs [i.e., the Koreans] or ours. And things like that. And I don't think, *war isn't good, it doesn't do good things to people.*

N: So what I'm hearing you say is, for you, patriotic service is true equality. That is, everyone having an opportunity.

AM: And voting, voting, everybody needs to vote.

N: Okay, so having a voice in whom our representatives are going to be. Okay, alright, that's totally different, I like it. What about you, how do you define *patriotism*? And are there other forms outside of military service?

MARY E. WORTHINGTON: I would agree with everything that Amanda said. I would add to that, that you know there's some countries where I believe after high school you're required to give two years of service to your country. Now, it does not necessarily mean military service, it can be service in community renewal; it can, you know. But I think that that would be a good thing for us to have, before we go to college that we give our country two years. I think we'd be a better people for that. I'm not one of these, I certainly don't believe in my country right or wrong. *I'm a patriot. I mean I definitely have a sense of patriotism. I hear "The Star-Spangled Banner" and I get tingles, you know.*

N: *Why do you get tingles?*

AM: *I always have. I mean, it's my country.* And as bad as the things we have done, I realize we have done horrible things in our history. However, I think that we've been driven by a desire to do right. *A desire for goodness, I guess.* I don't think that we were founded by, that our Founding Fathers were . . . you know most of them were deists.

N: They *were* deists. Yes, they were. Most people don't realize that. God is out there, but he doesn't . . .

MEW: Right. I know, and I get so mad because you know: "established a Christian *nation*." Well no, they established a nation where there's freedom of religion. You know, and this may be going into the second part, but I think it's real interesting—

N: Which is, does your faith, since you're going to let me segue, does your faith influence your understanding of patriotism? How? Then go ahead.

MEW: Okay. It's real interesting to me that the Methodist Church in America, and America as a nation took place at basically the same time in history.

N: In terms of birthing.

MEW: Uh-huh, yes. And that the structure of the Methodist Church is very much like the structure of our government.

N: So there's a judicial branch, an executive branch, and a legislative branch.

MEW: Right, yeah. And I think that growing up Methodist and growing up American kind of blends together in me. That respect for other religions, it's Methodist but it's also American you know. There's just a lot of things that I think like that, that it just kind of—and I think it may have to do with that birth, like you said, birthing of both around the . . . because this was like the age of reason, you know. And—

N: Yeah, exactly, we have a rational God who doesn't interfere in the affairs of the world; it's our responsibility. Go ahead.

MEW: Yeah. Well that's basically it.

N: Okay. Let me ask you the second part of that question that isn't there, which you had actually brought up. The impetus for this is the fact that in both the churches that have been my study churches, some version of the American flag is present in the sanctuary. I think for my black church it's the American flag, the Tennessee flag, and the Christian flag. So how do you understand the presence of the American flag in the sanctuary?

MEW: Well, I don't think it should be there.

N: You too? Tell me why. [Amanda had supplied me with the same answer.]

MEW: It's there because of our World War II veterans who want it there.

N: Okay, and tell me why they want it there.

MEW: Because when they were fighting, and I respect those men, they weren't just fighting for America, they were fighting for . . . I mean, I guess you know fighting for their church. And I guess we all were. I mean we all were, that's how you get into the freedom of religion. But I think when you stick the flag in the church that you cross the line between freedom of religion. I mean you're putting the government into the church.

Amanda Martinez' understanding of patriotism is that it ensures peace, mitigates suffering, and provides equality of education. These are the moral and civic values that the practice for which saying the Pledge of Allegiance stands. For her, public prayer is not an open demonstration of commitment to land and country. Rather, her moment of silence recognizes American plurality and desires the best of and for all children. Military service is patriotic service; but her husband's account of wartime conditions, which unquestionably involved brushes with death and indeed killing, colors Amanda's evaluation about war not being "good" and "not do[ing] good things to people."

On the other hand, Mary Worthington's patriotism would require each young person after high school graduation to serve the country in some way; service could include teaching in marginalized areas as a form of community renewal. Despite America's present problems, racial history, and record of human rights violations, Worthington is convinced the American public is motivated to do right; she consequently admits to feeling tingles upon reciting and hearing "The Star-Spangled Banner."

In responding to the question of American patriotism as civil religion, both women's accounts of American civil religion are dialectical. Their answers show there is no commonly agreed upon interpretation and explanation of this national faith, although civil religion is illustrative of socially constructed realities. In other words, each woman's social interactions— whether at church, home, or school—frames and determines how each one makes meaning in her social world. Socially constructed realities translate into ideas about what holds Americans together as citizens and a nation.

In the early 1970s, Martin Marty wrote about two kinds of civil religion. The *priestly* mode of a "nation under God" celebrated national identity, meaning, and purpose while highlighting the promise of America.[84] Worthington's perception of a "powerful" and "good" America supports this idea. By contrast, the *prophetic* articulation of a "nation under God" promotes the idea of a God as both overseer and judge of the American nation. This articulation embraces ecumenicity as the meaning of America.[85] Martinez' concept of a civil religion that ensures equality for everybody, rejects war for peace, and sees voting as an exercise of political freedom is an example of this idea. Each woman's evaluation of American patriotism as civil religion differs; yet there is consonance to their thinking.

Deeper analysis suggests that both women would agree with the following premises: that love of country does not demand blind allegiance or "blood" sacrifices and that showing profound respect for national symbols like "The Star-Spangled Banner" validates who we are as Americans. As it happens, Rappaport would name the singing of "The Star-Spangled Banner" a *speech-act*. He terms this type of speech-act a "factive." Factives are ritual performances that bring about a new personality and future for the performers—that is, a new state of affairs.[86] Martinez and Worthington both describe participation in singing "The Star-Spangled Banner" as producing "tingles" in them. The anthem's ability to produce "tingles" is a result of

"the factiveness of ritual acts and utterances [to] include the magical power
of words. Ritual words do, after all, bring conventional states of affairs, or
'institutional facts' into being, and having been brought into being they
are as real as 'brute facts.'"[87] The magic of "The Star-Spangled Banner"
lies in the words. The lyrics have two forces: "illocutionary" force, which
is the ability to effect new conditions, and "perlocutionary" force,[88] meaning the ability to persuade, convince, scare, enlighten, and otherwise affect
those listening. This leads to the following conclusion: when Martinez and
Worthington participate in and speak the lyrics or "magical words" of "The
Star-Spangled Banner," this ritual act contains the emotional force to precipitate the "tingles." Such ritual acts have the potential to transform and
bring together all ritual participants for they cement social bonds, hierarchy, arrangements, and orientations—which is its illocutionary force. They
reaffirm national and regional identity in the Bald Eagles community. That
is its perlocutionary force. Therein lies the strength of such civil religious,
historic, and national symbols.

Our conversation ends by deciphering the presence and meaning
of the flags in the First's worship space. World War II veterans, we learn,
are the inspiration behind the display of flags in the sanctuary. For this
population, the national and Christian flags symbolize two struggles—
the fight for country (i.e., to preserve constitutional freedoms) and the
fight for the church (i.e., religious freedom). Even though their views
prevent these two women from being included in the following assessment, we still leave the conversation extrapolating that most parishioners
have no problem inserting national symbols of the state into their private
religious spaces. Seen from a global perspective, the fact that these symbols are in worship spaces suggests that God is on America's side, further
fortifying the capacity of national and civil religious symbols to represent
"God and country."

Ancient Landmarks in Legitimizing
an American Nation at War

Institutional life and patriotism are inextricably joined for most Southern,
white, evangelical Christian, and rural dwellers of Bald Eagles. Each mirror the other. Landmark and legitimating symbols like the American flag,
the Pledge of Allegiance, and "The Star-Spangled Banner" are patriotic
identifiers that sustain and support leadership of institutions like family,
church, school, and military, among others. These legitimating institutions, in turn, stabilize landmark-oriented and summarizing key symbols.
Legitimizing institutions and landmark or national symbols fortify and

strengthen the morality, values, social norms, and identity of whites in this rural community.

For members of Bald Eagles First United Methodist Church, of utmost importance is protecting the rights of fellow Americans regardless of their ideologies and especially if such beliefs are contrary to their own religious, moral, and political stances. Here is the crux of civil religion as American patriotism for Bald Eagles' white residents, captured by the emotion-laden sentiments of Harry Ray, who declares his devotion in his willingness to fight for those with whom he disagrees: patriotism does not mean anything if he is unwilling and does that which is contrary.

Among congregants living in an American nation permanently at war, "God and country" means that patriotism is embodied in and produces American exceptionalism. It has to be something that all Americans live. Patriotism lives *in* landmark "national" symbols like the American flag and regional monuments, identifying religious and other freedoms guaranteed by our nation-state and experienced in our particular locales. It lives *through* legitimizing institutions like the family, school, church, and military—institutional anchors of American society. It lives *with* religious, racial, ethnic, class, and other tensions challenging our ecumenicity and multivocality, illuminating our equivocality, and calling into question our country's "goodness." It *demands* the "blood" sacrifices of a group willing to forfeit their lives to uphold the rights and responsibilities of a republican and liberal American democracy.

7

Black Patriotism and
Bloodstained Loyalty
Tabernacle Missionary Baptist Church

American civil religion selectively borrows beliefs, rituals, symbols, and myths from evangelical Protestantism in an effort to create a cohesive America. By doing so, it gives political legitimacy to the nation-state by implying that its citizens share its spiritual foundation, values, and moral principles. Yet salvation and religious sectarianism are not American civil religion's aims, even if it appropriates the vernacular of Protestantism. Instead, the goal of America's tradition of civil religion is a political process in which ostensibly God's will is carried out on earth, thus involving American civil religion in the most critical moral, religious, ideological, and political issues of a historical period.[1] Yet, this 1967 definition is not the only possible understanding of American civil religion. In *The Broken Covenant* (1992), Bellah would later offer another description of American civil religion, defining it as "that religious dimension, found in the life of every people, through which it [i.e., the people] interprets its historical experience in light of transcendent reality."[2] By not exclusively tying the concept to Protestantism, both nontheistic and other theistic variants of civil religion are included, while holding more closely to the phenomenological and sociological (i.e., Durkheimian) roots of the term.[3]

Indeed, blacks practice many regional and racial varieties of civil religion in rural Bald Eagles, where evangelical faith traditionally supports their civil religious and moral commitments. Yet these rural blacks derive their interpretations of Southern civil religion and therefore their view of and connection to transcendent reality from their historical and contemporary racial experiences in America. Such experiences both differ from, are conversant with, and yet at times also at odds with those of their white counterparts.[4] Many instances indicate regionalism as the tie that binds together both communities of rural and Southern whites and blacks, a regionalism usually displayed when they share similar civil religious sentiments and convictions. However, there are many more situations in which the racialized experiences of these black Baptists reinforce the "various deformations and demonic distortions"[5] that American civil religion—like all religions—has suffered.

In this chapter, I investigate how members of Tabernacle Missionary Baptist Church construe ideas about larger society, the black family, and leadership in the local community as such construals relate to their practice of civil religion formulated as ritualistic expressions of American patriotism. Black leadership and social behavior and activities are characterized as values driven, in-group oriented, and generationally linked with a focus on church, community, and the wider American society. By highlighting three church conversations and case studies about leadership, authority, and community in black Bald Eagles, the connections between those qualities are demonstrated.

A "nation-based paradigm of race"[6] partially explains why values-driven and in-group-oriented leadership and social practices operate within the everyday lives of these Southern black and Christian rural dwellers. Though they are residents of the community and citizens of the United States, they still exist in a social world or land that is often disconnected from their white counterparts. In offering this paradigm, sociologists of race Michael Omi and Howard Winant suggest that race is a master—though not a transcendent—category that profoundly and doggedly shapes the history, politics, polity, economic structure, and culture of the United States.[7] While this approach intimately connects race and nation through the concept of peoplehood, Omi and Winant observe the irony and problem with "race as peoplehood." That is, from the nation's founding and settlement, American social collectivity—encapsulated in the phrase "We the People"—has been metaphorically designated as a white nation.

Race as peoplehood employs a racial schema that distinguishes between oppressors and the oppressed, colonizers and the colonized, the "free" and the enslaved, and thus whites and other groups of people.[8] As such, the idea of "We the People" demands an Anglo-conformity that whites developed categorically and exclusively into a national image and culture of whiteness. Equating a multinational, multiethnic, multicreedal country to "whiteness" leads to questions raised by the likes of W. E. B. Du Bois as early as 1903 ("Your country? . . . How came it [to be] yours? . . . Before the Pilgrims landed we were here . . .")[9] or questions issued in 2015 ("What about the others?").[10] The trope of America as a white nation is paradoxical, for it represents both *nation building* and the zeal of the pioneering spirit to open up new frontiers and borders, contributing to social cohesion and national unity; but it is also the site of *racial division* that persistently dismisses, disregards, violates, and negates "other" races and ethnicities.[11]

This "nation-based paradigm of race" is the hallmark of the practice of black patriotism in this town of Bald Eagles, where black residents exhibit a high regard for democratic principles. For black townsfolk, the countercultural spaces where American liberty and equality—and where the exercise of rights and responsibilities—are played out are the black family, church, and community, and the military. The military was one of our nation's first social institutions to recognize the humanity, dignity, and equality of black "men," and this has translated into an equity that this racial group previously had not experienced, even though such equity was deformed by segregation in the early to mid-twentieth century and not maintained upon a black soldier's return after war. Even if being American born was not enough to be a racial equalizer, service to the country, to the point of death, was.

African American cultural and social memory surrounding military service sustains these black and rural Christians, even when such collective memories falter in the face of America's present social crisis and failure to attract large numbers of young blacks to military service. The inability to attract young blacks to military service is due in part to a breach in American democratic principles that regards black life as questionable and valueless, a contention supported by mass incarceration of and state violence against black bodies.

Wartime rites protect against invasion and enforce the safekeeping of geographic *borders*. Borders, as I explained in the previous chapter, define social identity and describe social belonging: that is, who we say we are and who can count as American. For these African Americans, such safeguarding comes at the price of blood(stained) devotion to a country that many times dishonors the birthright and territorial inheritance of American blacks.[12] Birthright claims are claims to nationhood justified and guaranteed by our country's highest and most sacred civil religious documents.

Territorial inheritance has to do with the benefits that accrue to those within a land's borders. In public talk the blending of "citizen" and "border" implies that "citizen" is fundamentally a legal status but sociologically and at its base is about social belonging and community recognition of membership by others.[13] "Even the legal status of citizen depends implicitly on borders and their meaningfulness in defining 'homeland.' Borders, when meaningfully regulated by sovereign authority, separate peoples and delimit cultures, all of which works to guarantee identities."[14] In other words, U.S. borders secure the full rights and responsibilities of American citizenship. However, what these black, rural, and southern Baptists communicate about their citizenship through "blood"(stained) patriotic narratives is a liminal identity (i.e., betwixt and between) based on their experience with and lack of surety about a homeland that both tolerates racial division *within* U.S. borders and fails to advocate for their status as full members of American society. Although black Americans are located within the confines of U.S. borders, their imposed ambiguous identity ensures and shows that they are still not being recognized as truly American.

The civil religion of black, rural, southern Baptists in Bald Eagles represents a metaphorical "one nation under God" that challenges and calls for social change of historically sanctioned legal and physical segregation as well as other social injustices that deny these blacks' humanity. At the heart of their public theology of war is *not* dichotomy but rather dialectic. For "liberty and justice for all" under the banner of one nation under God explicitly captures aspects of America's covenants—the Declaration of Independence and the Constitution, *for which* they would willingly offer their blood(stained) devotion and *to which* they would sacrificially give their lives. For these Southern, black, and rural church folk, the four case studies on black patriotism in this chapter express what it means to be a *soldier forever*—namely, service, allegiance to one's racial and cultural group, and readiness to abandon one's life and livelihood to a higher purpose, cause, or calling. These elements contribute to their religious and moral vision of a good society.

This vision is put on full display when they enact particular patriotic beliefs and embody practices that endeavor to answer the following questions: What activities connote service to this country? Why have these black and rural Baptists introduced nation-state symbols into their worship spaces? To what degree does military service and the ultimate sacrifice of willingly giving up one's life become an expression of black patriotism? How do they maintain their blood(stained) loyalty in the face of America's "broken" covenant with them? What do their public theologies of war and civil religion communicate about *their* America? To find out, I turn to my first case study.

The (Black) Church's "Soul of a Nation": Countercultural and Counterpublic Space

Deidre Abraham is a petite, dark-skinned woman of sixty-four years. She is married and is a church usher who drives a school bus during the day. She talks with me about black female-headed leadership given her experiences of "not having a man in the house."[15]

Abraham stresses the importance of parental and teacher involvement in a child's life. She implies that the lack of such involvement is stunting the growth and development of today's black youth. Even in her formative years in the 1940s and 1950s, alternative family structures existed. She learned values like honoring her elders, saying "yes ma'am" and "no sir," respecting herself, valuing a dollar, and earning an honest living in the confines of a matriarchal home and supportive black church environment.

Not having her father under the same roof as her mother did not adversely affect her. Although sociologist Patrick Moynihan wrote a 1965 report—*The Negro Family: The Case for National Action*—out of concern for a seemingly disintegrating black family, he blames its dysfunction on single black female-headed households rather than the myriad of social, political, economic, and other systemic causes and issues. Further, he blames single black female-headed households for emasculating black males and stripping them of their parental authority. However, Deidre's story (and many like hers) counters the report by defying the longstanding norms and myths about the ultimate value of the traditional and nuclear family. The black church likewise is not monolithic; yet it continues to be an extension of the black community and, thereby, of the black family unit. That is what this exchange exemplifies: the countercultural nature of black female-headed households that are communally focused and oriented toward values-driven, and generationally linked leadership, and that are fortified and sustained by participation in the church.

WWJD: "What Would Jesus Do?"

My second case is of Moses Synclair, a church deacon and a factory worker in his mid-fifties. He has lived in Bald Eagles for fifty years, having moved there with his family at the tender age of five. Moses Synclair strongly believes in the church's role in the community. Convinced about the church's role in shaping individuals into participatory and law-abiding citizens, he asserts that the black church has a role in socializing persons into active neighbors and community members. He talks about a form of leadership that is in-group and socially oriented as he reveals and declares a consonance between his actions toward Brother Simpson and Jesus' earthly ministry. His behavior toward Simpson, he surmises, actually answers the rhetorical question, "What would Jesus do?"[16]

> Alright man, I'll see you . . .
> Let's consider what am I doing this week with Brother Simpson and his wife. I feel like I've been working hard and I hope [that] helping

them works. It doesn't cost me nothing to help somebody if I know somebody needs help. Just like Brother Simpson and his wife, even though he has a felony and been in "the pen." He and his wife, they moved here and they don't have any income. And, I'm not doing nothing that Jesus wouldn't do and because I consider myself a Christian and want to help somebody. I will help him and his wife in any way I can. He doesn't have any transportation so I am willing to drive him where he wants to go. That's not my vehicle. That's not my gas, and Brother Terrence gave me a gas card so that I could drive him around and help him find a job, go apply for social resources and stuff: food stamps and all that. So, I did that.

We should always feel like we want to be Christlike. You know, we wear those "What Would Jesus Do?" bracelets, right? We wear those. So, you say to yourself, "What would Jesus do?" Would he, knowing this man needed a job, would he let him suffer because he was in the "pen" . . . just not help? I don't think . . . I *know* Jesus wouldn't do that. As I consider it, those bracelets have come through and gone, but the question still to ask is, "What would Jesus do?" He would do the right thing for people that needed help and everything. The church should reflect Jesus and his ministry. I think this church's doors should always be open. If this community is running right, [they] should. Now, the Lord has blessed us to have two more ministers, two more reverends. Somebody should be running this church phone, every day.

I think that would help. I include even myself because I am a deacon. If I've got the time, we've got seven deacons, I think we could all do it a day—come up here and run the phone because the community needs you first. *That's what churches are supposed to do—help the community.* People would stop all that bad talk about the church if they were doing something. If you ain't doing nothing, that's what's going to happen, you gonna turn on the church.

Tabernacle's supposed to be this and that, but, from what I see, some won't help with this, and they won't help that. . . . But, you know when you help somebody, that's where you get new members. We had a lady to come here that—what do they call it? She owns all the apartments down on the east side of town, everything. Tabernacle, if they'd have stepped forward and bought those apartments, got hold of those apartments and helped the people in the community, it would have been big for this church, for this community, it woulda helped a whole lot, and by helping that's how you get members.

I went to this church in Calumet City. In Calumet City, Chicago, called St. Matthews. My grandmother belongs to that church. We visited, me and my wife, visited that church. When we get back home two weeks later, we get a phone call. We pick up the phone call, and guess who is on the other end of the [phone] line? It's a person from St. Matthews, uh, saying prayers to us over the phone. Now, I've not suggested that to Tabernacle as something to do. However, we could do that for some of our members that are in nursing homes or that can't come to church every Sunday. That don't cost nothing to have the phone call out to members.

That would help.

"Jesus," says Moses Synclair, would resettle a former convict and his family into a new area while also spearheading efforts at finding employment opportunities for the family. That is personally "what Jesus would do." More important, Synclair proposes that Tabernacle should provide assistance to the doubly marginalized members of the black community like Brother Simpson. Although black people comprise only 13% of the U.S. population, they represent approximately 40% of the incarcerated population.[17] The numbers are disproportionate. Yet, those statistics contribute to the United States presently having the largest criminal justice system and the highest incarceration rates in the world.[18] Brother Simpson, having been incarcerated, stands for African American males who are six times more likely than white males to be incarcerated and two and a half times more likely than Latino males.[19] Yet, he is also one of the 636,000 people released from prison each year.[20] That raises two questions: Where do they go? And who helps them once they pass through the prison gates? Synclair would answer by suggesting that the black church should be one of the institutions to assist black families once a member of the family is released from "the pen."

In short, Moses Synclair names how seminal the institutional black church is to leadership and authority in this rural and Southern black community. More than that, however, he introduces the idea of the institutional black church as a public church. "The public church"[21] is described as Christian churches, primarily mainline Protestant groups, and other religious communities who live out their faith in American public life by providing a prophetic witness through their beliefs and actions and in their work for a more just society. While simultaneously critiquing and/or furnishing moral advocacy on social concerns and political issues affecting all Americans, the public church also models social teaching, focused policy research, and charitable service.[22] From the nation's start, the public church has articulated a range of public theologies.

Tipton has written extensively on the public church and includes the institutional black church in the category of the public church by confirming its public dimension: "Studies of the African American church in particular as a 'church with the soul of a nation,' in contrast to civil-religious visions of the 'nation with the soul of a church' tend to close the distance between civil religion and 'church religion' and expand the institutional range of public theology."[23] In Synclair's deliberations about Brother Simpson's plight, he not only implies but defends this public role and nature of the "black church." In articulating a public theology, he finds it to be a place where the formerly incarcerated can gain the support needed in order to be socialized back into society and to acquire assistance to become good citizens.

Like Moses Synclair, Deidre Abraham's conceptions of values-driven, in-group, and communal leadership and authority are motivated by the idea and image of "the black church" as the public church. Her interpretation of the strength of matriarchal and single-female-headed households is nurtured via her family and by the black church. Because the institutional black church serves a black public in this way, Abraham was informed about and benefits from the education she received in this space. It allowed her to develop a positive perspective on alternative families that has been formative all her life. Abraham's and Synclair's narratives illustrate the importance and relevance of the institutional black church in addressing subjects that pertain to the social welfare of black Americans—giving care and showing concern outside the realm of the "purely" spiritual. Tipton identifies this black church role as the public church. On the other hand, anthropologist Marla F. Frederick attributes this ability of the black church to the "black public sphere."[24]

Informed by the philosophies of Jürgen Habermas and historian Evelyn Brooks Higginbotham, Frederick writes about the black church as a black public sphere.[25] In this sphere, black oppositional discourse is cultivated, black collective will is developed, and black cultural identity is expressed and celebrated. The black church achieves each by being distinct from and, at times, in contention with prevailing white society and institutional racist structures.[26] The black church also functions as a counter-public space for Moses Synclair and Deidre Abraham, for it is in the church that they hear about possibilities for them beyond what is conventionally desired or delivered by ruling white classes and society.

Such a "counterpublic [space] holds special significance for those barred by racial caste, class, or gender from full standing in the public at large—or the church at large . . ."[27] and feeling betrayed by their invisibility and lack of representation in such institutions. As a cradle of democratic citizenship and civic aptitude,[28] the institutional black church remains a public and counterpublic space where blacks bring up social concerns that are being widely debated, where they work out their moral values and vision(s) of American society outside of the gaze of the broader and often hostile American public, and where they prepare for their involvement in democratic projects by encouraging civic engagement and furthering public theologies.

The Irony of "Postracial" Integration: Black Lives (Still) Don't Matter

In my third case study, a conversation with Cowboy "Wonderful" Tread-way and Sampson Frye Brown raises the question and poses the problem of post-1960s integration. In this conversation, both men consider the values African Americans presently possess. As well, they talk about the principles for which black people would likely sacrifice their lives. This subject opens up discourse about the irony of a presumed "postracial" American culture and society. Cowboy "Wonderful" Treadway and Sampson Frye Brown are deacons at Tabernacle, in their late fifties to mid-sixties, and military veterans. The erosion of some 1960s civil rights gains and the disintegration of black ideas about freedom and equality are the ironies of integration existing in a supposedly postracial America.

> N: What do you think are the values that African Americans or black people in America would die for in this day and age? Can you compare them to the values that were important to black people in the past? Are the values the same? Or are past values different from those in the present? Do you agree with Brother Jones' statement? Because it sounds like he is saying that we ain't dyin' for no values.
> Cowboy "Wonderful" Treadway: Well, no, that's what, that's what I would say. Today. And I really believe that. Okay, today, because—
> N: We're not dying for any values?
> CWT: No, because a lot of us think today that we have made it, so we don't have to put in any work anymore. I think there are some things we should be doin' now, like marchin' in the streets over some of these [government] policies. But we're too comfortable now. Now, back in the day, uh, in the civil rights movement, we were dying for all kinds of values—freedom and equality, all kinds of stuff! But see, our mindset today is totally different. We don't think we have to die for anything today.
> Sampson Frye Brown: Nope.

CWT: 'Cause we already made it. We think.

SFB: Yeah, we think.

CWT: So, I don't think there is no values that, that a black person would— now, there are some causes.

N: Okay, so tell me.

CWT: I think family. But, as far as values, I don't think there's any.

N: Really?!

CWT: I sure don't.

N: No?! That sounds so hopeless for my generation! Really?!

CWT: I really don't.

SFB: Your generation will do—

N: My—

SFB: They don't have no values.

N: That's what you're tryin' to, that's what you sayin' to me?

SFB: They don't have any values, they will . . . look at the system. *They really are dyin' because of the unfairness of the system. But they are even killin' each other.* Back in the day, we wouldn't kill ourselves because we had, ya' know, civil rights organizations. I marched in a few [protests]. There were a lotta things that uh, uh, let's say the civil rights organizations represented. I can really identify myself with that. But, there were other values that I didn't identify with and [marches] that I didn't participate in where people died [to uphold] those values. If it hadn't been for those values, though, you wouldn't be sittin' where you are today. You believe that?

N: (*thinking out loud*) Yeah . . . Okay . . . However, let me press you a little bit. What do you think are the values black young people exhibit, now?

CWT: Those that do have a set of values act like they are self-sufficient. [Their attitude is]: *It's about me.* What can I get? How can I get that house? How can I get that car? That's what it's about. *But, there's a reason for this decline.*

N: Okay. Why?

CWT: Because, if you think about Martin Luther King Jr., when he had gotten the civil rights bill passed, he was sittin' ponderin', and they wanted to know what was wrong with him. *He was concerned, because he says that: "I'm afraid for our people. I'm afraid that we are going to become what we have fought so hard to integrate into."*[29] That's what we had then. *We had a different value system back in the day that integration was going to threaten.*

N: And that was?

CWT: That was taking care of ourselves. Some of the old African tradition values: that it takes families to build a village, a village to raise

a family, kids or something like that. [A village to raise a child.] *All that's gone now because we have integrated into a society that never had those values. And, we have become what we integrated into, and that is what he was afraid of, and it happened today.*
N: Okay.
SFB: True, very true.
N: Okay. Alright.
CWT: Gotta be careful what you ask for.

Of great concern to Cowboy "Wonderful" Treadway and Sampson Frye Brown is the impact of integration on black life in a postracial era. For them, integration is connected to a devaluation of black life. They support such thinking by invoking Martin Luther King Jr.'s thoughts on blacks and integration in the aftermath of the passage of the Civil Rights Act of 1964. In a conversation with activist and humanitarian Harry Belafonte, King Jr. voiced fear that: "I am integrating my people into a burning house."[30] Hence, Treadway and Brown are convinced two of the aftereffects of integration are persistent systemic woes that keep black people marginalized and oppressed and the twisted thinking and logic of young(er) blacks who value neither their own lives nor the lives of other blacks.

News reports and other accounts frequently seem to corroborate the sense that young blacks are killing one another at alarming rates, at rates unseen by previous generations of African Americans. Having received the benefits of integration, Treadway and Brown are convinced younger generations no longer hold onto constitutional promises of life, liberty, and the pursuit of happiness but have coopted the values and principles of a dominant white social group as a result of integrating into their social institutions, hierarchy, and established social orders. This leads the pair to conclude that black life (still) does not matter because young(er) blacks are now experiencing a loss of the racial and collective ideals that anchored their parents' and grandparents' generations.

From what both men have witnessed, systemic injustice holds the key to the irony of "postracial" integration. Integration was supposed to level the playing field. Yet social and racial injustices endure and have a negative impact on young(er) blacks who seem not to possess or hold dear the values of life, liberty, and equality. These are principles and rights for which those in the civil rights generation sacrificed themselves and died.

The "politicization of race" maintains that race is altogether political. This means that regardless of race or ethnicity, Americans are intricately interwoven into *racial politics* and thus involved with the *racial state*. A racial state draws forth democratic and despotic practices, Omi and Winant explain. The *despotic* dimensions of a racial state refer to domination, dispossession, violence, confinement, coerced labor, exclusion, denial of rights and due process, and deprivation of life, liberty, or land, which have been state practices as long as the United States has existed.[31] Organized around race, these practices caused and produced the near genocide of Native Americans, the enslavement of African Americans, the internment and forced labor of Asian Americans, and the conquering of Latinos and other immigrants. At the same time, these practices reinforced a racial ideology of white supremacy that continues to create and maintain subaltern groups of people. For these reasons and many more, the "color line"[32] or racial division endures as the major schism in the U.S.A.[33]

Counterbalancing the despotism of a racial United States is its *democratic* dimension—for the "politics of race" in America are communicated also by democratic projects and practices that include "freedom dreams" like Martin Luther King Jr.'s now famous 1963 "dream" speech delivered at the March on Washington; social movements to resist domination; noncompliance of social and cultural groups with unjust laws; alternate ways of conceiving group and individual identities; and the display of racial and social solidarity in the presence of despotic challenges.[34] These projects not only galvanize individuals and groups but also produce energy-fueling practices of democratic politics and reform that counter unjust and inequitable treatment and inspire new visions of a moral and just society.

The irony of postracial integration is that these rural, Southern, black, and Christian townsfolk, like their black counterparts in cities, are operating under the dictates of a nation-based paradigm of race through which the despotic and democratic dimensions of a racial United States coexist. And thus, the reality that black lives still do not matter, even to young(er) blacks, can potentially be attributed to "a racial state that has been transformed over and over in unending efforts to deal with its contradictions: Its concept of freedom included slavery. It is a racial despotism that also claims to be democratic. It is an empire that rose out of anti-imperial revolution. It is a settler society (based on immigration) that is also exclusionist."[35] The despotic and democratic dimensions of life in the United States sum up Cowboy "Wonderful" Treadway and Sampson Frye Brown's assessment of the paradox and irony of a postracial state where integration should hold the promise for a brighter future. Yet, this in–group–oriented and communally focused discussion about the worth of black lives points out the problems of living and existing in a racial state not only for blacks but also for other racial and ethnic minorities, a state in which people of color are often diminished because of the color line.

True to Our God, True to Our Native Land:
Black America's Politics and Blood(Stained) Loyalty

Cowboy "Wonderful" Treadway chides his fellow veterans and active soldiers for their unpatriotic behavior during the 2008 presidential campaign in this first case study on black patriotism. Treadway was offended by Republican propaganda suggesting that those who were not in support of the war in Iraq are unpatriotic. Further, he takes exception to his plant manager's unwarranted assertion that servicemen and servicewomen are complicit with dying because they have volunteered to defend their country.

> N: Okay, okay, okay . . . How do you define *patriotism* and, um, outside of military service? Are there other forms of patriotic service to this country? If you say to me, "Well, I really believe that military service is the highest form," then I would like you to tell me why.
>
> COWBOY "WONDERFUL" TREADWAY: I'm gonna go first because I'm the youngest, I guess. I thought it was always age first, you know?
>
> SAMPSON FRYE BROWN: (*humorously*) The more he talks, the less I have to say, you know?
>
> N: (*laughing*) Oh no, you gonna have to say somethin'!
>
> CWT: In this area, I may be somewhat biased, okay, because if you look at my license plate, *my license plate—at least the vanity plate around it—says, "Soldier Forever."*
>
> N: Mm hm . . .
>
> CWT: Because that's the mentality of a soldier. Patriotism is in many forms. But, of course, I was a soldier for twenty-four years, you know? Vietnam and all of that stuff. So, I look at that as the highest form because what you're involved in is a matter of life and death, okay? Anytime, anywhere. You can't get any more higher than that. But, patriotism can be servin' your country in many forms: by volunteer work, community services—what you call it when you go overseas to work with the Peace Corps? Anyway, being a doctor . . . you may go to school, then serve your country and the community doing free medical clinics. Patriotism is doing something, at your will, for your country. You know? *So . . . that's what was so upsetting during the [presidential] campaign because soldiers and veterans allowed that ugly head to stick up and separate us. And, and just because we don't believe in certain people, we'll say, "Well, you're not patriotic."*
>
> N: Okay, help me out, you're going to have to be more specific.

CWT: More specific about that. During the [presidential] campaign when someone denounced the war in Iraq, the Republican Party was saying, "You're not a patriot, you're not patriotic." You know, "You don't support the troops." *I* support the troops, *I* support the troops, I *don't* support the war, you know? That's two different statements right there. And so, they were using that, using it, to distort and to deceive people, you know?

And fortunately nobody said that to me except one person who I thought was very ignorant. He said, *"You guys knew what you were doing. They knew what they were doing and still volunteered and went to Iraq." He responded that way because I was upset every time I woke up and found out there was two and three soldiers killed and stuff like that.* And I would make that statement to that guy. This guy responds, *"Well, they knew what they was doing." This guy was a big-time plant manager, and he says, "They knew what they were doin' when they volunteered."* I looked at him and I said, "You know, that's the most ignorant comment I have ever heard, and I find that really disturbing, you being a plant manager with this position and you gonna make an ignorant statement like that. *We don't join the military to die. You know what I'm sayin'? Even though we know that's a possibility."* A possibility.

N: Okay, but you didn't give me the definition—

CWT: Yeah, I did! Before—I said *patriotism* is defined as doing something for your country, on behalf of your country, for your fellow man whether it's stateside, or abroad, or across seas, or whatever it is, as long as you give it your service, on behalf of your country, for the best interest of people, protection, health, whatever it is.

Irritated and incensed, Treadway counters his white plant manager's declaration ("You guys knew what you were doing. They knew what they were doing and still volunteered and went to Iraq") with the retort: "We don't join the military to die. . . . Even though we know that's a possibility." Military men and women serve the nation by protecting fellow citizens and American interests at home and abroad, at times dying as a result of that service. Treadway does not mince words when he declares support for the troops but notes that like many other people he is averse to war.

Such devotion despite being opposed to war is captured by Langston Hughes' 1926 poem "I, Too [sing America]," written during the Harlem Renaissance and between the end of WWI and the start of WWII. More recently, the nation has been embroiled in a national conversation about black patriotism. Sergeant La David T. Johnson was a Green Beret. Killed in an ambush while on joint mission with the Niger military in West

Africa, he voluntarily "touched" death in order to represent American interests abroad and to keep the nation *and* the rest of the world safe. In the fight against terrorism, he lost his life. But his actions and his service— to provide national security—will always prove his allegiance to America. President Trump punctuated his condolence call to Sgt. Johnson's widow, Myeshia Johnson, with: "He knew what he signed up for . . . but when it happens it hurts anyway."[36] Offended by the statement were not only the sergeant's widow and other family members (particularly his mother) but also the U.S. representative Frederica Wilson, who overheard the call while riding in the car with the family as they headed to the airport to receive the fallen soldier's body as part of a ceremonial military homecoming.

Application of Rappaport's ritual theory helps to make sense of the exchange between Johnson's widow and President Trump and similarly Treadway and his plant manager. Advancing a Durkheim-inspired explanation of ritual, Rappaport identifies rituals as "speech–acts" or enacted beliefs that bring about social transformation, a change in social conditions and affairs. For this reason, a crucial component of ritual behavior is *performance*.

When America's young enlist in the armed forces, they are agreeing to participate in ritual performance and to fulfill the *liturgical orders* (i.e., a subset of ritual performance; mandates conferred by authority figures) dictating such performance. There is no ritual or liturgical order without performance.[37] *Acceptance*, *belief*, and *conformity* are intrinsic to and decisively affect ritual performances. Participation in war as military personnel implies engagement with liturgical orders. Liturgical orders are a "sequence of formal acts and utterances" connoting "authority" and "conformity."[38] Liturgical orders are public orders. By volunteering to serve in the armed forces, U.S. soldiers, should war break out, have already signaled their ready acceptance of the public order delivered by the president regardless of their personal beliefs about war. Ritual performances demarcate the boundaries between public and private processes, making it possible for individuals internally to contradict their external acceptance of public orders.[39] Acceptance, however, confirms that their participation in war as ritual performance is a public act.[40]

Rappaport further declares:

Acceptance is not only public, but clear. . . . While ritual participation may not transform the private state of the performer from one of "disbelief" to "belief," [my] argument is that in it the ambiguity, ambivalence and volatility of the private processes are subordinated to a simple unambiguous public act, sensible both to the performers themselves and to witnesses as well. Liturgical performance is, thus, a fundamental *social act* [based on] public orders and [not subject to volatile belief] or conviction.[41]

Treadway's rejoinder signals his understanding that American citizens who join the armed forces accept the public orders even if they do not ultimately believe in the justifiability of the orders to go to war issued by our nation's chief executive officer and/or congressional leadership. Yet, participation and acceptance of liturgical orders are socially and morally binding.[42] Enlistment assumes conformity and obligation to carry out the president's public orders. Compliance is where *morality* begins.[43] In other words, Treadway's statement is accurate and true because acceptance of military orders stipulates moral obligation.

So, our country's military personnel neither go to war nor choose to die because of personal belief or conviction, even if personal reasons might motivate their decision to enlist. Rather, they go to war to fulfill a moral obligation. Treadway's retort demonstrates the politics of American black patriotism; such a response is mindful of the sacrifices of *all* soldiers, including those of black servicemen and servicewomen. Treadway exhibits a blood(stained) loyalty to America, even when disagreement with his white plant manager ensues.

Treadway, like Sgt. Johnson, sings America as a black patriot. Yet, unlike Treadway, Sgt. Johnson paid with his life, the ultimate price—death—leaving behind his young family and his town to grieve his loss. Johnson's ritual offering gives reason for Treadway's previously implied proclamation and conviction: that patriotism demands that Americans recognize the sacrifices of men and women at home and on the battlefield, regardless of political or ideological preferences and positions and regardless of race. Sgt. Johnson's blood(stained) faith is a postmortem display and reminder of black patriotism. Despite the insensitive and insulting politics of our sitting president, Johnson's death epitomizes the practice of an abiding black civil religion in America, one that is always "True to our God, True to our native land."

Black Nationalism on Display

Cowboy "Wonderful" Treadway and Sampson Frye Brown discuss the meaning of the placement of the American and Tennessee state flags in Tabernacle's sanctuary. At one point, they recall that church leaders had placed a POW/MIA flag in the sanctuary but note that the flag was later removed.[44] Besides the regional and cultural tradition of exhibiting flags in worship spaces, for Tabernacle's demographic, flags are patriotic symbols of the freedoms Americans share and reminders of the country's military sacrifices.

These American, regional, and military symbols unquestionably showcase the African American connection to the U.S. homeland despite their, at times, "exilic"[45] treatment and experience. New Testament scholar Allen D. Callahan offers exile as a metaphor for the African American experience in his text *The Talking Book*, where he elevates the issue of the centrality of the Bible to the birth and development of African American religion and culture. He supplies a history of the antebellum and postbellum periods as basis for critical social commentary—from slavery to the present. He also explores how the Bible and Christianity both influence and shape American social and cultural context, particularly read from the perspectives of black literature, visual art, sermons, hip-hop music, and other African American cultural forms. When speaking of "exile" as one of the tropes that represents, communicates, and gives meaning to the black American experience, the Babylonian exile of Judean Israelites is compared to the trans-Atlantic enslavement and trade of African Americans.

Like the Israelites, African Americans experienced a savage exile. Yet, unlike the once subjugated and captive Jews that eventually returned home, African Americans never experienced such a return—a point made even more compelling and explicit when drawing on statesman and abolitionist Frederick Douglass' July 4, 1852, speech, "The Meaning of the Fourth of July for the Negro."[46] In his remarks, Douglass wrestles with the hypocrisy of having Fourth of July celebrations of independence in a land of bondage in which the laments of black abductees saturated American society. The consequence of their displacement and translocation from African homelands was them experiencing America as a strange land.

In a more contemporary treatment of this subject, Callahan draws upon theologian and Christian ethicist Cheryl Sanders' research to explain how an African American exilic sensibility evolved throughout their agonizing voyage into modernity to which African Americans have responded by expressing their longing for some place or space—geographical, cultural, spiritual—where they can feel at home.[47] An African American theology of exile asks: "What happens when the exilic place becomes the new 'homeland'?" That is still a pressing question for black America. Will black America ever ascend to a "postexilic" place?

Exile remains a part of black America's modern-day racial experience, thus cementing a nation-based paradigm of race. However paradoxical, the idea of being an exilic people contrasts with the homeland for which these rural, black, and Christian Southerners willingly sacrifice life and limb. The flags in the worship space are symbols that validate *who they are*—African American patriots—whose blood(stained) faith proudly animates their practice of a black civil religion.

Stars and Stripes and "One Nation under God"

The subject of my next case is Elizabeth Ainsley, who is married, retired, and sixty-three years old. She is also an usher in the church. We discuss the meaning of the American, Tennessee, and Christian flags in the church's worship space. Elizabeth interprets the presence of the three flags in Tabernacle's worship space as emblematic of America and all Americans identifying with being a part of "one nation under God."

N: So, in the front of the church when you enter, there's the American flag, there's the Christian flag, and there's the Tennessee flag. What do those three flags represent to you in terms of them being in the church? Had you ever seen [them]? (*pause*) (*laughter*)

Elizabeth Ainsley: They sittin' right up there?

N: Yeah.

Deidre Abraham: I was up there by the choir, up there, okay where Josh sit, there's a flag sittin' there, where Yvonne sits, there's two flags over there.

EA: Oh . . .

N: Okay, if you had something else that you wanted to say I'm gonna let you say it, then I'm gonna let her respond to that.

EA: I'll tell you this—what I think it ought to stand for.

N: Okay, what do you think it should stand for?

EA: *One nation under God.*

N: Oh. Okay.

EA: Uh, the . . . that flag, it's the United States flag hanging there, and I just [believe] without God, there is no nation. Without God, there is no church. And so, whatever we do, it's got to come through him. As I was about to say a while ago, I don't know. I was trying to think my best about that question when I was at home and before coming here for this conversation. But in my mind, I'm thinking missionary is about the closest thing to a man that's in the service.

N: Okay, and why's that?

EA: *Because missionaries are the people, they put their lives on the line also by goin' in to help people in other countries. They are on the battlefield, and a lot of time they do get killed for servin' their country. Or servin' whatever country.*

N: Okay, now are you talkin' about missionaries sent by church groups, or you talkin' about governmental, like . . .

EA: Yeah, any kind of missionary.

N: Ambassadors?

EA: It can be through church, [governmental] ambassadors, or whatever. I just think that they show a lot of patriotism and we need to stand behind a missionary and make every available means for them to go forward. I think that we can also put in service there. If you bein' faithful enough, if you see this missionary is goin' forth, you want to make sure that whatever means that can be available to them, that you give, in support of their efforts. Give, give, give. And so, I couldn't think of too many higher things that I could speak about as far as patriotism.

N: Okay. That's fine! I don't have a problem with that! Everybody has a different response. I'm just looking at the responses; I'm not judging the responses. For these questions, I'm not making a judgment; I'm really trying to get a better understanding of all these terms. That's it. Okay, now, I'm gonna move on.

God holds family, neighborhood, community, and nation together and in balance. Without God, none of these social institutions, especially in this part of the country, would function properly. Elizabeth provides an interesting twist on service to the country, likening missional service to the costliness of military service. That is how she answers the question about the presence of the flags and constructs meaning around their placement in the church's main sanctuary. Her thinking and rhetoric exemplifies sociologist Robert Wuthnow's explanation of civil religion as public religion.

In the late 1980s, he describes two elements, "public utterances" and the "unspoken assumptions" of the American people, that constitute and make civil religion, a public religion.[48] Together, public utterances and unspoken assumptions become foundational to the ways in which America defines and measures itself against other nations. For they furnish public discourse, revealing a matrix of shared understandings about the nation and leading to policies articulated, at times defended, but also sometimes contested, in the public square.[49] This public (thereby political) dimension of religion furnishes the premise(s) upon which the nation is legitimated.

By equating military and Christian soldiers, Elizabeth Ainsley voices the regional and therefore shared mindset of the residents of Bald Eagles. Like her, many in this community would liken the sacrificial life and deaths of military to faith-filled personnel like missionaries and ambassadors, who, in serving our country and depending on where they are placed in the world, will also likely face death. Her metaphor proposes that in life and death a soldier's job—whether military personnel, missionary, or ambassador—is subject to God, who charges all Christian soldiers in whatever capacity they might serve to uphold life, liberty, and justice for all. Here, her regional interpretation of patriotism reflects a civil religious understanding that has been raised to the level of a public religion, regardless of racial and social identities. Her rhetoric, like that of her white counterparts in this area of the country, represents public discourse about the United States that legitimates the country.

Although regionalism strongly ties Ainsley to Bald Eagles culture, I find it ironic that she conveys her understanding of the flags' positioning in the sanctuary in terms of one nation under God especially because American practice of civil religion is profoundly divided along religiously conservative and liberal lines. Each group offers distinctive versions of what America is and should be, because they speak out of different traditions. Religious conservatives espouse a "one nation under God" philosophy, elevating the connection between the biblical tradition of the kingdom of God and America. They often refer to a unified nation and to America's divinely ordained, special position and mission to the rest of the world, including economic leadership, the spread of democracy, and evangelizing the world.[50]

By contrast, religious liberals tend to refer to the United States as a place "with liberty and justice for all." That liberal version replaces the chosenness motif with the country's responsibility, based on its vast resources, to alleviate some of the world's problems.[51] Work on economic and ecological concerns, human and civil rights, and peace and social justice are subjects that religious liberals assert are biblically based, coming out of a tradition that addresses debilitating human conditions.

Although Ainsley employs this trope, she is not identifying as a religious conservative, since her racial identification also factors into and socially determines her comprehension of American civil religion. Rather, "one nation under God" is a conflation of conservative and liberal visions of America that, to her and many of Bald Eagles' black townsfolk, imply "with liberty and justice for all." She believes and practices a dialectical black civil religion—a black public religion—that is cultural (i.e., regional) and racial. And so, by putting her assumed yet contested moral visions of America—what the nation should be and how it should act (especially toward black Americans)—into conversation with each other, a convergence between the two inevitably happens.

Like Cowboy "Wonderful" Treadway and Sampson Frye Brown, Elizabeth Ainsley typifies in her response what it means to be a "soldier forever"—the ideology and application of black nationalism that is about metaphorically enlarging U.S. borders to recognize the rights and responsibilities of American citizenship as what elicits public service, racial loyalty, and submission to a higher calling, cause, or effort.

"Keeping Together in Time": Black Military Service in the Early Twenty-First Century

My next conversation partners are Mai Mai Watkins and Georgia Wilder. They talk about the ground-breaking nature of black men's service in the military during a historical time when the American military was a de facto racially prejudiced institution. Civil religious loyalties and patriotism for blacks in that era meant honoring and upholding democratic values in the face of the country's and the military's decidedly undemocratic actions toward them. Nevertheless, the opportunity to serve abroad and potentially die for American democratic principles instilled confidence, dignity, and racial pride in these black servicemen.

> MAI MAI WATKINS: Our young men don't seem to have the desire to think about enlisting in the armed forces. At one time, it was a very honorable thing for our black men, even though back then they had a hard time in our forces once they enlisted. I just wonder if it's being encouraged, if our boys are aware of what they can do. For instance, by joining the armed forces, they would get their education paid for and get to see the world.
>
> N: Okay. Let me ask you, historically, what did it mean, what do you think it meant for black men—because it was mainly black men at the time, what did it mean to enlist in the military? Like, you said it was honorable. Why was it honorable? What did it mean for black men to be in the military despite, and it sounds like you were implying, despite the racism in the military?
>
> MMW: Well, my mind is running long, and you don't need to hear about that history about the black men in the armed forces. But, let me see, to answer your question there, I would have to say . . . what made it honorable then . . .
>
> It was a sense of, first of all, of serving the country and feeling that "I am somebody, and I am representing, my people." Because you see, they [the military] was highly prejudiced, towards black men. It was not easy at all for them. And they [the military] was down and very dirty, too. Very, very dirty. But, the men had the strength to endure, and they also developed strong relationships with

their comrades. And, they, it was a growing, it was doing things for them, and [they] had a feeling of strength—worth. And they were praised by their family members and friends.

N: Mm hm . . . And they were praised because?

GEORGIA WILDER: To see what their parents had to go through in order to get through the walk of life's journey. And if this is what they could do in the military, they were willing to step and take this risk, 'cause [they believed] it will help them, their family, and help another person that's comin' this route. They thought: "It would be to my advantage to do what I can do."

MMW: I see the same thing with today's men, as we just expressed with the men of the days before.

N: You see what same things?

MMW: They see a way out, a way to improve, a way to grow.

N: Mm hm. Mm hm. But, I guess the difference, though, was also that they were breaking new ground.

MMW: Indeed. Indeed.

N: And I guess that may be the difference with this generation. It's not groundbreaking. Do you believe that is the case?

MMW: I do. Right, I guess that's true.

GW: When black men join the military, the way has already been paved for them. Back then, it was much easier for them to go in and do what they needed to do. Get the training they needed, you know, and go forward or come out.

Now one of my [brothers], the one that's still in Germany, he stayed twenty-nine years. Each time when his time would run out, he would reenlist. But he was doing that for himself. Rather than comin' back to Bald Eagles and trying to pick up a new job or find a new direction in life or get caught up with the wrong crowd, he stayed in the military. He said the kind of people that were gonna be here and do certain stuff was not for him. He knew there was something better for him. And when he got done with school, he was not going to go to school any further. You know, and he couldn't just sit at home.

See, that's the problem, today's young black men don't have the same social or community forces behind them. One of my brothers, he just did the four years. Billy Joe's the one. He just stayed four years. My son went and stayed the four years. My nieces and nephews, you know what I'm saying? Raymond John is the only one that made a career out of it. But the others got the same benefits. Raymond John's got the whole thing. Now he's retired, he will just work in another government job until he gets ready to retire from that.

N: Okay.

GW: Serving in the military just made a better way of life for him.

MMW: I've spoken to some young men and had some moms of young men who've told me: "Well, I don't want him going in to the military. He's gonna be sent straight to Iraq." Well, maybe so. But, the chances of bein' killed on the streets are just as strong for our young men today.

Both women point to the flagging interest in volunteering for military service among today's young black men, although many still join the institution. That so few continue to do so is surprising to these two women given the institution's history of traditionally being a place for black men (and women) to learn discipline and gain training and an education, positively impacting their growth and development. In fact, what Wilder and Watkins express is documented.

A 2015 article in the *Economist* entitled "Who Will Fight the Next War?" begins with a Southern military officer and recruiter's attempt to attract volunteers from Clayton County, Georgia, to the army. The county is described as Southern, predominantly black, and poorer than the national average.[52] It is one of the most likely places in the country and in the greater metro-Atlanta area to recruit potential volunteers because of its longstanding relationship with the armed forces. However, the article goes on to report the growing divide between the American public and our nation's armed forces, explaining that their inability to gain recruits will affect their ability to mobilize for future war.

This aversion to enlist has to do with many factors but includes negative coverage of recent wars (i.e., Afghanistan and Iraq), coverage that was focused primarily on battlefield deaths and the tens of thousands of soldiers wounded; the end of a 1973 draft that supplied previous wartime recruits; and disqualification from service based on potential recruits' criminal records, body tattoos, drug offenses, lack of rudimentary education, and even obesity. *All* have contributed to the disconnect between American society and the armed forces. Even if half of the recruits for the armed forces are ethnic and racial minorities, another social factor adding to stagnant recruiting efforts are the many upper-class Americans who not only avoid but are spurning military service. In addition, with low unemployment rates (less than 6%), recruiting a potential pool of volunteer applicants becomes challenging. Finally, many of America's young are disenchanted with the costliness of war: they are all too aware of soldiers returning home in body bags and/or broken—physically, spiritually, mentally, morally, and emotionally.[53] Hence, they are seeking alternative, more fulfilling, and more lucrative career options.

Although anxieties loom around recruiting personnel to serve in future wars, precipitating questions that pertain as well to African American communities, in my interviews Wilder and Watkins still insist that military service is both an exercise in black nationalism and a viable career option that comes with development and advancement. As they point out, black men who joined the armed forces in the twentieth century did so not only to make a way out of no way for their families back at home but also for reasons of manhood. Military service bestowed social dignity and graces that strengthened and bolstered their manhood by reinforcing these messages: "I am somebody, and I am representing my people." Further, enlisting men gained a sense of internal worth because of the praise they received from family members; because of the brighter future they were carving out for themselves upon their retirement; and by way of upholding the rights, responsibilities, and principles guaranteeing U.S. nationality and membership through their service. These points are more forcefully made when considering the concept *muscular bonding*, a feature of military exercises benefitting not only enlisted men but also marginalized groups. Muscular bonding specifically illustrates why military service has been advantageous to the African American community.

Author William H. McNeill notes in his book *Keeping Together in Time: Dance and Drill in Human History* that muscular bonding, a feature of religious practice and military drills, is enacted ritual, reflecting the thoughts of Durkheim, Rappaport, and Erving Goffman (i.e., interaction rituals).[54] McNeill's theory on muscular bonding reinforces and moreover extends Wilder's and Watkins' positions on the benefits of black military service especially when he suggests that in complex and hierarchical societies divided by social and economic class, muscular bonding may be the vehicle through which discouraged, discontented, and oppressed groups can gain the solidarity necessary for challenging the existing social order.[55] Given this assertion, *keeping together in time* is about the collective effervescence—the group emotions, unity, and community—produced when enlisted personnel participate in muscular bonding. Muscular bonding or keeping together in time further implies that coordinated rhythmic and shared movements—displayed in marching, drills, and dance—bond particular segments of a population and groups and thus sustain communities.

In the situation of African American military men (and women), keeping together in time disrupts the status quo despite social setbacks and in order to ensure equitable treatment and application of constitutional truths, values, and laws to all racial and ethnic groups. Keeping together in time supports a performance of black nationalism and black masculinity. These promote the social cohesion and solidify the self-respect that Watkins and Wilder express and that McNeill evaluates as being aspects of muscular bonding. Regardless of modern-day ambivalence(s) around and arising from efforts to enroll today's black youth—and particularly black men—Wilder and Watkins remain staunch supporters of African American military service as a noble profession partly because of the complex, rich, and honorable history of blacks in the military, a history that showcases black America's pride and investment in defending our country, and partly because of the benefits of fortifying and developing black manhood and womanhood.

Earning Your Bars and Stripes Despite America's Broken Covenant(s)

In this last interview, Moses Synclair and Ossie Terrence define *patriotism* as the ability and necessity to transcend the most humiliating situations in order to serve fellow citizens and the country. When they assert that patriotism is the reason why Synclair had to leave Bald Eagles, eventually to return, this is what they mean. Altruism is a "civil religious" quality that Synclair embraces and performs in order to prevail against racist barriers that had once prevented him from initially receiving his "bars and stripes."

> MOSES SYNCLAIR: Yeah, you know, I just feel that like I probably had a goal when I was a little fellow of what I wanted to be in life and if I didn't get to be that, I didn't want nobody to say, "Well, you didn't make it," you know? I probably could have been a professional athlete in any three sports: basketball, football, baseball—any three. I was pegged in the community to be the one to make it. But, it takes determination; it takes that drive; it takes that push. In our community, when I was coming up in high school—I probably would have been, I hate to boast, Terrence ain't never heard me brag or boast or ever heard me talk about what I used to do.
>
> OSSIE TERRENCE: Well, you said you played football.
>
> MS: I told everybody I played football. I would have been the first black quarterback that Bruce ever had (*all laughing*) if I had been here, but in Bald Eagles—
>
> OT: You can play now!
>
> MS: But, I had to leave Bald Eagles because—of patriotism.
>
> N: Meaning what?

MS: Because the doctor's kid, the president of the bank's kid, let's see—
the coach's son, there's some more names I could put in there, but,
uh, you know, "I could never get to the top." Being the best on the
team, you had to take second fiddle if you were black, for what was
coming. You know everybody in the stands knew you was the best,
but when it comes down to the awards, giving the awards—

*You get awards for being in the army, you get honorable mention—you
get them stripes and stuff.*

Okay, I don't think I reached, when I was here in Bald Eagles, I
didn't reach my stripes so I had to go to Paris, Tennessee [a predominantly black city in West Tennessee], to reach my stripes. I could go
to the state championship in Paris, Tennessee, all the time for somebody to know who Moses Synclair was. They would find out ahead
of time I was on my way there.

Everybody would say, "Well, Moses Synclair is in town." But, I
grew up here [in Bald Eagles]. I could have come back here a young
man and played basketball here. But if I had played basketball here
and they were winning, then everybody would say this is a black kid.
So, I didn't come up playing basketball. *Okay, it was okay then because
I was still the best around West Tennessee for a black kid. Now, however,
I have come back home knowing that I was one of the best that ever come,
doesn't matter, I was a black man, black kid. But, I didn't get my just due,
they messed me around in Bald Eagles.*

N: Okay, how did . . . because I really want to understand this. I guess
I don't really understand how, I understand that you had to leave in
order to get your just due. But, how did that leaving—

MS: I came back. I had to, when I came back, I tried to work in the community doing some things in the community of Bald Eagles; they
didn't have a black, they didn't have a black prom when I—

OT: He wanted, he wanted ours to be better. He came back after he
left.

MS: I wanted—

OT: He saw the same thing that happened to him was still happening
here. So, when he left and got into another environment that opened
his eyes and he saw things differently so he came back here and
said, "Look!"

N: Oh! That's what—

OT: That's a patriot!

N: That's a patriot. Okay that's what you're saying.

MS: They didn't have any proms when I was here. But when I came back
they had to have two proms: a black and a white.

OT: Yeah! We know and understand that in Philadelphia a historical figure rode down with a gun, saying, "The British are coming! The
  British are coming!"
N: Paul Revere.
OT: Paul Revere. He was also a patriot, but you know, but hey, if he
  had come down to Bruce, he'd have [kept] going on that horse!
  (*all laughing*)

"Bars and stripes" is an apt metaphor for achieving success and recognition since it evokes national images and imagery concerning *what it
means to be American*. Synclair uses this military image of bars and stripes
to communicate social belonging—his Americanness—and pledge to
nationhood. However, in doing so, Synclair confesses he was denied his
bars and stripes as a youngster, for the Bald Eagles community disregarded
and dismissed his athletic prowess. Instead of recognizing his gifts and
talents, the community conferred honors upon the children of the town's
white leadership and elites, and Synclair left town in hopes of finding
recognition for his talents elsewhere. In being compelled to leave town
for lack of recognition of his talents, Synclair experiences that as a breach
of the sacred documents that are a blueprint for American democracy—a
violation of these enduring principles that Robert Bellah calls America's
"broken" covenant.

The Broken Covenant: American Civil Religion in Time of Trial offers
a late twentieth-century social and cultural critique on the corrosion
of morality and erosion of religious understanding at a place and time
in which common moral and religious orientations and interpretations
were being upended. American society, once based on the "freedom
to do good" (i.e., liberal utilitarianism) with an implied moral obligation toward others, was being replaced with the freedom to pursue self-
interest.[56] Revival of common sets of moral and religious understandings
is argued for and upon which, sociologically speaking, any viable society rests; from which American society is culturally legitimated; and by
which individual and social behavior can be judged as good or bad, just
and unjust, right and wrong.

A revival of this sort could address some of the ills and problems facing
late twentieth-century American society. Later, *The Broken Covenant* offers
a more definitional statement about American civil religion, written as an
American jeremiad "alternately denouncing and lamenting the American public"[57] for the radical individualism that had become the source
of major problems by undermining social and moral obligation. A
return to the common good, to practice the better instincts of American

patriotism,[58] and the call for democratic and social change motivates the writing the text.

Moses Synclair's active engagement with a black civil religion is reminiscent of Bellah's appeal to practice the better instincts of American patriotism. He puts his actions in terms of figuratively earning military bars and stripes. Nevertheless, his story's twist is that racial discrimination prevented him from gaining his metaphorical bars and stripes. To his detriment, the town's white leadership and elites dismissed and ignored his athletic talent while praising those of their children, although he was more talented than them. Bellah would in all probability identify Synclair's experience as a malfunction and collapse of American democracy. *The Broken Covenant* responds to the deficiencies and failures of the American experiment:

> Instead of one civil religion, it is argued, there are many civil religions; instead of one covenant, many. (It is ironic that late in its history the great Protestant word "covenant" should have been used in the phrase "restrictive covenant" as *a symbol of the exclusion of others*.) A few critics feel that the American experiment has been so badly botched that it is even questionable that we can survive as a single society.[59]

Synclair's confession is an admission of a black nation-based paradigm of race controlled by "restrictive" borders.

His inability to earn his metaphorical bars and stripes can be imputed to the fact that black Americans have long operated under restrictive (national) covenant(s). Synclair's narrative likewise points to a historical fact: the Declaration of Independence and the Constitution, when initially composed, were paradoxical national and covenantal documents. While the preamble guaranteed equality, our constitutional "We the People" kept out the enslaved, American Indians, and other indigenous and immigrant groups. Neither was meant to apply to *all* Americans, but instead they functioned by excluding some. At the point of the Civil War, the purposes of our sacred and national covenants were still unfulfilled. So, another reason for fighting was to have both documents eventually live up to their rhetorical standards—the inclusion of all peoples. Nevertheless, Moses Synclair's story reminds us that even in our modern America, individuals, people, and groups continue to be excluded.

Another feature of this verbal exchange worth noting is the way in which Ossie Terrence distinguishes yet compares Moses Synclair to Paul Revere—an illustrious historical and iconic-turned-mythical figure summoned and commonly identified as a model American patriot. In Terrence's re-visioning, Synclair is likewise a historic, mythical, and iconic figure. He is an American patriot. Terrence's metaphor appears to be said jokingly, but his words hold deeper meaning. They reframe Synclair's unfortunate condition; they restore him to a position of honor from one of dishonor. Even so, Terrence and Synclair are sure to communicate the cost attached to black patriotic service, ethical conduct, and moral commitments. The sacrificial cost is loss of a black person's "home[land]"—the place where community groups bestow individual and social identity.

Expulsion from home(land) is the lot of an exile, a person without a home. Racial segregation forced Synclair to leave home in order to have his giftedness realized. He does not say, so we do not know to what degree he experienced his expulsion as something violent. Yet, we can assume that certain white families or leaders found his athletic talent to be a threat, triggering a nativistic response in white townsfolk whose protective response was to reward their own children with what was rightly due Synclair, thus securing their current regard and their future leadership of the city. Bellah puts into words an inexplicable concept—nativism—words that when applied do not excuse but offer more profound interpretation and understanding of these white townsfolk's behavior.

There is cost to social groups for reacting in this way. There are serious political implications for groups who feel they must safeguard their property and privilege against the threat of competing groups—to the extent that "one man's 'cultural pluralism' can then become another man's 'nativism' with all the classic elements of violence and repression that that entails."[60] In other words, nativism is a reaction to a perceived threat; groups respond nativistically in the face of presumed social and cultural disintegration—a calamity over which groups feel they have no power. Thus, there are no merits to cultural diversity when groups deem their social status, position, and power is potentially placed at risk. That is why Synclair's athletic performance and acumen was dismissed by the white townsfolk.

Nevertheless, Synclair's black patriotic beliefs helped him to triumph over the breach he experienced in America's contract based on this racial experience—for his practice of a black civil religion required devotion to country and community while instilling racial pride and security. He and Terrance have reconciled with having to claim a home(land) that many times does not claim them. Sacrificing oneself to a higher cause is a feature of black patriotism, made more apropos when black people remain true to the rhetoric and principles found in America's sacred documents—the Declaration of Independence and the Constitution—and kept relevant even though the United States continually breaks its covenant with this group of people. Black patriotism might demand relinquishing and refusing refugee status—and moving past dishonor—to return home to assist new generations of black folk presently living under the guise of nativistic and restrictive covenants. But that is the blood(stained) sacrifice demonstrating the better instincts of American patriotism that black patriotism is willing to make.

Patriotism, American Exceptionalism, and a Matter of Black Lives

Soldiers forever, whether in civilian or military life, is how black patriotism plays out in Bald Eagles and other parts of the country. A nation-based paradigm of race dictates the form of black leadership and authority that remains vital and sustains these evangelical Christian, Southern, black, rural dwellers. In a country where race is a master, albeit not a transcendent, category, what matters most to these rural black folks is communal-values-inspired, in-group-oriented, and generationally linked social activity, behavior, and practices connecting families, churches, and the community to wider society.

Although contestable, the black church still serves as the leading institution for finding countercultural, public, and counterpublic space(s) where black folk come to acquire the support and skills they need to maintain healthy family lives, whether headed by single- or two-parent households. The church is a gathering spot where members and the larger black public sphere raise social concerns and debate political issues pertinent to black America's cultural longevity. It continues to be the place where the work of determining and ensuring black inclusion in American democracy is done.

One nation under God encapsulates the two broad categories of liberty and justice for all. Both animate a black civil religion focused on uplifting the rights and privileges of American citizenship, regardless of aberrations in American national character that result in broken promises and restrictive covenants. Historically, they have inspired black fealty despite despotic features of U.S. democracy. They are the reason why black America's blood(stained) allegiance and moral convictions endure, despite dislocation, alienation, and exile, all for country and particularly for the well-being of black lives.

8

"We the People" . . .
White and Black
Dying to Defend Our Nation

Death in "Political" Production: White and Black

Southern civil religion emerged in the aftermath of Confederate defeat. Centered on evangelical Protestantism, the religion of the Lost Cause had developed as a postbellum social movement in response to this fall. Connecting the church and Confederacy, the religion of the Lost Cause celebrated white Southern identity through the elevation of dead heroes, symbols, hymns, wartime artifacts, and institutions to which it imputed mythic status. The elements of this regional form of civil religion included mythology, ritualistic practices, theology, and ideologies about the virtuous and religious nature of white Southerners, despite their failure at founding a separate political nation.

In an atmosphere marked by despondency, division, destitution, death, and anxiety, white Southerners developed the religion of the Lost Cause to redeem themselves by restoring the divine approbation lost in their military campaign against the North. Even though war defeat quickly disabused them of their purpose for fighting, Lost Cause civil religion nevertheless reconfirmed white Southerners' transcendent mission and special assignment to the American nation and world and supported their cultural and religious orientation.

In *Baptized in Blood: The Religion of the Lost Cause, 1865–1920*, Charles Reagan Wilson declares that each time a Confederate veteran died and flowers were placed on graves on Southern Memorial Day, Southerners recalled and relived *the death of the Confederacy*.[1] Religious concerns were central to the practice of the religion of the Lost Cause: a cult of the dead. Southerners faced emotional turmoil, suffering, doubt, and guilt—having to confront their seeming evil and having lost what they considered a holy war.[2] Above all, death loomed out of the darkness. Through civil religion's ritualistic and organizational activities, Southerners tried to overcome existential worries and to live with their sense of loss and tragedy.[3]

While the demise of "martyred" heroes signaled the downfall of the Confederacy, the rise of Southern civil religion solidified white Southern identity and reinforced Southerners' moral values, religious commitments, and democratic ideals. A politics of death only strengthened this. Writing in the 2009 preface to his book *Baptized in the Blood*, Wilson continued to explore twentieth-century Southern civil religion, reaffirming that the concept's strength lies in the belief that the South has a special destiny to play in America and throughout the world. Recent scholarship confirms its enduring power in the minds of many white Southerners and especially the Lost Cause version. However, in modern times, different Southerners have shared and advanced new visions of the region's civil religion.[4]

The Lost Cause version of Southern civil religion remains unconsciously active in the dispositions, mindset, political attitudes, and religious affairs of some "traditional" white Southerners—Southern born, bred, and with a historical legacy. Using Martin Luther King Jr. as an example, other people and groups have offered variations to the Lost Cause version of Southern civil religion, thus supporting the idea that the Lost Cause and Southern civil religion continue to initiate lively debate.[5] The idea is unyielding and remains alive via twenty-first-century media, American popular culture, and—I would add—Confederate monuments and statues.

While the Lost Cause version of Southern civil religion no longer predominates the modern understanding of this regional form of American civil religion, American popular culture continues to fuel interest in the South as a geographic locale with its own unique and sacred missions.[6] One gathers that is because Southern civil religion endures, but in more than one form. Whites and blacks practice and believe in more than one version of it, adding to the mystique of the South. Nevertheless, the Lost Cause version of Southern civil religion is yet another construal of American civil religion that complexifies *what it means to be Christian, Southern, and American* as well as *who* and *which* of the fallen—leaders, military service personnel, and common citizens—can serve as acceptable "human" blood sacrifices to maintain the mission of the nation. At the same time, the different versions of Southern civil religion draw attention to the very apparent regional and color-coded variations of civil religion and concomitant public theologies practiced by Americans.

Akin to Charles Reagan Wilson, Karla F. C. Holloway's scholarship treats the politics of death, but from a different perspective. In *Passed On: African American Mourning Stories*, she explores twentieth-century death and dying in the African American community. Admitting to the limitations of trying to cover "black death"[7] fairly over such a long period, she nevertheless argues three positions: black America's peculiar vulnerability to untimely death; how others represent them culturally; and how blacks represent their own death and dying.[8] Throughout her text, she draws upon literature, the visual arts, song (i.e., spirituals, the blues, and hip-hop music), film, media images, news programming, and articles to demonstrate the pervasiveness of death as a subtext for black culture and life: "Instead of black death and dying being unusual, untoward events, or despite being inevitable end-of-lifespan events, the cycles of [black] daily life is so persistently interrupted by specters of death that [black people] have worked this experience into the culture's iconography and included it as an aspect of black cultural sensibility. In this macabre revision of CPT (colored people's time), death is an untimely accompaniment of the life of black folk—a sensibility that was, unfortunately, based on hard facts."[9]

Holloway's ominous words make a strong case for why African Americans are particularly vulnerable to death and dying. Black mortality is measured by a litany of causes: childhood morbidity, maternal death in childbearing, cardiac-related deaths of elders, suicide, death at the hands of the police, and other violent deaths of youth.[10] Even when controlling for economic, social class, and sex, African Americans died and die at statistically significant and comparatively higher rates than any other racial or ethnic group in the United States. Given these facts, black people operate under a familiar and functional cultural code of death. History bears this out, showing that from post–Civil War lynchings of black men and women to the mob-related homicides of black veterans upon returning home from World Wars I and II to modern-day police brutality, black death has been political, testing and interrogating American democratic principles.

From infant mortality rates to death from preventable diseases like hypertension and diabetes, from bullying and suicide to prison and gang-related deaths of youth, the politics of black death display the egregious social inequalities that continue to plague a presumed postracial and post-9/11 United States of America. Charles Reagan Wilson's and Karla F. C. Holloway's contentions augment mine regarding the political nature of death and its role in revealing and distinguishing the sociopolitical concerns of whites and blacks. This chapter is about this "politics of death." It shows that certain public theologies articulated by members of Bald Eagles' rural and religious communities still reflect this civil religion. The chapter's four case studies illustrate the civil religious loyalties and public theologies of whites and blacks in Bald Eagles County arising around a politics of death. Both groups question and debate the meaning of a democratic republic and liberal democracy in a postracial, post-9/11, militarized America as both feel the effects of economic insecurity because of the housing crisis, market crash, and global impact of war.

Whether white or black, these citizens argue for democratic principles they believe divinely guide this country, even if their public theologies are in conflict with civil religious commitments. Death in "political" production exposes the civil religious allegiances of white and black townsfolk, which are at times in tension with distinctive public theologies expressed through the sociopolitical affairs they raise. Each case study argues for group rights and responsibilities as liberties that "We the People" must exercise, protect, and uphold. These group rights and responsibilities effect the process of "dying to defend the nation" and produce heterogeneous moral traditions that still stress what it means to be American.

Protecting Children at All Costs: An American Value

The first case engages the public theologies of Cindy Jones and Naomi Smith on a subject of serious concern to these rural, Southern, and black residents—protecting our nation's children at all costs. Cindy Jones is thirty-four years old, college educated, and an African American elementary school educator who has lived in Bald Eagles for twenty-nine years. She is a married mother of two children who self-identifies as socially and theologically moderate. She is also a member of a predominantly black nondenominational congregation in the area. Naomi Smith is also African American. She has lived in Bald Eagles all thirty years of her life. She is a member of a black church in the area. A single mother of an elementary-school-aged daughter, Naomi works for the Corrections Department and self-identifies as theologically liberal but socially moderate.

> N: What do you think, given your age, and given the times in which we live, are the causes, or the values that, um, African Americans would die for, presently?
>
> CINDY JONES: You know, my answer to that would be, as a younger person—mature person—they would die for their family. You know, they would die for, moral beliefs within their family, first. That's just a first response. Now, that doesn't make it right. You know, we should want to die for Christian beliefs, but the emotional side of me is sayin', "If you touch my daughter, or if you harm my son . . . I would be caught in a bind."

If it means I gotta go to jail, what have you, to protect my children, then I would have to go to jail. However, if you burned a Bible, then I would probably say, "Well, the law gonna take care of that. You know?"

I'm not gonna shoot you 'cause you burned a Bible. But what's wrong is wrong, and what's right is right. I'm human with flaws, too, so that would be my belief. Now in terms of what people of the younger [black] generation would die for—it's money. Anything that has to do with money, or materialistic things, they're willin' to die for that kind of stuff. Now, that to me is insane. Mature-minded, young adults and the older generation, they just, they ain't dyin' for nothin' [insignificant]; it just don't make sense. However, the younger folk, their thinking is like, "I'm gonna die anyway, so I'm not gonna premeditate [think about the consequences of] my death—especially not for children or my family, 'cause I know God gonna take care of them." They make the decision early on that "God gonna take care of them anyway." [However], they should be thinkin' like the more mature and older generations [who think contrary to them].

[For instance, as a more mature person], I'm thinkin, if they hurt my child, I have strong feelin's about that, I'm gonna give you my anger, which is not right, but, my first response would be to attack . . .

N: Okay . . .

CJ: And, hopefully, in my attack mode somebody with some good Christian sense is gonna say, "Look, here, girl, don't you go do nothin' crazy." It would take somebody strong, more, uh, elderly or an older person to come and say, "Okay, you crazy right now, and I know how you feel." It can't be somebody my age 'cause [they] don't know how I feel. You have to live a little to know how I would feel about my children . . .

N: Okay, okay. I'm gonna get your response, and then I'm gonna ask this a different way.

Naomi Smith: I totally agree with what Cindy just said. For me it would be the same—family. You know, I feel the same way, if anybody harmed my child that would be the only thing right now that I feel like I would die for. I don't really see anything that would make me lay down my life other than family.

N: Okay.

NS: Anything I would wanna give my life for [besides my children].

N: Okay. Well, the reason why I asked is because in the past, historically, black people have given their lives for the value of freedom and equality. And, I'm just wondering, outside of your family, or maybe in addition to your family, are there any values for this generation of black people that you see that we would die for? I am talking about lofty values like equality and freedom and so on, so forth. Or are we not living in that type of historic moment?

NS: I don't think so.

CJ: I agree, I don't think we livin' in that type of moment right now. But eventually I think we will come to cross-purposes about religion [and the state]. You gonna have to make a decision [about your religious belief], and you may have to die for that decision. You know, it's just not at its head right now [i.e., at the point of explosive tension]. You know, 'cause we so liberal. We live in a liberal society, and we have so many freedoms that we don't have to deal with that because we have it all.

Back in the civil rights movement, you *didn't* have it all. You know? Everything you had was somethin' to fight for. But there's not much to fight for right at this point in history because you can do it all, and you can live it all. You can be a homosexual, and you can be my neighbor, and I have to like it. You know, it's just we live in a world where you don't have to do that anymore, you don't have to continue to fight because . . . We were brought up to think the law will take its course. Or God will take his course.

Take it to the Supreme Court if you feel that procedures were violated. Everything now has procedures. You gotta go here, you gotta do that, you gotta do this, you got to petition. Whereas then, back in those civil rights days to petition you would go straight to the court and protest, you know? You would prepare for protest. You'd be walkin' up there right now with your signs and chants.

Now, you walk straight up there and they're like you didn't even follow this, you didn't follow this, and now you goin' go to jail. So now if you want to be heard, you got to follow procedures. You know, you didn't bother to even follow the fact that there is a certain degree of respect that you supposed to give as you talk one man to another.

The conversation arouses deep emotions in Cindy Jones as she contemplates the mere threat of harm to her children. The protection of children is an American belief and nationalistic sentiment. Ironically and poignantly, however, it is not yet a reality, particularly because sizable segments of our children experience poverty, inadequate housing and homelessness, hunger and malnutrition, income and wealth inequality, juvenile and gun violence, and exploitation and abuse. As well, they face disparities in early childhood development, healthcare, education, juvenile justice, and child welfare. As the Children's Defense Fund's *The State of America's Children 2017* reported, nearly one in five and more than 13.2 million children were poor in 2016. Of 550,000 people living in homeless shelters, in transitional housing, or on the streets in 2017, children comprised more than one in five persons. Additionally, 1.2 million homeless children were enrolled in public schools in 2014–2015. Close to 14.8 million or one in five children struggle with hunger in food-insecure households, and every year thousands of children die because of gun violence. Between 2013 and 2015, that number was 7,768 children. Each day, 1,854 children are confirmed as neglected and abused; and with the worsening opioid epidemic, the number of children in family foster homes, child care institutions, and group homes is 433,201 and growing rapidly.[11]

When analyzed by race and ethnicity, the numbers among Hispanic, Black, Asian / Pacific Islander, and American Indian / Alaskan Native are even more staggering, even though the demographic trends for all childhood populations include significant portions of white American children. Protection of children guarantees the well-being and continuance of future generations of Americans. While Cindy Jones and Naomi Smith eloquently communicate their conviction about family and community responsibility toward children, and more explicitly the role of black families and the community in caring for and sheltering black children, such shocking numbers also indicate the importance of government in securing the safety of *all* children, and particularly through policies geared toward those most in need, safety that the numbers clearly show is not yet true for black children.

This subject draws Jones and Smith into conversation about an ideology for which they are willing to die. Jones artfully draws a parallel to those who "would take a bullet" in defense of the Bible to convey how strongly she feels about protecting her children. Moreover, she communicates that "taking a bullet" for a child is a fixed belief akin to the civil religious principle of defending religious freedom. Yet, Jones and Smith's public theological commitments are at variance with the civil religious devotion displayed by those who actually would "take a bullet" to safeguard the Bible (i.e., for religious liberty).

The Bible is thus both a political and a religious symbol for Bald Eagles' residents and other citizens who confess to being willing to "shoot to kill and [to] die" if it were being desecrated. Disagreeing, Jones remarks, "I'm not gonna shoot you 'cause you burned a Bible." Yet in the same breath she declares, "If it means I gotta go to jail, what have you, to protect my children, then I would have to go to jail." In that statement, she justifies violence against anyone who threatened to harm her children. Her comment discloses the moral value she places on the safety of children; to her, such safety is part of the "American way of life."

Anthropologist Sherry Ortner recognizes the "defense of children" as an "elaborating" symbol. Elaborating symbols sort out experience; they have the capacity to order experience by their use as vehicles for sorting through complex and undifferentiated feelings and ideas, making them comprehensible to oneself, communicable to others, and translatable into orderly action.[12] Elaborating symbols are instrumental in enlarging our worldview and our capacity to conceive of ourselves and others. Hence, for Jones, the defense of children is a moral obligation disclosing the formative roles of both Bald Eagles' and her black church's religious cultures on developing her into a conscientious rural resident and U.S. citizen.

While Jones and Smith elaborate on the values for which they would die—the safety of children—they also critique the ideals for which young blacks are dying today. In contrast to their moral values, they note materialism and consumerism as twin and overpowering forces that encourage the wasteful and life-altering actions of some black youth. Jones notes their actions as being contrary to the ethos of black elders and mature young adults whose choices seem to lead them down a different path, one of lifetime longevity versus the premature death that unfortunately at times accompanies these young people's pursuit of material objects and earthly comforts.

Jones' pointed critique of certain aspects of black youth culture warrants a discussion about a U.S. market system animated by a liberal democracy that has produced and aggravated grave inequities between those who "have" and those who "have-not." The chasm between American producers and consumers prompts the following ethical questions: What American ideologies and beliefs can possibly legitimate the death-dealing lifestyle of a black youth culture shaped and influenced by American consumerism and materialism? How are we to think about the future of all young Americans growing up in a society where a great chasm exists between the über-wealthy and the dismally poor?

Declaring that we live in a liberal and progressive society where African Americans no longer wrestle with desires for freedom, Jones closes her commentary by noting provocatively: "But eventually I think we will come to cross-purposes about religion." Jones understands what Wuthnow named the "restructuring of American religion"[13] in the late 1980s—except she and the rest of the United States population are living through a period that is actualizing new historical shifts. In this post-9/11 world, religious pluralism and secularization are competing trends, captured by the emergence of the religiously diverse (e.g., adherents of Islam, Buddhism, and Hinduism) and religious "nones."[14] Social changes form and precipitate changes to religious orthodoxy, religious practice, and the religious landscape. Religious adaptation unquestionably involves complexity. An example of this is the intricate interactions between religious communities as social collectives and the ways that the character of these collectivities' social and cultural environments are modified and changed.[15] Even if she senses that African Americans have become lax in fortifying their social and political liberties, Jones nonetheless prophesies that the next major battle for all Americans will be about the ties between American political liberties and the moral ideals stemming from national religious communities.

Said another way, religious communities and groups might need to adapt to rapidly changing American social and political environments—which undoubtedly will challenge their belief systems. That will inevitably spark debate and potentially raise questions and concerns about the state's role in leveraging public morality as well as the role of religious (i.e., Christian) groups in politics, leading to conflict about which constituency (or constituencies) holds the power to shape and to determine the future of American culture.

The American Jeremiad and the Irony of Black Patriotism

The second case study involves Frances Trumpton and Roger Charles Courtney speaking on how the American jeremiad in relationship to black civil religion can ironically be translated into a display of black patriotism. Frances Trumpton is a black American, college-educated, and a retired auto dealer. The sixty-two year-old married father of two daughters has lived in Bald Eagles for twenty-four years. Trumpton served his country in the Vietnam War and now serves in the Baptist Church as a deacon. He is sociopolitically moderate and theologically moderate. Roger Charles Courtney is a college-educated retiree from the West Coast who worked as a telecommunications engineer. He moved to Bald Eagles two and a half years ago to pursue a quieter and more reflective life. Not currently active in a local congregation, he identifies as a Christian who "speaks up for what I believe is right and am willing to help out when and where I can." An African American, he served in the armed forces from 1955 to 1959. At seventy-one years of age, he is a social and theological conservative. Here, Trumpton responds to my question about patriotism:

FRANCES TRUMPTON: Patriotism is obviously love for your country, but aside from that, it is love for the prosperity and the future of the country and the nation as a beacon and as a pattern for how justice and peace are revered and handled. Just because there are symbols of patriotism such as the Liberty Bell and the flag and just because the guy doesn't salute the flag . . . if he goes and supports his family and does the things that his country expects of him as a contributor and he doesn't do anything that is subversive, he is a patriot. Now, *we overstate the symbolisms of patriotism* because say a guy didn't salute the flag, but let's say he fought in the war and was willing to give his life, his person for the country, that is patriotism. *But the fact that he served in a war that he may or may not have believed in . . .* that is a form of patriotism. But to see a child not saluting the flag or whatever—that's just the sum of the symbols. The real sign is in the heart, when the person believes in what that country stands for and the advancement of that country.

N: Let me ask you a question as you two are talking. Can you criticize your country and still be a patriot? For example, let's consider Obama's former pastor, Jeremiah Wright. Outside of how the media has portrayed him and the language that he has used like "*God Damn America.*" Can his criticisms make him a patriot?

FT: He is a patriot! When he said, "God Damn America," it ain't like me telling you, "Goddamn you." *To damn a country or a person is like "cursing" them.*

ROGER C. COURTNEY: . . . meaning you not going to get your blessings.

FT: Right. That is to put a curse on 'em.

N: But can he be patriotic by saying that "God is not going to bless America"?

FT: Yeah. He didn't say . . . but . . . he is ex-military.

RCC: He is a marine.

FT: He served his country; he is actually a brilliant man. Now, to take what he said in that context or [even if] you take it out of context, in my mind that does not disqualify him from being a patriot.

N: Oh, okay.

FT: He fought for the right to express himself as a human being—life, liberty, and the pursuit of happiness. Now, he has the liberty and *the right* of the First Amendment for saying it.

N: Do you think he is a patriot?

RCC: Now he has got that *right, no doubt about it.* But myself? I wouldn't have said that. I don't feel that in my heart. I don't know how he could have expressed himself that way, be that divisive, and still be a patriot.

I just don't, I wouldn't go there. Just like with Rush Limbaugh; I listen to him—he expresses himself, he says—however, if you are out in the public like that, in the forefront, I think you have to choose your words more carefully. You have to take into consideration that you are going to alienate people, and you have to decide whether or not you want to. So, I don't know. I wouldn't have gone there.

FT: I wouldn't have gone there because of my poise and tact and savoir faire . . .

N: (*laughing*)

RCC: Savoir faire? . . . *Frenchie.*

FT: But there . . . who was the patriot who said, "I may not agree with what you say, but I absolutely defend *your right* to say it."

RCC: Patrick Henry.

FT: It might have been Patrick Henry. What [Jeremiah Wright] said was not antipatriotic. It might have been dumb, but it was not antipatriotic. To me it was a statement about how he felt about why America is in the quandary it is in now. Because it has . . . we talk about the violation of human rights. America has always violated human rights. *This current war we are in right now, it is nothing but genocide.* It has taken out a large segment of our society who could be doing something else. We left here after 9/11 and went into Afghanistan for bin Laden. *How did we end up in Iraq?* I ain't that smart in geography but . . . *Iraq?*

RCC: Iraq was payback.

FT: Yes, but was 9/11, the spill that caused that? We went into Afghanistan looking for bin Laden if he was in fact the mastermind behind 9/11, but we end up over in Iraq! Is that patriotic [for Bush] to send our young men and women into harm's way? *For what?!?!?!*

RCC: The reason for Iraq is strictly oil. We are an oil-based economy. And if there is a disruption, or any kind of interruption, our economy will suffer and everything will die. This country will die. Everything is propelled by plane, train, ship, and truck. Everything in your marketplace, to get to the marketplace, everything has to travel in one of those ways or all four of those ways. So, to make sure to save the economy we had to go there, to make everything flow. That is what this is all about. The same thing with Russia and Georgia when they went over there, Hussein cut their pipelines. So you mess with our pipelines and we are going to come over here and kill everybody. That's what Iraq is all about. It's all about oil. So the man is making sure we get an uninterrupted flow of oil.

N: Are black people patriotic?

RCC: For the most part, yea. I'm thinking back to Roosevelt. Black people would take a bullet for Roosevelt, take a bullet for John Kennedy,
take a bullet for Bill Clinton. And then their patriotism is a lot different than what we would normally consider patriotism. *It is based on
loyalty and the reward system. These men represented America, represented
what is good about America.* And black folks want to be part of it. So
they flock to these people.

FT: Well, you take obviously the military side of it. *Black people would have
to be patriotic to participate in a segregated army. To go off to a foreign land
fighting for your country that treats you as a second-class citizen.* Then you
come into the Tuskegee experiment . . . Was it one of the presidents'
wives—Eleanor Roosevelt—who said, "Let's let them fly"?

N: Are we patriotic now?

FT: We have our issues with America and how America has executed
its promise to us. We don't live in a perfect society. Still, still, still I
think the number-one issue in America still is racism.

RCC: You think so?

FT: Yes.

RCC: That hasn't been my experience.

From historical luminaries Ida B. Wells and Frederick Douglass to
present leaders like Jeremiah Wright, black leadership has typically armed
itself and the black community against the vagaries of the American experience using the jeremiad. A rhetorical format that emerged out of Puritan
literary and homiletical tradition, American political and religious leaders have applied the American jeremiad to inveigh against an anomalous
public life, where the promise of the American dream is often shattered
by the reality. The American jeremiad assumes the form of a lamentation,
allowing the speaker to unleash a critique of the moral and political inept-
itude of the nation, demand correctives, and support a hope and a vision
for progress.

Frances Trumpton might not be familiar with the American jeremiad, but he remains resolute about Jeremiah Wright's patriotism despite
Wright's prophetic pronouncement: "God Damn America!"[16] Trumpton
is convinced of this because Wright is accustomed to using his rhetoric
both in civic discourse and as prophetic critique, and also because Wright
is a marine veteran. Wright's familiarity with this literary and homiletical
device brought attention to the American jeremiad as a feature—albeit
understudied and even less understood—of the vernacular of a black civil
religious tradition. He participates in a pre– and post–Civil War black
jeremiad tradition that continues today and that characteristically and

intricately weaves together the messianic destinies of blacks and whites in America. Though distinct, the two groups claim "chosenness" as a feature of their "Americanness."[17] When employing this version of the American jeremiad, spokespersons use this rhetorical and literary instrument as a form of black protest against all forms of racial injustice and to anticipate future black flourishing. In line with the three components of the American jeremiad, black leaders will cite a democratic promise; furnish a criticism of moral declension; and resolve the social declension with a prophecy about God deliberately and mysteriously aiding society to fulfill its mission toward its black sons and daughters, which redeems the enduring and sacred promise.[18]

In Wright's critique, he focuses on the abuse and exclusion of certain social and cultural groups from American democracy (particularly blacks) to imply that better treatment of them and inclusion of normally excluded (racial, religious, and ethnic) groups will contribute to America, delivering on "a stronger and more national 'We.'"[19] In a rejoinder to Philip Gorski's article on Barack Obama and civil religion, Joseph Gerteis reaffirms covenant theology and civic republicanism as the two primary elements of Gorski's and Bellah's definition of civil religion to debate the meanings of a politics of belonging.[20] Wright's fiery religious and political rhetoric also pledges allegiance to and argues for an American politics of belonging based on the traditions of covenant theology and civic republicanism. Any violation of these fundamental concepts and *American* truths warrant censure—which is what Wright's rhetoric intended.

In the early and developing nation, this covenant theology created meaning and social belonging based on a shared religious language. Even in a now religiously diverse U.S. context, that covenant theology continues to hold significance by supplying a shared language in which believers and nonbelievers can potentially speak to, rather than past, each other.[21] At the same time, civic republicanism still inspires public participation, while making a moral demand to uphold the common good.

In fact, black Americans have been engrafted into an American civil *religious* tradition that embraces the common discourse and language of an inspired covenant theology and spirited civic republicanism despite the occasional failures of American democracy. They have *adopted* and *adapted*—based on their racial experiences and social contexts—the republicanism and covenantal language of the early Puritans in order to lay claim to their "We"-ness. Yet, they are always mindful that shared stories are not always culturally available to all Americans,[22] reinforcing the fact that the American experiment developed not only around inclusion—but also around brutal national, racial, linguistic, and ethnic exclusions. And so, to address the cultural, racial, and ethnic *boundaries* and *borders* that prevent African American prosperity, Wright relies on the jeremiad to stress the areas where America has broken its covenant with this group and to demand a reckoning and rectifying of this situation, in hopes of producing stronger shared beliefs about social belonging. Wright's civil religious discourse prompts Trumpton to invoke this aphorism: "I may not agree with what you say, but I absolutely defend *your right* to say it."[23]

However, the converse is true for Roger Charles Courtney. Though he recognizes that the First Amendment guarantees Wright protection against retribution, he still does not consider this former soldier a patriot. Wright's demeanor, from Courtney's perspective, reflects Rush Limbaugh's, whose behavior has alienated a good segment of the American population.

Discussion about Jeremiah Wright's patriotism leads these two men to a discussion of America's perceived human rights abuses and the spoils of war being the loss of life. In this shift, Trumpton questions the patriotism of American leadership in conscripting young men and women to enter, fight, and die in a seemingly unjustifiable Iraq war. His critique, fueled by ruminations on death and dying, brings forward four value-laden subjects: the merits of war, justifications for war, young people's role in fighting America's wars, and the nation's present fight against the elusive enemy called terrorism in a battle that, according to Courtney, is meant to maintain our oil-based economy. These comments anticipate the following questions: Are we at war with Iraq to build an oil-based empire? Is it moral for a country to risk the lives of its young in order to fight a never-ending war (and to build an empire)? If not the young, then who will fight America's next wars?

In the last part of the conversation, Trumpton and Courtney ponder African American patriotism. Their line of argumentation diverges from the previous conversation to Courtney declaring: "Black people would take a bullet for Roosevelt, take a bullet for John Kennedy, take a bullet for Bill Clinton. . . ." Courtney's assessment is that these men represent America, and represent, for blacks, what is good about America. And black folks want to be part of it. So they flock to these people. For black people, "taking a bullet" means dying to ensure that constitutional promises, liberty and equality, and other rights guarantee black America's thriving and surviving. Courtney, however, ends the conversation with a rhetorical twist as he explains how black patriotism is unlike white patriotism. For him, black patriotism is based on a socially constructed loyalty and reward system. Agreeing, Trumpton makes this distinction even clearer by emphasizing the role of the "color" line in a postracial America: it

still dictates the success of a black civil religious tradition and the operation of black patriotism. The "color" line has the capacity to limit black
patriotic expression and to circumscribe a black civil religious tradition.
Trumpton's final statement points to the slippery nature of American civil
religion, which stipulates what is justifiable patriotic protest depending on
who is protesting.

Religio-political Paradoxes and Moral Bifurcations

In this third conversation, Carmello Kelley, Jessica Parker, and Muffin
Morgan wrestle with the ways in which public theologies that address
the abortion issue condition the religious beliefs, political ideologies, and
moral impulses of white townsfolk. Carmello Kelley is a white American,
thirty-nine-year-old, married mother of two preteen girls and one teenage
girl. Originally from Little Rock, Arkansas, Kelley is a college-educated
"cradle" Episcopalian who works for Habitat for Humanity. She and her
husband moved to Bald Eagles more than fifteen years ago to pursue job
opportunities. Kelley identifies as moderate socially and theologically.

Jessica Parker grew up in Atlanta. She had made several moves with
her husband and young family before settling into Bald Eagles, where
she owns a dance studio. A college-educated, thirty-eight-year-old, white
American woman, she converted to Catholicism from Lutheranism to
match her husband's religious affiliation. Parker describes herself as conservative, theologically and sociopolitically.

Born in Chicago, Muffin Morgan was raised in Bald Eagles from the
age of five. A stay-at-home mother, Morgan is now a thirty-five-year-old,
white American woman who is married with children. Though she is
not college educated, she is heavily invested in her children's education.
Morgan is in the midst of switching from her more conservative nondenominational church to join Kelley in the more liberal Episcopal parish in
town. She self-identifies as a social and theological liberal.

> MUFFIN MORGAN: Let's see . . . the healthcare thing bothers me,
> because I don't understand; sometimes I just don't understand, like,
> Republicans—you know like the Republicans and the different . . .
> I just don't understand their thinking. They don't want everyone to
> have healthcare, but yet they don't want people to have abortions;
> how are they supposed to pay for the babies? You know what I mean,
> how are you—
> N: So, once you have your baby, how are you supposed to care for it?
> MM: Yeah, what are you supposed to do?

N: . . . if you don't have the resources.

MM: Exactly. You know, it just doesn't make sense to me, at all. And let's see, what else is there? (*chuckling*)

N: Okay, so, you don't understand the rhetoric, you don't see how the pro-life rhetoric fits in with actual, real-life circumstances.

MM: Yeah! You know, in a perfect world, wouldn't it be nice? But it's not! And there's got to be other plans, like, who's gonna take care of these kids and . . . but you don't wanna give out any kind of programs to care for the children—duh! You know, what's gonna happen [to them]? That bothers me. That doesn't have anything to do with my congregation, but . . .

N: Well, it doesn't have to, you or your congregation. Whatever's easier to answer.

MM: Well, I mean I don't really see things like a lot of people at church do, so—

N: How do they see things?

MM: Well, basically, if you're a Democrat, you can't be a Christian!

N: (*lots of laughter, all laughing*) Well, that's just . . .

MM: I have a bumper sticker on my Facebook page declaring, "I think, therefore I'm a Democrat," and then I have another one that says, "I'm a Christian and a Democrat. Yeah, believe it." Or something like that—

N: I'm sorry. I read something to the same effect in an opinion letter in the newspaper that said if you don't vote Republican, then you're not a Christian.

MM: Now, these are things that bother me, now they may not be my own personal beliefs. *You know, it's not . . . like myself, I wouldn't have an abortion, but what are you gonna do with these women out here?* You've got to have plans, and you've got to have life choices. It's wonderful to have children, but you have to teach things in school . . . but then I read something that they don't want programs in the schools either! You know, safe-sex programs and whatnot.

N: So, no comprehensive [sex education]; it's abstinence only.

MM: I don't see how it connects. Yeah. I just, I don't.

N: Now, I'm going to, *now.* (*laughing*)

JESSICA PARKER: Well, in the Catholic Church, of course, they're always fighting the abortion issue. Um, but it's kind of, I don't know how much I agree with it [abortion]. *I do agree with it in the instance of rape and incest, you know.* But then, you've got the culture; certain cultures believe that having young babies and having lots of them [is] okay, and they're not usually the ones that seek the abortions; they're usually the ones that *want* to have the children.

So, sometimes the people that want the abortions are, you know, maybe the young, young moms that are thinking: "Oh, I don't want my boyfriend to find out," or "I don't want my mom to find out." It just, I guess it all depends on the circumstances, which is just not what the Catholic Church would support. I mean, I do believe [in abortion] in situations like rape or incest, you know, if this happens then you should have that option.

N: Okay.

JP: 'Cause, you know, there's always adoption, there's always . . . people are beggin' for babies every day.

MM: When I was in high school, though, I had a friend who would have stuck a hanger up herself before she would have told her parents [about her pregnancy].

JP: Yeah.

N: Oh, lord.

JP: Oh yeah, it makes it . . .

MM: Yeah, she would have thrown herself down the stairs.

JP: And that's the thing, somehow, they're gonna somehow get rid of the baby, so . . . *We're in 2008, people.*

MM: Well, I just read the other day that abortion is illegal in certain countries and that they have, you know, prison terms. But the report also said that abortion is actually four times higher in those countries.

JP: Where it's illegal?

MM: . . . and the bedroom abortions . . .

JP: Right.

MM: It affects thousands of women, too. So, like I was saying, there has to be steps. I just don't think you can cut [abortion] off. You have to make programs and steps . . .

JP: Yeah, you've got to assist the people who, you know, because it does change your life, especially if you're young and you're in a situation where you're considering that. There's gotta be some other options for you so you don't feel overwhelmed. Of course, there's always family values, for abstinence, and birth control. *But that's the thing, we've got all these laws and things to take care of people's mistakes.*

That's what aggravates me. Let's work on the things to deal with the *aftermath of all these mistakes, but let's not work on the prevention?* It all boils down to *family values*, you know? I don't know. Sometimes kids do make mistakes. They can come from a great family and just happen to get pregnant; it happens. But usually if you're in that kind of situation, your parents help you out and you work through it.

N: Mm hm . . . But does the abortion issue only impact children? I mean, or teenagers? I'm asking about grown women.

MM: I don't know of any of my friends or how many times my friends aborted as adults, unless, you know the amniocentesis came back indicating something was wrong with the pregnancy.

JP: I think it does mainly affect primarily low-income and, um, young moms. Or people with no options or [who] just don't feel they have any options.

MM: I dealt with that in high school. I drove a friend to the abortion clinic. You know, now she has four kids. *You know, but she's hardcore pro-life, now.*

N: Why is she so given to—

MM: She's become very evangelical, feels like she really made a mistake.

JP: It can really affect you.

MM: Yeah, I think it really affected her. She's become a strong person afterward and regretted it deeply.

N: Mmm . . .

JP: Yeah, you don't consider [that] it's gonna affect you.

MM: Yeah, when you're fifteen, sixteen years old, you're thinking, "Oh, my God, my parents are gonna find out!" But, yeah, I agree. *I'm very much pro-choice, but personally I would be pro-life.*

Muffin Morgan and Jessica Parker have an exchange about abortion, a topic that elicits an eye-opening and profound conversation about how political rhetoric, ideological belief, and religious and moral values mix and how they shape personal opinion. Even though the city and county of Bald Eagles is described as populist, the Bible Belt culture of this region influences the theological and social conservatism practiced by a majority of the residents. Theological conservativism is pan-denominational and often identified with Pentecostal, Holiness, Charismatic, and conservative evangelical movements.

Frequently guiding the faith of theological conservatives are creeds and doctrines that uphold the authority of the Bible and the salvific nature of Jesus Christ. On the other hand, sociopolitical conservatives generally support the traditional nuclear family in family-values debates, a definition of marriage as being only between heterosexuals, a pro-life position concerning the inception of human life, and the death penalty. They bemoan the secularization of American society, sexually saturated media, and lack of governmental regulation in the private affairs of citizens.

That the intentional death of the fetus is labeled infanticide in this Bible Belt community points up what to Morgan is a contradiction in the Republican rhetoric. She wonders: How can a party support health-care policies that limit abortions but be averse to social policies that mandate funds to care for children born to mothers who decide to have their babies? This exemplifies the disconnect between Republican (i.e., political) belief and action. Complicating the matter for Morgan is a Bald Eagles educational system that teaches abstinence-only education versus comprehensive sex education that is meant to expose young people to safer sexual conduct options. This is what prompts her to comment: "You've got to have plans, and you've got to have life choices. It's wonderful to have children, but you have to teach things in school." Additionally, in this cultural milieu the abortion debate is tied to political and ideological propaganda that is pervasive throughout the town and in the church communities. Such propaganda identifies the religio-moral conduct of Republicans as upright and typifies Democrats as less Christian than Republicans.

The more theologically and socially conservative Jessica Parker both contradicts and affirms the Republican Party's political rhetoric. However, her evaluation is based on her religious and ideological orientations and not her political party affiliation. Despite her long-term practice of Lutheranism, the Catholic Church's imprint seems to have been left on Parker, whose stance on abortion is informed by a family-values perspective. She remarks: "But that's the thing, we've got all these laws and things to take care of people's mistakes. That's what aggravates me. Let's work on the things to deal with the aftermath of all these mistakes, but let's *not work* on the prevention? It all boils down to *family values*, you know?" Although Parker admits there are exceptions to the "family values" rule, having an abortion is the less favorable of two options that come down to either "taking care of people's mistakes" or "having the unborn child."

Morgan's and Parker's abortion deliberations, by the end of the conversation, can be reduced to the following. Morgan, while socially and theologically progressive, confesses she is pro-choice *and* pro-life, as the circumstance dictates. Though she would "never have an abortion herself," in high school she had a friend "who would have stuck a hanger up herself before she would have told her parents [about her pregnancy]." Clearly, Morgan is split on the subject of abortion. Her comments betray the religio-political paradoxes and bifurcations of her public theological convictions and moral claims. Her conversation partner, Jessica Parker, concedes that teenage pregnancy can happen even to young people who hail from "good" families, but she later asserts: "I think [abortion] does mainly affect primarily low-income and, um, young moms. Or people with no options or [who] just don't feel they have any options." Parker's assessment is correct, although she offers no rationale for her statement.

Economic disadvantage, higher pregnancy rates, and higher rates of conception do indeed contribute to higher abortion rates among racial and ethnic minorities, low-income women, and poor women, according to the 2002 report "Patterns in the Socioeconomic Characteristics of Women Obtaining Abortions in 2000–2001."[24] From 2000 to 2001 (and much later studies), the Alan Guttmacher Institute conducted a national survey that included approximately 10,700 women across different races, ethnicities, ages, and social (i.e., unmarried, married, divorced) and economic levels. It is common for women across racial and ethnic subgroups (e.g., white, Hispanic, and black) to have abortions and for abortions to be the result of unintended pregnancies.

Yet research data reveals that abortions are typical among women who have never married, are twenty to thirty years old, have one child, live in a metropolitan area, are impoverished, and identify as Christian (whether evangelical or non-evangelical). The authors of this particular study explored factors that contribute to increasing or decreasing pregnancy and abortion rates—namely, contraceptive use, sexual patterns, and changes in public policy.[25] In fact, researchers found higher abortion rates among poor and low-income women (meaning those 200% below the poverty line) due to higher pregnancy rates. Pregnancy and abortion rates for middle- and higher-income women are dramatically lower. For economically disadvantaged females, investigators propose changes in welfare policy to parallel increased pregnancy and abortion rates.

Amendments to welfare policy benefitted low-income women who gained more job opportunities, economic development of families, and access to college tax credits. Nonetheless, these benefits were met with a decline in Medicaid coverage for a great majority of women and a proportional increase in the numbers of poor women who no longer had insurance. For these women, contraceptive and family-planning services were covered by Medicaid; these services were not replaced by free or low-cost services when Medicaid was removed. Accordingly, the authors of this study concluded that effective contraceptive use and family-planning services might curb the pregnancy and abortion rates of the economically disadvantaged.

These statistics support Parker's position, but, like Morgan, paradox characterizes her public theological claims and moral convictions. She does not believe in abortion *except for* cases of rape and incest. More than that, she realizes: "certain cultures believe that having young babies and having lots of them [is] okay, and they're not usually the ones that seek the abortions; they're usually the ones that *want* to have the children." Her comment about these cultures contradicts her implied assumption that women with large families automatically should want to have abortions. She also trivializes the reality that women and girls in middle-income and stable families have abortions. Abortions might disproportionately affect racial and ethnic minorities and women in lower-income groups, but the fact is that terminations of pregnancies are performed across races, ethnicities, and socioeconomic classes.

The paradoxes of Morgan's and Parker's religious, moral, and ideological positions reflect historian George Marsden's evaluation of the development of American evangelicalism and fundamentalism. Adherents to both forms of conservative Christianity, he reports, exhibited tensions between their moral and political-cultural viewpoints. Such incompatibilities he attributes to many factors, including the "fus[ion] of many traditions . . . [and] of being two minds on the question of personal and social application of the Gospel."[26] Morgan and Parker are likewise of two minds, their political-cultural and religio-moral stances at times pulling them in opposite directions.

The public morality and stances of the religious communities in which these women have been socialized at times align with and at other times contrast with the women's personal and moral commitments. Holding them in tension produces an internal ambivalence. In an unusual way, such ambivalence manifests in these women as religio-political paradoxes and moral bifurcations that curiously become signatures of their U.S. citizenship.

Endless War and the Local Men Sent to Fight It

This final exchange is between Sue Simpson and Louise Hall, who consider the potential drawbacks of an American civil religion that supports modern-day U.S. expansionism and imperialistic democratic projects abroad as part of the fight against terrorism. Such freedom projects require sending a continual supply of local men into war.

Sue Simpson is a white American woman in her seventies who has lived in Bald Eagles for fifty years. A retired state worker for Tennessee, she is active in the ministries of the Bald Eagles First United Methodist Church. She describes herself as a moderate, both theologically and socially. Louise Hall is a retired school teacher in her seventies who has lived in Bald Eagles for fifty-four years. Engaged in caring for her grandchildren, she is a grandmother who participates in church ministries at Bald Eagles First United Methodist Church. A white American woman, she identifies as a conservative, both theologically and socially.

N: I've got the issues in your local community. So what concerns you, nationally? Are there any national issues that are pressing to you?

SUE SIMPSON: Well, I think crime, and then I think, like the war. Afghanistan. Iraq.

N: People are still concerned about that? Why?

SS: What? The war?

N: I mean, you know . . .

LOUISE HALL: *Well, we still have men from Bald Eagles there . . .*

N: Okay. Mm hm.

LH: *. . . and from other areas that we know. Anytime you have a loved one, or someone you know . . . in the Bible Belt it's constantly on your mind.*

SS: And it seems like, uh, how long has it been going on—six years?

N: Yeah, it's been going on awhile.

SS: It seems senseless to me. It hasn't gotten, so far, it hasn't done any good.

N: Alright. Okay, okay. It's actually been going on, since September 11th, 2001, so it has been longer than that. At this point, maybe eight years.

LH: *Well, even before that we had the Gulf—*

N: Gulf War, yeah.

SS: I don't know, seems like we want everyone to do what we want 'em to do and everyone doesn't want to. They've got their own cultures, and we're tryin' to make every dag . . . I better get off of my—

N: Soapbox.

SS: *Soapbox here, but it seems like that. That we want everybody to do, have a government like we do. They may not want it like that.*

LH: I know that there have been . . . that there are governments that need to be overthrown.

SS: But, it seems like we try to step in there too often. I don't know.

N: Okay.

LH: And the thing is, today, if something happens on the other side of the world, we hear it tonight. You know, when we were growing up . . .

SS: Well, you hear it just right after it happens on CNN or—

LH: And sometimes we get one picture, and sometimes we get another picture, and you don't really, unless you're there in the circumstance, you don't really know what's going on.

N: Do you feel like the government sometimes keeps certain things away from its citizens?

LH: Yeah. I think that there are sometimes things that *need* to be kept away, like when my brother was serving in Vietnam. If it would have saved his life, then keep it away from me. If it would save his life . . . but we are, nationally . . . it seems like we're too concentrated on money.

Death is the subject that hangs in the air as Sue Simpson and Louise Hall speak, react, and respond to concerns about local men from Bald Eagles serving in the Afghanistan and Iraq wars. Rural Americans have a tradition of sending their young and local men into military service because placing rural youth on this path exposes them to greater educational and job opportunities. The downside to this trend is that fulfilling their patriotic duty on the battlefield comes with a price—high casualties.[27] These local men (and women) disproportionately return from the battlefield and to U.S. soil in body bags. No wonder Simpson and Hall object to America's occupation of Iraq, Afghanistan, and, much earlier, the Persian Gulf. War is endless (especially war on terrorism), and death hits hard and close to home. Hence, Louise reflects: "Anytime you have a loved one, or someone you know . . . in the Bible Belt [the wars are] constantly on your mind." That comment can neither be ignored nor denied.

In fact, the widening gap between the American people and the armed forces can partially be attributed to a developing military caste that is disproportionately constituted by the financially disadvantaged and economically insecure; by sons and daughters of career service men and women; and by racial, ethnic, and rural Americans—characteristics that insulate the rest of the American public from war realities.[28] In 2001, the Department of Defense reported that 19% (about 60 million) of the U.S. population were rural Americans; however, through 2006, rural Americans suffered 27% of the casualties in the wars in Afghanistan and Iraq. Higher rates of armed services enlistment account for why young folk (and local men and women) from rural regions of the country have higher death rates than their urban and suburban counterparts.[29] These numbers were not much different in 2016. Whereas the rural population of the United States made up about 17% of the total population, 23% of the war casualties came from rural regions and small towns. By contrast, 29% of Americans live in U.S. metropolitan areas of more than 1 million people. The war casualties from these urban and suburban areas also equaled about 23%.[30]

The deaths of these fighting men (and servicewomen) are connected to modern-day U.S. expansionism. Ironically, it is the civil religious and exceptionalist traditions that identify America as a "city on a hill" that typically supports such expansionism. National myths reinforce this trope, a trope communicated as America's divinely guided, special mission to the rest of the world. And so, America's virtue is purportedly found in its ability to redeem countries where oppression, violence, and injustice run rampant.[31] In those countries where war inevitably brings American social and political involvement, the spread of democracy seems inevitable. Bellah names this the new American empire,[32] because Americanization/globalization of these nations happens as a result of war—military strategy, maneuvering, and force—in order to expand American spheres of influence through building up those nations.

Yet, U.S. engagement with these countries, peoples, and cultures is not always welcomed. In spite of U.S. standing and its self-interpretation as a liberator nation (though by military power and pressure), some nations and their peoples choose not to be receptive to the changes that democratic reform might bring (or the ways in which it is brought) and consequently resist adopting the democratic social and political system the United States has to offer. Those feelings are captured by Sue's statement: "seems like we want everyone to do what we want 'em to do and everyone doesn't want to." That sentiment is at the heart of Simpson's and Hall's protest and desire to have their local men and women return home from war and active duty—alive.

Louise closes with a critique about living in a "sound bite" culture in which American citizens never receive enough information to know what is actually happening at home or abroad, though media outlets like CNN have the technology to flash news stories across the airwaves as they unfold. When I prod her about whether she wants to have more information about what is happening, she answers in both the affirmative and the negative: not if such information will place our soldiers in harm's way.

This final comment captures the essence of this exchange: that fighting war demands sacrifice, causes death, and supports the rebirth of nations. That comes at a high price. Military service personnel and particularly local men deployed to the battlefield pay the cost for endless war—with their lives. Americans believe and practice a civil religion that makes demands on these local and rural men (and women) to enter war(s) for the public welfare and in defense the nation. Interestingly, by consent of the governed, through divine mandate and because of moral obligation, they unwittingly volunteer for more, placing their lives at risk to encourage U.S. expansionism and the ongoing work of building an empire.

Interaction, Contradiction, and Contestation: Peoplehood in White and Black

"We the People" is an enduring metaphor and lasting symbol for U.S. nationality and peoplehood. It is a concept that includes not only nation and democracy-building projects but also unfulfilled promises and broken covenants. It is a metaphor that stands for a politics of social belonging, yet it excludes some. "We the People" also brings about the processes involved in and the multiple facets that comprise the U.S. nation-state. It is a clarion call to the people to shape and solidify the nation-state through U.S. expansionism. That prominent feature holds the potential to develop into American imperialism. While it limits U.S. citizenship to membership *within* borders, it sometimes intentionally obstructs U.S. residency by constructing walls and boundaries between many who live *inside* such borders.

As a metaphor for American regional and national identities as well as exceptionalism, "We the People" is vital for our country's stability, and for our sociopolitical, moral, and cultural order. Therefore, to make meaning of "We the People" in white and black during this period of incessant war, it is essential to establish the ways in which our civic republic and liberal democracy either supplies order and balance or fails to do so. As we consider this, we must examine the unresolved tension between the constitutional liberalism and civic republicanism that make up what it means to live out the trope "We the People" as representing America's social experiment and dream.

Contradictory and at times conflicting viewpoints characterize these white and black, rural, Christian, and Southern townsfolk. At times their public theologies are at variance with their civil religious loyalties. Yet they underscore what it means to be American in a representative democracy. When public theology vies with civil religion, fundamental struggles with dialectical moral traditions are revealed. This conceptual tug of war will always end in conflict and concession. Because this is so, the trope of "We the People" fails to serve as an enduring ideal for comprehending *what makes America great*, although it remains an adequate metaphor for social belonging and public participation in democratic governance and processes.

Nevertheless, "We the People" is the ideal to which we aspire, and it stands for what it means to be American. For this community, what it means to be an American in an age of terrorism is the willingness to die defending the political ideologies, religious traditions, and moral values that anchored the covenant theology, public-spiritedness, and common good that guided this nation's early settlers. For the people of these towns, what it means to be American is a common language and shared values around the protection of *every child* in the United States. What it means to be American acknowledges that patriotic protest can display profound love of country and a desire for excellence despite a less than perfect *union*. It demands tolerance in the face of political-cultural paradoxes and moral bifurcations because these exemplify what it means to be American. It recognizes the irony of service to the nation: that local men (and women)— here, rural Americans—willingly place themselves in harm's way in order to uphold American democracy at home and to maintain American power, influence, presence, and interests abroad.

9

A "New" American Exceptionalism

American National Identity in a Global Civil Society

War, Faith, and Visions of the Common Good

Bellah and his coauthors published *The Good Society* in 1991 to explore the power of institutions in shaping American public and private life and to argue for their role in helping Americans lead more fulfilling lives. "How ought we to live? How do we think about how to live?" are the central questions of this text whose responses come down to the patterned ways Americans have developed for living together, what sociologists call institutions.[1] U.S. citizens in general do not have a clear sense of the extent to which institutions shape and influence daily existence, nor are they aware of the ways in which their everyday lives rely upon them.

Institutions are both subject to American social conditions and hold the power and potential to transform and to reform civic life. These public institutions facilitate the pursuit of the "public good" or the "good of the common,"[2] one such institution being the "public church."[3] The public church calls to mind American civil religion's place for religious bodies inculcating morality into public life, seen in the infrastructural role of religion in political processes that serve to clarify the relationship while mediating the tensions between our liberal democracy and civic republic.[4] The public church has historically and conventionally shaped conscientious citizens and the American conscience because religious communities are concerned not only with the common good of the nation but also with the common good of all human beings,[5] an idea consistent with the religious conviction that "here on earth God's work must truly be our own."[6]

The public theology articulated by national religious communities and the American public church draws on biblical resources for a vision of a just society defined by mutual care and responsibility, not simply by individual rights, fair contracts, and due process of law.[7] Public theology is both argument and conversation *within* and *among* communities of faith.[8] Studies of the First United Methodist Church and the Tabernacle Missionary Baptist Church suggest this. However, one of the concerns of this chapter is to interpret the quest after the common good under religiously inspired, early twenty-first-century wartime conditions given the diverse and divergent public theologies articulated by Bald Eagles' rural and Southern, evangelical communities of faith and especially when whites and blacks advance differing understandings of regional and American national identities. Asked another way, is the search after religious visions of the common good possible in a postracial, post-911, globalized, and militarized America that is in the midst of radical religious and social changes?

And what of the morality that plays out in public institutions but derives from a civil religion that offers a well-defined set of religious symbols, myths, and rituals that legitimize political authority but is not fused with the church or the state?[9] Speaking to the subjects of religion, democracy, and the social life puts forth questions about how we should live. Yet, to these, add: Who are we, as Americans? What is our character?[10] The theory and practice of an American civil religion offers an answer.

By virtue of unfolding in the political realm, civil religion is a public faith that accords multiple and distinct constituencies and cultures the ability to participate in ongoing moral arguments, civic debates, and social reform conceived of as dramatic conversations.[11] Yet, this discourse comes out of dialogical and dialectical moral traditions often counterbalanced by public theologies that contest and rework the meaning of civil religion.[12] Civil religion lends coherence to cultural conflict during key "times of trial,"[13] starting from the American Revolution, leading into the Civil War, and continuing with the civil rights era and on into the Cold War era.

It is debatable whether the United States is presently in an extended "third time of trial" or the beginning of a "fourth time of trial." "Times of trial" make the operation of our civil religious tradition most apparent and our national commitments and group loyalties more evident. Such times raise deep questions about national self-understanding and meaning as they permit us the liberty to judge and/or to justify such meanings. From 2001 up to now, the United States has been involved in a succession of wars precipitated by religiously inspired and international terrorism. America's Civil War brought up grave and profound concerns about national meaning and self-definition. Death, sacrifice, martyrdom, and national rebirth were introduced into the idea of a civil religion with the life and death of then U.S. president Abraham Lincoln.[14]

Our engagement in this early twenty-first-century war on terrorism is doing the same—but to the degree of engendering a crisis in American national identity by provoking questions about self-definition and meaning in a pluralistic society and more global world.

Our present-day generations are living through macrostructural shifts prompted by social and human rights revolutions throughout North Africa and the Middle East—Tunisia, Egypt, Syria, Libya, and Yemen— the Arab Spring, as well as global climate change. We along with our world partners are witnessing Brexit, that by referendum vote sealed the United Kingdom's departure from the European Union. That economic decision was incited by a white working-class' perception of inequality and loss of political authority and social status. A vote like that will likely impact international agreements with close allies like the United States. It will affect international immigration of war refugees to the United Kingdom and throughout border states since economic changes also impact social and other public policies.

In the United States, we have lived through a national crisis spawned by corruption, greed, and the mismanagement of economic institutions leading to a housing crash and recession. Though the United States is now in the midst of a purported economic recovery, what remains are deep divides between lower, middle, and upper socioeconomic classes. This fissure is spawning distrust and nationalistic fervor because of fear and anger over anticipated demographic shifts that by 2040 are expected to create a white, working-class minority that even now has feelings of economic insecurity and therefore a perceived loss of social and political position and power. Hence, global reordering produced by social revolutions and the reprioritizing of economic systems is affecting American strivings toward self-definition, the common good, and the creation of a "good society."

Seismic social, structural, and worldwide transformations leave Bald Eagles' white and black, Southern and rural dwellers, who self-describe as "evangelical" and "politically populist," feeling marginalized and isolated from the rest of the country. Bound by regionalism, both groups respond similarly, and yet differently, to these drastic changes. The election of the first president of African descent and participation in an enduring war only compound such jarring social turbulence and systemic shifts.

All of these have precipitated a crisis in American national identity and have opened the way to exclusionary reformulations of American exceptionalism. Bald Eagles' Southern and rural whites and blacks exemplify why this might be the case. Feeling marginalized and isolated from the rest of the country, they feature human "sacrificial" death prominently in their thinking and rhetoric. The trope taps into their sense of social belonging best represented by dying to preserve the country's moral commitments, constitutional values, and freedoms. Dying for country creates belonging.

Their disenchantment can be ascribed to two causes. First, they are an American cultural subgroup that traditionally delivers their young men and women to the frontlines of war. Second, they are a subgroup that is feeling the adverse effects of economic restructuring, postmodern globalization, and technological innovations on their once-predictable, peaceful, and comfortable lives. And for these reasons, their messaging becomes: "Don't forget the dead!"; "Don't forget our sacrifice!"; and therefore "Don't forget us!" The rest of America can ill afford to be blind to their sacrifices or to the unsettling effects of war and postmodern globalization on their Southern, rural, family and communal life.

In the end, I aim to answer the following questions garnered from my study of race, religion, patriotism, and the "politics of death" in the Bald Eagles community: In an age of terrorism, global reordering, and social ruptures, what is the role of public theology and civil religion in producing a religious vision of the good society? How will the United States define itself? And what is just and good for society alongside such growing nationalism and pluralism?

A more inclusive understanding of American national identity and a reformulated political tradition of American exceptionalism, rooted in an American dream that accommodates diverse interpretations of rites of faith and rites of war, might be one pathway to a response to those questions. This "new" American exceptionalism will reshape the narrative about American national identity outside of the communal effects and despite white church members' and black residents' views of and disappointment with our nation's continuous participation in the War on Terror. This new American exceptionalism calls for greater democracy in our global and civil society.

The following sections treat the connection between Bald Eagles' ritual life and the political process, democracy and rhetoric of cosmic warfare, and religious ideology. All simultaneously reflect and mold the American patriotism Bald Eagles' residents believe in and practice. As well, all are essential steps toward actualizing a good society and fashioning new definitions of American national identity and exceptionalism in this age.

Ritual, Religion, Politics, and Power

Faith and politics in Bald Eagles enjoy a symbiotic relationship made possible by the ease with which religious symbol and language, belief, history, and myth enter into its centers of political activity and equally by the ease with which political symbols, language, belief, history, and myth are welcomed into the church house. For example, earlier I recounted separate white and black Memorial Day ceremonies and detailed the black and white versions of worship services that addressed America's 2008 economic crisis to illuminate the power of religious ritual in fortifying group allegiance and identity regardless of race. In public and private "worship" circles, where ritualizations, symbols, belief, and language mimic each other, group and regional commitments are solidified and sustained.

Elaborating on this idea, Émile Durkheim asserts that sacred and adored objects release an emotive power that is harnessed by religious ritual and enacted by the cult (i.e., religious adherents). Faithful devotees practice a religion that stimulates feelings of joy, inner peace, serenity, and enthusiasm, which comes to represent the proof of their beliefs. Faith is created and re-created when it centers around sacred and adored objects and is outwardly expressed.[15] Symbols like the cross, the American flag, the Tennessee State flag, the Bible, and the Christian flag demarcate the sacred centers of ritual space and performance in Bald Eagles.

When performance grows up around what ritual subjects consider symbolically sacred and where ritual action is repeatedly expressed, faith is strengthened and produces an emotionally charged social interdependence among participants. Habitual and repetitive action that surrounds a sacred center cements group behavior. By regularly assembling and participating in symbolic ritual action, townsfolk propagate collective ideas and sentiments, and they make and remake their moral universe(s).[16]

Religious and political power in Bald Eagles is sacralized and regulated by webs of ritual. Rituals concretize social identities and ideologies, induce conformity and allegiance, and reassert order and structure of groups. Thus, rites of intensification are peculiar to these civil religious and ritual spaces; they ultimately cultivate particular political realities and legitimize religious authority in the community. As anthropologist David I. Kertzer writes: "Through participation in rites, the citizen of the modern state identifies with larger political forces that can only be seen in symbolic form. And through political ritual, we are given a way to understand what is going on in the world, for we live in a world that must be drastically simplified if it is to be understood at all. . . . Such symbol systems provide a 'shield against terror.' They are a means, indeed the primary means, by which we give meaning to the world around us; they allow us to interpret what we see, and, indeed, what we are."[17] Rituals make it possible for these white and black rural Southerners to be involved with political life, even when political beliefs are at odds with religious conviction. And rituals also help them to manage the social chaos that invariably comes with human experience.

In Bald Eagles' civil religious public spheres, ritual life mirrors and reinforces ritual activities in private (i.e., church and home) worship arenas. While public worship spaces attract all segments of the Bald Eagles population, private worship spaces are limited by denominational, age, and racial affiliations. Liturgy, symbols, religious belief, and myth embody and organize each space. The spaces each parallel and fortify the other. Because ritual spaces induce social and moral order, the Bald Eagles small-town atmosphere draws residents who relish quiet and safe living, reflected in what can be considered a balanced and stable environment. Ritual geographies are extensions of this deliberately planned and orchestrated milieu.

For these residents, ritual spaces are also cultural spaces. Therefore, religious practices are cultural practices. Civil religious and evangelical faith-centered rituals suffuse both public *and* private domains. Regarding this, religion is a cultural system,[18] for it stands for conventionally transmitted patterns of meanings that are embodied in symbols. Comprising inherited ideas, this symbolic system becomes the means by which human beings communicate, perpetuate, and develop their knowledge about and attitudes toward life.[19] The symbols that dwell in ritual spaces—myth, language, art, sacred artifacts, words, hymns, and song and more—are "meaning-full" containers that become the blueprint for what people believe (their worldview) and how they behave (their ethos). Religion is a primary cultural system dictating social thought and action. And so, in this civil religious and evangelical community, ritual furnishes a schema for how to believe and to act.

Furthermore, ritual spaces are repositories for the "emotional" life that underlies humanity's contradictory and at times dialectical nature. Death, in general, elicits emotions, but politically laden death definitively inflames passion. Harry Ray's patriotic and emotional display is an example of this, reminding us that all deaths are not the same. Cowboy "Wonderful" Treadway expresses similar patriotic sentiments when he describes his exchange with his supervisor where he states: "We don't join the military to die. You know what I'm sayin'? Even though we know that's a possibility."

Each man—white and black—conveys strong rhetoric, opinions, and patriotic sentiments about dying to defend the nation. Still, their patriotic assertions lack uniformity even if the subject elicits a consensus of opinions. This can be explained in terms of the *multivocality* of symbol systems. That is, a variety of meanings are attached to the same ritual symbols.[20] In fact, the polysemous nature of symbols employed in ritual action makes ritual useful in cultivating solidarity without consensus (i.e., uniformity). In spite of each participant's differing interpretation, symbols strongly influence people's emotions and are capable of rallying them around an organizational flag. Human thought processes neither calls for conflict resolution nor consistent symbolic use to bond people together or create social cohesion.[21]

Ritual theorist Catherine Bell would agree. She attests to the dialectical nature of ritual defined by the underlying dichotomy between thought and action,[22] and by arguing that ritual furnishes provisional synthesis of some form of the original opposition. Provisional convergence of those antithetical forces is achieved by means of ritual's dialectical nature. This interaction forms culture in particular ways.[23] Although the above examples show social consensus and not uniformity, in both cases dead "loyalists" and "soldiers" morph into sacred symbols, unconsciously augmenting the merits of sacrificing one's life for one's nation in order that the United States might continue to be a worldwide democratic leader and wield military power.

Sacred symbol systems are also cultural patterns that provoke moods and motivations, thus affirming *models for* and *models of* reality. Said another way, sacred symbols as the content of ritual action induce emotions and attitudes that shape how we live (ethos) and the ways in which we think about our universe (worldview). In like manner, the ways in which we carry out our daily tasks and conceive of nature, of self, and of society give meaning to the symbols we find sacred.[24] Our emotions and attitude bear heavily on our sociology (how we interact with others) and psychology (how we think, see ourselves, and respond to the world) and by contrast how our sociology and psychology inform emotional life. That implies that the political value of rituals is that they foster allegiances nurtured by an emotional life, since social identification with groups is what frequently reinforces people's political allegiances instead of shared beliefs with other members.[25] In short, ritual life firmly establishes residents' social realities and worlds.

Moreover, ritual space can withstand the dialectics of cosmology and ontology—the self in relation to the universe—which distinguishes humans from animals. The emotional life lays bare the dialectical nature of humanity. In the case of these rural whites and blacks, their Southern regionalism reflects a ritual life that promotes social solidarity because rituals resolve the dialectical tension that emerges as a consequence of ritual participants not sharing or holding the same values. In this region, rites of intensification effect social forces that reaffirm rural and Southern life and resolve the dialectical nature of public and private ritual spaces.

Add to this the fact that liminal spaces are also properties of public ritual and private worship. Liminality is structured by forces that compel individual compliance to the group as both the means to and the price of belonging, which strengthens group identity while creating balance and safety. In Bald Eagles, regardless of race, group pressure to conform is based on a disciplinary system (and military culture) comprised of three major components: pride, respect, and honor. This disciplinary system is a socializing force, delineating for residents, both young and old, black and white, the boundaries of good and bad behavior. However, this disciplinary ("honor") system fosters marginalization and isolation from other parts of our country because not everyone can hold membership in this special group. These rural dwellers teach us that marginalized groups compensate for being on the periphery by developing and/or complying with a system that operates in liminal space and that creates social dignity and adulation.

Communitas also functions in liminality. *Communitas* is the liberation of human capacities from the normative constraints of social status and order,[26] and it is an attribute of and predicated upon "antistructure." In liminal space, *communitas* creates the leveling of distinctions between us/them, superior/inferior, male/female, leader/follower. In simultaneously supporting "antistructure and structure," liminal space carved out in ritual space distinguishes the individual from the group while also fortifying human interconnectedness, inciting human beings to action as well as thought.[27] Where cultural conservatism exists, rituals provides continuity of communal life because of ritual consistency and the constancy of ceremonial practices over time. Yet where cultural innovation can occur, rituals are also a force for political action and change because ritual participants have the ability to develop new rituals and alter old ones.[28] Whites and black participate in Bald Eagles' rich ritual life. It is one that supports regional customs and active evangelical religious cultures and that builds religious and political agreement, even if social consensus lacks uniformity. This can be attributed to community members' ritual behavior and action being able to support the *multivocality* and *ambiguity* of ritual symbols. Ritual life allows for the coexistence of disparate moral traditions as residents aim for religious visions of the good society.

Ritual, Institutions, and the Emotional Life

Previously, we met Muffin Morgan, who finds Republican political rhetoric on healthcare and abortion both frustrating and discordant. For her, a conservative pro-life stance is anomalous to real-life circumstances. Party politics leave many women and children to suffer in silence and especially those with no other alternatives to a "good" life except for a life of poverty.

If abortion is not an option and if healthcare is not an option, she asks, then who is going to care for the babies? While Morgan is pressed about the care of the children, her faith convictions drive her into another direction made apparent by the following confession: "You know, it's not . . . like myself, I *wouldn't* have an abortion, but what are you gonna do with these women out here?"

In this example, Morgan's personal politics and public faith collide. Her case epitomizes the incongruous nature of the many public theologies that comprise this civil religious milieu as well as its diverse religious communities and traditions into which these whites and blacks are socialized. Such diversity holds potential to materialize as religio-political paradoxes and moral bifurcations. Where ritual sacralizes institutional spaces, institutional cultures oblige the tension(s) between political beliefs and religious practices. In Bald Eagles, public institutions sustain and preserve ritual behavior that object-relationally speaking makes them Winnicottian "holding" environments for ambivalent feelings.

Object relations theory is a post-Freudian theory, inspired by Freudian thought. Freud suggested an individual's emotional attachments to primary persons (i.e., father and mother) figure prominently in one's self-representation and God-representation. Moreover, Freud understood that an important aspect of healthy psychic as well as physical growth and development is one's ability to relate to an "object," meaning individuals and/or things outside of the "self," be that a parent figure, a blanket, or a cause.

Freud's notion of object-relatedness has been extended, confirmed, and replaced by different object relations theorists; yet, his thoughts remain the framework for psychoanalytically influenced object relations theories. Even if theorists cannot agree on a definition of object relations, they all agree on the supremacy of relationships, rather than drives, as the building blocks for healthy self-development.[29] A child's psychic development and maturation process happens in relationship to a primary caregiver who is attuned and adapted to the needs of the developing child, according to physician, psychoanalyst, and twentieth-century object relations theorist Donald W. Winnicott.

The "good" mother provides care to the developing infant by creating a "holding" environment. The holding environment is nontraumatic and unobtrusive, guaranteeing the safety of the child. The sphere additionally reflects the sensitivity of a mother who "holds" the emotionally developing child. This environment is the basis of "normal" (nondefensive) splitting in a maturing child.

With regard to the holding environment and normal splitting, James S. Grotstein in *Splitting and Projective Identification* writes:

In the meanwhile, I hope it suffices to say that normal splitting—
cognitive, phenomenological, or defensive—is a narcissistic luxury
bequeathed by an empathic self-object which serves as a background of
safety for the infant and helps it symbiotically to experience its own separation (primal splitting) safely from the background object and, further,
to conduct splitting "in front," so to speak, in the field of perceptual
view. . . . As trust in object constancy develops, the infant is enabled to
utilize the object as a reservoir or container of its temporarily postponed
feelings.[30]

In the case of a maturing child, a successful holding environment will
accommodate a child's initial forays into the emotional life. At the start,
the child is unable to keep contradictory feelings together (e.g., pleasure
vs. frustration) and so chooses to hold onto one of the two emotions. However, as the child matures, the child develops the ability to sort through
conflicting emotions and additionally to contain the more sensitive and/
or explosive of his or her emotions. Through developing an increasingly
trusting relationship with the "good" mother (i.e., the holding environment), the child ultimately gains the ability to postpone defensive feelings,
with the end result of maintaining ambivalent emotions.

In Bald Eagles, "institutional spaces are ritual spaces." And they behave
in like manner to the "holding" environment of the growing child. As
healthy spheres where individuals and groups interact, and where individuals and group members are protected and therefore trusting, these spaces
enable ritual participants to respond creatively to associates in close proximity but outside their spheres of influence and to persons in the larger
world. More importantly, "institutional space as ritual space" accords
individuals and social groups the ability to experience, sort through, and
contain the ambivalences of emergent conflicting emotions due to incom-
patible Christian beliefs and political practices.

This, too, might be a response to realizing the common good in a
postracial, post-911, globalized, and militarized America. This further
explains the role of rituals in shaping political beliefs. Rituals "contain"
the rise in cognitive dissonance that derives from people holding mutually inconsistent views, and even when those views differ from significant
others.[31] I am pointing out the fact that religious visions of the common
good are characterized by cognitive dissonance. However, the complex
and ritual-rich Bald Eagles setting furnishes institutional spaces as ritual
spaces—a mechanism for "holding," "sorting through," and "contain-
ing" diverse religious and political antagonisms, which has the potential
to minimize the probability of social conflict and disruptions on the road

toward redefining American national identity and realizing a vision of the good society.

In Bald Eagles, the dialectical character of institutional spaces as ritual spaces makes room for the "structure" of institutions and the "anti-structure" of ritual and liminal spaces. Here, individuals and social groups maintain binary and tensive attitudes, feelings, and emotions. Because they are contained by ritual life, such oppositions lessen the chance of social ruptures on the way toward envisioning what is "new" and "good" about the pluralistic and ecumenical U.S. age.

Rhetoric, Cosmic Warfare, Democracy, and Ritual Space(s)

Religious rhetoric, whether theological or more civil religiously oriented, emerges in ritual spaces to become a defining feature of rites of intensification in rural Bald Eagles. To recognize the ways in which blacks and whites employ "God vs. devil" is to begin to understand the distinctiveness of each social group. Both groups in this rural community use the "God vs. devil" trope to explain good versus evil (ethical conduct). However, each has different understandings of "God vs. devil" with respect to their lived experiences.

For blacks, the "devil" is anything that produces black distress and suffering. For instance, what blacks would consider "demonic" is the racial disparity in the criminal justice system in which black men are disproportionately convicted and sentenced for crimes for which others might not face prosecution or would receive shorter sentences. The percentage of black men in prison negatively impacts the well-being of black families. When I asked these rural townsfolk to share their concerns about national and local leadership, James Bond, a fifty-nine-year-old African American business owner, declared: "Locally and nationally, the war on drugs tends to bother me because we continue to let drugs enter the U.S. because it creates millions of dollars. Our government don't care to put a stop to drug trafficking and drug lords; yet, eighty percent of criminals incarcerated are black." Ironically, the U.S. government seems to tolerate a drug culture that is ravaging many of America's small and working-class communities. What Bond considers demonic is America's monetary gain from illegal drug activity, and the judicial system's unfair profiling and imprisonment of black men—at high rates and in large numbers.

For whites, the "devil" is embodied in the threat of secularization. For example, what is "demonic" for whites would be young people's media exposure to extremely relaxed morals, especially sexually explicit content, and the apparent increased violence directed toward and experienced among members of American society. Asked about local and national leadership, Selita Judson, a forty-nine-year-old accountant, remarked: "The issue of self-regulation is of great concern to me. If we constantly rely on the government to keep us in line, then we are in danger of becoming a communist society. We do need some government regulations to keep a livable balance, but we also need to practice restraint on our own. As for religious issues, we don't stand up for our religious beliefs enough. We have moved from a community to a 'me-first' way of life that has little love for our neighbors. American culture has also become accepting of relaxed morals." Besides the debauchery of immoral lifestyles, to have America—a democracy—ever become communist is an oxymoron to Selita. Both are demonic.

"God vs. devil" language assumes two forms in these communities. Both forms judge and justify American democracy as a commentary on the social and political condition of their region and the U.S. nation and as coming from perceptions about the spirit world generated from each group's respective evangelical Christian beliefs and practices. In this sense, "God vs. devil" language refers to their spiritual walk—how they work out their salvation as "born-again" (evangelical) Christians. In the former sense, "God vs. devil" is anthropomorphized. Corporal Essary's funeral, described at the start of this volume, displays the dominance of battlefield imagery to these religious adherents who profusely use "God vs. devil" language to construct their social worlds and realities.

Preachers stressed the battle with the enemy (Satan, Afghanis) as located in spiritual and physical realms; emphasized the war as an oppositional conflict between evil (Afghanis) and good (the United States and Essary, the fallen soldier); and characterized the Taliban (and Afghanistan) as losers while Essary and America were conquerors and thereby triumphant winners. That rhetoric reified what it meant to be American.

To practitioners of evangelical faith, the apocalypse and eschatology are revelatory, end-of-time historical events. Spiritual warfare signals God's effort to establish a new kingdom. That kingdom building will require fighting with the devil. And humans are expected to participate in this battle of good over evil.[32] That eschatological expectation has been realized in Christian practice (i.e., prayer, fasting, Bible study, scriptural readings) and struggles against oppressive human conditions (e.g., slavery, poverty, homelessness, war)[33]—the subjects of public theological and moral matches.

Bald Eagles' black and white communities show us that eschatological and apocalyptic expectations are mainstays of the town's religious cultures and disclosed by the language of cosmic warfare—in public and private ritual spaces. Nonetheless, there is a danger associated with "God vs. devil" language and rhetoric.[34] Believers and nonbelievers should be concerned with the ways in which religion, religious discourse, and social violence are associated with each other. Jeffrey Williams writes that religion provides both meaning and value and a container for aggression, self-hatred, sacrifice, and multitudinous anxieties.[35] Characteristics that scholars have associated with religious violence are a belief in cosmic struggles between good and evil; God's divine judgment of the sinful world via apocalyptic traditions; theologies that portray the world as profoundly flawed, sinful, and in need of purification; and images of humans as divine warriors.[36]

We must defend against the use of inflammatory religious discourse, for it has the power to intensify social grievances and to transform benign and dormant emotions into violent behavior. In the faith convictions and democratic practices of both church communities as well as the rest of Bald Eagles, the cosmological conflict of "good vs. evil" is lived out. Williams' caution is supported by Kertzer's idea that ritual can be seen as a form of rhetoric since messages are advanced through complicated symbolic performances. Of special note is the political use of ritual as a form of rhetoric that promotes an emotionally compelling structure of we/they imagery by establishing a thesis–antithesis construct that unfailingly includes some and excludes many others.[37]

Blacks and whites in this rural and Southern town might differ on social, religious, and political issues. However, they all resonate with the language used to communicate their desires for change to their local community and to the larger, democratic U.S. society. Their public theological rhetoric captures visions of the good life, and yet their civil religious language condemns and sets the group up for social conflict. However, consider that "the belief in cosmic warfare helps orient people in the world and can help them make sense of social marginalization and feelings of anger."[38] For the people of Bald Eagles, "good vs. evil" language conveys many feelings associated with their perception of being a subpopulation on the periphery. Such rhetoric indicates their discontent with being marginalized; the evil of conspicuous consumption; their fear of a "godless" nation-state; their anxiety about public moral laxity, especially with regard to their children; and their resistance to being stripped of religious freedoms and other constitutional rights.

Churchill and Howard: Religious Ideology and American Dreaming

Civil religious rhetoric and behavior on display in ritual space conveys white and black understandings of a public theology of war and "politics of death," as related to American patriotisms that have emerged out of recent terrorist-inspired war conditions. For whites, war conditions alongside the election of the nation's first black president have resulted in a form of Southern civil religion expressive of civic Americanism. This brand of American patriotism upholds Christian faith, symbols, history, and myths while concomitantly offering their description of regional and conceptions of American national identities. Consider Larry Churchill's speech at the 2009 Bald Eagles Veteran's Day parade as an example of civic Americanism:

> **Folks, we live in the greatest country in the world.** Tell your children and family about the sacrifice made on behalf of them. Folks, God sent his son here for us. America is the greatest nation on earth because we have citizens who are willing to give back and sacrifice their lives. There has been more done in the last hundred years than we can stop to count. We went through World War I and the Depression. Japan bombed Pearl Harbor. We sent our men over there to keep this country free.
>
> **Women did a whole lot also to keep this country free.** Look at how great a military we have now. We have the best technology to contribute to the progress of America. We love each other, here. We might have our differences and our disagreements, but the rest of the world knows do not mess with Americans. We are not going to let another country take this away from us. . . . Folks remember this. . . . *Look at the monuments here and in Washington, D.C. Men have given their lives.*
>
> **Have they ever said, "You owe me"? No, they have not.** Instead, they will say, "Love your family, neighbor. Love the Lord, and do something good for somebody." We are proud of the state of Tennessee. It is the Volunteer State. A volunteer will always do ten times more than a person who is getting paid. Volunteer to serve this country and fight for this country. Do not forget to tell your children about the service to this country.

For blacks, war conditions and the election of former president Barack Obama have produced a Southern civil religion exercised as civic responsibility. That demands defending democratic principles and displaying loyalty to the U.S. nation despite the imperfections of our union. Marshall Howard's words spoken at the 2009 citywide worship service for Martin Luther King Jr. Day sums this up:

> **Why are we here today?** We're not here because of Dr. King but because of Rosa Parks. If not for Rosa Parks, we would not have Martin Luther King Jr. Had there not been a Dr. King, there would not be a Barack Obama! Dr. King said that our dream is rooted in the American dream.
>
> **What is the American dream?** The American dream is, *first, the right to vote.* Cheryl Simpson registered 180 people in Bald Eagles County on the weekend because of Barack Obama and because of Dr. King's dream. The American dream is, *second, the right to shelter and jobs.* Dr. King fought for shelter and better jobs. Black folks went north from the South because we did not want to be in the fields all our lives. The American dream is, *thirdly, about education.* Dr. King fought for education. We must commit ourselves to education not just as children but even also as adults. Take classes at Bald Eagles State Community College even if it is to learn a trade. *Dr. King's dream is deeply rooted in the American dream, and you too can achieve it.*

In *Religious Ideology in American Politics: A History*, Nicole Guétin explains the religio-political term *Manifest Destiny*, its historic entrance into political discourse, and its strength as an American and religious ideology even in today's political arena. She claims:

> The concept of "American exceptionalism," inscribed in the genes of the country's forbears, still appears to be linked to the myth of a historical redemptive mission. Many Americans are, as in the past, convinced that America has a divine mission, but, as in the past, this opinion is not shared by everyone worldwide. This, obviously, generates political tensions. In American historiography, the religious interpretation of many events may have denatured the core of the Christian faith and contradicted its truthfulness and its authenticity. If American exceptionalism today gives rise to serious questioning, one must admit that such ideological patterns were largely reproduced in many nations throughout the centuries. Since the origin of the world, nations and empires have claimed their supremacy over other countries or continents. However, what makes it original when it comes to America is the deep conviction that this supremacy is expressed in moral, religious, and missionary terms.[39]

How shall we interpret Churchill and Howard in light of Guétin's declaration and critique of American exceptionalism with its missionizing message? While the civic Americanism of Larry Churchill calls attention to the sacrifices of American military on foreign soil, encourages volunteerism and service to the region and country, and charges us to share in moral lessons with future generations, his political discourse embraces and illumes American superiority over other countries in the world. The American exceptionalism of Churchill appeals to a "heritage"—applied here as a racialized term—that can be claimed only by a select group of Americans. Historian David Lowenthal argues, "Heritage passes on exclusive myths of origins and continuity, endowing a select group with power and prestige."[40] Ergo, American exceptionalism, as articulated by Churchill, implies a white racial nationalism that does not extend U.S. membership to all Americans and for this reason is not an inclusive ideal.

Marshall Howard's civic responsibility is an acknowledgment of our responsibilities to our families, ourselves, and others as American citizens—to vote, to work, to have access to housing, and to get an education. As simple as Marshall's ideas are, civic responsibility stipulates levels of accountability in the pursuit of freedom, equality, and justice. That is why the American dream can certainly be a critique of American exceptionalism; it is *not* exclusionary. It calls forth the best in all of us—to live full lives; to grow and develop; and to put to good use acquired skills and innate talents for the betterment of America and the rest of humankind.

The myth of American exceptionalism can diminish the degree to which we will admit that our regionalisms, racialisms, and genderisms—biases, prejudices, and ethnocentricisms—contribute to our failing to achieve a more perfect union, the Beloved Community, or the public good. American exceptionalism further holds the potential for violence if misunderstood or misused. Larry Churchill inadvertently justifies the use of violence in preserving democratic and American liberties. Yet, this is in glaring contrast to the evangelical faith and civil religion that Bald Eagles' townsfolk commonly depict, accept, and profess—one formulated around our country's sacred documents, upheld by the community's Christian congregations and the rest of the American public.

Scholar of religion Conrad Cherry outlines two forms of American exceptionalism and civil religion when he writes:

> The civil religion, like any religion which becomes an established part of culture, is always in danger of sanctifying the virtues of a society while ignoring its vices. . . . America's present position as a great world power intensifies the peril; Americans have long lived under the conviction that

their nation always comes to the defense of other countries for the sake of "free institutions" and "democratic governments." Can we admit . . . that we have also rushed to the aid of military dictatorships when we believe such action will serve our national interests?[41]

Here, America's greatness is tied to its ability to assist countries that want our help to move toward democratic leadership and free and public institutions. Yet the other side of this is an American exceptionalism that grants "insider" status to its enthusiasts, but at a cost—the cost of the threat of violence stirred by an expansionist and messianic imperialist project. Cherry observes this as the cost of imperialism and notes that it is measured by America's inability to be self-critical or to see its blind spots. This inability Cherry critiques and speaks of as "[America's] rush to aid military dictatorships." Is there another way to make America great without the violence of militarism?

Guétin moreover adds that American exceptionalism blinds us to the importance of creating and maintaining connections to a more global world, a world that cannot be overlooked, especially in a technological age in which the tools of science place us in more immediate contact with the other. If nothing else, the Middle Eastern and North African social movements and our illegal and undocumented immigrant problem (e.g., DACA) teach us that our expansionist and missionizing leanings will require us to expand instead of limit our *borders* (e.g., social, political, religious, etc.) and in more ways than can be counted. This is not to say we do not need the boundaries of nationhood, however.

The civic Americanism practiced by Bald Eagles whites ascribes both exceptional and exclusionary meanings to key symbols. In some places, it overlaps with and strengthens the civic responsibility practiced by blacks, but in other places meaning is not shared, and subsequently the concepts become diametrically opposed to each other. Civic responsibility nurtures American dream-ing. It embraces values, commitments, and a way of life similar to but different from the civic Americanism of American exceptionalism. Except in cases of war (i.e., young persons' deaths) and the presence of a new outsider (specifically illegal immigrants), where there is seeming agreement, the ritual spaces where whites and blacks remain present are dialogical, dialectical, and contested spaces, spaces that reflect the civic Americanism and civic responsibility embraced and exercised by individuals and white and black social groups in this rural and Southern town.

Reformulated definitions of American identity and "new" formulations of American exceptionalism would recognize the complexities of living in America; would realize no single social group or culture can adequately represent America because, from its origins, America has been syncretistic (insiders were once outsiders, and outsiders who eventually become insiders will always exist); and would appreciate that America's "exceptionalism" rests with the ability of Americans to resolve cultural conflicts on American soil and without necessarily resorting to explosive violence.[42]

A "New" Exceptionalism for a Global U.S. Civil Society

In an age of terrorism, global reordering, and social ruptures, what is the role of public theology and civil religion in producing a religious vision of the good society? How will the United States define itself? Who are we, as Americans? And what makes for a just and good American society alongside growing nationalism and pluralism? These have remained abiding questions throughout this interdisciplinary empirical study on self-identified evangelical and politically populist Bald Eagles, a rural and Southern community, where members were wrestling with their multidimensional identities under religiously inspired war conditions and upon the election and presidency of Barack H. Obama. In so doing, this study demonstrates how structural and global innovations and developments affected white and black residents who were dealing with shifting and changing understandings of American national identity; such disquieting transitions signaled the beginning of a crisis in national identity. For that reason, new interpretations of American exceptionalism presently include the more triumphalistic and nativistic brand that *makes America great again.*

Social alienation and isolation offer to these rural and Southern whites and blacks reasons why human "sacrificial" death features so prominently in their thinking and rhetoric. It also taps into their feelings of inclusion in a nation where dying for country preserves constitutional rights and responsibilities, freedoms, and dignity as well as creates an atmosphere of social belonging. Bald Eagles is a farming community whose sons and daughters have and still faithfully serve our country. Military service is a "family business." Moreover, townsfolks' sons and daughters, grandsons and granddaughters, now fill the ranks of a "self-perpetuating" military caste largely segregated from the rest of the U.S. society because, by serving our country, they live with the peculiar experience of having to regularly experience the horrors of war. So, these Southern and rural dwellers become the face of the fallen who sacralize the land and preserve America from its "enemies."

By its very nature, this subpopulation not only symbolizes the confusion around but also makes claims to and displays strong emotions about *who is* and *who is not* American. Such confusion is plausible whenever groups are ill prepared for or succumb to rapid social changes, especially ones brought on by tumultuous financial markets, new technologies, and increased cultural plurality caused by the movement of migrants, immigrants, and refugees. Each is a hallmark of an early twenty-first-century postmodern nation. Especially for those who are white, the election of Barack H. Obama embodied such rapid and turbulent changes. He had come to stand for the unsettling nature of twenty-first-century postmodernity realized as threats to national security and as religiously inspired terrorist activity, and resulting in alternative interpretations of American regional and national identities.

Knowing this, what makes for a just and good American society alongside growing nationalism and pluralism? Civil religion is the religious dimension of American public life that is conceived less as a single template or fixed foundation for moral life. Rather, it frames and accommodates multivocal moral arguments because it extends through multiple moral traditions, practices, and institutional arrangements.[43] It is counterbalanced by the public theologies of national religious communities and the American public church. When both work in concert, they augment each other, even though public theology has the power and authority to contest civil religious ideals that fall short of how Americans should live together.

Bald Eagles' white and black, rural and Southern residents have particular lessons to teach us about our nation's attempts at self-definition and pursuit of the common good in a postmodern, globalized, postracial, and post-911 U.S. society. First, civil religion and public theology implicitly offer conceptions of how Americans should live together because both are mediums for interpreting diverse yet debatable and multiple moral traditions. Because of and not in spite of the civil religious and the public theological atmosphere of Bald Eagles and its religious communities, we discover how conflict can lead to moral and spiritual growth and greater social openness instead of struggles that threaten to turn into schisms, the result of uncontainable moral traditions and opinions.[44] Rites of intensification, particularly those in institutional and ritual spaces, and exaggerated by the "politics of death," reveal and contain opposing thoughts, behaviors, and emotions, while reaffirming this population's social and regional identities. So, Bald Eagles' Southern civil religion(s) and public theologies translate into a canopy for social diversity, regardless of race, age, gender, or political or denominational affiliation.

Second, because of the civil religious and public theological environment in Bald Eagles, we learn that the quest after the public good is possible despite early twenty-first-century postmodern globalism. In fact, the search after the common good is necessary in a pluralist U.S. society. By actively socializing community members into American citizenship and public life, religious communities still hold keys to teaching individuals and groups how to be ecumenical, ways to face pluralism, and how to become interdependent, work, and live together. Yet, in a global U.S. civic society, pursuing the common good means having to confront issues around nationalism.

A good society can still be produced if nations practice "responsible nationalism,"[45] which would recognize "the right of every people to self-government and the responsibility they share for their common fate."[46] That would acknowledge nations' rights and responsibilities to determine the parameters for common membership (i.e., citizenship) and would demand the exercise of moral and political ethics. That means we do not abuse our least advantaged citizens and immigrants or refugees.[47] It understands that countries' main objectives should be the pursuit of their citizens' economic welfare and elsewhere circumscribe their ability to harm the interests of citizens.[48]

Third, the quest to achieve the public good is always fraught with dialectics, contradictions, and ambivalences—all of which must be contained. The whites and blacks of rural and Southern Bald Eagles gift us with examples of their rich ritual life that translates into "holding" environments or "containers" for disparate and contestable thoughts, beliefs, behaviors, and emotions. As the struggle between religious and political rites ensues, ritual space implies and reveals residents' conflicts of interest.[49] There is no way to speak of the common good without having dialogue that produces, at times, symphonious—but more often manifests discordant—moral traditions.

Another powerful aspect of Bald Eagles' ritual life is the fact that ritual spaces serve as containers for rhetorical categories that are verbal expressions of the common good.[50] In other words, white and black community members possess contrary conceptions of American national identity and American exceptionalism. However, ritual spaces disclose their shared interpretation and understanding of the "covenant" model as furnishing the means to pursue the moral community and common good.[51] Here, again, is an example of ritual spaces holding disparate notions of what it means to be American and creating a moral community. Yet, these white rural Southerners, like their black counterparts, rely on and utilize a historic, civil religious, and sacrificial covenant model to inspire political action, to aspire to social reform, and to express differing conceptions about American greatness and American identity.

The existing tenor of the nation can be attributed to the start of the War on Terror, if not before. For an example of the tension between a pluralistic *and* nationalistic country, consider that whites and blacks in Bald Eagles practice divergent patriotisms that have developed into assorted public theologies of war. Because of this circumstance, the current formulation of American exceptionalism exposes a national identity crisis that can be imputed to a void that needs to be filled. Specifically, President Trump must lay out a civil religious description of American national identity that meets the needs of the American public during this "time of trial" and particularly because he has only clearly avowed a racially tinged version of American exceptionalism that is proving controversial. It is contributing to confusion and conflict, and in particular cases producing social violence and questions about our national identity.

This signals that a "new" American exceptionalism is in order for our more global American civil society. It requires vigorous application of democratic principles and (civil) religious work. For it holds the potential to reconstrue and weave together the "civic Americanism" of white residents and the "civic responsibility" of black residents to create a more inclusive and just society where multiple global constituencies meet and where the connection between race, ethnicity, public theology, and civil religion comes to represent reformulations of national identity and the more nativistic expressions of American exceptionalism.[52] Hopefully, this "untested" value, theory, and principle will course its way through the minds, hearts, and actions of those striving against as well as those supportive of the ideology and rhetoric that *makes America great again* by replacing it with democratic and religious work always yearning to *make America better again.*

Appendix 1

Methodology and Research Process

Overview

I employed three methodologies to advance my field research and for this mixed-methods (i.e., qualitative and quantitative) study. First, ethnographic fieldwork in Bald Eagles included participating in and observing public events on holidays like Veterans Day and Martin Luther King Jr. Day; conducting unstructured and semi-structured interviews with residents; and leading a macrolevel case study of two congregations—one white, the other black—in this community. Upon entering the West Tennessee farming community of Bald Eagles, I used ethnographic research methods to understand how residents synchronize their religious and political worldviews. Ethnographic research captured the thoughts, opinions, and vernacular voices and actions of community members. Ethnographic research also enabled me to approach the broad question fueling this project: How should we live in America?

I observed the town's public events on civic holidays (e.g., Memorial Day, Juneteenth, and Independence Day). Being present at town ceremonies like military funerals and being invited to participate in church events permitted me entrée into spaces where religion was inserted into political life and politics introduced into religious life. Knowledge about this rural culture I also culled from local newspaper, television, and radio.

I used participant observation to study individual and group behavior and to record information about group and individual thought, speech, actions, and feelings in field notes. Unstructured and semi-structured interviewing of townsfolk, church, and political leadership paralleled participant observation as tools for gathering more information. Reading and writing field notes stimulated conscious awareness of the relevance of

civic holiday rituals to this town's people in both public and private settings. Alongside this, conversation with community members and event
observation over a two-year period prompted my return to Bald Eagles in
spring 2008 to late summer 2009.

In the next stage of ethnographic research, I secured permission to
conduct my studies in congregational settings from two of the community's key informants: the white pastor of a leading church (Bald Eagles
First United Methodist Church) and the black pastor of a historic congregation (Tabernacle Missionary Baptist Church) in the city of Bald Eagles.
Participant observation of both church communities included attending
weekly Bible studies, Sunday school, Sunday worship services, Christian
liturgical calendar worship services (e.g., Ash Wednesday, Easter), special
services reinforcing American nationhood (e.g., Martin Luther King Jr.
Day, Memorial Day, Independence Day, Thanksgiving), church events
to which townsfolk were invited (e.g., Women's Sunday, Mission Blitz),
church business meetings, and church socials. I also attended public events
and conversed with townsfolk about life in Bald Eagles. In many instances,
I conducted individual interviews formally.

In the third stage of my fieldwork, I generated a questionnaire and distributed it to members of the Bald Eagles First United Methodist Church
and the Tabernacle Missionary Baptist Church. A total of thirty questionnaires were completed: six from the predominantly black Tabernacle Missionary Baptist Church and twenty-four from the predominantly
white First United Methodist Church. Each questionnaire had a cover
sheet requesting information about ethnicity/race, age, gender, occupation, years living in Bald Eagles, veteran status, theological status (e.g.,
conservative, moderate, liberal), and sociopolitical status (e.g., conservative, moderate, liberal). These nominal variables were used to conduct
categorical analyses of the demographic data according to the theological
and sociopolitical distribution of research participants.

I asked respondents to answer a series of questions. Sample questions included:

-What sociopolitical issues are important to you, locally and
    nationally? Why?
-Do you believe that American culture (media, the arts, social beliefs,
    etc.) affects your religious belief and practice?
-Do you identify as an Evangelical Christian? Please define the term.
-How do you define patriotism?
-Do we live in a postracial society?
-What are your beliefs and practices around death and dying?[1]

Members in both congregations initially found the questionnaire complex and asked for simplification. I clarified terms and questions using a clarification sheet with definitions of terms.[2] Emerging later as new concerns, the following two questions factored into my data analysis:

-What is the relationship between American national identity and American exceptionalism? Are the concepts equal or different?

-In what ways have ideas about "peoplehood" and an "exceptional" America remained the same or changed under the duress of endless war?

I used the questionnaire to inform the development of a semi-structured interviewing format subsequently conducted with fifty-five volunteers from the Bald Eagles First United Methodist Church, the Tabernacle Missionary Baptist Church, and the outside Bald Eagles community, who were placed into focus groups. This was the fourth phase of field research. Formal focus groups were composed of two to four participants per group and were organized along veteran, age, gender, church, community, and racial lines. Fifty-five research participants formed twenty-five semi-structured focus groups. Black participants in the study represented fourteen focus groups, and white participants eleven focus groups.

I interviewed participants in the study rooms of the Bald Eagles State Community College. A few interviews I held in naturally occurring settings (e.g., homes, church, personal businesses). Informed consent of interviewees and focus-group sessions were audiotaped. Interviews lasted from one and a half to four hours. However, the average length of group interviews was two hours. Interviews were later transcribed. In total, the questionnaires and focus-group interviewing yielded eighty-three research participants (n=83) for this study, although after using a computer-generated randomization program,[3] sixty-five (n=65) research participants became my study's focus. With their permission, I retained the names of the two local churches that were the focus of this research and those of public figures (e.g., clergypersons, politicians, community leaders, military personnel). However, I used pseudonyms to identify parishioners, private citizens, and other residents in the city and county.

Ethnographic field notes, questionnaires, and individual and focus-group interviews gave me four data sets with analyzable content. I read material in this collection of data to find emergent themes and analyzed it to develop coding categories. I used the software program NVivo-8 to code the data into twenty-four categories that in some cases were divided into subcategories. Sample categories included American culture on religion, defining evangelicalism, gender, leadership, patriotism as civil religion (subcategories: blacks on patriotism, whites on patriotism, faith and patriotism, military), regional culture, ritual (subcategories: myth, symbolism), sociopolitical issues (subcategories: family/youth, rights vs. responsibilities), sociopolitical issues with moral bent, and violence. I also conducted statistical analysis on these data sets. From them, I amassed comprehensive and rich knowledge about race, evangelical faith, and the nature of civil religious practice and ritual life in this community of rural dwellers from this collection of data, which I interpreted to understand how they were constructing and reconstructing their regional identity and the identity of the American nation.

Second, as an exercise in Clifford Geertz' theory on "religion as a cultural system,"[4] I completed a "thick description" to argue for a "critical hermeneutic theory of society,"[5] interpreting these rituals through the sublenses of sociology and anthropology.

Third, I employed a "critical correlational" method to advance critical theories (including theology and social psychology) for understanding these residents' interpretation of American national identity during wartime (and specifically during the War on Terror); evangelical faith; Southern civil religion expressive of polyvalent and polysemic death rites of soldiers and rituals commemorating the service of nonmilitary men and women also considered America's fallen; and multiple interpretations of American exceptionalism.

Appendix 1.A: Evangelical Faith and Southern Civil Religion Survey

*Name: _____   Gender: Male   Female

Ethnicity: African American   Caucasian American

Age Range: 20–45   46–69   70–beyond

Occupation: _____   Years in Bald Eagles ___

Veteran: Yes___   No___   Wars served in? _____

Theologically: Conservative___ Moderate___   Liberal___

Socially: Conservative___ Moderate___   Liberal___

1) What sociopolitical and religious issues are important to you, locally *and* nationally? Why?

2) Do you believe that American culture (media, the arts, social beliefs, etc.) affects your religious belief and practice? How and why?

3) Do you identify as an Evangelical Christian? Please define the term.

4) Do you participate in activities that identify you as an Evangelical Christian? And what causes and/or church ministries do you participate in?

5) a) How do you define patriotism? b) If military service, are there other forms of patriotic service to the country? c) Does your faith influence your understanding of patriotism? How?

6) In this age of Harold Ford and President Obama, do we live in a postracial society? Why or why not?

7) What are your beliefs and practices around death and dying? Please provide an example of a particular practice.

Appendix 1.B: Clarification Sheet for Evangelical Faith and Southern Civil Religion Survey

Definition of Terms

Very generally speaking, **theological conservatism** is often identified with *religious movements* such as Holiness, Pentecostal, Charismatic, and Conservative Evangelical Movements. Most *theological conservatives* uphold specific beliefs and practices associated with *creedal statements* like the Apostle's Creed and Nicene Creed. *Theological conservatives* also believe in the virgin birth, death, and resurrection of Jesus Christ; Jesus' second coming; and the authority of the Bible, even if they are not confessional Christians (meaning that the denomination does not uphold any particular doctrines).

A **theological moderate**, as the name suggests, holds beliefs and practices between that of **theological conservatism** and **theological liberalism**.

Speaking generally, **theological liberalism** has been identified with *mainline Protestant churches* like the Episcopal and United Methodist Churches. However, that is not necessarily the case, today. Instead of being guided by a particular belief system (creedal statements), *theological liberals* understand the "truth" of the Bible from cultural perspectives (i.e., class, race, gender, the social and political). God's movement is seen from the perspective of what is happening in the world and how these events impact individuals, today.

Social conservatism is usually described as a belief in traditional values. Most *social conservatives*, for example, are pro-life, for traditional nuclear families (meaning wife, husband, and children), and for the death penalty. They are generally against issues like same-sex marriage and stem-cell research.

A **social moderate**, as the name suggests, has beliefs and values that cut across **social conservatism** and **social liberalism**.

Social liberals are also described as *social progressives*. They usually stress a redistribution of wealth and the social welfare provisions for individuals. Most *social liberals*, for example, are pro-choice, for stem-cell research, for educational reform, and for the legalization of same-sex marriage. They are generally against the death penalty and choose diplomacy over military action.

PLEASE NOTE: These definitions do not fully encompass the meaning of these terms. For instance, a *theological conservative* can be *socially liberal*, and a *social conservative* can also be a *theological moderate*. Use your discretion in describing yourself and belief systems. This sheet is merely meant to CLARIFY these terms.

Updated Survey

1) a) What community (social) issues are important to you? What national (social) issues are important to you?
   b) What community religious issues are important to you? What national religious issues are important to you?
2) Do you believe American culture (the media, arts, societal beliefs, etc.) affects your religious belief *and* practice? How *and* why?
   For example: I was speaking with a resident who believed that MTV, VH1, and BET aired too many sexually explicit videos and programs that could easily impact a young person's religious belief system.
3) a) Are you an Evangelical Christian? Yes or No
   b) Please describe what being an Evangelical Christian means to you.
4) What *organizations* and/or *church activities* do you believe are reflections of your Christian faith?
5) a) Please define the word *patriotism*.
   b) Are there *other forms of patriotism* besides military service?
   c) Does your Christian faith *influence* your understanding of patriotism? How?
6) Do we live in a *postracial* society? (*Postracial* means we no longer categorize people according to race.) Why or why not?
7) Explain *death and dying* according to your Christian faith. Please give an example of a death practice.

Appendix 1.C: True Randomness

The questionnaires, individual, and focus-group interviewing yielded eighty-three research participants (n=83) for this study, although after using a computer-generated randomization program, sixty-five (n=65) research participants became the study's focus. For this small study, a simple randomization was performed by assigning numbers to the questionnaires, individual interviews, and focus groups that met minimal requirements for inclusion in the study. For instance, completed surveys included participants' answering questions and demographic information. Individual and focus group interviewees were required to provide informed consent for data usage. To maintain complete randomness, the computer program, "true randomness," produced integers that fell within the questionnaire, individual, and focus group assignment ranges. Randomly assigned data became the focus of this mixed-methods study (i.e., qualitative and quantitative), which produced data from sixty-five research participants, although statistical analysis was also performed on results from the eighty-three (n=83) research participants.

Computer randomization of the questionnaires, individual interviewing, and focus-group interviewing was applied for the three reasons. Randomization is used in human subjects research including social research and clinical trials to ensure against selection bias and accidental bias. It guarantees equal application of treatment conditions for participants in a study. Further, research participants should not differ systematically or research results will be biased. For example, after initial randomization a greater proportion of older subjects (i.e., sixty and older) were yielded. Therefore, a double randomization was conducted to correct for this imbalance and to ensure younger voices (i.e., fifties and younger) were equally represented in the study. Along these lines, individual and focus group interviews were assigned to two groups—A and B. Proper randomization was required to guard against a priori knowledge of group assignments. Both groups were included in the randomization process to ensure against selection bias.

RANDOM.ORG Site Description

"Perhaps you have wondered how predictable machines like computers can generate randomness. In reality, most random numbers used in computer programs are *pseudo-random*, which means they are generated in a predictable fashion using a mathematical formula. This is fine for many purposes, but it may not be random in the way you expect if you're used to dice rolls and lottery drawings. RANDOM.ORG offers *true* random numbers to anyone on the Internet. The randomness comes from atmospheric noise, which for many purposes is better than the pseudo-random number algorithms typically used in computer programs. People use RANDOM.ORG for holding drawings, lotteries and sweepstakes, to drive online games, for scientific applications and for art and music. The service has existed since 1998 and was built by Dr Mads Haahr of the School of Computer Science

and Statistics at Trinity College, Dublin in Ireland. Today, RANDOM.
ORG is operated by Randomness and Integrity Services Ltd."

Random Integer Generator

"Generate 11 random integers (maximum 10,000). Each integer should
have a value between 1 and 22 (both inclusive; limits ±1,000,000,000).
Format in 1 column(s)."

The random integer generator yielded the following:

3
15
13
14
9
8
21
1
6
19

Appendix 2

Theological Orientations and Social Perspectives
against Age Groups for N=83[1]

Age	Theological		Social			Total
			Conservative	Liberal	Moderate	
20–45	Conservative	Count	6	1	3	10
		% within theological	60.0%	10.0%	30.0%	100.0%
		% within social	100.0%	14.3%	30.0%	43.5%
		% of total	26.1%	4.3%	13.0%	43.5%
	Liberal	Count	0	4	1	5
		% within theological	.0%	80.0%	20.0%	100.0%
		% within social	.0%	57.1%	10.0%	21.7%
		% of total	.0%	17.4%	4.3%	21.7%
	Moderate	Count	0	2	6	8
		% within theological	.0%	25.0%	75.0%	100.0%
		% within social	.0%	28.6%	60.0%	34.8%
		% of total	.0%	8.7%	26.1%	34.8%
	Total	Count	6	7	10	23
		% within theological	26.1%	30.4%	43.5%	100.0%
		% within social	100.0%	100.0%	100.0%	100.0%
		% of total	26.1%	30.4%	43.5%	100.0%

(Continued on next page)

[1]   Appendix 2 is particularly relevant to the section entitled "The Theology and Politics of Race" in chapter 5 of this volume.

Age	Theological		Social			Total
			Conservative	Liberal	Moderate	
46–55	Conservative	Count	4		0	4
		% within theological	100.0%		.0%	100.0%
		% within social	100.0%		.0%	30.8%
		% of total	30.8%		.0%	30.8%
	Liberal	Count	0		2	2
		% within theological	.0%		100.0%	100.0%
		% within social	.0%		22.2%	15.4%
		% of total	.0%		15.4%	15.4%
	Moderate	Count	0		7	7
		% within theological	.0%		100.0%	100.0%
		% within social	.0%		77.8%	53.8%
		% of total	.0%		53.8%	53.8%
	Total	Count	4		9	13
		% within theological	30.8%		69.2%	100.0%
		% within social	100.0%		100.0%	100.0%
		% of total	30.8%		69.2%	100.0%
56–69	Conservative	Count	11	0	1	12
		% within theological	91.7%	.0%	8.3%	100.0%
		% within social	91.7%	.0%	8.3%	41.4%
		% of total	37.9%	.0%	3.4%	41.4%
	Liberal	Count	0	1	1	2
		% within theological	.0%	50.0%	50.0%	100.0%
		% within social	.0%	20.0%	8.3%	6.9%
		% of total	.0%	3.4%	3.4%	6.9%

Age	Theological		Social			Total
			Conservative	Liberal	Moderate	
56–69 *(cont.)*	Moderate	Count	1	4	10	15
		% within theological	6.7%	26.7%	66.7%	100.0%
		% within social	8.3%	80.0%	83.3%	51.7%
		% of total	3.4%	13.8%	34.5%	51.7%
	Total	Count	12	5	12	29
		% within theological	41.4%	17.2%	41.4%	100.0%
		% within social	100.0%	100.0%	100.0%	100.0%
		% of total	41.4%	17.2%	41.4%	100.0%
70+	Conservative	Count	7	0	1	8
		% within theological	87.5%	.0%	12.5%	100.0%
		% within social	87.5%	.0%	14.3%	44.4%
		% of total	38.9%	.0%	5.6%	44.4%
	Moderate	Count	1	3	6	10
		% within theological	10.0%	30.0%	60.0%	100.0%
		% within social	12.5%	100.0%	85.7%	55.6%
		% of total	5.6%	16.7%	33.3%	55.6%
	Total	Count	8	3	7	18
		% within theological	44.4%	16.7%	38.9%	100.0%
		% within social	100.0%	100.0%	100.0%	100.0%
		% of total	44.4%	16.7%	38.9%	100.0%

Note: In this cross-tabulation of three variables, theological and sociopolitical positions are measured against age. By reading vertically, "% within social" generates the intragroup statistic for each of the three sociopolitical statuses against theological position and age group. However, reading across horizontally, "% within theological" produces the intergroup statistic for theological position along age group and against sociopolitical status.

Appendix 3

Interviews[1]

Leadership in Black Female-Headed Households in the 1940s and 1950s

The following conversation was held at the Tabernacle Missionary Baptist Church with Deidre Abraham and Elizabeth Ainsley on March 21, 2009. However, here I highlight the exchange I had with Deidre Abraham on the black church, family, and black female-headed households in the 1940s and 1950s.

> N: What I'm also hearing you say is there was value in coming to church when you were growing up that you've seen lost now. So, historically, what was the value of coming to church? What are the values now? How did those values change? When you were growing up, why was the church so valuable here?
>
> DEIDRE ABRAHAM: Okay now, I'm gonna tell you the truth. As far as me, I was made to come to church. I'm gonna tell you somethin'. Now it [the Bible] says "train up a child in the right way and they will not depart from it." Like I said, my mama made me come to church, I was even grown, I had finished high school and I still was, as long as I was under her roof, I had to come to church. Okay. Coming to church I learned a little something and I had, like you said, values instilled in me, you know. I did. I strayed away after I got grown, got in a house myself. I left church, you know. 'Cause those streets seemed like they were more important to me at the time [I was in

---

[1]   Appendix 3 is particularly relevant to chapter 7 of this volume.

church]. I had to get out and see what was going on in those streets. It seemed like they were havin' more fun in those streets than in the church. But see, that wore out. You know, and I found out it really ain't nothin' out there. You see? And then I came back to the church. And, I'm glad the Lord spared me enough because he coulda left me out there . . . Like I said my mama taught me a lot of stuff that I didn't always abide by. But, like I said . . . I came back.

N: Now, tell me, the values that your mother taught you.

DA: To respect my elders. I had to say "yes ma'am" and "no ma'am." Kids nowadays say "yes" and "no." You know? And, she taught me how to respect—show respect for myself and [if you respect yourself] then other people will respect me. You know? I can't get respect if I'm half-naked. I walk down the street and some man says something, you know, out of—I'm asking for it. There's no reason for him to go . . .

N: Be disrespectful.

DA: Uh huh. But, if he sees me, he assumes certain things, you know?

N: You're saying scantily clothed?

DA: Uh huh. I've got to dress, I've got to carry myself in a way that I can be respected. If you don't have respect then, you know, she taught me this. She taught me the value of a dollar. She taught me to earn my living honestly. And, it wasn't—growing up, I didn't have a man in the house but my mama taught me—it was as if a man was there, you know? I don't feel like I have lost anything because a man wasn't there.

N: So, you're saying your father wasn't present.

DA: No, huh uh. But I don't feel like I missed that. Because I feel like my values and growing up was just as good as the person that did have a mother and a father in their house. Because, man, it was full of those women, but you couldn't [get away with anything]. If you didn't know which one was my mother, you was like, "Now I know it's my mother," because one will reach and grab you just as quick as the other one will, you know? And see, that's another thing, you know? Because, nowadays kids—say, for instance, with going to school.

If they went to school and they were cutting up [acting up] in school . . . see they got a whoopin' in school back in my day. And then they would go home and get another whoopin'. Or, if somebody in the streets saw your child doin' something, they may whoop your child there, and then you would go home and you got *another* whoopin', you know? But, you can't do that nowadays. 'Cause half the time when the children come home and tell you [parents], well the teacher was pickin' on me—you go to the school and half the time that parent's gonna be on that child's side when they should look at both sides of the situation. You know? They don't try to. . . . But that's also the way it was in church back in my day. Church folks would also discipline children who were cutting up.

Faith, Flags, and Guns: Black Civil Religion

The following conversation was held at the Bald Eagles State Community College with Sampson Frye Brown and Cowboy "Wonderful" Tread-way on March 25, 2009. I highlight the exchange I had with both men about the presence of national, state, and Christian flags in the Tabernacle Missionary Baptist Church sanctuary and worship space. In the conversation, I am inquiring about their interpretation of this version of black civil religion.

N: What does it mean for you to see the American flag in the church, the Tennessee flag, and the Christian flag? 'Cause that's a form of civil religion in the house of worship. So, how should a person understand that?

SAMPSON FRYE BROWN: First of all, the American flag is there because they are bein' patriotic. The state flag, I really don't have a lot of comment on the state, the flag can be there if it has to be. That is if the church decides. But by all means have the church flag. I believe in that. Now, I've gone to five churches, five churches in the area and my church, our church, I know it has the American flag in there 'cause I put one of them in there. It had the MIA flag, but I don't know what they did with that.

COWBOY "WONDERFUL" TREADWAY: I ain't seen that.

SFB: You ain't seen it? Well, I had one in there. I don't know what they did with it. The church flag has always been there as far as I can remember. What do they represent? Nothing really in God's house.

N: So, why are they there? That's my question.

CWT: Patriotic.

SFB: Bein' patriotic, I guess. I guess uh, it's a symbol. I guess.

N: What do you think?

CWT: That's really some of it. We symbolize a lot. We also follow suit a lot. For instance, so and so church they got this. Well let's get that too, you know? We wanna be like them. But, it's symbolism, that's what it is. Of course, in the church the [Christian] flag symbolizes "Well, this is the church." I guess, "We in a church, this is God's house," you know? The American flag means "We in America," you know? And that's patriotism bein' inserted into the church space. Tennessee [flag] symbolizes "We in the State of Tennessee." We got the flag, they got it in the capitol building, so we got it in the church. All symbolizin' . . . that's all it is.

N: But does it, does it trump God at any point?

CWT: I don't think it trumps God, because I think we look at those symbols differently than how we look at God. We have those there to symbolize and to represent tradition. It is recognition. Where God, we understand that the church is all about the Creator.

N: Okay.

CWT: So—

N: Okay, okay. Now, just related to this—do you think your faith influences your patriotism?

CWT: Yes. I think your faith influences everything about your being a human. For instance, patriotism is how you feel about certain things and what you are able to do with yourself in order to be able to get into those feelings. For instance, for instance, there was a time where people were killed [martyred], based upon their religions. Okay? If I lived within that time, my faith would tell me, "No I'm not doin' it even if I am a soldier. There are things that I just ain't gonna do." Even the military says to soldiers, "Okay, we can't make you do certain things if it's against your religion," because they understand that certain things are faith based.

Bibliography

Anderson, Ray S. *Theology, Death and Dying.* New York: Blackwell, 1986.

Anderson, Victor. *Beyond Ontological Blackness: An Essay on African American Religious and Cultural Criticism.* New York: Continuum, 1995.

Anglin, Mary K. *Women, Power, and Dissent in the Hills of Carolina.* Urbana: University of Illinois, 2002.

Balmer, Randall. *Encyclopedia of Evangelicalism.* Louisville: Westminster John Knox, 2002.

Barna Group. "Report Examines the State of Mainline Protestant Churches." December 7, 2009. https://www.barna.com/research/report-examines-the-state-of-mainline-protestant-churches/ (accessed February 2, 2011).

Barnes, Albert. *Notes on the New Testament: Explanatory and Practical.* Vol. 1, *Matthew and Mark.* Edited by Robert Frew. 1832. London: Blackie and Son, 1868.

Becker, Ernest. *The Denial of Death.* New York: Free Press Paperbacks, 1973.

Becker, Penny Edgehill. "What Is Right? What Is Caring?" In *Contemporary American Religion: An Ethnographic Reader,* edited by Penny Edgehill Becker and Nancy L. Eiesland, 121–45. Walnut Creek, Calif.: AltaMira, 1997.

Beinart, Peter. "How Trump Wants to Make American Exceptional Again." *Atlantic,* February 2, 2017.

Bell, Catherine. *Ritual Theory and Ritual Practice.* New York: Oxford University Press, 1992.

Bellah, Robert N. *Beyond Belief: Essays on Religion in a Post-traditionalist World.* Paperback ed. Berkeley: University of California Press, 1991.

———. *The Broken Covenant: American Civil Religion in Time of Trial.* 2nd ed. Chicago: University of Chicago Press, 1992.

———. "Civil Religion in America." *Journal of the American Academy of Arts and Sciences* 96, no. 1 (1967): 1–21. Reprinted in Bellah and Tipton, *Robert Bellah Reader,* 225–45; and in Richey and Jones, *American Civil Religion,* 21–43.

———. "Durkheim and Ritual." In Bellah and Tipton, *Robert Bellah Reader,* 150–80.

———. "Durkheim and Ritual." In *The Cambridge Companion to Durkheim*, edited by Jeffrey C. Alexander and Philip Smith, 183–210. Cambridge: Cambridge University Press, 2005.

———. "God and King." In Bellah and Tipton, *Robert Bellah Reader*, 357–75.

———. Foreword to *Myths America Lives By*, by Richard T. Hughes. Urbana: University of Illinois Press, 2003.

———. "Heritage and Choice in American Religion." Paper presented at *Daedalus* conference on religion and American culture, American Academy of Arts and Sciences, Brookline, Mass., October 15–16, 1965.

———. "Religion and the Legitimation of the American Republic." In Bellah and Tipton, *Robert Bellah Reader*, 246–64.

———. "The New American Empire." In Bellah and Tipton, *Robert Bellah Reader*, 350–56.

———. "Religious Evolution, Civil Religion and Public Theology in Global Perspective." Edited by Steven M. Tipton. Unpublished essay, 2012.

Bellah, Robert N., Richard Madsen, William M. Sullivan, Ann Swidler, and Steven M. Tipton. *The Good Society*. New York: Vintage Books, 1991.

———. *Habits of the Heart: Individualism and Commitment in American Life*. 3rd ed. Berkeley: University of California Press, 2008. First edition, 1985. Second edition, 1996.

Bellah, Robert N., and Steven M. Tipton, eds. *The Robert Bellah Reader*. Durham, N.C.: Duke University Press, 2006.

Bercovitch, Sacvan. *The American Jeremiad*. Madison: University of Wisconsin Press, 1978.

Berger, Peter L. *The Sacred Canopy: Elements of a Sociological Theory of Religion*. Garden City, N.Y.: Random House, 1967.

Berger, Peter L., and Thomas Luckmann. *The Social Construction of Reality: A Treatise in the Sociology of Knowledge*. New York: Anchor Books, 1966.

Bettie, Julie. *Women without Class: Girls, Race, and Identity*. Berkeley: University of California Press, 2003.

Bevans, Stephen B. *Models of Contextual Theology*. Rev. ed. Maryknoll, N.Y.: Orbis Books, 2002.

Bhabha, Homi K. *The Location of Culture*. New York: Routledge, 1994.

Blight, David W. "The Battle for Memorial Day in New Orleans." *Atlantic*, May 29, 2017.

———. *Beyond the Battlefield: Race, Memory, and the American Civil War*. Boston: University of Massachusetts Press, 2002.

———. "Forgetting Why We Remember." *New York Times*, May 30, 2011.

———. *Race and Reunion: The Civil War in American Memory*. 4th ed. Cambridge, Mass.: Harvard University Press, 2001.

Bloesch, Donald G. *Essentials of Evangelical Theology: Two Volumes in One*. Peabody, Mass.: Hendrickson, 2006.

Bromley, David G., and J. Gordon Melton, eds. *Cults, Religion, and Violence*. Cambridge: Cambridge University Press, 2002.

Browning, Don S. *Fundamental Practical Theology*. Minneapolis: Fortress, 1991.

Browning, Don S., and Terry D. Cooper. *Religious Thought and the Modern Psychologies*. 2nd ed. Minneapolis: Augsburg Fortress, 2004.

Burdette, Amy M., Christopher G. Ellison, and Terrence D. Hill. "Conservative Protestantism and Tolerance toward Homosexuals: An Examination of Potential Mechanisms." *Sociological Inquiry* 75, no. 2 (2005): 177–96.

Burwick, Frederick. "The Grotesque: Illusion vs. Delusion." In *Aesthetic Illusion: Theoretical and Historical Approaches*, edited by Frederick Burwick and Walter Pape, 122–32. Berlin: de Gruyter, 1990.

Butler, Jineea. "Integrating into a Burning House." *Final Call*, December 12, 2014.

Calhoun, Craig, ed. *Habermas and the Public Square*. Cambridge, Mass.: MIT Press, 1992.

Callahan, Allen Dwight. *The Talking Book: African Americans and the Bible*. New Haven: Yale University Press, 2006.

Campbell, Dennis M., William B. Lawrence, and Russell E. Richey, eds. *Doctrines and Discipline*. Vol. 3, *United Methodism and American Culture*. Nashville: Abingdon, 1999.

Casey, Edward S. *Remembering: A Phenomenological Study*. Bloomington: Indiana University Press, 1987.

Chapman, Mark L. *Christianity on Trial: African American Religious Thought before and after Black Power*. Eugene, Ore.: Wipf & Stock, 1996.

Chapple, Eliot Dismore, and Carleton Stevens Coon. *Principles of Anthropology*. New York: Henry Holt, 1942. See esp. "Rites of Intensification" (507–28) and "Rites of Passage" (484–506).

Cherry, Conrad, ed. *God's New Israel: Religious Interpretations of American Destiny*. Chapel Hill: University of North Carolina Press, 1998.

Children's Defense Fund. *The State of America's Children 2017*. http://www.childrensdefense.org/library/state-of-americas-children/2017-soac.pdf (accessed January 24, 2018).

Cohen, Howard. "'He Knew What He Signed Up For,' Trump Reportedly Tells Widow of Fallen Miami Gardens Soldier." *Miami Herald*, October 17, 2017.

Cone, James A. *A Black Theology of Liberation*. Twentieth anniversary ed. with critical reflections by Dolores S. Williams, Gayraud Wilmore, Rosemary Ruether, Pablo Richard, Robert McAfee Brown, K. C. Abraham. Maryknoll, N.Y.: Orbis Books, 1990.

———. *The Cross and the Lynching Tree*. Maryknoll, N.Y.: Orbis Books, 2011.

Duckitt, John H. "Authoritarianism and Group Identification: A New View of an Old Construct." *Political Psychology* 10, no. 1 (1989): 63–84.

Durkheim, Èmile. "The Elementary Forms of Religious Life." In *A Reader in the Anthropology of Religion*, edited by Michael Lambek, 34–49. Malden, Mass.: Blackwell, 2002.

———. *The Elementary Forms of Religious Life*. Translated by Carol Cosman. 2001. Repr., New York: Oxford University Press, 2008.

Economist. "Who Will Fight the Next War?" October 24, 2015.

Edison Media Research and Mitofsky International. "Tennessee Election Results 2008." *New York Times,* December 9, 2008. https://www.nytimes.com/elections/2008/results/states/exitpolls/tennessee.html.

———. "Tennessee: Presidential County Results 2008." *New York Times,* December 9, 2008. https://www.nytimes.com/elections/2008/results/states/president/tennessee.html.

Eikenberry, Karl W., and David M. Kennedy. "Americans and Their Military, Drifting Apart." *New York Times,* May 26, 2013.

Emerson, Michael O., and Christian Smith. *Divided by Faith: Evangelical Religion and the Problem of Race in America.* New York: Oxford University Press, 2000.

Erikson, Erik. *Childhood and Society.* 35th anniversary ed. New York: Norton, 1993.

———. *Dimensions of New Identity.* New York: Norton, 1974.

Erikson, Joan M. Preface to *The Life Cycle Completed,* by Erik H. Erikson. New York: W. W. Norton, 1997.

Erll, Astrid. *Memory in Culture.* Translated by Sara B. Young. New York: Palgrave MacMillan, 2011.

Evans, James H., Jr. *We Have Been Believers: An African American Systematic Theology.* Minneapolis: Augsburg Fortress, 1992.

Fonagy, Peter. *Attachment Theory and Psychoanalysis.* New York: Other Press, 2001.

Foster, Durwood. "Wesleyan Theology: Heritage and Task." In *Wesleyan Theology Today: A Bicentennial Theological Consultation,* edited by Theodore Runyan, 31–37. Nashville: Kingswood Books, 1985.

Frazier, E. Franklin. *The Negro Church in America.* 1964. Repr., New York: Schocken Books, 1974.

Frederick, Marla F. *Between Sundays: Black Women and Everyday Struggles of Faith.* Berkeley: University of California Press, 2003.

Freud, Sigmund. *The Future of an Illusion.* Translated by W. D. Robson-Scott. Garden City, N.Y.: Anchor Books, 1964.

———. *New Introductory Lectures on Psychoanalysis.* Translated by W. J. H. Sprott. New York: W. W. Norton, 1933.

Gadamer, Hans-Georg. *Truth and Method.* 2nd rev. ed. Translation revised by Joel Weinsheimer and Donald G. Marshall. New York: Continuum, 2000.

Gallagher, Sally K. "Where Are the Antifeminist Evangelicals? Evangelical Identity, Subcultural Location, and Attitudes towards Feminism." *Gender & Society* 18, no. 4 (2004): 451–72.

Geertz, Clifford. *The Interpretation of Cultures: Selected Essays.* New York: Basic Books, 2000. First published in 1973 by Basic Books. See esp. "Ethos, Worldview, and the Analysis of Sacred Symbols" (126–41) and "Religion as a Cultural System" (87–125).

Gerstle, Gary. *American Crucible: Race and Nation in the Twentieth Century.* Princeton, N.J.: Princeton University Press, 2001.

Gerteis, Joseph. "Civil Religion and the Politics of Belonging." *Political Power and Social Theory* 22 (2011): 215–23.

Gilkes, Townsend Cheryl. Afterword to *The Souls of Black Folk*, by W. E. B. Du Bois. New York: Signet Classics, 2012.

Glock, Charles Y. "The Churches and Social Change in Twentieth Century America." *Annals of the American Academy of Political and Social Science* 527 (1993): 67–83.

Gorringe, Timothy. *God's Just Vengeance: Crime, Violence, and the Rhetoric of Salvation*. New York: Cambridge University Press, 1996.

Gorski, Philip S. "Barack Obama and Civil Religion." *Political Power and Social Theory* 22 (2011): 179–214.

Graham, Janice. "I Fear I May Have Integrated My People into a Burning House." Our Common Ground Media and Communications, August 20, 2013. https://ourcommonground.com/2013/08/20/i-fear-i-may-have-integrated -my-people-into-a-burning-house-martin-luther-king-jr/.

Greenberg, Jay R., and Stephen A. Mitchell. *Object Relations in Psychoanalytic Theory*. 12th ed. Cambridge, Mass.: Harvard University Press, 1983.

Greene, Emma. "A Resolution Condemning White Supremacy Causes Chaos at the Southern Baptist Convention." *Atlantic*, June 14, 2017.

Grotstein, James S. *Splitting and Projective Identification*. New York: Scribner Books, 1985.

Guétin, Nicole. *Religious Ideology in American Politics: A History*. Jefferson, N.C.: McFarland, 2009.

Gutmann, Amy. "Communitarian Critics of Liberalism." *Debates in Contemporary Political Philosophy: An Anthology* (2003): 182–94.

Haidt, Jonathan. "The Ethics of Globalism, Nationalism, and Patriotism." *Minding Nature* 9, no. 3 (2016): 18–24.

Haidt, Jonathan, Jesse Graham, and Craig Joseph. "Above and below Left-Right: Ideological Narratives and Moral Foundations." *Psychological Inquiry* 20 (2009): 110–19.

Hall, John R., Philip D. Schuyler, and Sylvaine Trinh. *Apocalypse Observed: Religious Movements, Social Order, and Violence in North America, Europe and Japan*. New York: Routledge, 2000.

Harris, Frederick C. *The Price of the Ticket: Barack Obama and the Rise and Decline of Black Politics*. New York: Oxford University Press, 2012.

Hauerwas, Stanley, and L. Gregory Jones, eds. *Why Narrative? Readings in Narrative Theology*. Grand Rapids: William B. Eerdmans, 1989.

Hempel, Lynn M., and John P. Bartkowski. "Scripture, Sin, and Salvation: Theological Conservatism Reconsidered." *Social Forces* 86, no. 4 (2008): 1647–74.

Henshaw, Stanley K., and Kathryn Kost. "Trends in the Characteristics of Women Obtaining Abortions, 1974 to 2004." Guttmacher Institute, August 2008. https://www.guttmacher.org/sites/default/files/report_pdf/ trendswomenabortions-wtables.pdf (accessed January 26, 2018).

Higginbotham, Evelyn Brooks. *Righteous Discontent: The Women's Movement in the Black Baptist Church, 1880–1920.* Cambridge, Mass.: Harvard University Press, 1993.

Hodgson, Godfrey. *The Myth of American Exceptionalism.* New Haven: Yale University Press, 2010.

Holloway, Karla F. C. *Passed On: African American Mourning Stories; A Memorial.* Durham, N.C.: Duke University Press, 2003.

Hopkins, Dwight N. *Introducing Black Theology of Liberation.* 5th ed. Maryknoll, N.Y.: Orbis Books, 1999.

Howard-Pitney, David. *The African American Jeremiad: Appeals for Justice in America.* Philadelphia: Temple University Press.

Hudson, Jack, Jr. "A History of the First Methodist Church." Bald Eagles, Tenn.: Memphis Annual Conference, 1973.

Hughes, Langston. *The Collected Poems of Langston Hughes.* Edited by Arnold Rampersaud and David Roessel. New York: Alfred A. Knopf, 1994.

Hunter, James D. *American Evangelicalism: Conservative Religion and the Quandary of Modernity.* New Brunswick, N.J.: Rutgers University Press, 1983.

———. *Before the Shooting Begins.* New York: Free Press, 1994.

———. "Conservative Protestantism." In *The Sacred in a Secular Age: Toward Revision in the Scientific Study of Religion,* edited by Phillip E. Hammond, 150–66. Berkeley: University of California Press, 1985.

———. *Culture Wars.* New York: Basic Books, 1991.

Ignatiev, Noel. *How the Irish Became White.* New York: Routledge, 1995.

Janoff-Bulman, Ronnie. "To Provide and to Protect: Motivational Bases of Political Liberalism and Conservatism." *Psychological Inquiry* 20 (2009): 120–28.

Jensen, Gary F. "Religious Cosmologies and Homicide Rates among Nations." *Journal of Religion and Society* 8 (2006): 1–14.

Jones, James W. *Blood That Cries Out from the Earth: The Psychology of Religious Terrorism.* New York: Oxford University Press, 2008.

———. *Contemporary Psychoanalysis and Religion.* New Haven: Yale University Press, 1991.

Jones, Rachel K., Jacqueline E. Darroch, and Stanley K. Henshaw. "Patterns in the Socioeconomic Characteristics of Women Obtaining Abortions in 2000–2001." *Perspectives on Sexual and Reproductive Health* 34, no. 5 (2002): 226–35.

Juergensmeyer, Mark. *Terror in the Mind of God: The Global Rise of Religious Violence.* 3rd ed. Berkeley: University of California Press, 2003.

Jüngel, Eberhard. *Death: The Riddle and the Mystery.* Translated by Iain and Ute Nicol. Philadelphia: Westminster, 1971.

Kazin, Michael. "Trump and American Populism: Old Whine, New Bottles." *Foreign Affairs* 95, no. 6 (2016): 17–24.

Kertzer, David I. *Ritual, Politics, and Power.* New Haven: Yale University Press, 1988.

Kimball, Charles. *When Religion Becomes Evil.* Rev. and updated ed. New York: HarperOne, 2008.

Kohut, Heinz. *How Does Analysis Cure?* Chicago: University of Chicago Press, 1984.

Laderman, Gary. *Rest in Peace: A Cultural History of Death and the Funeral Home in Twentieth-Century America.* New York: Oxford University Press, 2003.

Landler, Mark, and Yamiche Alcindor. "Trump's Condolence Call to Soldier's Widow Ignites an Imbroglio." *New York Times*, October 18, 2017.

Larsen, Timothy, and Daniel J. Treier, eds. *The Cambridge Companion to Evangelical Theology.* New York: Cambridge University Press, 2007.

LeCompte, Margaret D., and Jean J. Schensul. *Designing and Conducting Ethnographic Research.* 2nd ed. Lanham, Md.: Altamira, 2010.

Lester, Andrew. *Hope in Pastoral Care and Counseling.* Louisville: Westminster John Knox, 1995.

Levine, Lawrence W. *Black Culture and Black Consciousness: Afro-American Folk Thought from Slavery to Freedom.* 30th anniversary ed. New York: Oxford University Press, 2007.

Liberman, Mark. "The Third Life of American Exceptionalism." *Language Log* (blog), February 23, 2012. http://languagelog.ldc.upenn.edu/nll/?p=3798.

Lincoln, Charles Eric. *The Black Church since Frazier.* New York: Schocken Books, 1974.

Lincoln, Charles Eric, and Lawrence H. Mamiya. *The Black Church in the African American Experience.* Durham, N.C.: Duke University Press, 1990.

Lipka, Michael. "A Closer Look at America's Rapidly Growing Religious 'Nones.'" *Fact Tank* (blog), Pew Research Center, May 13, 2015. http://www.pewresearch.org/fact-tank/2015/05/13/a-closer-look-at-americas-rapidly-growing-religious-nones/.

———. "Mainline Protestants Make Up Shrinking Number of U.S. Adults." *Fact Tank* (blog), Pew Research Center, May 18, 2015. http://www.pewresearch.org/fact-tank/2015/05/18/mainline-protestants-make-up-shrinking-number-of-u-s-adults/.

———. "Why America's 'Nones' Left Religion Behind." *Fact Tank* (blog), Pew Research Center, August 24, 2016. http://www.pewresearch.org/fact-tank/2016/08/24/why-americas-nones-left-religion-behind/.

Long, Charles H. "Civil Rights—Civil Religion: Visible People and Invisible Religion." In *American Civil Religion*, edited by Russell E. Richey and Donald G. Jones. New York: Harper & Row, 1974.

Lowenthal, David. "Letter to the Editor." *Perspectives: Newsletter of the American Historical Association* 32 (1994): 17–18.

Lyerly, Cynthia Lynn. *Methodism and the Southern Mind, 1770–1810.* New York: Oxford University Press, 1998.

Manis, Andrew M. *Southern Civil Religions in Conflict: Civil Rights and the Culture Wars.* Macon, Ga.: Mercer University Press, 2002.

Marcel, Gabriel. *Homo Viator: Introduction to a Metaphysic of Hope.* Translated by Emma Craufurd. Gloucester, Mass.: Peter Smith, 1978.

Marsden, George M. "Preachers of Paradox: The Religious New Right in Historical Perspective." In *Religion and America: Spiritual Life in a Secular Age,* edited by Mary Douglas and Steven Tipton, 150–68. Boston: Beacon, 1982.

Marty, Martin E. Foreword to *Theological Roots of Pentecostalism,* by Donald W. Dayton. Peabody, Mass.: Hendrickson, 1987.

———. *The Public Church: Mainline, Evangelical, Catholic.* New York: Crossroad, 1981.

———. "Two Kinds of Civil Religion." In *American Civil Religion,* edited Russell E. Richey and Donald G. Jones, 139–57. New York: Harper and Row, 1974.

Marvin, Carolyn, and David W. Ingle. "Blood Sacrifice and the Nation: Revisiting Civil Religion." *Journal of the American Academy of Religion* 64, no. 4 (1996): 767–80.

———. *Blood Sacrifice and the Nation: Totem Rituals and the American Flag.* New York: Cambridge University Press, 1999.

Maslow, Abraham. *Toward a Psychology of Being.* Princeton, N.J.: Van Nostrand, 1962.

McCann, Dennis. "The Good to Be Pursued in Common." In *The Common Good and US Capitalism,* edited by Oliver F. Williams and John W. Houcks, 158–78. Lanham, Md.: University Press of America, 1987.

McCoy, Terrence. "How Joseph Stalin Invented 'American Exceptionalism.'" *Atlantic,* March 15, 2012.

McGhaughey, M. A. "A History of Our Church—1892." In "A History of the First Methodist Church," by Jack Hudson Jr., photocopy, local church archives, 1–10. Bald Eagles, Tenn.: Memphis Annual Conference, 1973.

McLoughlin, William G., ed. *The American Evangelicals 1800–1900: An Anthology.* 1968. Repr., Gloucester, Mass.: Pete Smith, 1976.

———. *Revivals, Awakenings, and Reforms: An Essay in Religion and Social Change in America, 1607–1977.* Chicago: University of Chicago Press, 1978.

McNeill, William H. *Keeping Together in Time: Dance and Drill in Human History.* Cambridge, Mass.: Harvard University Press, 1997.

Mead, Sidney E. "The Nation with the Soul of a Church." In *American Civil Religion,* edited by Russell E. Richey and Donald G. Jones, 45–75. New York: Harper & Row, 1974.

Metz, Johann Baptist. "A Short Apology of Narrative." In *Why Narrative? Readings in Narrative Theology,* edited by Stanley Hauerwas and L. Gregory Jones, 251–62. Grand Rapids: William B. Eerdmans, 1989.

Miller, Katya. "A Statue Called *America, Liberty,* and *Freedom.*" U.S. Capitol Historical Society, Washington, D.C., 2007. http://www.ladyfreedom.net/history.html (accessed December 19, 2016).

Miller-McLemore, Bonnie. *Death, Sin, and the Moral Life: Contemporary Cultural Interpretations of Death.* Atlanta: Scholars Press, 1988.

Miller-McLemore, Bonnie, and Brita Gill-Austern, eds. *Feminist and Womanist Pastoral Theology.* Nashville: Abingdon, 1999.

Mitchem, Stephanie Y. *Introducing Womanist Theology.* 2nd ed. Maryknoll, N.Y.: Orbis Books, 2002.

Morgan, Ted. *A Covert Life—Jay Lovestone: Communist, Anti-Communist, Spymaster.* New York: Random House, 1999.

Morrison, Toni. "On the First Black President." *New Yorker,* October 5, 1998.

Obama, Barack. "A More Perfect Union." Delivered on March 18, 2008. Transcription available at *American Rhetoric,* http://www.americanrhetoric.com/speeches/barackobamaperfectunion.htm (accessed July 25, 2017).

O'Hare, William P. "US Rural Soldiers Account for a Disproportionately High Share of Casualties in Iraq and Afghanistan." Carsey Institute: University of New Hampshire, Fall 2016. https://scholars.unh.edu/cgi/viewcontent.cgi?article=1015&context=carsey (accessed February 22, 2018).

Olson, Roger E. *Pocket History of Evangelical Theology.* Downers Grove, Ill.: InterVarsity, 2007.

Omi, Michael, and Howard Winant. *Racial Formation in the United States.* 3rd ed. New York: Routledge, 2015.

Ortner, Sherry B. "On Key Symbols." In *A Reader in the Anthropology of Religion,* edited by Michael Lambek, 158–67. Malden, Mass.: Blackwell, 2002.

Osmer, Richard R. *Practical Theology: An Introduction.* Grand Rapids: William B. Eerdmans, 2008.

Patterson, Orlando. *Slavery and Social Death: A Comparative Study.* Cambridge, Mass.: Harvard University Press, 1982.

Pew Research Center. "America's Changing Religious Landscape." May 12, 2015. http://www.pewforum.org/2015/05/12/americas-changing-religious-landscape/.

Phillips, Michael M. "Brothers in Arms: The Tragedy in Small-Town America." *Wall Street Journal,* September 22, 2017.

Philpot, Tasha S. *Conservative but Not Republican: The Paradox of Party Identification and Ideology among African Americans.* Cambridge: Cambridge University Press, 2017.

Price, Melayne T. *The Race Whisperer: Barack Obama and the Political Uses of Race.* New York: New York University Press, 2016.

Raboteau, Albert J. "Americans, Exodus, and the American Israel." In *Religion and American Culture,* 2nd ed., edited by David G. Hackett, 73–87. New York: Taylor & Francis, 2003.

———. *Slave Religion: The "Invisible Institution" in the Antebellum South.* Updated ed. New York: Oxford University Press, 2004.

Rappaport, Roy A. *Ritual and Religion in the Making of Humanity.* Cambridge: Cambridge University Press, 1999.

Richey, Russell E., and Donald G. Jones, eds. *American Civil Religion.* New York: Harper & Row, 1974.

Rizzuto, Ana-Maria. *The Birth of the Living God.* Chicago: University of Chicago Press, 1979.

Robeson, Jerry, and Carol Robeson. *Strongman's His Name . . . What's His Game: An Authoritative Biblical Approach to Spiritual Warfare*. New Kensington, Penn.: Whitaker House, 2000.

Sakala, Leah. "Breaking Down Mass Incarceration in the 2010 Census: State by State Incarceration Rates by Race/Ethnicity." Prison Policy Initiative, May 28, 2014. https://www.prisonpolicy.org/reports/rates.html.

Scull, Danielle. "Women, Art, and the Capitol." U.S. Capitol Historical Society, Washington, D.C., 1999. https://uschs.org/explore/historical-articles/women-art-united-states-capitol (accessed July 5, 2006).

Seales, Chad E. *The Secular Spectacle: Performing Religion in a Southern Town*. New York: Oxford University Press, 2013.

The Sentencing Project. "Shadow Report to the United Nations on Racial Disparities in the United States Criminal Justice System." August 31, 2013. http://www.sentencingproject.org/publications/shadow-report-to-the-united-nations-human-rights-committee-regarding-racial-disparities-in-the-united-states-criminal-justice-system/.

Simpson, Robert. "The Circuit Riders in Early American Methodism." General Commission on Archives and History, United Methodist Church. http://www.gcah.org/history/circuit-riders (accessed July 31, 2018).

Smith, Christian. *The Secular Revolution*: *Power, Interests, and Conflict in the Secularization of American Public Life*. Berkeley: University of California Press, 2003.

Smith, Christian, with Michael Emerson, Sally Gallagher, Paul Kennedy, and David Sikkink. *American Evangelicalism: Embattled and Thriving*. Chicago: University of Chicago Press, 1998.

Smith, Theophus H. *Conjuring Culture: Biblical Formations of Black America*. New York: Oxford University Press, 1994.

Stenner, Karen. "Three Kinds of 'Conservatism.'" *Psychological Inquiry* 20 (2009): 143–50.

Stone, Jon R. *On the Boundaries of American Evangelicalism: The Postwar Evangelical Coalition*. New York: St. Martin's, 1997.

Stuckey, Sterling. *Slave Culture: Nationalist Theory and the Foundations of Black America*. New York: Oxford University Press, 1987.

Sweet, Leonard I. *Black Images of America, 1784–1870*. New York: W. W. Norton, 1976.

———. *The Evangelical Tradition in America*. Macon, Ga.: Mercer University Press, 1984.

Telford, John. *The Life of John Wesley*. Niagara Falls, N.Y.: Wesleyan Heritage, 1998.

Thomson, Philip. *The Grotesque*. London: Methuen, 1972.

Thurman, Howard. *Jesus and the Disinherited*. Nashville: Abingdon, 1949.

———. *The Negro Spiritual Speaks of Life and Death*. New York: Harper & Row, 1947.

Tillich, Paul. *The Courage to Be*. 2nd ed. New Haven: Yale University Press, 2000.

Tipton, Steven M. "Civil Religion in the Making." Unpublished essay, 2012.

———. *Getting Saved from the Sixties.* Berkeley: University of California Press, 1982.

———. *Public Pulpits*: *Methodists and Mainline Churches in the Moral Argument of Public Life.* Chicago: University of Chicago Press, 2007.

Turner, Victor. *From Ritual to Theatre: The Human Seriousness of Play.* New York: Performing Arts Journal Publications, 1982.

———. *The Ritual Process: Structure and Anti-structure.* New York: Aldine de Gruyter, 1995.

Turner, William C. "Black Evangelicalism: Theology, Politics, and Race." *Journal of Religious Thought* 45, no. 2 (1989): 40–56.

Tylor, Edward B. *Primitive Culture.* New York: J. P. Putnam's Sons, 1920.

Van Gennep, Arnold. *The Rites of Passage.* Translated by Monika B. Vizedom and Gabrielle L. Caffe. Chicago: University of Chicago Press, 1960.

Volkan, Vamik D. "Psychoanalytic Aspects of Ethnic Conflicts." In *Conflict and Peacemaking in Multiethnic Societies,* edited by Joseph V. Montville, 81–92. Lexington, Mass.: Lexington Books, 1990.

Wagner, Peter, and Bernadette Rabuy. "Mass Incarceration: The Whole Pie 2016." Prison Policy Initiative, May 14, 2016. https://www.prisonpolicy.org/reports/pie2016.html.

Wald, Kenneth D., and Allison Calhoun-Brown. *Religion and Politics in the United States.* 7th ed. Lanham, Md.: Rowman & Littlefield, 2014.

Warner, William Lloyd. *The Living and the Dead: A Study of the Symbolic Life of Americans.* Yankee City Series 5. New Haven: Yale University Press, 1959.

Webber, Robert E. *Common Roots: A Call to Evangelical Maturity.* Grand Rapids: Zondervan, 1978.

The White House, Office of the Press Secretary. "Remarks by the President at the National Defense University." May 23, 2013. https://www.whitehouse.gov/the-press-office/2013/05/23/remarks-president-national-defense-university.

Williams, Jeffrey. *Religion and Violence in Early American Methodism: Taking the Kingdom by Force.* Bloomington: Indiana University Press, 2010.

Williams, Rhys II. "Civil Religion and the Cultural Politics of National Identity in Obama's America." *Journal for the Scientific Study of Religion* 52, no. 2 (2013): 239–57.

———. "Constructing the Public Good: Social Movements and Cultural Resources." *Social Problems* 42, no. 1 (1995): 124–44.

Willis, Andre C. "Theology in Post Democracy." *Political Theology* 10, no. 2 (2009): 209–23.

Willoughby, Earl. "Historical Society Sets Goals for Coming Year." *Bald Eagles State Gazette*, October 29, 2007.

Wilmore, Gayraud S. *Last Things First.* Philadelphia: Westminster, 1982.

Wilson, Charles R. *Baptized in the Blood: The Religion of the Lost Cause, 1865–1920.* With a new preface. 2009 ed. Athens: University of Georgia Press, 2009.

————. "The Religion of the Lost Cause: Ritual and Organization of the Southern Civil Religion." *Journal of Southern History* 46, no. 2 (1980): 219–38.

Winnicott, Donald W. *Playing and Reality.* New York: Basic Books, 1971.

Wuthnow, Robert. *The Restructuring of American Religion: Society and Faith since World War II.* Princeton, N.J.: Princeton University Press, 1988.

Notes

Acknowledgments

1. Langston Hughes, "Let America Be America Again," in *The Collected Poems of Langston Hughes*, ed. Arnold Rampersaud and David Roessel (New York: Alfred A. Knopf, 1994), 189–93.

Preface

1. Rhys H. Williams, "Civil Religion and the Cultural Politics of National Identity in Obama's America," *Journal for the Scientific Study of Religion* 52, no. 2 (2013): 241. Although Williams *does not* name the relationship between "blood-land-religion" a "politics of death," it is simply implied in his terminology. I am suggesting the connection represents a *politics of death* especially in light of the following. The relationship between the three connects the bloodshed because of the religiously inspired, violent, and extremist attack on America in 2001 to the nation's political response of declaring war.

2. *Bald Eagles* is a pseudonym for the largest of the three cities where I conducted my research. The midsized city is pseudonymously named *Screaming Eagle*, and the smallest of the three is pseudonymously identified as *Hummingbird*. Bald Eagles, Screaming Eagle, and Hummingbird are the three cities comprising *Bald Eagles County*. Church parishioners and Bald Eagles' residents, per their request, were assigned pseudonyms. However, public figures chose to retain their actual names.

3. Robert Bellah, "Religious Evolution, Civil Religion and Public Theology in Global Perspective," ed. Steven M. Tipton (unpublished essay, 2012), 7.

4. Robert N. Bellah, "Civil Religion in America," *Journal of the American Academy of Arts and Sciences* 96, no. 1 (1967): 15–16.

5. Godfrey Hodgson, *The Myth of American Exceptionalism* (New Haven: Yale University Press, 2009), 23.

6. Civil-military relations: "Who Will Fight the Next War? Failures in Iraq and Afghanistan Have Widened the Gulf between Most Americans and the Armed Forces," *Economist*, October 24, 2015, paragraphs 2, 8, http://www.economist.com/news/united

-states/21676778-failures-iraq-and-afghanistan-have-widened-gulf-between-most
-americans-and-armed.
   7. Bellah, "Religious Evolution," 5–8.
   8. Bellah, "Religious Evolution," 6.

Introduction

   1. Bellah, "Civil Religion in America," 3, 9; and R. Williams, "Civil Religion and the Cultural Politics," 240.
   2. Charles R. Wilson, *Baptized in the Blood: The Religion of the Lost Cause 1865–1920*, with a new preface, 2009 ed. (Athens: University of Georgia Press, 2009), x.
   3. Charles H. Long, "Civil Rights—Civil Religion: Visible People and Invisible Religion," in *American Civil Religion*, ed. Russell E. Richey and Donald G. Jones (New York: Harper & Row, 1974), 211–21; Andrew M. Manis, *Southern Civil Religions in Conflict: Civil Rights and the Culture Wars* (Macon, Ga.: Mercer University Press, 2002), 42–43, 49–55; Albert J. Raboteau, "Americans, Exodus, and the American Israel," in *Religion and American Culture*, 2nd ed., ed. David G. Hackett (New York: Taylor & Francis, 2003), 81–83; and David Howard-Pitney, *The African American Jeremiad: Appeals for Justice in America* (Philadelphia: Temple University Press, 2005), 1–3, 10–13.
   4. Long, "Civil Rights—Civil Religion," in Richey and Jones, *American Civil Religion*, 211–21; Leonard I. Sweet, *Black Images of America, 1784–1870* (New York: W. W. Norton, 1976), 175; Albert J. Raboteau, "Americans, Exodus," in Hackett, *Religion and American Culture*, 83–86; Howard-Pitney, *African American Jeremiad*, 10–14.
   5. Residents of Bald Eagles City and County vote Democratic in local elections and Republican in national elections.
   6. Eliot Dismore Chapple and Carleton Stevens Coon, *Principles of Anthropology* (New York: Henry Holt, 1942), 508, 528. "Rites of Intensification" are "Rites of Passage," writ large, "making up the great periodic ceremonies of a society, as well as the less spectacular daily, weekly, monthly and yearly rituals . . . [which] help to reinforce the habitual relations within the society."
   7. William Lloyd Warner, *The Living and the Dead: A Study of the Symbolic Life of Americans*, Yankee City Series 5 (New Haven: Yale University Press, 1959), 248–51. I am contending that Bellah's work is rooted in Warner's studies. In Bellah's seminal essay "Civil Religion in America" (9–11), he discusses the merits of Warner's scholarship. In doing so, he establishes a clear intellectual history and connection to Warner's social anthropological research. Moreover, he introduces themes of sacrifice, death, and rebirth to the concept of an American civil religion with the "martyrdom" of President Abraham Lincoln.
   8. R. Williams, "Civil Religion and the Cultural Politics," 241.
   9. R. Williams, "Civil Religion and the Cultural Politics," 241.
   10. Bellah, "Religious Evolution," 7.
   11. Bellah, "Religious Evolution," 7.

Chapter 1

   1. Chapple and Coon, *Principles of Anthropology*, 507–8. Chapple and Coon both developed and described the term.
   2. Chapple and Coon, *Principles of Anthropology*, 507. These disturbances are cyclical in nature. They emerge during circadian, seasonal, annual, and other cycles.
   3. Bellah, "Civil Religion in America," 3; and R. Williams, "Civil Religion and the Cultural Politics," 240.

4. Carolyn Marvin and David W. Ingle, "Blood Sacrifice and the Nation: Revisiting Civil Religion," *Journal of the American Academy of Religion* 64, no. 4 (1996): 767–80; and Marvin and Ingle, *Blood Sacrifice and the Nation: Totem Rituals and the American Flag* (New York: Cambridge University Press, 1999), 64, 71.

5. R. Williams, "Civil Religion and the Cultural Politics," 241.

6. R. Williams, "Civil Religion and the Cultural Politics," 241.

7. R. Williams, "Civil Religion and the Cultural Politics," 241.

8. Émile Durkheim, *The Elementary Forms of Religious Life*, trans. Carol Cosman (2001; repr., New York: Oxford University Press, 2008), xxii.

9. Durkheim, *Elementary Forms of Religious Life*, xiii.

10. Durkheim, *Elementary Forms of Religious Life*, xxii.

11. Durkheim, *Elementary Forms of Religious Life*, xxiii.

12. Bellah, "Civil Religion in America," 3.

13. Robert Bellah has written numerous articles since 1967 further developing and refining the definition of "civil religion" to include "the religious dimension of a people through which it interprets its historical experience in light of transcendent reality" and being a form of moral discourse in America by its involvement with moral, religious, and political crises during particular periods of trial. Robert Bellah, *The Broken Covenant: American Civil Religion in Time of Trial*, 2nd ed. (Chicago: University of Chicago Press, 1992), 3. *Civil religion*, according to Robert Bellah, ultimately expresses the deep-seated values, commitments, and ethical principles of a people, not articulated in everyday life. Bellah, "Civil Religion in America," 2. Social philosopher and sociologist of religion Will Herberg defined *civil religion* as "the common religion of the people." *Civil religion* has also been understood as "ritualistic expressions of patriotism."

14. Bellah, "Civil Religion in America," 2.

15. Martin E. Marty, "Two Kinds of Civil Religion," in Richey and Jones, *American Civil Religion*, 139–57.

16. R. Williams, "Civil Religion and the Cultural Politics," 240.

17. Charles R. Wilson, "The Religion of the Lost Cause: Ritual and Organization of the Southern Civil Religion," *Journal of Southern History* 46, no. 2 (1980): 222. On page 222, Wilson explains that Southern civil religion was concerned with the "Southern Way of life" and stressed "'democracy' less than the conservative concepts of moral virtue and an orderly society."

18. Wilson, "Religion of the Lost Cause," 223, 228.

19. David W. Blight, "Forgetting Why We Remember," *New York Times*, May 30, 2011; Blight, *Race and Reunion: The Civil War in American Memory*, 4th ed. (Cambridge, Mass.: Harvard University Press, 2001), 68–86; Blight, "The Battle for Memorial Day in New Orleans," *Atlantic*, May 29, 2017. Scholar of American history David Blight writes about the grave-decorating rituals of Northerners and Southerners at the end of the Civil War. These rituals memorialized the approximately 700,000 soldiers who had died fighting for the Confederacy and the Union, eventually transforming into sacred memorial events. Memorial Day, initially recognized as Decoration Day, was practiced by communities and was filled with speeches, religious and cultural practices, as well as other festivities, as different states strove toward national reconciliation. Reconciliation of a divided nation coalesced around the sacrifices of soldiers, regardless of region, and war dead. The first officially recorded Memorial Day in the North was in 1868. Decoration Days in the South were recorded on April 26, May 10, and June 3, 1866, and were held in honor of fallen soldiers and Confederate leaders: General William T. Sherman, General Stonewall Jackson, and President of the Confederate States Jefferson Davis. While Blight's scholarship addresses the differences in white and black cultural memories of the Civil War, his work also recognizes and pays tribute to the extraordinary beginnings of

Memorial Day. The earliest record of Decoration Day (i.e., Memorial Day) proceedings was May 1, 1865, in Charleston, South Carolina, and led by 10,000 former slaves, including abolitionists. In the final year of the Civil War, Union soldiers were held captive in an outdoor prison in the port city of Charleston, South Carolina. After converting the inner track of the Washington Race Course and Jockey Club, Confederates maintained the dismal conditions contributing to the death by disease of 257 Union soldiers being held as captives. These dead were hastily buried in a massive grave. Once the remaining Confederate soldiers vacated the city, newly freedmen traveled to the site and commenced to rebury the dead Union soldiers properly. These formerly enslaved workmen secured the cemetery and thereafter wrote "Martyrs of the Race Course" on the fence constructed around the cemetery. Three thousand black schoolchildren led the cemetery dedication in a parade that included "black women holding baskets of flowers, wreathes, crosses and black men marching in cadence and followed by black Union infantrymen." On that day, the crowd sang spirituals, patriotic songs like "We'll Rally Around the Flag" and "The Star Spangled Banner," as black ministers read from the Bible.

20. Blight, "Forgetting Why We Remember"; Blight, "Battle for Memorial Day."

21. Wilson, *Baptized in the Blood*, x.

22. Long, "Civil Rights—Civil Religion," in Richey and Jones, *American Civil Religion*, 211–21; Sweet, *Black Images of America*, 175; and Manis, *Southern Civil Religions in Conflict*, 42–43, 49–55.

23. Pitney, *African American Jeremiad*, 11–12.

24. Pitney, *African American Jeremiad*, 11–12; and Raboteau, "Americans, Exodus," in Hackett, *Religion and American Culture*, 81–83.

25. Long, "Civil Rights—Civil Religion," in Richey and Jones, *American Civil Religion*, 211–21; Pitney, *African American Jeremiad*, 10–12; and Manis, *Southern Civil Religions in Conflict*, 42–55.

26. Warner, *Living and the Dead*, 4.

27. Warner, *Living and the Dead*, 4.

28. Warner, *Living and the Dead*, 248, 249, 279.

29. Warner, *Living and the Dead*, 248.

30. Noel Ignatiev writes about the arrival of Irish Catholic immigrants to the urban North, whom "native" evangelical Protestant, Anglo-Americans categorized as equal to freed slaves. Upon realizing the competitive advantage they would have by identifying as white American, these Irish immigrants and other ethnically "white" immigrant groups quickly embraced a pan-European identity and racially differentiated themselves from their black counterparts, entering the racial sorting pattern institutionalized by Southern slavery. Ignatiev, *How the Irish Became White* (New York: Routledge, 1995), 42; cited in Chad E. Seales, *The Secular Spectacle: Performing Religion in a Southern Town* (New York: Oxford University Press, 2013), 55. Drawing upon Ignatiev's scholarship, Seales further explains that much of the earliest "blackface" minstrel performers were Irish-descended immigrants whose participation in nineteenth-century America's "most popular form of entertainment" assisted them in "associating their ethnicity with a nationalized whiteness" (55).

31. Warner, *Living and the Dead*, 256.

32. Warner, *Living and the Dead*, 253.

33. Warner, *Living and the Dead*, 256, 263, 261.

34. Warner, *Living and the Dead*, 263.

35. Bellah ("Civil Religion in America," 3) coined the term and described *American civil religion* as "certain common elements of religious orientation that the great majority of Americans share [and] that have played a crucial role in the development of American institutions . . . including the political sphere. This public religious dimension is expressed

in a set of beliefs, symbols, and rituals." *Civil religion*, according to Bellah, also ultimately expresses the deep-seated values, commitments, and ethical principles of a people, not articulated in everyday life.

36. The White House—Office of the Press Secretary, "Remarks by the President at the National Defense University," May 23, 2013, paragraph 3, https://www.whitehouse.gov/the-press-office/2013/05/23/remarks-president-national-defense-university.

37. White House, "Remarks by the President," paragraphs 3, 5.

38. White House, "Remarks by the President," paragraphs 3, 30, 47.

39. Nicole Guétin, *Religious Ideology in American Politics: A History* (Jefferson, N.C.: McFarland, 2009), xx.

40. For more information on the racial distinctions in Southern civil religion, consider the work of Andrew M. Manis (*Southern Civil Religions in Conflict*, 43). Expanding Charles Reagan Wilson's thesis, Manis explains that white and black Southerners between 1917 and 1947 displayed *ambivalence* in their civil religious loyalties. He continues, "Southern whites [were] torn between being Americans and being Southerners, while Southern blacks experienced what W. E. B. Dubois called a 'double-consciousness' of simultaneously being black and American."

41. Hodgson, *Myth of American Exceptionalism*, 16. Hodgson describes *exceptionalism* as a political tradition, closely related to and shaping the foreign affairs of countries. With respect to *American Exceptionalism,* he writes: "The core of the belief is the idea that the United States is not just the richest and most powerful of the world's more than two hundred states but is also politically and morally exceptional. Exceptionalists minimize the contributions of other nations and cultures to the rule of law and to the evolution of political democracy" (10). Hodgson also refers to John Winthrop and his classic sermon "A Model of Christian Charity," which he preached in the presence of fellow Puritans, members of the Massachusetts Bay colony, before setting sail to New England in 1630 aboard the Arbella. Its most famous passage compares America to a "city on a hill." Based on this "civil religious" metaphor, the church and civil society were destined to carry the covenantal responsibilities for actualizing the common good; the metaphor also establishes the spiritual foundations for the "newly" settled colony meant to be an exemplar for English colonies throughout North America and other places. The sermon's most famous passage and metaphor, "a city on a hill," develops around the idea of America possessing a special "divinely inspired" destiny to expand its power and influence over nations and institutions throughout the world (2, 10), leading Hodgson to point to the sermon as the earliest model of *American Exceptionalism.*

42. Hodgson, *Myth of American Exceptionalism*, 16.

43. Hodgson, *Myth of American Exceptionalism*, 16.

44. Hodgson, *Myth of American Exceptionalism*, 14.

45. Memorial Day public ceremony at Fairview Cemetery, May 29, 2016.

46. The American jeremiad is described in Sacvan Bercovitch's 1978 text, *The American Jeremiad*, as a rhetorical device, mainly used in sermons or politically themed speech, employed by speakers in the Puritan period as a commentary on the dissonance between the realities of American social life and the promise of the American dream. Invoked at the point of strain between the ideal and real public life, the jeremiad exhorted individuals and communities to provide correctives to public life while also encouraging hope for the future. It is noteworthy not only because of its religious undertones but also as a constructive critique of Puritan society that has remained part of the American (political) rhetorical tradition into the present. Refer to Bercovitch, *The American Jeremiad* (Madison: University of Wisconsin Press, 1978); and Pitney, *African American Jeremiad*, 1–12.

47. Memorial Day public ceremony at Memorial Park Cemetery, May 29, 2016.

48. Michael O. Emerson and Christian Smith, *Divided by Faith: Evangelical Religion and the Problem of Race in America* (New York: Oxford University Press, 2000), 7–9. Emerson and Smith consider the gulf in race relations between blacks and whites from the perspective of evangelical faith, particularly because race scholars have tended not to study race relations and racial divides from religious dimensions. As they study the dividing lines between blacks and whites, they argue that group distinctions are based on a *racialized (American) society.* Using this term, both authors move beyond discrimination, prejudice, and racism to evaluate the ways in which race factors into each group's different life experiences, opportunities, social behaviors, and relationships (7). More importantly, race matters when "a society allocates differential economic, political, social and psychological rewards to groups along racial lines" (7). Further, racialization happens around the social construction of race, revealing and reproducing racial hierarchies, inequities, and divisions that are often hidden, systemic, institutional, avoided, and invisible to most whites (9).

49. Wilson, "Religion of the Lost Cause," 222.

50. Nichole Renée Phillips, interview with Mayor Bill Revell, June 7, 2006.

51. Wilson, "Religion of the Lost Cause," 232.

52. Donald G. Bloesch, *Essentials of Evangelical Theology: Two Volumes in One* (Peabody, Mass.: Hendrickson, 2006), 14.

53. Respecting the nature of evangelical Christianity, in addition to epistemology (the authority of Scripture and biblical revelation), ontology (the sinfulness of humanity), and soteriology (salvation through experiential commitment to Jesus Christ), ecclesiology and eschatology rank as primary concerns among Evangelicals. Bloesch comments that "in evangelical theology we do not try to bring together the answer of faith and the creative questions of culture (as in Paul Tillich); instead our aim is to challenge the culture to begin to ask the right questions" (Bloesch, *Essentials of Evangelical Theology,* 14–15).

His scholarship sparks conversation with the "liberation" and "narrative" theologies of James Cone and Stanley Hauerwas. I also engage the scholarship of Jon R. Stone (*On the Boundaries of American Evangelicalism*: *The Postwar Evangelical Coalition* [New York: St. Martin's, 1997]), who argues for a "boundary (social-cultural)" model to defining Evangelicals because "boundaries incorporate and enclose difference" and serve as "a focal point of group distinctiveness" (40, 43–49). This approach aims to explain the diversity within the evangelical community using sociological and anthropological concepts.

54. Psychology provides another lens for interpreting the cult of the dead and the rituals associated with Memorial Day, other civic holidays, and other public ceremonies commemorating the dead, particularly in the American South. Psychoanalytic psychology assists me in deciphering the intrapsychic motivations and emotional life of community members as well as how their emotional and psychological lives play out in ritual settings. Using psychological theory, I gain to better understand: How have the attitudes and behaviors of townsfolk toward death developed? What does death mean in this rural culture and among different social groups (i.e., black and white) in this community? Why does death function in this way? What psychic functions do the death rituals play in the minds and emotions of participants in these rituals?

Object relations theory generally claims that a matrix of relationships nurtures the developing self. Psychiatrist Ana-Maria Rizzuto (author of *The Birth of the Living God*) and her predecessor David W. Winnicott figure prominently in this school of thought. Winnicott describes the "transitional space as a space of play for creative living" in his 1950s text *Playing and Reality*. It is an imaginative intrapsychic space where art, religion (i.e., "god"), superheroes, angels, demons, and death are located.

It is also a place that includes the relationship between individuals and society and, hence, is a space for the formation of culture. Winnicott's and Rizzuto's scholarship compels discussion about the role of familial attachments in the formation of thought and practice. Their writings also address how the mutual relationship between individual and society shapes culture. I will employ psychoanalytic psychology to assist in explaining the significance of ritual space as a "holding environment" to contain emergent and incongruous emotions. Rizzuto, *The Birth of the Living God* (Chicago: University of Chicago Press, 1979); and Winnicott, *Playing and Reality* (New York: Basic Books, 1971).

Chapter 2

1. See Appendix 1: "Methodology and Research Process."

2. As noted above, *Bald Eagles* is a pseudonym for the largest of the three cities where I conducted my research. The midsized city is pseudonymously named *Screaming Eagle*, and the smallest of the three is pseudonymously identified as *Hummingbird*. Bald Eagles, Screaming Eagle, and Hummingbird are the three cities comprising *Bald Eagles County*. Church parishioners and Bald Eagles' residents, per their request, were assigned pseudonyms. However, the congregations and public figures chose to retain their actual names.

3. Source: 2008 Demographic Data Bald Eagles / Bald Eagles County Chamber of Commerce (Orange, Calif.: DemographicsNow, 2007), 2, 11. Demographics based on the 2000 Census remained constant in the 2010 Census and continued to be so in 2016 according to U.S. Census Bureau data reports. Statistical data results account for multiracial persons who self-identify in more than one racial category. The 2000 Census allowed people to check any one of six racial/ethnic categories or respective combinations. For example, a respondent might be biracial and self-identify as both Asian and Anglo. Data results reflect such combinations.

4. Source: 2008 Demographic Data Bald Eagles / Bald Eagles County Chamber of Commerce (Orange, Calif.: DemographicsNow, 2007), 4. Demographics based on the 2000 Census remained constant in the 2010 Census and continued to be so in 2016 according to U.S. Census Bureau data reports.

5. Source: 2008 Demographic Data Bald Eagles / Bald Eagles County Chamber of Commerce (Orange, Calif.: DemographicsNow, 2007), 13. Demographics were very similar in 2010 and 2016. Demographics based on the 2000 Census remained constant in the 2010 Census and continued to be so in 2016 according to U.S. Census Bureau data reports.

6. Bald Eagles / Bald Eagles County Chamber of Commerce Statistical Directory (2008), 1–2.

7. According to Tennessee exit polls, in 2008, blacks overwhelmingly voted for Barack Obama (94%) compared to whites (34%). Edison Media Research and Mitofsky International, "Tennessee Election Results 2008," *New York Times*, December 9, 2008, https://www.nytimes.com/elections/2008/results/states/exitpolls/tennessee.html. Yet, race is not factored into the 2008 Tennessee, Bald Eagles County, presidential election results, which stood at 31% for Barack Obama compared to 68% for John McCain. In other words, geographic region (i.e., rural and conservative) and race (i.e., black or white) must be considered in order to more accurately assess voting patterns. Some blacks do share the same voting patterns as their white counterparts because of regional influences. That accounts for individual variation, from common social-group voting patterns, in each of the racial entities. Edison Media Research and Mitofsky International, "Tennessee: Presidential County Results 2008," *New York Times*, December 9, 2008, https://www.nytimes.com/elections/2008/results/states/president/tennessee.html.

8. American religious historian Evelyn Brooks Higginbotham writes about the creation of the early 1900s Women's Convention, an auxiliary of the National Baptist Convention. In the face of rampant racial prejudice and in the shadow of an early twentieth-century

women's suffrage movement, black Baptist women carved out "sacred space" in the institutional black Church for the purposes of self-definition, self-determination, and self-esteem. With the church serving as a springboard for organizing, these women entered the public arena stressing "respectability." Respectability connoted "manners and morals" required to combat the stigma around "blackness." While black women were characterized as immoral, promiscuous, and lazy, black men were stereotyped as hypersexualized and brutish. Emphasizing reform of individual attitudes and behavior, blacks, as a social group, would benefit from the racial uplift accorded by these race women's "politics of respectability."

Yet, these black Baptist women would face criticism for employing the "politics of respectability" as an assimilationist tool. To that end, Higginbotham writes: "For the Women's Convention, the politics of respectability constituted a counter-discourse to the politics of prejudice, but it was aimed dually at white and black Americans. Respectability held an identifiable and central place in the philosophy of racial self-help. It entrusted to blacks themselves responsibility for constructing the 'Public Negro Self' (to borrow from Henry Louis Gates, Jr.), a self presented to the world as worthy of respect. . . . Uplift, however, encoded the church women's assimilationist leanings. Organized black church women disseminated throughout the black community the assimilationist message implicit in respectability, and they endeavored to implant middle-class values and behavioral patterns among the masses of urban blacks who retained rural folkways of speech, dress, worship, and other distinct cultural patterns. With evangelical fervor, they strove to win converts from the ranks of the poor and 'unassimilated.' . . . The evangelical message, like the historic work of Home Missions among other ethnic and racial groups, sought to bring black America in line with the both religious and class values of the dominant society." *Righteous Discontent: The Women's Movement in the Black Baptist Church, 1880–1920* (Cambridge, Mass.: Harvard University Press, 1993), 195–96.

9. As historian Evelyn Brooks Higginbotham explains, *race women* during the Reconstruction era (1865–1877) would enter Southern states to better the dismal conditions of formerly enslaved blacks. However, they were often looked upon with the same suspicion as whites coming south because they were educated and not from the area. Also, Southern blacks did not want anyone—including their own—patronizing them.

10. Nobel Prize–winning author Toni Morrison introduced the belief that former president William Jefferson Clinton was America's first black president in a 1998 article for the *New Yorker* magazine. There she compared his impending impeachment proceedings to the daily indignities of black men in America. She comments: "African-American men seemed to understand it right away. Years ago, in the middle of the Whitewater investigation, one heard the first murmurs: white skin notwithstanding, this is our first black President." Morrison wrote that Clinton was "blacker than any actual black person who could ever be elected in our children's lifetime." She continued: "Clinton displays almost every trope of blackness: single-parent household, born poor, working-class, saxophone-playing, McDonald's-and-junk-food-loving boy from Arkansas." Further, she said: "When the President's body, his privacy, his unpoliced sexuality became the focus of the persecution, when he was metaphorically seized and body searched, who could gainsay these black men who knew whereof they spoke? The message was clear: 'No matter how smart you are, how hard you work, how much coin you earn for us, we will put you in your place or put you out of the place you have somehow, albeit with our permission, achieved. You will be fired from your job, sent away in disgrace, and—who knows?—maybe sentenced and jailed to boot. In short, unless you do as we say (i.e., assimilate at once), your expletives belong to us.'" Morrison, "On the First Black President," *New Yorker*, October 5, 1998, https://www.newyorker.com/magazine/1998/10/05/comment-6543.

11. Melayne T. Price, *The Race Whisperer: Barack Obama and the Political Uses of Race* (New York: New York University Press, 2016), 1–8. Price's text investigates how Obama used racial rhetoric and tropes that drew upon his mixed-race heritage to advance national discussions about race during his presidencies. However, her writings are more about his ability to master race and racial narratives as political instruments to contextualize and appeal to voter preferences while connecting with the fluidity and malleability of a racialized American society, at given points in time, than about his contributions to the country's racial discussions. Knowing this, Price talks about the "Obama phenomenon" by describing it and comparing him to previous seminal and luminary black figures like Jesse Jackson and W. E. B. Dubois. The "Obama phenomenon" highlights Obama's use of his charismatic personality not to achieve black political legitimacy or to offer black policy concessions or promises but to galvanize loyalty and a black voting base.

12. Frederick C. Harris, *The Price of the Ticket: Barack Obama and the Rise and Decline of Black Politics* (New York: Oxford University Press, 2012), 9–10, 18–20. Jackson was a "native son"—local black politicians committed to strategically building black power bases (10). Influenced by his predecessor Shirley Chisholm and having the support of a black grassroots and political base, Jackson ran for president having developed a national campaign that grew out of the black experience and from the perspective of marginalized American social groups. His 1984 presidential campaign bid grew into and out of what is now nationally known as the Rainbow Coalition, with the premise being that blacks are America's primary disaffected group. Other groups also on the periphery would ultimately join Jackson's campaign efforts, which were primarily tied to "black special interests" and highlighted issues of relevance to blacks via mobilization in a political system that was heretofore dismissing their concerns.

13. Harris, *Price of the Ticket*, 3–5. Although Shirley Chisholm was the first black person and woman to declare candidacy for president of the United States, Harris suggests the path toward that goal had been paved earlier. In the mid-1960s upon the passing of the 1965 Voting Rights Act, black leaders began to discuss ways for blacks to have more influence in national decision making, which included finding a way to gain greater access to political positions and the ballot box. In such ways, these leaders determined that black causes and agendas would be taken more seriously because blacks had pledged their loyalties to the Democratic Party but failed to see what the party was doing for them and their plight.

14. "Ontological blackness," according to Victor Anderson, "is a covering term that connotes categorical, essentialist, and representational languages depicting black life and experience." Anderson desires not only to enlarge this idea but also to move beyond its limitations by extracting African Americans from situations, events, and practices stifling to the progress of black people. He asserts: "Unfortunately, the need among African Americans to promote a positive racial community has too often taken binary dialectical formation against individuality. In the dialectic of community and individuality, where community is totalized, blacks who pursue goods that contribute to their fulfillment as individuals (whether in selecting marriage partners, exercising freedom of movement, acting on gay and lesbian preferences, or choosing political parties) often find themselves ostracized and their cultural fulfillment repressed by an *ontological blackness*. My attempt is not to negate but to displace, decenter, and transcend the determinative transactions and practices of ontological blackness over black life and experience." Anderson, *Beyond Ontological Blackness: An Essay on African American Religious and Cultural Criticism* (New York: Continuum, 1995), 11, 16–17 (emphasis added). See also Anderson's discussion of Philip Thomson's *The Grotesque* on p. 127.

15. Anderson, *Beyond Ontological Blackness*, 127–28.

16. Frederick Burwick, "The Grotesque: Illusion vs. Delusion," cited in Anderson, *Beyond Ontological Blackness*, 129.

17. Homi K. Bhabha, *The Location of Culture* (New York: Routledge, 1994), 5, 37. Bhabha is a foremost scholar of postcolonial studies who developed and popularized many of the field's concepts, such as *hybridity*. *The theory of cultural hybridity* is a form of cultural criticism that refers to the relationship between the colonizer and the colonized and that illustrates the emergence of new histories and cultures in the encounter between the colonizer and the colonized peoples. The colonized disrupt the colonizer's dominant culture upon this encounter, producing a deconstruction of the dominant culture. This cultural collision creates a fissure, not only opening up a "third space" for the formation of new culture, but also making room for the histories, cultures, and narratives of the once-excluded and colonized subjects. Bhabha talks about *cultural hybridity* as leading to political change in the following ways: "The interstitial passage between fixed identifications opens up the possibility of cultural hybridity that entertains difference without an assumed or imposed hierarchy. . . . A place of *hybridity*, figuratively speaking [is where] the construction of a political object that is new, *neither the one nor the other*, properly alienates our political expectations, and changes as it must, the very forms of our recognition, of the moment of politics. The challenge lies in the time of conceiving the moment of political action and understanding as opening up a space that can accept and regulate the differential structure of the moment of intervention without rushing to produce unity of the social antagonism or contradiction" (5, 37; emphasis added).

18. Philip S. Gorski, "Barack Obama and Civil Religion," *Political Power and Social Theory* 22 (2011): 185, 203–4. In this article, Gorski attempts to revive interest in the study of American civil religion, a concept initially presented by Robert Bellah. In his writing, he weighs three traditions demonstrating the relationship between religion and politics in America. Arguing along (Max) Weberian lines and in support of Bellah's Durkheimian approach, Gorski suggests that the civil religion tradition outperforms the other two competing traditions of religious nationalism and liberal secularism. Religious nationalists are defined as those who would "fuse religious and political communities," and who would uncritically support an American government that encourages viewing the country as a "Judeo-Christian nation." Religious nationalists are characterized as blind patriots who believe blending religious beliefs and political commitments are necessary for the country's survival and prosperity (185). Liberal secularists, conversely, would like to remove religious language from political discourse and from the public square. They are convinced the nation will advance only if there is a separation of church and state (185). In between both strands resides *American civil religion*, a "multi-stranded" social theory upholding civic republicanism and a covenant theology; therefore, in elevating both, civil religion achieves the common good, human flourishing, and egalitarianism (201). To showcase and to prove the strength of civil religion, Gorski conducts a historical survey of leading civil theologians, from John Winthrop to Frederick Douglass, and from Robert F. Kennedy to Barack Obama.

19. Gorski, "Barack Obama and Civil Religion," 185, 203–4.

20. Gorski, "Barack Obama and Civil Religion," 203.

21. Gorski, "Barack Obama and Civil Religion," 204.

22. Terrence McCoy, "How Joseph Stalin Invented 'American Exceptionalism,'" *Atlantic*, March 15, 2012, https://www.theatlantic.com/politics/archive/2012/03/how-joseph -stalin-invented-american-exceptionalism/254534/; Ted Morgan, *A Covert Life—Jay Lovestone: Communist, Anti-Communist, Spymaster* (New York: Random House, 1999).

23. McCoy, "How Joseph Stalin."

24. Hodgson, *Myth of American Exceptionalism*, 43.

25. Mark Liberman, "The Third Life of American Exceptionalism," *Language Log* (blog), February 23, 2012, http://languagelog.ldc.upenn.edu/nll/?p=3798.

26. Liberman, "Third Life of American Exceptionalism."

27. Hodgson, *Myth of American Exceptionalism*, 108.

28. Hodgson, *Myth of American Exceptionalism*, 108.

29. Hodgson, *Myth of American Exceptionalism*, 107.

30. McCoy, "How Joseph Stalin"; Hodgson, *Myth of American Exceptionalism*, 107–9.

31. Hodgson, *Myth of American Exceptionalism*, 23.

32. Hodgson, *Myth of American Exceptionalism*, xvii.

33. Hodgson, *Myth of American Exceptionalism*, xvii.

34. Michael Omi and Howard Winant, *Racial Formation in the United States*, 3rd ed. (New York: Routledge, 2015), 194.

35. Omi and Winant, *Racial Formation in the United States*, 194.

36. Omi and Winant, *Racial Formation in the United States*, 219.

37. Hodgson, *Myth of American Exceptionalism*, 110–11; Omi and Winant, *Racial Formation in the United States*, 221–22.

38. Hodgson, *Myth of American Exceptionalism*, 2–3. Because John Winthrop was still an Englishman upon arriving to the New World, Hodgson debates if Winthrop's metaphor can appropriately be applied to America, especially since many scholars contend he likens the United States to a "city upon a hill." Always a loyal British subject in spite of leading his life in America, Winthrop (and the rest of the colonists) did not have any awareness of the American potential to develop into a freestanding nation. Therefore, from Hodgson's perspective, Winthrop must *not* have been referring to America as a "city upon a hill." Instead, writes Hodgson: "He was preaching to Englishmen, and expressing his determination that the colony, or in contemporary language the 'plantation,' that he and his friends were setting out to found, would be an example to other English colonies, in North America and elsewhere" (3).

39. McCoy, "How Joseph Stalin." In 1980, journalist Richard J. Tofel earnestly asked Jimmy Carter and Ronald Reagan to defend the ideology in light of America's waning stature on the world stage.

40. Bellah, "Civil Religion in America," 9–12, 16–19.

41. Hodgson, *Myth of American Exceptionalism*, 10.

42. Peter Beinart, "How Trump Wants to Make America Exceptional Again," *Atlantic*, February 2, 2017, https://www.theatlantic.com/politics/archive/2017/02/how-trump-wants-to-make-america-exceptional-again/515406/; Hodgson, *Myth of American Exceptionalism*, 100.

43. McCoy, "How Joseph Stalin."

44. Barack Obama, "A More Perfect Union," delivered on March 18, 2008, transcription available at *American Rhetoric*, http://www.americanrhetoric.com/speeches/barackobamaperfectunion.htm (accessed July 25, 2017).

45. Gorski, "Barack Obama and Civil Religion," 204.

46. Price, *Race Whisperer*, 1–8, 19. Price describes a race whisperer as "one who is seamlessly and agilely able to employ racial language and tropes by using personal experiences or common historical themes to engage and mobilize diverse racial constituencies."

In *The Race Whisperer*, she argues that Barack Obama is uniquely situated to appeal to diverse racial groups and not necessarily specific and mutually exclusive groups. Without being white, he has the ability to appeal to whiteness through authentic and politically expedient connections to multiple groups. His broad-based racial appeals serve as instruments of mobilization that bring together many and varied groups. He was able to tailor his multiracial background, experiences living abroad, Ivy League education, and organizing skills to reach across and into diverse social groups, identities, and sectors of the American public. "In this way, he is able to tap into narratives of Blackness, whiteness, migration, and other things with a good amount of credibility." Price's book examines how Barack Obama is able to do this and the implications for understanding his racial legacy and black politics in the future.

47. Harris, *Price of the Ticket*, 170–72.

48. Harris, *Price of the Ticket*, 173–75.

49. Astrid Erll, *Memory in Culture*, trans. Sara B. Young (New York: Palgrave MacMillan, 2011), 14, 17, 56. French sociologist Maurice Halbwachs, who was trained by Henri Bergson and Emile Durkheim, is notable in the development of cultural memory studies. He, alongside Aby Warburg in the 1920s, coined the term "collective and social" memory and systemized memory studies, identifying such studies as a part of culture. He offered three fundamental and related concepts of collective memory. Regarding Halbwachs' second fundamental concept concerning *family and intergenerational memory*, he surmised those memories developed from shared versions of a past emerging through social interaction, communication, media, institutions, and the association of small social groups and cultural communities. Through social relationships, connections, and repeating past events, those community members who did not experience an event firsthand can participate and share in the memory. In this way, states Erll, an *exchange of living memory* happens between eyewitnesses and descendants. Similar to *inter*generational memory, *intra*generational memory is the formation of memory between generations, except that *intra*generational memory "sees age groups as communities of memory" (56).

50. Erll, *Memory in Culture*, 14, 17.

51. Omi and Winant, *Racial Formation in the United States*, 145.

52. Beinart, "How Trump Wants to Make America Exceptional Again."

53. Omi and Winant, *Racial Formations in the United States*, 192.

54. Edward S. Casey, *Remembering: A Phenomenological Study* (Bloomington: Indiana University Press, 1987), 186, 189, 201. In his study, Casey demonstrates the connection between "place" and "memory." He contends that memory is not simply a temporal phenomenon but attached to particular "places" that facilitate remembering. "Place" is a container for lived experiences and is selective for specific memories. Nostalgia functions by transporting us back to the time and space in which an event occurred. A commemorative activity, we experience *re-implacing* when we are nostalgic—a *re-experiencing of past places*.

55. Omi and Winant, *Racial Formations in the United States*, 236–37. Both explain the emerging and anticipated "majority-minority" demographic as "politically unprecedented" and the effect of the removal of "overtly racist components" of immigration laws that had been established in the United States since the 1920s (236–37). These revisions to 1920 and 1986 laws precipitated seismic changes to the American racial and ethnic composition. Most importantly, the shift means that "no single racially defined group, including those considered white, will be a majority in the country" (237).

56. Hodgson, *Myth of American Exceptionalism*, 41. While Hodgson does not make this claim, he does recount the post–Civil War social changes that gave all white men, regardless of "class" distinction, the right to vote. However, as American society experienced drastic changes with immigration and urbanization during that period, he asserts that an "anti-democratic" reaction set in, targeting women, free blacks, paupers, felons, and migrants—all who lost the right to vote.

Chapter 3

1. Christian Smith, *The Secular Revolution: Power, Interests, and Conflict in the Secularization of American Public Life* (Berkeley: University of California Press, 2003), 35; James

D. Hunter, "Conservative Protestantism," in *The Sacred in a Secular Age: Toward Revision in the Scientific Study of Religion*, ed. Phillip E. Hammond (Berkeley: University of California Press, 1985), 150; and Seales, *Secular Spectacle*. Smith's and Hunter's works engage twentieth-century modernity as the historical benchmark for the onset of America's modern secularization process and how evangelical Protestants responded to the process. Each holds a different view on how Evangelicals approached secularization. In his present and earlier scholarship, Smith justifies Evangelicals' response to modernization as being "embattled but thriving," primarily based on the concept of an "engaged orthodoxy," a display of their full commitment to Protestant belief and theology, and their simultaneous participation in social, political, cultural, and political life in America. Hunter, on the other hand, considers Evangelicals' response to modernity in terms of the "privatization" of religion, rooted in a *structural pluralism* that emerges and structures American public life into public and private spheres. Educational, scientific, technological, healthcare, military, modern state, and other large institutions, according to Hunter, reside in the public sphere, but family life, religion, social relationships, and other identifiers of human experience are circumscribed to the private sphere, forced out of the public sphere. Religious belief is depoliticized as a consequence of secularization and other effects of modernity. However, irrespective of the secularization process each presents, both sociologists affirm through their theorizing that evangelical Protestantism does the work of *accommodating and resisting* secularism and the modernization process, whether through embattlement or privatization. In his work *The Secular Spectacle: Performing Religion in a Southern Town*, Chad Seales presents yet another perspective on secularization. He writes about a Southern variety of secularism in proximity to and constitutive of public performances of Southern religion that residents of a North Carolina town enact throughout the twentieth century to maintain class, gendered, religious, and racial hierarchies in public places. On the basis of the town's local religious history and extensive archival research, he delineates the path of secularization (informed by Durkheimian theory of social performativity) by showing how these Southern Protestants wielded the powers of secularism and religious performance to shape a socioeconomic and racial class who reinforced community members' interpretation of the sacred as well as the profane nature of social difference.

2. Christian Smith, with Michael Emerson, Sally Gallagher, Paul Kennedy, and David Sikkink, *American Evangelicalism: Embattled and Thriving* (Chicago: University of Chicago Press, 1998), 4.

3. Smith et al., *American Evangelicalism*, 5.

4. James Davison Hunter describes *modernity* in terms of the *modernization process* in both Western and non-Western, premodern and modern societies. Forces behind the economic, social, and political growth of underdeveloped and developed nations push the modernization process forward. Hunter writes, "Modern societies are characterized by a population concentrated in urban areas. There is a highly intensified division of labor as well as a high degree of institutional specialization and segmentation. The economic sphere—the production apparatus in particular—is based on a highly sophisticated technology. Social relationships are largely impersonal and arbitrary; the primary mode of social organization in all spheres is bureaucratic. Political power is, at least ideologically, based in the populace. The gesellschaft is further characterized by sociocultural pluralism—a curious admixture of social and cultural worlds in various degrees of contact with one another. The worldview of modern man is typically rational and secular, not bound by traditional sanctions but critical and open to innovation and experimentation." See Hunter, *American Evangelicalism: Conservative Religion and the Quandary of Modernity* (New Brunswick, N.J.: Rutgers University Press, 1983), 4–5.

5. "Engaged orthodoxy" showed neo-Evangelicals' adherence and loyalty to conservative Protestant theology and practice while promoting their active participation in social,

cultural, and political life in America. Smith et al., *American Evangelicalism*, 10; and Emerson and Smith, *Divided by Faith*, 3–4.

6. Smith et al., *American Evangelicalism*, 188.

7. Smith et al., *American Evangelicalism*, 14.

8. Hunter, *American Evangelicalism*, 17.

9. Smith et al., *American Evangelicalism*, 90.

10. In their text *American Evangelicalism: Embattled and Thriving*, authors Smith et al. argue for a "subcultural identity" theory of religious strength, presupposing that evangelicalism continues to be strong because adherents struggle with, instead of stray away from, the forces that make up American modernity. In other words, evangelicalism is not shielded from a pluralistic American society. Rather, it is strengthened and *thrives* because of its robust encounter with diversity bringing to itself a certain degree of *distinction* as it sits in *tension* and *conflict* with pluralism. Modern evangelicalism confronts and perceives itself to be embattled with *threats* that ironically maintain its strength. Distinction, tension, conflict, and threat characterize and fortify American evangelicalism.

Pulling together eight basic sociological principles, Smith et al. combine these principles to propose what they call a "subcultural identity" theory of religious strength. The first principle contends: "Individuals find meaning and belonging in social groups furnishing collective identities and distinctive moral orientation" (90). The second asserts: "Social groups distinguish themselves from outside groups by drawing symbolic boundaries that construct and sustain collective identities" (91). The third suggests: "Religious traditions respond to changing sociocultural environments by strategically renegotiating their collective identities and revising their constructed orthodoxies" (97). The fourth principle proposes: "Modern religious believers establish stronger religious identities and commitments based on individual choice" rather than the sway of social circles. The impact of personal choice is more effective at shaping and reinforcing identity than is the influence of somebody else's beliefs (102–3). The fifth principle advances the idea that social groups and individuals define themselves, their identities, and their behavior according to specific and selected reference groups; antagonistic and dissimilar outgroups serve as negative reference groups (104). According to the sixth principle, instead of a decline in religion as proposed by modern secularization theories, engagement with modern pluralism produces strong subcultures and potentially "deviant" identities, including that of religious subcultures and alternative religious identities (107). The seventh proposal views diverse contexts as spaces where intergroup conflict enhances in-group identity, resources, membership retention, and unity (113). The eighth principle suggests that modernity bolsters instead of detracts from religion's appeal, creating social conditions that heighten religion's ability to fulfill social needs and desires (116). By coordinating these eight individual and social identity principles, Smith et al. showcase a "subcultural identity" theory of religious strength, reinforcing the belief in religion's ability to survive pluralistic modernity as well as secularization. Religious cultures are capable of doing so because religion remains active and flourishes in subcultures, offering adherents meaning and belonging in moral orienting collective identities. Smith et al., *American Evangelicalism*, 89–119.

11. A "subcultural identity" theory of religious strength is informed by the social identity theories developed in the 1970s and 1980s by social psychologists Henri Tajfel and John Turner. In their theorizing, they proposed and developed interpretations and understandings of human social selves and of interpersonal and intergroup behaviors.

12. In historic church architecture, the area that holds the pulpit, altar, and altar-table is the *religious sanctuary* or *presbytery*. The religious sanctuary is a sacred place in the church, temple, mosque, etc. and is designated as a place of holiness and safety. It is also identified as the presbytery.

13. Edward Burnett Tylor was a British anthropologist and originator of cultural anthropology who—in his famous two-volume work *Primitive Culture* (1871)—defines *culture* as follows: "Civilization taken in its broad, ethnographic sense, is that complex whole which includes knowledge, belief, art, morals, law, custom, and any other capabilities and habits acquired by man as a member of society." See Tylor, *Primitive Culture* (New York: J. P. Putnam's Sons, 1920), 1:1. For a more up-to-date description of *culture*, consider that sociologist Margaret D. LeCompte and medical anthropologist Jean J. Schensul write: "Culture also consists of the beliefs, behaviors, norms, attitudes, social arrangements, and expressions that form a describable pattern in the life of members of a community or institution. Culture can be *mental phenomenon* like what people know, believe, understand, think, and feel, about what they do. Culture is also *the actual product*—what people do and practice (describable patterns) versus norms, what they say that they do. Culture involves the *social arrangements and institutions* where people interact that are designed to fulfill their emotional needs. Culture is also *socially agreed upon* patterns and meanings as well as behavior." See LeCompte and Schensul, *Designing and Conducting Ethnographic Research*, 2nd ed. (Lanham, Md.: Altamira, 2010), bk. 1, p. 24 (emphasis added).

14. Hunter writes about Evangelicals' cultural conformity to modernity as a domestication of belief. As they had done in the early 1900s, Evangelicals adjusted features of their religious orthodoxy by responding to the demands of social change precipitated by a contemporary process of modernization in the very late twentieth century (1980s and beyond). Yielding their religious beliefs and practices to the influence of American culture, this religious subculture's adaptability is laid out and made evident through the interactions between social structure and local culture, even as they continued determinedly to hold strong core beliefs and practices. See Hunter, *American Evangelicalism*, 71–119.

15. Kenneth D. Wald and Allison Calhoun-Brown, *Religion and Politics in the United States*, 7th ed. (Lanham, Md.: Rowman & Littlefield, 2014), 208, 210, 215. Until the 1920s, evangelical Protestantism was an active force in American political life via cultural issues. While it had contributed greatly to the growth of Northern states' antislavery movements during the period leading up to the Civil War, it had, paradoxically, reinforced Southerners' commitment to maintenance of the slave economy. Following the Civil War, Evangelicals led movements to cleanse American politics of profane influences. For instance, led by William Jennings Bryan, Evangelicals initiated and were a force behind currency reform, women's suffrage, regulation of corporate abuses, arbitration of international conflicts, and adoption of "direct democracy" through the initiative, referendum, and recall election. These reforms were assumed to maintain the economic interests and social values of traditional Protestantism. As evidence of evangelicalism's centrality to American culture, widespread adoption of these reforms occurred in the period leading up to WWI.

Later, as many Northern Protestant denominations embraced modernity, the center of evangelicalism shifted decisively to the South. Increasingly, the orientation of traditional Protestantism turned toward the South with grave political implications. For instance, social and economic deprivation denied Evangelicals sustained political participation and isolated them from experiences that would have promoted tolerance, compromise, and other democratic values from the 1920s to the 1970s. Lesser educational opportunities disadvantaged them in the democratic political arena, causing them to lose their competitive edge. Furthermore, their otherworldly Southern and religious orientation disengaged them from social conditions and discouraged their participation in the political process. However, after WWII and heading into the 1960s civil rights movement, Evangelicals reengaged the political process and were counseled to "reject the division of human affairs into the 'secular' and 'sacred' and insist, instead, that there is no arena of human activity, including law and politics, which is outside of God's lordship. The task is not to avoid this world, but to declare God's Kingdom in it." Invigorated by this idea, Evangelicals passionately applied themselves to the political arena in the same way they had traditionally been evangelizing.

16. Smith et al., *American Evangelicalism*, 33.

17. Smith et al., *American Evangelicalism*, 90.

18. William G. McLoughlin, ed., *The American Evangelicals, 1800–1900: An Anthology* (1968; repr., Gloucester, Mass.: Pete Smith, 1976), 1. Citations are to the 1976 edition.

19. See Danielle Scull, "Women, Art, and the Capitol," U.S. Capitol Historical Society, Washington, D.C., 1999, https://uschs.org/explore/historical-articles/women-art -united-states-capitol (accessed July 5, 2006); Katya Miller, "A Statue Called *America, Liberty*, and *Freedom*," U.S. Capitol Historical Society, Washington, D.C., 2007, http:// www.ladyfreedom.net (accessed December 19, 2016).

20. Smith et al., *American Evangelicalism*, 92–93.

21. Smith et al., *American Evangelicalism*, 92.

22. Smith et al., *American Evangelicalism*, 99.

23. Hunter, *American Evangelicalism*, 14.

24. Guétin, *Religious Ideology*, 174.

25. In "The Poison Book," ch. 2 from *The Talking Book: African Americans and the Bible* (New Haven: Yale University Press, 2006), Allen Dwight Callahan launches the chapter by detailing the heated 1850s debate about soliciting funds to send Bibles to Southern slaves between African American luminaries and leaders Henry Highland Garnet and Frederick Douglass. Callahan reminds the reader that both men had different experiences and therefore held different perspectives on "slavery, literacy, religion" (22). A Presbyterian minister, Garnet believed the Bible was key to liberation of the Southern slave because the Bible had inspired his West African Mandinka father to flee from Southern slavery to the North with his wife, his son (Garnet), and the rest of his children. Douglass, the abolitionist, held an opposing view as the product of a black enslaved mother and white slave-master father. He had toiled and survived the harshness of slavery to receive manumission papers to move into Northern freedom. "Long before Lincoln," writes Callahan, "Douglass had learned that the Bible was the highest authority of American slavery and the strongest link in the chain of oppression and violence that warranted slavery as the sacred basis for the Christian culture of the Confederacy. . . . Bitter experience had taught Douglass and other slaves and former slaves that the master class of the United States bore a whip in one hand and a Bible in the other" (23).

26. M. A. McGhaughey, "A History of Our Church—1892," in "A History of the First Methodist Church," by Jack Hudson Jr., Memphis Annual Conference, Bald Eagles, Tenn., 1973, photocopied, 1.

27. "Early History of Bald Eagles," *Bald Eagles State Gazette*, n.d.

28. Robert Simpson, "The Circuit Riders in Early Methodism," General Commission on Archives and History, United Methodist Church, http://www.gcah.org/history/ circuit-riders (accessed July 31, 2018).

29. Simpson, "Circuit Riders in Early Methodism."

30. McGhaughey, "History of Our Church," in Hudson Jr., "History of the First Methodist Church," 2.

31. Albert J. Raboteau declares: "More than the Presbyterians, the Separate Baptists and the Methodists reaped a revival harvest of black and white members in the South. By the end of the century these two denominations were in the ascendancy in the South. Slaves and free blacks were among those swelling the Baptist and Methodist ranks. Methodist itinerants frequently commented on the presence of blacks in their congregations. Joseph Pilmore wrote to Wesley in 1770 that 'the number of blacks that attend the preaching affects me much.' . . . The increase in conversions of Negroes

under the impact of revivalism was due to several factors. The evangelical religion spread by the revivalists initiated a religious renaissance in the South, as a somnolent religious consciousness, was awakened by revivalist preachers. The revival itself became a means of church extension for Presbyterians and, particularly, for Methodists and Baptists. The mobility of the Methodist circuit rider and the local autonomy of the Baptist preacher were suited to the needs and conditions of the rural South. In the heat of religious fervor, planters became less indifferent about their own religious involvement and, potentially, about that of their slaves. The individualistic emphasis of revivalism, with its intense concentration on inward conversion, fostered an inclusiveness which could border on egalitarianism. Evangelicals did not hesitate to preach the necessity of conversion to racially mixed congregations. Revivalist preachers had little doubt—indeed they were enthusiastic—about the capacity of slaves to share the experience of conversion." Raboteau, *Slave Religion: The "Invisible Institution" in the Antebellum South*, updated ed. (New York: Oxford University Press, 2004), 130, 132.

32. McGhaughey, "History of Our Church," in Hudson Jr., "History of the First Methodist Church," 3.

33. William G. McLoughlin, *Revivals, Awakenings, and Reform: An Essay on Religion and Social Change in America, 1607–1977* (Chicago: University of Chicago Press, 1978), 132.

34. Charles Reagan Wilson explains that evangelical Protestantism with its stress on a theology of inward conversion was not antithetical to the development of a Southern civil religion. Both, in the South, openly supported each other. Wilson, "Religion of the Lost Cause," 232.

35. Smith et al., *American Evangelicalism*, 107.

36. Smith et al., *American Evangelicalism*, 107.

37. Smith et al., *American Evangelicalism*, 108.

38. John Telford, *The Life of John Wesley* (Niagara Falls, N.Y.: Wesleyan Heritage, 1998), 101.

39. Dennis M. Campbell, William B. Lawrence, and Russell E. Richey, eds., *Doctrines and Disciplines*, vol. 3, *United Methodism and American Culture* (Nashville: Abingdon, 1999), 4–5.

40. Cynthia Lynn Lyerly, *Methodism and the Southern Mind, 1770–1810* (New York: Oxford University Press, 1998), 29.

41. Lyerly, *Methodism and the Southern Mind*, 29.

42. Campbell, Lawrence, and Richey, *Doctrines and Disciplines*, 3:6.

43. In *The Sacred Canopy*, Peter L. Berger introduces the term "sacred canopy" to explain the role of religion in the face of chaos and threat. Religion serves to bind all of life together under an overarching "canopy" that protects against terror and lawlessness because individuals experience ultimate meaning in the bonds solidified by a common world. Berger, *The Sacred Canopy: Elements of a Sociological Theory of Religion* (Garden City, N.Y.: Random House, 1967), 133; and Smith et al., *American Evangelicalism*, 106.

44. Smith et al., *American Evangelicalism*, 106.

45. Smith et al., *American Evangelicalism*, 106.

46. Smith et al., *American Evangelicalism*, 105.

47. *Reference groups* affirm who groups are and their identities, decisions, and actions. However, Smith and his coauthors write about "negative reference groups": "People also construct for themselves '*negative reference groups*': categories of people who are unlike them, who actively serve in their minds as models for what they do *not* believe, what they do *not* want to become, and how they do *not* want to act. Having to interact with others who are dissimilar to oneself, perhaps even antagonistic to one's own religious views, does not necessarily need to disconfirm one's own commitments, practices, and identity.

Indeed, they can serve as ongoing reminders of one's desire to be quite different from them." Smith et al., *American Evangelicalism*, 105 (emphasis added).

48. Lawrence W. Levine, *Black Culture and Black Consciousness: Afro-American Folk Thought from Slavery to Freedom*, 30th anniversary ed. (New York: Oxford University Press, 207), 103–4.

49. Johann Baptist Metz, "A Short Apology of Narrative," in *Why Narrative? Readings in Narrative Theology*, ed. Stanley Hauerwas and L. Gregory Jones (Grand Rapids: William B. Eerdmans, 1989), 253.

50. Hunter, *American Evangelicalism*, 18.

51. Sam Cooke, "A Change Is Gonna Come."

52. Jeffrey Williams, *Religion and Violence in Early American Methodism: Taking the Kingdom by Force* (Bloomington: Indiana University Press, 2010), 39.

53. J. Williams, *Religion and Violence*, 38–39.

54. Smith et al., *American Evangelicalism*, 114–16.

Chapter 4

1. Elaborating on the tradition of "lining" hymns, Allen Dwight Callahan writes about Harriet Ware, who was an abolitionist and member of Gideon's Band. Describing the worship meetings of the enslaved, Ware reports that "at regular intervals one hears the elder 'deaconing' a hymnbook hymn, which is sung two lines at a time" (12). Callahan continues by relating that the practice of worship-meeting leaders "lining" or singing the first two stanzas of a hymn in advance and in the hearing of the rest of the congregation became a tool for the illiterate population to learn the Bible. He further writes: "The slaves' Bible became musical, even as the slaves' music became biblical. Through the peculiar liturgies of the Peculiar Institution, slaves could become biblically articulate without the benefit of letters" (12). Callahan, *Talking Book*, 12.

2. In *Conjuring Culture*, author Theophus H. Smith analyzes and critiques African American Christian tradition, positing that a European-influenced, African spirituality is central to the black North American religious experience. More intentionally, he argues for the Bible's vital role as a *conjure* book. In other words, blacks have used the contents and figures of the Bible as a "kind of magical formulary for prescribing cures and curses, and for invoking extraordinary powers," writes Smith, "in order to reenvision, revise and transform the conditions of human existence" (6). Basically, *conjure* is magic. Enslaved blacks and later African Americans would seek out the black conjurer, who would use a "magical" system of manipulating human artifacts and herbal remedies and use its curative properties to transform social reality; hence, the black American conjurer "hoodoo"/"root" doctor was both magician and healer. Smith extends the meaning of *conjuring culture* to include African American cultural performances (i.e., religious and folklore practices) that use "biblical figures and biblical configurations of African American cultural experience" (6) to produce healing and social transformation. Smith, *Conjuring Culture: Biblical Formations of Black America* (New York: Oxford University Press, 1994), 4, 6; Callahan, *Talking Book*, 89–93.

3. Smith, *Conjuring Culture*, 6.

4. Smith, *Conjuring Culture*, 4.

5. Smith, *Conjuring Culture*, 5, 6.

6. Smith, *Conjuring Culture*, 5.

7. Smith, *Conjuring Culture*, 6.

8. Smith, *Conjuring Culture*, 5.

9. Callahan, *Talking Book*, 89–93.

10. Charles Y. Glock, "The Churches and Social Change in Twentieth Century America," *Annals of the American Academy of Political and Social Science* 527 (1993): 67–83; Penny Edgehill Becker, "What Is Right? What Is Caring?" in *Contemporary American Religion: An Ethnographic Reader*, ed. Penny Edgehill Becker and Nancy L. Eiesland (Walnut Creek, Calif.: AltaMira, 1997), 123 (emphasis added).

11. James D. Hunter, *Culture Wars* (New York: Basic Books, 1991); Hunter, *Before the Shooting Begins* (New York: Free Press, 1994); Becker, "What Is Right?" in Becker and Eiesland, *Contemporary American Religion*, 124.

12. Steven M. Tipton, *Getting Saved from the Sixties* (Berkeley: University of California Press, 1982), xiv; Becker, "What Is Right?" in Becker and Eiesland, *Contemporary American Religion*, 122.

13. Becker, "What Is Right?" in Becker and Eiesland, *Contemporary American Religion*, 124, 130, 140.

14. Howard Thurman, *Jesus and the Disinherited* (Nashville: Abingdon, 1949), 7–11.

15. Callahan, *Talking Book*, 83.

16. Smith, *Conjuring Culture*, 56.

17. Raboteau, *Slave Religion*, 311.

18. Smith, *Conjuring Culture*, 56.

19. Smith, *Conjuring Culture*, 55.

20. Smith, *Conjuring Culture*, 58.

21. Earl Willoughby, "Historical Society Sets Goals for Coming Year," *Bald Eagles State Gazette*, October 29, 2007.

22. E. Franklin Frazier, *The Negro Church in America* (1964; repr., New York: Schocken Books, 1974), 14–16. Citations are to the 1974 edition.

23. Frazier, *Negro Church in America*, 11–16.

24. Frazier, *Negro Church in America*, 23–24.

25. Frazier, *Negro Church in America*, 35–51.

26. Charles Eric Lincoln, *The Black Church since Frazier* (New York: Schocken Books, 1974), 106–8, 125–28.

27. James H. Cone, *The Cross and the Lynching Tree* (Maryknoll, N.Y.: Orbis Books, 2011), xv.

28. Tabernacle Baptist Church Centennial Celebration 1880–1983, p. 3. This source is a combination of Mrs. Whitelaw's oral history, as described in this volume, and also of a centennial celebration pamphlet that contains church history written throughout the years.

29. Tabernacle Baptist Church Centennial Celebration 1880–1983, p. 5.

30. Tabernacle Baptist Church Centennial Celebration 1880–1983, p. 8.

31. Tabernacle Baptist Church Centennial Celebration 1880–1983, p. 15.

32. In Bald Eagles, the "east and west sides" of town traditionally were and continue to be predominantly the black areas of the city. The "west side" of town is "across the railroad tracks" and is considered the poorer of the two sections. The Bruce Community Center is symbolic of the west side of town. Railroad tracks are still physically present, and on occasion residents will hear freight trains crossing. The "east side" of town is considered the more economically stable of the two black areas and is mainly residential.

33. Charles Eric Lincoln and Lawrence H. Mamiya, *The Black Church in the African American Experience* (Durham, N.C.: Duke University Press, 1990), 12.

34. Price, *Race Whisperer*, 4, 7, 10.

35. Price, *Race Whisperer*, 10–11.

36. Raboteau, *Slave Religion*, 132.

37. Thurman, *Jesus and the Disinherited*, 7–11; quoted in James H. Evans Jr., *An African American Systematic Theology: We Have Been Believers* (Minneapolis: Augsburg Fortress, 1992), 83.

38. Thurman, *Jesus and the Disinherited*, 7–11; quoted in Evans Jr., *African American Systematic Theology*, 83.

39. Matthew 10:34-36 describes Jesus telling the disciples that he came to bring not peace to the world but a sword. Biblical commentators suggest Jesus' sword is figurative and not literal. In fact, Matthew 26:52 reports that Jesus tells Peter to put away his sword after Peter takes it out to defend Jesus in the Garden of Gethsemane, "for all who draw the sword will die by the sword." What then did Jesus mean when he said, "Do not suppose that I have come to bring peace to the earth. I did not come to bring peace, but a sword" (NIV)? Jesus knew that the type of sword he would bring would inevitably divide families, separating nonbelievers and believers, good and evil, children of the light (God) and children of darkness (devil). The sword that Jesus brings is the word of Truth, the Gospel. Commentator and American theologian Albert Barnes supported this and concluded: "Christ did not here mean to say that the object of his coming was to produce discord and contention, for he was the Prince of Peace, Isaiah 9:6; Isaiah 11:6; Luke 2:14; but he means to say that such would be one of the effects of his coming. One part of a family that was opposed to him would set themselves against those who believed in him. The wickedness of men, and not the religion of the gospel, is the cause of this hostility." Barnes, *Notes on the New Testament: Explanatory and Practical*, ed. Robert Frew, vol. 1, *Matthew and Mark* (1832; London: Blackie and Son, 1868), 115.

40. Callahan, *Talking Book*, 193–96.

41. Callahan, *Talking Book*, 217.

42. Callahan, *Talking Book*, 194, 196.

43. Callahan, *Talking Book*, 201.

44. James A. Cone, *A Black Theology of Liberation*, twentieth anniversary ed. with critical reflections by Dolores S. Williams, Gayraud Wilmore, Rosemary Ruether, Pablo Richard, Robert McAfee Brown, K. C. Abraham (Maryknoll, N.Y.: Orbis Books, 1990), 32.

45. Smith, *Conjuring Culture*, 218.

46. Evans Jr., *African American Systematic Theology*, 74–75.

47. Cone, *Black Theology of Liberation*, 3.

48. Smith, *Conjuring Culture*, 160.

49. Smith, *Conjuring Culture*, 160.

50. Cone, *Black Theology of Liberation*, 4–5.

51. Dwight N. Hopkins, *Introducing Black Theology of Liberation*, 5th ed. (Maryknoll, N.Y.: Orbis Books, 2005), 8.

52. Cone, *Black Theology of Liberation*, 6.

53. Cone, *Black Theology of Liberation*, 7.

54. Cone, *Black Theology of Liberation*, 4.

55. Mark L. Chapman, *Christianity on Trial: African American Religious Thought before and after Black Power* (Eugene, Ore.: Wipf & Stock, 1996), 25–27.

56. Jerry and Carol Robeson, *Strongman's His Name . . . What's His Game: An Authoritative Biblical Approach to Spiritual Warfare* (New Kensington, Penn.: Whitaker House, 2000).

57. Robeson, *Strongman's His Name*, 13.

. Robeson, *Strongman's His Name*, 17.

59. Cultural unity amongst enslaved Africans, by Sterling Stuckey's account, began to be forged in the coffles of slave ships making their way across the Atlantic Ocean to the New World. Stuckey's text describes and explains the conditions and settings under which Africans from disparate ethnic groups started to relate to one another in the New World and especially in the midst of U.S.-based plantation life. His comprehensive study

of particular cultural artifacts like storytelling, song, dance rituals, ancestral rites, and religion shows how these Africans moved toward oneness. Taking religion, for example, Stuckey identifies small numbers of Africans in the Pennsylvania area in the 1790s who might have retained features and essential patterns of African religion like youth initiation by transplanting the ceremony to the New World, where plantation life required meeting the people's needs in a different way (24). Into the 1850s, aspects of religious life among Africans in America like preaching, dance, and the shout (i.e., the ringshout) were defined by the power of freedmen and slaves' adaptation of African culture into the Christian faith. Stuckey argues such religious practices represented an "Africanization of Christianity" (54) because the Christian message was being delivered in an African form. He argues that case into the twentieth century, where these ancient and transcultural religious forms have endured based on adoption and adaptation of traditions and transmission of cultural memories throughout each historic period. And, thus, I argue this African religiosity is a feature of the traditional Christianity practiced by the Southern blacks in rural Bald Eagles. This is all the more apparent as Pastor Matthews preaches about the "buzzards" having adapted this folktale to his Christian message rooted in the African / African American tale of "King Buzzard," traditionally shared amongst American slaves and recounting the "spirit of the traitor who took the form of a buzzard selling them to slave traders," betraying thousands (4). Stuckey, *Slave Culture: Nationalist Theory and the Foundations of Black America* (New York: Oxford University Press, 1987), 4, 24, 54–56.

60. Smith, *Conjuring Culture*, 36 (emphasis added).

61. Evans Jr., *African American Systematic Theology*, 151–52.

62. Gayraud S. Wilmore, *Last Things First* (Philadelphia: Westminster, 1982), 77; quoted in Evans Jr., *African American Systematic Theology*, 151–52.

63. Evans Jr., *African American Systematic Theology*, 151–52.

Chapter 5

1. Stone, *Boundaries*, 24.

2. Sociologists James D. Hunter, Christian Smith, and Michael O. Emerson; historian of American Christianity (i.e., Pentecostalism and Evangelicalism) Richard Quebedeaux; and theologian Robert E. Webber are examples of scholars who conduct research on American Evangelicals.

3. Hunter, *American Evangelicalism*, 86–87.

4. Robert E. Webber, *Common Roots: A Call to Evangelical Maturity* (Grand Rapids: Zondervan, 1978), 31; quoted in Stone, *Boundaries*, 35–36.

5. Webber, *Common Roots*, 31; quoted in Stone, *Boundaries*, 35–36.

6. Stone, *Boundaries*, 36.

7. The National Association of Black Evangelicals began in 1963 and is a cross-denominational organization that espouses a statement of faith privileging evangelical commitments and values and that advances a black racially conscious tradition of religious, theological, cultural, and historical practice. The association holds local meetings where chapters have been established, and it organizes an annual national convention, prints a journal, participates in global missions, and encourages participation in black higher education, while supplying the membership with networking resources. "Values and Distinctions," National Black Evangelical Association, http://www.the-nbea.org/about/values-and-distinctions/ (accessed March 17, 2017).

8. Stone, *Boundaries*, 36.

9. Emerson and Smith, *Divided by Faith*, 3, 76–78. Both authors declare that Evangelicals come from diverse racial and ethnic backgrounds. However, in 2000, close to

90% of Americans who called themselves Evangelicals were white. The authors' volume focuses primarily on white Evangelicals and how this subgroup used religion to address the problems inherent to black-white race relations in the United States. They found that white Evangelicals hardly ever addressed the problem of a racialized society in structural terms. But the onus of race-based practices, inequality, discrimination, and intergroup conflict fell upon a freewill-individualist tradition (i.e., individuals are free to make their own choices, whether wrong or right), relationalism (i.e., interpersonal relationships held strong influence over decision-making processes, which included encouraging people to make the right choices), and antistructuralism (i.e., structural influence was lacking when thinking about race issues and solutions).

10. Karen Stenner, "Three Kinds of 'Conservatism,'" *Psychological Inquiry* 20 (2009): 150. Though I use the terms (i.e., racial, moral, and political intolerance) to describe and point out how the American public perceives white Evangelicals, Stenner discusses racial intolerance, political intolerance, and moral intolerance as examples of "status quo conservatism" and as statistical measures of general intolerance of difference. Earlier she defines "status quo conservatism" as an inclination to favor stability and preservation of the status quo over social change.

11. Stenner, "Three Kinds," 150.

12. Stenner's analyses are based on source data sets from the General Social Survey (GSS) 1972–2000 and World Values Survey (WVS), particularly her comparisons of social conservatism (i.e., authoritarianism), status quo conservatism, and laissez-faire conservatism. The GSS is a sociological and psychological instrument that measures the social trends, demographics, attitudes, and behaviors of Americans over periods of time. This survey gives information about the stability, functioning, and structure of American people and society as social changes occur and in comparison to other nations. The WVS collects and publishes data about social trends, values, and beliefs of representative samples of people in countries throughout the world, also giving cross-national statistics about how these countries vary. Stenner, "Three Kinds," 150.

13. Stenner, "Three Kinds," 150.

14. Emma Greene, "A Resolution Condemning White Supremacy Causes Chaos at the Southern Baptist Convention," *Atlantic*, June 14, 2017, https://www.theatlantic.com/politics/archive/2017/06/the-southern-baptist-convention-alt-right-white-supremacy/530244/. This article clarifies the earlier statement pointing out race and gender as being fault lines in evangelical circles; but its more specific focus is the subject of race. Recently Dwight McKissic, a prominent black pastor in Texas, presented a resolution on race to the Resolutions Committee at the Southern Baptist Convention Annual Meeting in Phoenix, held the week of June 17, 2017. Greene writes of this resolution:

> It affirmed that "there has arisen in the United States a growing menace to political order and justice that seeks to reignite social animosities, reverse improvements in race relations, divide our people, and foment hatred, classism, and ethnic cleansing." It identified this "toxic menace" as white nationalism and the alt-right, and urged the denomination to oppose its "totalitarian impulses, xenophobic biases, and bigoted ideologies that infect the minds and actions of its violent disciples." It claimed that the origin of white supremacy in Christian communities is a once-popular theory known as the "curse of Ham," which taught that "God through Noah ordained descendants of Africa to be subservient to Anglos" and was used as justification for slavery and segregation. The resolution called on the denomination to denounce nationalism and "reject the retrograde ideologies, xenophobic biases, and racial bigotries of the so-called 'alt-right' that seek to subvert our government, destabilize society, and infect our political system."

The Resolution Committee twice denied McKissic's proposal review until the denial, publicized by other black and prominent members of the convention, precipitated a chaotic reaction. At that point the convention, functioning in crisis mode because of the resolution and subsequent denials for its review, forced the committee to pay attention. In the end, the convention resolved to accept McKissic's proposal, but the situation revealed fault lines around race in this evangelical institution and by extension in other corporate evangelical bodies.

15. Andre C. Willis, "Theology in Post Democracy," *Political Theology* 10, no. 2 (2009): 212.

16. Lynn M. Hempel and John P. Bartkowski, "Scripture, Sin, and Salvation: Theological Conservatism Reconsidered," *Social Forces* 86, no. 4 (2008): 1650.

17. *Intragroup analyses* can be observed and are based on the statistics in vertical columns. In the vertical columns, racial designation is measured against sociopolitical and theological categories. Cross-tabulations compare respondent answers against "totals" *within* each racial group (i.e., % within ethnicity) and for individuals who responded along three sociopolitical dimensions (i.e., social conservative, liberal, and moderate). *Intergroup analyses* are based on and can be observed in horizontal columns. In other words, the horizontal columns compare both racial groups—blacks versus whites signified by "% within groups." "Totals" in the horizontal columns combine black *and* white participants in each group to produce cross-tabulations of race, theological, and sociopolitical positioning.

18. Tasha S. Philpot, *Conservative but Not Republican: The Paradox of Party Identification and Ideology among African Americans* (Cambridge: Cambridge University Press, 2017), 5.

19. Philpot, *Conservative but Not Republican*, 59, 206.

20. Philpot, *Conservative but Not Republican*, 15.

21. Philpot, *Conservative but Not Republican*, 16.

22. Philpot, *Conservative but Not Republican*, 9, 12, 14, 192. For instance, based on the 2012 American National Elections Studies (ANES), Philpot reports: "Blacks' ideological self-identification weakly correlates with party identification. Black conservatives (who are not Black Republicans) behave more like Black liberals than White conservatives when it comes to vote choice. 96 percent of Black liberals and 78 percent of Black conservatives identified with the Democratic party. In contrast, 81 percent of White liberals identified as Democrats while only 13 percent of White conservatives did so." The primary differences between black Republicans and black conservatives are the following. Black Republicans are black conservative elites who are more likely to have college degrees, have higher incomes, and be connected to elite conservative organizations, including the Republican Party. However, black conservatives are a mass of people more likely to be female and live in Southern states but less likely to own a home, be married, or be employed. Unlike these two groups, white Republicans and white conservatives look more demographically similar.

23. Philpot, *Conservative but Not Republican*, 13, 207–8.

24. Philpot, *Conservative but Not Republican*, 205–7.

25. Jonathan Haidt, Jesse Graham, and Craig Joseph, "Above and below Left-Right: Ideological Narratives and Moral Foundations," *Psychological Inquiry* 20 (2009): 111.

26. Haidt et al. describe the social psychological and moral foundations of political behavior in the following way. *Harm/care* displays elementary concerns for another's suffering and includes virtues of caring and compassion. *Fairness/reciprocity* shows basic concerns for unjust treatment, inequality, and more abstract notions of justice. *In-group/loyalty* targets members' responsibilities to groups such as loyalty, self-sacrifice, and vigilance against betrayal. *Authority/respect* is related to concerns about social order and hierarchy as well as obligations to hierarchical relationships such as obedience, respect, and fulfilling proper roles and positions. *Purity/sanctity* is about controlling desires, wholesomeness, and

values chastity as well as regulating physical and spiritual contagion. Haidt, Graham, and Joseph, "Above and below Left–Right," 113–15.

27. Haidt, Graham, and Joseph, "Above and below Left–Right," 111, 112–13.

28. Haidt, Graham, and Joseph, "Above and below Left–Right," 113.

29. Social and moral psychologist Ronnie Janoff-Bulman deals with conservatism and liberalism very differently from Haidt, Graham, and Joseph ("Above and below Left–Right"). She defines "conservatism" as being oriented toward *protection from* harm of group members and "liberalism" as *providing for* the welfare of others. However, she does point out that the strong moral values operating in each political group do not negate the lesser values, which are still present and acting. Janoff-Bulman, "To Provide and to Protect: Motivational Bases of Political Liberalism and Conservatism," *Psychological Inquiry* 20 (2009): 121.

30. Haidt, Graham, and Joseph, "Above and below Left–Right," 114.

31. Haidt, Graham, and Joseph, "Above and below Left–Right," 114.

32. Haidt, Graham, and Joseph, "Above and below Left–Right," 117.

33. Gary Gerstle, *American Crucible: Race and Nation in the Twentieth Century* (Princeton, N.J.: Princeton University Press, 2001), 44–47.

34. Michael Kazin, "Trump and American Populism: Old Whine, New Bottles," *Foreign Affairs* 95, no. 6 (2016): 17–18.

35. Kazin, "Trump and American Populism," 18.

36. Stenner, "Three Kinds," 144.

37. Stenner, "Three Kinds," 142.

38. John H. Duckitt, "Authoritarianism and Group Identification: A New View of an Old Construct," *Political Psychology* 10, no. 1 (1989): 71–72; quoted in Stenner, "Three Kinds," 143.

39. Stenner, "Three Kinds," 143.

40. Duckitt, "Authoritarianism and Group Identification," 71.

41. Stenner, "Three Kinds," 143.

42. Stenner, "Three Kinds," 143.

43. Stenner, "Three Kinds," 143.

44. Stenner, "Three Kinds," 144.

45. Stenner, "Three Kinds," 143–44.

46. Philpot, *Conservative but Not Republican*, 156, 160.

47. Philpot, *Conservative but Not Republican*, 160.

48. Philpot, *Conservative but Not Republican*, 160.

49. Janoff-Bulman, "To Provide and to Protect," 120–21.

50. Janoff-Bulman, "To Provide and to Protect," 124.

51. Janoff-Bulman, "To Provide and to Protect," 124.

52. Smith et al., *American Evangelicalism*, 121.

Chapter 6

1. Steven M. Tipton, "Civil Religion in the Making" (unpublished essay, 2012), 6–7; Robert N. Bellah, "Civil Religion in America," 5–8.

2. Bellah, "Civil Religion in America," 5–8.

3. Bellah, "Civil Religion in America," 4.

4. Tipton, "Civil Religion in the Making," 6–7.

5. Tipton, "Civil Religion in the Making," 6–7; Bellah, "Civil Religion in America," 4, 8.

6. Bellah, "Civil Religion in America," 8.

7. Bellah, "Civil Religion in America," 10–11.

8. Bellah, "Civil Religion in America," 10–11.

9. As discussed above in chapter 1, Reverend Branscomb names the Declaration of Independence, the Constitution, and the word of God (i.e., the Bible) as examples of ancient landmarks. They are patriotic and national symbols that, according to him, identify who Americans are and what they stand for.

10. Robert N. Bellah, "Religion and the Legitimation of the American Republic," in *The Robert Bellah Reader*, ed. Robert N. Bellah and Steven M. Tipton (Durham, N.C.: Duke University Press, 2006), 246.

11. Bellah, "Religion and the Legitimation," in Bellah and Tipton, *Robert Bellah Reader*, 246, 251.

12. Bellah, "Religion and the Legitimation," in Bellah and Tipton, *Robert Bellah Reader*, 251–52.

13. Bellah, "Religion and the Legitimation," in Bellah and Tipton, *Robert Bellah Reader*, 253; Steven M. Tipton, *Public Pulpits: Methodists and Mainline Churches in the Moral Argument of Public Life* (Chicago: University of Chicago Press, 2007), 39.

14. Bellah, "Religion and the Legitimation," in Bellah and Tipton, *Robert Bellah Reader*, 253.

15. Bellah, "Religion and the Legitimation," in Bellah and Tipton, *Robert Bellah Reader*, 254.

16. Bellah, "Religion and the Legitimation," in Bellah and Tipton, *Robert Bellah Reader*, 255; Tipton, *Public Pulpits*, 40.

17. Bellah, "Religion and the Legitimation," in Bellah and Tipton, *Robert Bellah Reader*, 256; Tipton, *Public Pulpits*, 40. Religious historian Martin Marty proposed the motivation for the American Revolutionary period derived from "national" and religious communities that were also important to the birthing of the nation. Unlike that of civil religion, the public theology of these national and religious communities depended on religious metaphors and symbolism like "chosen people" and "God's new Israel" to communicate the transcendent story and history of Americans. Marty calls this "civil millennialism" because, "namely," Bellah writes, the metaphors supplied "the providential religious meaning of the American colonies in world history" (256).

18. Bellah, "Religion and the Legitimation," in Bellah and Tipton, *Robert Bellah Reader*, 257.

19. Bellah, "Religion and the Legitimation," in Bellah and Tipton, *Robert Bellah Reader*, 257; Tipton, *Public Pulpits*, 40.

20. Bellah, "Religion and the Legitimation," in Bellah and Tipton, *Robert Bellah Reader*, 257; Tipton, *Public Pulpits*, 40; and Tipton, "Civil Religion in the Making," 10.

21. Tipton, *Public Pulpits*, 41.

22. Tipton, *Public Pulpits*, 42; Tipton, "Civil Religion in the Making," 11; Bellah, "Religion and the Legitimation," in Bellah and Tipton, *Robert Bellah Reader*, 258–59 (emphasis in original). Bellah further states that Alexis de Tocqueville believed religion had the force to curb self-interest, transforming it into "self-interest rightly understood," meaning a self-interest inspired by public interest and self-sacrifice. "In this way," writes Bellah, "Tocqueville showed how religion mitigated the full implication of American liberalism and allowed republican institutions to survive" (259).

23. Bellah, "Religion and the Legitimation," in Bellah and Tipton, *Robert Bellah Reader*, 259.

24. Tipton, "Civil Religion in the Making," 11.

25. Tipton, "Civil Religion in the Making," 11; Tipton, *Public Pulpits*, 43.

26. Marvin and Ingle, *Blood Sacrifice and the Nation*, 20–23, 30–33, 66; Marvin and Ingle, "Blood Sacrifice and the Nation," 767–69. Freudian studies and Durkheim's totem

taboo theory are foundational to Marvin and Ingle's application of knowledge and theorizing about the relationship between blood sacrifices, the nation-state, and religion. In fact, their work shaped Rhys H. Williams' scholarship around blood-land-religion. Based on early investigations of premodern societies, Durkheim proposed the following. The taboo totem—a consecrated symbol and/or representation that kinship groups identify themselves with—is an object that controls, rules, and guides social relationships. Rituals are created to maintain the sanctity of the taboo totem and to ask for blessings of the totem god. Maintaining the totem demands sharing in sacrificial obligations. Hence, the idea behind Durkheim's totem taboo theory is that social solidarity happens around a contract created by group members who agree on the following guidelines and rules: (a) how to handle the totem-object; (b) what counts as sacrificial behavior of group members; and (c) acceptable terms for group regeneration. In the case of America and civil religion, the taboo totem object is the flag. The flag is both totem object and totem god, "serving to designate the clan collectively" (Marvin and Ingle, *Blood Sacrifice and the Nation*, 25). The rhetoric and rituals surrounding the flag represent the group's affirmation of this symbol as a sign of group membership. Upholding and guarding the principles of the flag, particularly during wartime, calls for the sacrifices of "blood kinsmen," a relationship stronger than familial bonds. The sacrifice of these social bodies becomes a sacred gesture. Death not only maintains existing group loyalties thereby making sure the group remains together but also starts the process of group regeneration because those who have "touched death" have been expunged from the community, thus preserving the nation.

27. Marvin and Ingle, *Blood Sacrifice and the Nation*, 66.

28. Marvin and Ingle, "Blood Sacrifice and the Nation," 768.

29. Marvin and Ingle, "Blood Sacrifice and the Nation," 769.

30. Marvin and Ingle, "Blood Sacrifice and the Nation," 769.

31. When Bald Eagles community members spoke of war, living in a military culture often implied maleness and/or militaristic constructions of masculinity even though residents were cognizant of women's active involvement with the military and participation in service to the nation as soldiers. Until 2015, American women were not trained to participate in combat. Since that time, combat positions once limited to men have opened up to qualified women. Thus, Bald Eagles' community mindset and vernacular was as follows: women serve the country but in different ways than men even though they are members of the armed forces. Most casualties from fighting wars are men (not women). That is a unique aspect of this community influenced by American military culture (a culture reinforced by the community's practice of Southern evangelicalism). Military culture is predominantly male and tends to bred a militaristic masculinity. The Bald Eagles community maintained a lively, family-oriented, military culture structured by unspoken and even possibly unconscious yet gendered rules and roles for men and women.

32. Hodgson, *Myth of American Exceptionalism*, 23. Hodgson explains that Franklin Delano Roosevelt was reflecting Wilsonian ideology by being convicted that the United States needed to enter World War II to fight against fascism in order to safeguard the country. In addressing Congress about the nation's security, almost a year away from Pearl Harbor, he stated that Americans should fight to uphold four freedoms: freedom of speech, freedom of worship, freedom from want, and freedom from fear. Hodgson then goes on to suggest Roosevelt was also convinced America should enter the war to put an end to imperialism.

33. *Pax Americana* is a history and foreign affairs term that means something different depending upon the era to which it is applied. Today the concept pertains to the relative peace in the Western Hemisphere and the rest of the world because of America's dominance as a world power, beginning from around the mid-twentieth century. It has come to represent not only the economic and political position of the United States in relation to

other nations but also the nation's ability to shape, influence, and direct global events. Its most contemporary connotation is the "peace" and international order established among post–World War II superpowers, with the United States of America holding its position at the apogee. Nonetheless, world leaders suggest that America's preponderant position is on the decline because of global upheavals, social movements, and security issues.

34. Erll, *Memory in Culture*, 14, 17, 56.

35. Erll, *Memory in Culture*, 14, 17.

36. Omi and Winant, *Racial Formations in the United States*, 236–37. Residents' interpretation of this American creed has been affected by macrostructural changes to worldwide migration and immigration patterns caused by war, violence, and the threat of Islamic extremism, which are also precipitating a global refugee crisis. Each of these social factors has contributed to anticipated but feared "majority-minority" population dynamics throughout the United States, in certain parts of Europe, and in other areas of the world.

37. Hodgson, *Myth of American Exceptionalism*, 41. While Hodgson does not make this claim, he does recount the post–Civil War social changes that gave all white men, regardless of "class" distinction, the right to vote. However, as American society experienced drastic changes with immigration and urbanization during that period, he asserts that an "anti-democratic" reaction set in targeting women, free blacks, paupers, felons, and migrants—all who lost the right to vote.

38. Tipton, "Civil Religion in the Making," 2–3.

39. Tipton, "Civil Religion in the Making," 2.

40. Barna Group, "Report Examines the State of Mainline Protestant Churches," December 7, 2009, https://www.barna.com/research/report-examines-the-state-of -mainline-protestant-churches/ (accessed February 2, 2011). The Barna Group conducted several national telephone surveys for this report. In 1998 the surveys among mainline adults included 267 adults; in 2008, 1,148 mainline attenders were interviewed. The surveys among pastors involved 492 mainline senior pastors drawn from random samples of Protestant churches. Sampling error associated with the sample of 267 adults was between the range of ±2.7 and ±6.4 percentage points at the 95% confidence level. Sampling error associated with the sample of 1,148 adults was between the range of ±1.3 and ±3.0 percentage points at the 95% confidence level. Other types of error (known as nonsampling error) that can occur in surveys—such as errors arising from question wording, question sequencing, and the recording of responses—were not included in these ranges.

41. Barna Group, "Report Examines the State"; Michael Lipka, "Mainline Protestants Make Up Shrinking Number of U.S. Adults," *Fact Tank* (blog), Pew Research Center, May 18, 2015, http://www.pewresearch.org/fact-tank/2015/05/18/mainline -protestants-make-up-shrinking-number-of-u-s-adults/.

42. Pew Research Center, "America's Changing Religious Landscape," May 12, 2015, http://www.pewforum.org/2015/05/12/americas-changing-religious-landscape/; Lipka, "Mainline Protestants."

43. According to the "changing religious landscape" reporters, the decline could be as small as 3 million or as large as 7.3 million between 2007 and 2014, when taking into account combined margins of error. Pew Research Center, "America's Changing Religious Landscape"; Lipka, "Mainline Protestants."

44. Robert N. Bellah, *Beyond Belief: Essays on Religion in a Post-traditionalist World*, paperback ed. (Berkeley: University of California Press, 1991), 42.

45. Sidney E. Mead, "The Nation with the Soul of a Church," in Richey and Jones, *American Civil Religion*, 45–48.

46. Mead, "Nation with the Soul," in Richey and Jones, *American Civil Religion*, 54–59.

47. Mead, "Nation with the Soul," in Richey and Jones, *American Civil Religion*, 59.

48. Tipton, *Public Pulpits*, 4.

49. Marvin and Ingle, *Blood Sacrifice and the Nation*, 65–66.

50. Marvin and Ingle, *Blood Sacrifice and the Nation*, 66.

51. Marvin and Ingle, "Blood Sacrifice and the Nation," 777.

52. Tipton, *Public Pulpits*, 38

53. Amy Gutmann, "Communitarian Critics of Liberalism," *Debates in Contemporary Political Philosophy: An Anthology* (2003): 182–94; "Amy Gutmann, 'Communitarian Critics of Liberalism,'" *Political Not Metaphysical* (blog), May 23, 2016, https://politicalnotmetaphysical.wordpress.com/2016/05/23/amy-gutmann-communitarian-critics-of-liberalism/ (accessed September 17, 2017).

54. Tipton, *Public Pulpits*, 38.

55. Tipton, "Civil Religion in the Making," 5.

56. Tipton, *Public Pulpits*, 38.

57. Robert N. Bellah, "Heritage and Choice in American Religion," paper presented at *Daedalus* conference on religion and American culture, American Academy of Arts and Sciences, Brookline, Mass., October 15–16, 1965; Tipton, "Civil Religion in the Making," 5.

58. Tipton, "Civil Religion in the Making," 4.

59. Marvin and Ingle, *Blood Sacrifice and the Nation*, 71.

60. Marvin and Ingle, *Blood Sacrifice and the Nation*, 69.

61. Marvin and Ingle, *Blood Sacrifice and the Nation*, 69.

62. Marvin and Ingle, "Blood Sacrifice and the Nation," 770.

63. Marvin and Ingle, "Blood Sacrifice and the Nation," 772.

64. Marvin and Ingle, "Blood Sacrifice and the Nation," 770.

65. Robert N. Bellah, "Durkheim and Ritual," in Bellah and Tipton, *Robert Bellah Reader*, 170–72.

66. Marvin and Ingle, *Blood Sacrifice and the Nation*, 89.

67. Erll, *Memory in Culture*, 58. Public and social memories are subareas of the discipline, sociology of memory. Social memories determine "how societies remember" and are "an expression of collective experience which identifies a group and gives the group a sense of its past as it aspires towards the future." Social memories with a focus on being "public" connect how societies remember to the public realm with the end result of forming collective and public group identities. For instance, memories of the Holocaust are often related to German guilt and defeat, and slavery in America not only connects to African American identity but also forms it.

68. Marvin and Ingle, *Blood Sacrifice and the Nation*, 89.

69. Marvin and Ingle, *Blood Sacrifice and the Nation*, 89.

70. Marvin and Ingle, *Blood Sacrifice and the Nation*, 67–68.

71. Marvin and Ingle, *Blood Sacrifice and the Nation*, 67–68.

72. Marvin and Ingle, *Blood Sacrifice and the Nation*, 74.

73. Roy A. Rappaport, *Ritual and Religion in the Making of Humanity* (Cambridge: Cambridge University Press, 1999), 107, 112, 113; Bellah, "Durkheim and Ritual," in Bellah and Tipton, *Robert Bellah Reader*, 161–62.

74. Rappaport, *Ritual and Religion*, 114–15.

75. Rappaport, *Ritual and Religion*, 119–20.

76. Rappaport, *Ritual and Religion*, 120.

77. Sherry B. Ortner, "On Key Symbols," in *A Reader in Anthropology of Religion*, ed. Michael Lambek (Malden, Mass.: Blackwell, 2002), 158–67.

78. Tipton, *Public Pulpits*, 35–38.

79. Tipton, *Public Pulpits*, 37.

80. Bellah, "Durkheim and Ritual," in Bellah and Tipton, *Robert Bellah Reader*, 163–64.

81. Bellah, "Durkheim and Ritual," in Bellah and Tipton, *Robert Bellah Reader,* 164. A similar concept, explains Bellah, is Abraham Maslow's "peak experiences," which can be religious. Maslow, *Toward a Psychology of Being* (Princeton, N.J.: Van Nostrand, 1962).

82. Bellah, "Durkheim and Ritual," in Bellah and Tipton, *Robert Bellah Reader,* 164.

83. Bellah, "Durkheim and Ritual," in Bellah and Tipton, *Robert Bellah Reader,* 164.

84. Marty, "Two Kinds of Civil Religion," in Richey and Jones, *American Civil Religion,* 145–47, 151.

85. Marty, "Two Kinds of Civil Religion," in Richey and Jones, *American Civil Religion,* 145, 147–49.

86. Rappaport, *Ritual and Religion,* 114–15.

87. Rappaport, *Ritual and Religion,* 117.

88. Rappaport, *Ritual and Religion,* 114.

Chapter 7

1. Bellah, "Civil Religion in America," 4–5, 15.

2. Bellah, *Broken Covenant,* 3.

3. Gorski, "Barack Obama and Civil Religion," 182.

4. Historian Andrew Manis, explaining Southern civil religion, writes: "What I am calling southern civil religion is one of the subcultural, or regional, manifestations of the American civil religion. It is an American faith, but one with its peculiar distinctions. It is, above all, a system of mixed symbols. The images of this public faith resemble a mythic Rorschach. At one glance they embody and communicate the faith of an American's America; another peek, and they gather before the undulating Stars and Bars and intone, 'Forget Hell!'" Manis, *Southern Civil Religions in Conflict,* 23.

5. Bellah, "Civil Religion in America," 33, 12.

6. Omi and Winant, *Racial Formation in the United States,* 75.

7. Omi and Winant, *Racial Formation in the United States,* 106. Both authors developed a *theory of racial formation* to describe how the concept of race works in the United States. To understand their theory is to know that *race* is a way of "making up people" (105), meaning people use *race* in two ways: (a) to shape and guide social interactions while telling them where they fit in social hierarchies; and (b) to categorize people as friend or foe, which often includes assigning people to the category of "other." When subordinate status is attached to labeling an-"other," that is injurious and damaging. With this as the foundation, one of the features of their theory is that "race" is a *master category* because the concept is fundamental to, has shaped, and continues to influence U.S. history, politics, economics, culture—in other words, all spheres of American life. However, race does not *transcend*—work above or separately from—other social indicators of inequality and difference such as gender, class, and sexual orientation. Rather, race when interconnected with these other axes of difference, termed *intersectionality* by legal scholar Kimberlé Williams Crenshaw, compounds social marginalization, inequality, and difference.

8. Omi and Winant, *Racial Formation in the United States,* 83.

9. Omi and Winant, *Racial Formation in the United States,* 78, 81.

10. Omi and Winant, *Racial Formation in the United States,* 79.

11. Omi and Winant, *Racial Formation in the United States,* 76.

12. R. Williams, "Civil Religion and the Cultural Politics," 253.

13. R. Williams, "Civil Religion and the Cultural Politics," 253.

14. R. Williams, "Civil Religion and the Cultural Politics," 247.

15. See Appendix 3: "Leadership in Black Female-Headed Households in the 1940s and 1950s."

16. In his widely acclaimed book *In His Steps*, Charles Monroe Sheldon, a Congregationalist minister, liberal Protestant, and leader of the Social Gospel Movement, introduced the question-turned-principle, "What would Jesus do?" Sixty years after its 1897 publication, his book was second to the Bible in sales with an estimated 8 million copies distributed. The question—"What would Jesus do?"—was popular in the early twentieth century and experienced a revival in the late twentieth century, almost one hundred years after Sheldon had introduced it into Christian circles. Kansapedia, Kansas Historical Society, July 13, 2018, https://www.kshs.org/kansapedia/charles-monroe-sheldon/12201.

17. Leah Sakala, "Breaking Down Mass Incarceration in the 2010 Census: State by State Incarceration Rates by Race/Ethnicity," Prison Policy Initiative, May 28, 2014, https://www.prisonpolicy.org/reports/rates.html.

18. The Sentencing Project, "Shadow Report to the United Nations on Racial Disparities in the United States Criminal Justice System," August 31, 2013, http://www.sentencingproject.org/publications/shadow-report-to-the-united-nations-human-rights-committee-regarding-racial-disparities-in-the-united-states-criminal-justice-system/, paragraph 1.

19. Sentencing Project, "Shadow Report," paragraph 2.

20. Peter Wagner and Bernadette Rabuy, "Mass Incarceration: The Whole Pie 2016," Prison Policy Initiative, May 14, 2016, https://www.prisonpolicy.org/reports/pie2016.html.

21. Martin E. Marty, *The Public Church: Mainline, Evangelical, Catholic* (New York: Crossroad, 1981), 16.

22. Marty, *Public Church*, 16; and Tipton, *Public Pulpits*, 3–4, 11–17, 40, 44.

23. Long, "Civil Rights—Civil Religion," in Richey and Jones, *American Civil Religion*, 211–21; Mead, "Nation with the Soul," in Richey and Jones, *American Civil Religion*, 45–74; and Tipton, *Public Pulpits*, 42. In his 1973 essay, historian of religion Charles Long examines civil religion from the perspectives of racial and ethnic national communities—black Americans, Native Americans, and Jewish Americans. He dissents with the concept of an American civil religion capable of furnishing a "consensus" model of culture and community and thereby promoting unitary moral arguments in the midst of a socially diverse public. Such a model renders segments of the population invisible. Instead, Long insists on a "new hermeneutic" when it comes to the civil religious form of American religion. An inclusive American civil religion would ably pursue a just, equitable, and diverse society, and it would have the strength to overcome the invisibility of American Indians and blacks and other racial and ethnic religious communities (213–14, 216, 220).

24. Higginbotham, *Righteous Discontent*, 9; and Marla F. Frederick, *Between Sundays: Black Women and Everyday Struggles of Faith* (Berkeley: University of California Press, 2003), 232.

25. Frederick, *Between Sundays*, 232.

26. Craig Calhoun, ed., *Habermas and the Public Square* (Cambridge, Mass.: MIT Press, 1992), 4; Higginbotham, *Righteous Discontent*, 9, 11; and Frederick, *Between Sundays*, 96, 232. Relying on Calhoun, Frederick explains Habermas' notion of the "democratic public sphere" as comprising two elements: "the quality or form of rational-critical discourse" and the "quality, or openness to, popular participation" (232).

27. Tipton, *Public Pulpits*, 42, 456.

28. Tipton, *Public Pulpits*, 42.

29. In one of his final conversations before his death, Martin Luther King Jr., speaking with humanitarian and activist Harry Belafonte about black people and integration, professes: "I've come upon something that disturbs me deeply. We have fought hard and long for integration, as I believe we should have, and I know we will win. But I have come to

believe that we are integrating into a burning house. I'm afraid that America has lost the moral vision she may have had. And I'm afraid that even as we integrate, we are walking into a place that does not understand that this nation needs to be deeply concerned with the plight of the poor and disenfranchised. Until we commit ourselves to ensuring that the underclass is given justice and opportunity, we will continue to perpetuate the anger and violence that tears the soul of this nation. I fear I am integrating my people into a burning house." Startled by King Jr.'s response, Belafonte asks: "What should we do?" Dr. King tells him that we "become the firemen. Let us not stand by and let the house burn." Janice Graham, "I Fear I May Have Integrated My People into a Burning House," Our Common Ground Media and Communications, August 20, 2013, https://ourcommonground.com/2013/08/20/i-fear-i-may-have-integrated-my-people-into-a-burning-house-martin-luther-king-jr/; and Jineea Butler, "Integrating into a Burning House, *Final Call*, December 12, 2014, http://www.finalcall.com/artman/publish/Perspectives_1/article_101996.shtml.

30. Graham, "I Fear"; and Butler, "Integrating into a Burning House."

31. Omi and Winant, *Racial Formation in the United States*, 138–39.

32. Cheryl Townsend Gilkes, afterword to *The Souls of Black Folk*, by W. E. B. Du Bois (New York: Signet Classics, 2012), 17. In 1903, Du Bois pointed out, "The problem of the twentieth century is the problem of the color-line," which is a phrase that scholars of race continue to use to discuss race issues in America.

33. Omi and Winant, *Racial Formation in the United States*, 131.

34. Omi and Winant, *Racial Formation in the United States*, 147.

35. Omi and Winant, *Racial Formation in the United States*, 147.

36. Howard Cohen, "'He Knew What He Signed Up For,' Trump Reportedly Tells Widow of Fallen Miami Gardens Soldier," *Miami Herald*, October 17, 2017, http://www.miamiherald.com/news/local/community/miami-dade/miami-gardens/article179433356.html; and Mark Lander and Yamiche Alcindor, "Trump's Condolence Call to Widow Ignites an Imbroglio," *New York Times*, October 18, 2017, https://www.nytimes.com/2017/10/18/us/politics/trump-widow-johnson-call.html?smid=fb-share.

37. Rappaport, *Ritual and Religion*, 118.

38. Rappaport, *Ritual and Religion*, 118.

39. Rappaport, *Ritual and Religion*, 121.

40. Rappaport, *Ritual and Religion*, 121–22.

41. Rappaport, *Ritual and Religion*, 122–23 (emphasis added).

42. Rappaport, *Ritual and Religion*, 122.

43. Rappaport, *Ritual and Religion*, 123–24.

44. The POW/MIA flag was created to recognize the National League of Families of American Prisoners and Missing in Southeast Asia. Congress still continues to acknowledge the flag, which was affiliated with the Vietnam War prisoner-of-war/missing-in-action issue. It serves as an emblem and to remind the nation about U.S. Public Law 101–335, which establishes "our concern and commitment to resolving as fully as possible the fates of Americans still prisoner, missing and unaccounted for in Southeast Asia, thus ending the uncertainty for their families and the Nation." The motto inscribed in white on the flag is: "You are not forgotten." It has a silhouette of a "prisoner of war" before a guard tower and white barbed wires on a black field. See "Faith, Flags, and Guns: Black Civil Religion," in appendix 3.

45. Callahan, *Talking Book*, 49–51.

46. Callahan, *Talking Book*, 50.

47. Callahan, *Talking Book*, 59.

48. Robert Wuthnow, *The Restructuring of American Religion: Society and Faith since World War II* (Princeton, N.J.: Princeton University Press, 1988), 241–42.

49. Wuthnow, *Restructuring of American Religion*, 242.

50. Wuthnow, *Restructuring of American Religion*, 244, 246–47.

51. Wuthnow, *Restructuring of American Religion*, 250–53.

52. *Economist*, "Who Will Fight the Next War?" 25–26.

53. *Economist*, "Who Will Fight the Next War?" 28.

54. William H. McNeill, *Keeping Together in Time: Dance and Drill in Human History* (Cambridge, Mass.: Harvard University Press, 1997), i–ii; cited in Bellah and Tipton, *Robert Bellah Reader*, 173.

55. McNeill, *Keeping Together in Time*, 86–90; cited in Bellah and Tipton, *Robert Bellah Reader*, 174.

56. Bellah, *Broken Covenant*, xix.

57. Bellah, *Broken Covenant*, xi.

58. Bellah, *Broken Covenant*, xii.

59. Bellah, *Broken Covenant*, 108 (emphasis added).

60. Bellah, *Broken Covenant*, 109–10.

Chapter 8

1. Wilson, *Baptized in the Blood*, 36.

2. Wilson, *Baptized in the Blood*, 36.

3. Wilson, *Baptized in the Blood*, 36.

4. Wilson, *Baptized in the Blood*, xvii.

5. Wilson, *Baptized in the Blood*, xvii.

6. Wilson, *Baptized in the Blood*, xviii.

7. Karla F. C. Holloway introduces the concept of "black death" in *Passed On: African American Mourning Stories; A Memorial* (Durham, N.C.: Duke University Press, 2003), 1.

8. Holloway, *Passed On*, 2.

9. Holloway, *Passed On*, 6.

10. Holloway, *Passed On*, 6.

11. Children's Defense Fund, *The State of America's Children 2017*, http://www .childrensdefense.org/library/state-of-americas-children/2017-soac.pdf (accessed January 24, 2018), 6–7.

12. Ortner, "On Key Symbols," in Lambek, *Reader in Anthropology of Religion*, 161–63.

13. Wuthnow, *Restructuring of American Religion*, 297, 308.

14. Religious "nones" describe themselves as atheists, agnostics, as well as individuals who grew up in traditional religious congregations and denominations and who were socialized into religious belief and practice yet now identify as religiously unaffiliated, no longer connected to a religious community, organization, or group. Atheists and agnostics comprise a minority of religious "nones," while many others identify as religious and declare the importance of religion in their lives despite not being formally associated with a religious body or group. About 23% of the U.S. adult population self-identifies as religious "nones" across educational and income levels, races, ethnicities, native-born and immigrant statuses, as well as geographic regions. Michael Lipka, "A Closer Look at America's Rapidly Growing Religious 'Nones,'" *Fact Tank* (blog), Pew Research Center, May 13, 2015, http://www.pewresearch.org/fact-tank/2015/05/13/ a-closer-look-at-americas-rapidly-growing-religious-nones/; Lipka, "Why America's 'Nones' Left Religion Behind," *Fact Tank* (blog), Pew Research Center, August 24, 2016, http://www.pewresearch.org/fact-tank/2016/08/24/why-americas-nones-left -religion-behind/.

15. Wuthnow, *Restructuring of American Religion*, 301, 308.

16. Jeremiah Wright, retired senior pastor of Trinity United Church of Christ in Chicago, Illinois, made news headlines during President Obama's national campaign for office in 2008. Wright is President Obama's former pastor. Employing the technique and rhetoric of the American jeremiad, Wright preached a 2003 sermon where he held America accountable for the events of September 11, 2001, concluding it was a result of America's own international and domestic terrorism. During the sermon, he also indicted America for its ill treatment of blacks, proclaiming: "Blacks should not sing 'God Bless America' but 'God Damn America.' The government gives them drugs, builds bigger prisons, passes a three strike law and then wants us to sing 'God *Bless* America.' No, No, No, God *Damn* America! that's in the Bible for killing innocent people. God *Damn* America for treating our citizens as less than human. God *Damn* America for as long as she acts like she is God and is supreme." Educated at the University of Chicago, Wright is still considered one of the country's leading black pastors as he mixes the social gospel with contemporary sociopolitical issues in his sermonizing. Brian Ross and Rehab El-Buri, "Obama's Pastor: God Damn America, U.S. to Blame for 9/11," ABC News, March 13, 2008, http://abcnews.go.com/Blotter/DemocraticDebate/story?id=4443788&page=1.

17. Howard-Pitney, *African American Jeremiad*, 10.

18. Howard-Pitney, *African American Jeremiad*, 7, 10, 13.

19. Joseph Gerteis, "Civil Religion and the Politics of Belonging," *Political Power and Social Theory* 22 (2011): 219.

20. Gerteis, "Civil Religion and the Politics of Belonging," 219–22.

21. Gerteis, "Civil Religion and the Politics of Belonging," 220.

22. Gerteis, "Civil Religion and the Politics of Belonging," 220.

23. Shrouded in mystery is the original author of this dictum traditionally attributed to Voltaire. However, the maxim cannot be located in any of his works. Commentators suggest that later, writing under the pseudonym Stephen G. Tallentyre in *The Friends of Voltaire* (1906), Evelyn Beatrice Hall penned the saying to summarize Voltaire's attitude. This phrase has also been attributed to Founding Father Patrick Henry, a politician and orator, who is thought to have made the statement during America's founding.

24. Rachel K. Jones, Jacqueline E. Darroch, and Stanley K. Henshaw, "Patterns in the Socioeconomic Characteristics of Women Obtaining Abortions in 2000–2001," *Perspectives on Sexual and Reproductive Health* 34, no. 5 (2002): 226–35; and Stanley K. Henshaw and Kathryn Kost, "Trends in the Characteristics of Women Obtaining Abortions, 1974 to 2004," Guttmacher Institute, August 2008, https://www.guttmacher.org/sites/default/files/report_pdf/trendswomenabortions-wtables.pdf (accessed January 26, 2018).

25. Jones, Darroch, and Henshaw, "Patterns in the Socioeconomic Characteristics," 229–34; and Henshaw and Kost, "Trends in the Characteristics," 3–13.

26. George M. Marsden, "Preachers of Paradox: The Religious New Right in Historical Perspective," in *Religion and America: Spiritual Life in a Secular Age*, ed. Mary Douglas and Steven Tipton (Boston: Beacon, 1982), 160–61.

27. William P. O'Hare, "US Rural Soldiers Account for a Disproportionately High Share of Casualties in Iraq and Afghanistan," Carsey Institute: University of New Hampshire, Fall 2016, https://scholars.unh.edu/cgi/viewcontent.cgi?article=1015&context=carsey (accessed February 22, 2018).

28. Karl W. Eikenberry and David M. Kennedy, "Americans and Their Military, Drifting Apart," *New York Times*, May 26, 2013, http://www.nytimes.com/2013/05/27/opinion/americans-and-their-military-drifting-apart.html. Civil-military relations: *Economist*, "Who Will Fight the Next War?" paragraph 2, 8.

29. O'Hare, "US Rural Soldiers."

30. Michael M. Phillips, "Brothers in Arms: The Tragedy in Small-Town America," *Wall Street Journal*, September 22, 2017, https://www.wsj.com/articles/brothers-in-arms -the-tragedy-in-small-town-america-1506092151?.

31. Robert N. Bellah, "God and King," in Bellah and Tipton, *Robert Bellah Reader*, 370; and Hodgson, *Myth of American Exceptionalism*, 22.

32. Robert N. Bellah, "The New American Empire," in Bellah and Tipton, *Robert Bellah Reader*, 350.

Chapter 9

1. Robert N. Bellah, Richard Marsden, William M. Sullivan, Ann Swindler, and Steven M. Tipton, *The Good Society* (New York: Vintage Books, 1991), 4; idem, *Habits of the Heart*, 3rd ed. (Berkeley: University of California Press, 2008), xlvii.

2. Dennis McCann, "The Good to Be Pursued in Common," in *The Common Good and US Capitalism*, ed. Oliver F. Williams and John W. Houcks (Lanham, Md.: University Press of America, 1987), 158–78; cited in Bellah et al., *Good Society*, 9.

3. Bellah et al., *Good Society*, 179–215.

4. Bellah et al., *Good Society*, 181.

5. Bellah et al., *Good Society,* 182.

6. Bellah, "Civil Religion in America," 4; Tipton, "Civil Religion in the Making," 4.

7. Bellah et al., *Good Society*, 194.

8. Tipton, "Civil Religion in the Making," 11; Bellah et al., *Habits of the Heart*, vii–ix, 27–51, 250–96.

9. Tipton, "Civil Religion in the Making," 17.

10. Bellah et al., *Habits of the Heart*, vii–ix, 27–51, 250–96.

11. Bellah, "Religious Evolution," 6; Bellah, "Civil Religion in America."

12. Bellah, "Religious Evolution," 5.

13. Bellah, "Civil Religion in America," 16–19; Bellah, "Religious Evolution," 5; Gorski, "Barack Obama and Civil Religion," 219.

14. Bellah, "Civil Religion in America," 10.

15. Emile Durkheim, "The Elementary Forms of Religious Life," in Lambek, *Reader in the Anthropology of Religion*, 47.

16. David I. Kertzer, *Ritual, Politics, and Power* (New Haven: Yale University Press, 1988), 62.

17. Kertzer, *Ritual, Politics, and Power*, 1–2, 4.

18. Clifford Geertz, "Religion as a Cultural System," in *The Interpretation of Cultures: Selected Essays* (New York: Basic Books, 1973), 89

19. Geertz, "Religion as a Cultural System," 89.

20. Kertzer, *Ritual, Politics, and Power*, 11.

21. Kertzer, *Ritual, Politics, and Power*, 69.

22. Catherine Bell, *Ritual Theory, Ritual Practice* (New York: Oxford University Press, 1992), 21.

23. Bell, *Ritual Theory, Ritual Practice*, 23.

24. Clifford Geertz, "Ethos, Worldview, and the Analysis of Sacred Symbols," in *Interpretation of Cultures*, 127.

25. Kertzer, *Ritual, Politics, and Power*, 67.

26. Victor Turner, *From Ritual to Theatre: The Human Seriousness of Play* (New York: Performing Arts Journal Publications, 1982), 44.

27. Turner, *From Ritual to Theatre*, 44–46.

28. Kertzer, *Ritual, Politics, and Power*, 12.

29. Jay R. Greenberg and Stephen A. Mitchell, *Object Relations in Psychoanalytic Theory*, 12th ed. (Cambridge, Mass.: Harvard University Press, 2000), 3–4.

30. James S. Grotstein, *Splitting and Projective Identification* (New York: Jason Aronson, 1985), 6.

31. Kertzer, *Ritual, Politics, and Power*, 97.

32. J. Williams, *Religion and Violence*, 173.

33. J. Williams, *Religion and Violence*, 173, 176.

34. In writing *Religion and Violence in Early American Methodism*, Jeffrey Williams attends to a topic that historians have often neglected: the military rhetoric and warfare imagery of early Methodism. A history of the Methodist tradition, his narrative traces the religious life of Methodists to ascertain how the language of spiritual conflict was translated religiously and socially. Redemptive aspects of violence played out in the lives of this religious group. James W. Jones scribes *Blood That Cries Out from the Earth: The Psychology of Religious Terrorism* (New York: Oxford University Press, 2008) to unearth the psychological dimensions of religious terrorism and to add to a body of knowledge scarcely studied: the religious understandings of terrorism. The thrust of his work is found in this question: Are there dynamics inherent to particular religious systems that lead to violence? (Jones, *Blood*, introduction, xvii).

35. Jones, *Blood*; cited in J. Williams, *Religion and Violence*, 168.

36. For example, see Timothy Gorringe, *God's Just Vengeance: Crime, Violence, and the Rhetoric of Salvation* (New York: Cambridge University Press, 1996); Gary F. Jensen, "Religious Cosmologies and Homicide Rates among Nations," *Journal of Religion and Society* 8 (2006): 1–14; David G. Bromley and J. Gordon Melton, eds., *Cults, Religion, and Violence* (Cambridge: Cambridge University Press, 2002); John R. Hall, Philip D. Schuyler, and Sylvaine Trinh, *Apocalypse Observed: Religious Movements, Social Order, and Violence in North America, Europe and Japan* (New York: Routledge, 2000); Mark Juergensmeyer, *Terror in the Mind of God: The Global Rise of Religious Violence*, 3rd ed. (Berkeley: University of California Press, 2003); Charles Kimball, *When Religion Becomes Evil*, rev. and updated ed. (New York: HarperOne, 2008); cited in J. Williams, *Religion and Violence*, 202.

37. Kertzer, *Ritual, Politics, Power*, 101.

38. J. Williams, *Religion and Violence*, 175.

39. Guétin, *Religious Ideology*, 173–74.

40. David Lowenthal, "Letter to the Editor," *Perspectives: Newsletter of the American Historical Association* 32 (1994): 17–18.

41. Conrad Cherry, ed., *God's New Israel: Religious Interpretations of American Destiny* (Chapel Hill: University of North Carolina Press, 1998), 17; quoted in Guétin, *Religious Ideology*, 161.

42. I gleaned these evaluations from a conversation with Alyson Dickson, July 29, 2011.

43. Tipton, "Civil Religion in the Making," 11.

44. Bellah et al., *Good Society*, 214.

45. Jonathan Haidt, "The Ethics of Globalism, Nationalism, and Patriotism," *Minding Nature* 9, no. 3 (Fall 2016): 23.

46. Bellah, "Religious Evolution," 6.

47. Bellah, "Religious Evolution," 6.

48. Haidt, "Ethics of Globalism," 23.

49. Kertzer, *Ritual, Power, Rites*, 175.

50. Rhys H. Williams, "Constructing the Public Good: Social Movements and Cultural Resources," *Social Problems* 42, no. 1 (1995): 129–30.

51. R. Williams, "Constructing the Public Good," 130–31.

52. Bellah, "Religious Evolution," 6.

Appendix 1

1. See Appendix 1.A: "Evangelical Faith and Southern Civil Religion Survey."

2. See Appendix 1.B: "Clarification Sheet for Evangelical Faith and Southern Civil Religion Survey."

3. See Appendix 1.C: "True Randomness."

4. Geertz, "Religion as a Cultural System," 87–125.

5. Sociologist Robert N. Bellah and his coauthors offer a theory on the "good society" in their book *The Good Society*, based on critical social theory. Social ethicist and practical theologian Don S. Browning both applauds and critiques the ways in which the social sciences have submitted to a critical social theory. Browning proposes broadening critical social theory by "taking history, its religious classics, and hence theology as sources for its vision of the good person and the good society." He notes, "Critical theory alone tends to neglect history and its religious classics." Browning includes history and religion in his reformulation of a "critical social theory" and considers them essential to understanding what constitutes the "good society." Don S. Browning and Terry D. Cooper, *Religious Thought and the Modern Psychologies*, 2nd ed. (Minneapolis: Augsburg Fortress, 2004).

Index

racial group consciousness, 160–61, 172–73

racial politics, 43, 44, 48–49, 156–58, 160–61, 225–26, 327n7. *See also* postracial society

racial state, 48–49; democratic and despotic practices, 225–26

Rainbow Coalition, 329n12

randomization, 295, 298–300

Rappaport, Roy A., 206, 207–8, 212, 229–30

regional identity, 62–63, 66, 88, 90, 133, 213; and race, xiii, 52–53, 105. *See also* American national identity

religion: of Jesus, 136–39; of the Lost Cause, 19, 245–46; and politics, 35, 62, 63, 183–86, 200, 330n18; superstructural and infrastructural roles, 184–85, 271; of the warmed heart, 80–84, 97. *See also under* American exceptionalism; American national identity; culture

religious evolutionary process, 190

religious history, xix, 37–38, 70, 121–22

religious nationalism. *See* patriotism: religious

religious "nones," 253, 352n14

religious rhetoric, 52, 66, 90, 101, 181, 184, 284

Religious Right, 44, 153. *See also* Christian Right

religious sanctuary, 334n12. *See also* presbytery

representative democracy, xiv, 153, 154, 157, 178, 269

restructuring of American religion, 252–53

Revere, Paul, 241, 242

ringshout, 340–41n59

rites: of blood sacrifice, 13, 187; of faith, 2, 13, 52–53, 85, 95, 98–101, 144, 274; of faith, and race, 105–6, 108, 129, 147–48, 150; of intensification, 2, 10–11, 275, 277, 281, 289, 322n6; of war, 2, 13, 182, 186, 187, 274

ritual, and power, 274–75, 283

ritual performance, 148, 206, 212–13, 229

sacred and profane, 17, 203, 332–33n1. *See also* Durkheimian theory

sacred canopy, 89, 337n43

sacred umbrellas, 53–54, 85, 89–90

Satan, 68, 71, 87–89, 93, 94, 145–46, 151, 282. *See also* devil; strongman

Screaming Eagles, 6

sectarianism, 186, 194, 215

secularism, 51, 70, 89–91, 330n18, 332–33n1

secularization, 51–52, 79, 253, 281–82, 332–33n1, 334n10

Smith, Theophus H., 105–6, 338n2

social effervescence, 208

social gospel, 52, 154, 353n16

Social Gospel Movement, 184, 350n16